MW01090088

Bootstrap Liberalism

Bootstrap Liberalism

Texas Political Culture in
the Age of FDR

Sean P. Cunningham

University Press of Kansas

© 2022 by the University Press of Kansas

All rights reserved

Published by the University Press of Kansas (Lawrence, Kansas 66045), which was organized by the Kansas Board of Regents and is operated and funded by Emporia State University, Fort Hays State University, Kansas State University, Pittsburg State University, the University of Kansas, and Wichita State University.

Library of Congress Cataloging-in-Publication Data

Names: Cunningham, Sean P., author.
Title: Bootstrap liberalism : Texas political culture in the age of FDR / Sean P. Cunningham.
Other titles: Texas political culture in the age of FDR
Description: Lawrence, Kansas : University Press of Kansas, 2022. | Includes bibliographical references and index.
Identifiers: LCCN 2021033101
  ISBN 9780700633005 (cloth)
  ISBN 9780700633012 (ebook)
Subjects: LCSH: Texas—Politics and government—1865–1950. | United States—Politics and government—1933–1945. | Roosevelt, Franklin D. (Franklin Delano), 1882–1945—Influence. | New Deal, 1933–1939—Texas. | Right and left (Political science)—Texas—History—20th century. | Political culture—Texas—History—20th century.
Classification: LCC F391 .C86 2022 | DDC 976.4/06—dc23
LC record available at https://lccn.loc.gov/2021033101.

British Library Cataloguing-in-Publication Data is available.

Printed in the United States of America

10 9 8 7 6 5 4 3 2 1

The paper used in this publication is acid free and meets the minimum requirements of the American National Standard for Permanence of Paper for Printed Library Materials Z39.48–1992.

For Mom and Dad

Contents

Preface

My grandparents were children of the Great Depression. My maternal grandmother was born in 1920, the oldest of ten kids raised by farmers struggling to survive in the Texas Panhandle, right in the middle of what was later called the "Dust Bowl." My maternal grandfather was also born in 1920, but he began his life in western Arkansas, just across the Oklahoma and Texas borders. Sadly, he began smoking just a few years later, around the age of ten—a bad but not uncommon habit formed at roughly the same moment he and his mother and brother were shoved out of a car and abandoned by the side of a road somewhere in East Texas by his biological father—a man whose membership in the Ku Klux Klan provided little in the way of a moral compass, let alone appreciation for "family values." Shortly thereafter, my grandfather dropped out of third grade. He spent the rest of his childhood learning to survive off the land, becoming especially good at fishing, a fact I was blessed to discover with him as a child. My grandparents married in 1941, shortly before his deployment to England as a soldier in the United States Army. They did not see each other again until 1945. In the years after World War II, they raised two children, one of whom—my uncle, Frank—became the first in the family's history to go to college.

My grandfather died of lung cancer in 1988. My grandmother subsequently moved to Lubbock to be closer to her daughter, my mom. For the next fifteen years, Sunday-afternoon lunch at Mama's house became a can't-miss event. My grandmother was a God-fearing woman, but she rarely went to church, in part because she didn't know how to drive, but primarily because preparing a scratch lunch for her family was the highlight of her week—and took hours to finish. A woman of limited means, Mama still managed a dining-room table overflowing with abundance and ostentation, belying an ever-present insecurity that another great depression could snatch away the bounty at any moment. She filled her garage with canned vegetables and preserves, resembling food stockpiles from a Cold War–era bomb shelter. She decorated her house with as much crystal and gold as she could afford, though none of the gold was real. Table topics varied, but it was never a surprise to hear my grandmother recall a story that was somehow related to her childhood. I don't know how many times I must have heard the tale of her Depression-era move from the rural Texas Panhandle to the "big city" of Amarillo, during which she "rode down Polk Street" in the back of a pickup truck, sitting next to one of her little sisters . . . and a cow. She described it as one of the most humiliating events of her life, not because of the cow, but because of what it symbolized: abject poverty. The Depression never seemed very far from the forefront of her consciousness.

My grandmother was a high-school graduate, but not an "educated woman" in the classical sense. Her experiences growing up in the Texas Panhandle were common. I would not describe her as politically engaged, though by the time I came to know her well, it would be fair to describe her as a social conservative. "Old-fashioned," really. She believed in hard work, perseverance, and self-reliance. She did not wear boots, but certainly would have agreed that pulling oneself up by the bootstraps was part of what made a person honorable. And she never forgave the Japanese for Pearl Harbor.

In so many ways, my grandmother was a typical Texas conservative of her generation. And yet, at the same time, no political figure ever captured her heart quite like Franklin D. Roosevelt did. She in fact spoke of FDR with such reverence that one might have suspected she was talking about her own grandfather. As Mama often put it, Roosevelt was for the "forgotten people" like her, while Republicans were for bankers and country club "fat cats." Simply put, my grandmother trusted FDR. She believed that he cared about her and her family. She did not see the New Deal as a welfare giveaway. Yes, by the end of her life, she believed that government had grown inefficient and wasteful. She opposed the progressive identity politics that characterized the modern Democratic Party, particularly on social issues. And yet somehow none of that led her to reassess FDR's stature or legacy, at least not as it stood in her mind. Nor did it lead her to switch parties. She remained a loyal Democrat to the day she died in 2003. Moreover, she remained convinced that no politician would (or could) ever match President Roosevelt, whose steady, brilliant leadership had steered her generation—the "Greatest Generation," as Tom Brokaw taught her to say—through the twin calamities of depression and war.

One of my goals in writing this book is to explain how my grandmother could be as conservative as she was for most of her life, and yet consider Franklin Delano Roosevelt the greatest president—and possibly the greatest man, other than Jesus and her husband—who ever lived.

Few presidents have ever been as polarizing as FDR, particularly during the late 1930s and early 1940s. He remains anathema to ideological conservatives, who lament the growth of big government that began (more or less) under his watch, before growing even more expansive under the administration of his most famous protégé, Lyndon Baines Johnson. My grandmother despised LBJ, but she loved FDR. This book tries to make sense of that apparent paradox. I don't know if it does, but at the very least, I tend to think it would have made perfect sense to my grandmother.

Acknowledgments

There is an old proverb that says, "It takes a village to raise a child." The same might be said of this book, which would not exist without the guidance and support of dozens of colleagues, friends, and loved ones during the past eight years.

First, I would like to thank the amazingly responsive staff at the University Press of Kansas (UPK), especially Dr. David Congdon, whose enthusiasm for this project never waned, and whose encouragement and insight proved invaluable throughout the entire process. I would also like to thank UPK's Colin Tripp for guiding me through the production process with remarkable clarity, patience, and ease, as well as Carol A. Kennedy for her excellent copy edits and communication skills. Thanks also go to the dozens of archivists and archival assistants who helped me—sometimes by phone, sometimes by email, and often in person—during my various research trips. This includes entire staffs at the Dallas Historical Society; the Dolph Briscoe Center for American History at the University of Texas at Austin; the Franklin D. Roosevelt Presidential Library in Hyde Park, New York; the Southwest Collection/Special Collections Library at Texas Tech University in Lubbock; the Lyndon B. Johnson Presidential Library in Austin, Texas; and the Texas State Library and Archives Commission, also in Austin. Special mentions go to Monte Monroe and Weston Marshall at the Southwest Collection, Stacy Flood at the Sam Rayburn House State Historical Site, Sarah Cunningham (no relation) at the LBJ Library, Chris Bohannan and Kaitlyn Price at the Dallas Historical Society, Aryn Glazier at the Briscoe Center, Mike Miller at the Austin History Center, and Matthew Hanson at the FDR Library, as well as Sarah Wilson of the Willis Library and Oral History Program at the University of North Texas in Denton. In various ways, each of these individuals went above and beyond to help me get what I needed, particularly as the COVID-19 pandemic interrupted travel plans and impeded access to certain collections throughout most of 2020.

I also appreciate the support of my colleagues at Texas Tech, as well as those at Humanities Texas, the Texas State Historical Association, and various other entities. Particular notes of thanks go to Saad Abi-Hamad, Alwyn Barr, Walter Buenger, Paul Carlson, Amanda Chattin, Stefano D'Amico, Mayela Guardiola, Barbara Hahn, Justin Hart, Karlos Hill, Miguel Levario, Richard Lutjens, Randy McBee, Ron Milam, Ted Miller, Jeffrey Mosher, Michelle Nickerson, Tim Nokken, Nina Pruitt, Travis Snyder, Mark Stoll, Don Walker, Julie Willett, Aliza Wong, and Nancy Beck Young—each of whom on at least one occasion counseled, read, commented, and/or assisted me in some way as I vented through various stages of a seven-year research and writing process, most of which coincided with my service as chair of Texas Tech's Department of History. Likely dozens of others helped in various other ways. I am indebted to them all.

Professional assistance is always critical, but emotional support is often just as (if not more) important, and no individual bore the burdens of this project, or offered more support, than my amazing wife and best friend, Laura. She, along with my daughters, Caitlin and Samantha, put up with several research trips, not to mention numerous evening and weekend writing sessions (and periods of general exhaustion). I also want to thank my brother, Eric, for more thought-provoking conversations about politics than I can count, including many that either directly or indirectly shaped at least a few of the arguments in this book. Tyson Purdy and Eric Washington joined several of those conversations and deserve thanks as well, as do, for various reasons, Joshua Abraham, Brad Agee, Doug Allen, Chris Benner, Clint Bingham, John Boyle, Averi Cunningham, Jeremy Dalton, Justin Duncan, Paul Foeldvari, Adam Foley, Jeramey Gillilan, Reis Goldberg, Nicole Grandjean, Peter Griffith, Mike Hall, Trace Hunt, Chris Kramedjian, Larry LaFreniere, Jeff Lashaway, Jennifer Mayfield, Brandon Mulkey, Steve Percifield, Ronnie Rowe, Ryan Scheckel, Tom Sell, Mike and Sally Shelton, Matthew Smith, Jonathan Towell, and Dustin Williams, each of whom provided a listening ear and asked constructive questions on at least one occasion during the past several years.

Finally, I want to thank my parents and grandparents, whose unconditional love I have never questioned, even amid oft intense (and occasionally overheated) political disagreements, particularly in recent years. Each of my four grandparents—Frank and Margaret Allen (aka Mama and Papa) and J. Pat and Eleanor Cunningham (aka Mema and Poppy)—grew up during the "Age of FDR," though their experiences during those years varied dramatically. Each of my grandparents has passed on, but the effect of their love and support still reverberates through my parents, Kirk and Kay Cunningham (aka Grammy and Pops to my two daughters). I am immeasurably blessed to have had parents who are also great friends. I deeply appreciate their support and love and respect them dearly. We don't always agree, especially when it comes to politics, but I would not be the husband, father, teacher, or scholar that I am without their parental guidance. This book is dedicated to them.

Introduction
"Men of Constructive Minds and Patriotic Motives"

In April 13, 1935, politicians of all ages gathered in Fort Worth for the annual Thomas Jefferson Society Dinner. As usual, the Young Democrats of Texas hosted the event, which was nothing short of a who's who among state leaders both current and aspirational. The evening's highlight came when the organization unveiled a life-size portrait of President Franklin Delano Roosevelt, as captured by Douglas Chandor, an eminent English artist and recent transplant to nearby Weatherford. Chandor told reporters from the *Dallas Morning News* that Roosevelt was the "greatest man" he had ever met, and Elliott Roosevelt—the president's son and himself a transplant to the area—hailed the portrait as "the best likeness ever painted" of his father. With great fanfare, the Young Democrats then presented the painting as a gift to the State of Texas, adding proudly that it would hang at the capitol building in Austin, alongside portraits of Stephen F. Austin and Sam Houston.[1] Less than a month later, Bob Barker, secretary of the Texas State Senate, telegrammed the president to confirm the portrait's placement inside the capitol. In Barker's words, the portrait would allow "generations to honor and admire [FDR] as the greatest leader of all time," also noting Roosevelt's "supreme efforts to bring this nation out of the Depression."[2]

Later that year, on October 16, 1935, the Chamber of Commerce in Amarillo, Texas, held a banquet to honor their local representative in Washington, DC, Congressman Marvin Jones. Already in his sixteenth year representing the Texas Panhandle, Jones had long since established an unshakable reputation as a friend to farmers, an ally to ranchers, and an advocate for the common, oft-forgotten citizens of his district. It was Jones's work in direct support of the New Deal, however, that elevated his stature to another level. Before an audience of more than five hundred attendees, one speaker said of Jones: "To us in Texas, he is our pilot, and of him we all acclaim, 'Sail on, oh noble pilot, sail on—our hearts, our hopes, are all with thee, are all with thee!'" It was an effusive display of praise stylistically befitting the occasion. A standing ovation beckoned Jones to the stage, where the evening's hosts presented the congressman with a new cowboy hat. "My friends," the speaker said, "this type of hat is a symbol and emblem of an unconquered and unconquerable race of men—pioneer cowmen."[3]

All things considered, there was little unique about either of these events. Politicians had long utilized banquets to reaffirm their own importance or to honor their friends, colleagues, benefactors, and preferred candidates. However, events like these in 1935 reflect an underappreciated duality within Texas political culture during the Great Depression and New Deal era. Franklin D. Roosevelt—champion of unprecedented federal experimentation and economic intervention—became one of the most beloved national leaders in Texas history, winning reelection to the White House four times, each by astoundingly high margins. In a state noted for its perceived commitment to conservative, rugged individualism, self-help, and limited government, FDR brandished coattails for state, county, and municipal candidates, the vast majority of whom—for at least a time—not simply endured Roosevelt's New Deal, but embraced it, sold it, and capitalized on it. Marvin Jones, who prior to the New Deal had a reputation as a fiscally conservative traditionalist, became one of Roosevelt's most valued advocates and advisors, backing the New Deal at almost every turn while somehow maintaining (and even strengthening) his standing with an otherwise conservative West Texas base. A contradiction on one level, and yet seamlessly rational to most Texas voters living through the greatest economic disaster in the nation's history, the alliance between federal activism in Washington and traditional Democratic loyalties in Texas was, for a time, strong. Eventually that alliance crumbled. Among party leaders, the divisions between pro- and anti–New Deal factions were arguably sharper than in any other state. Yet, when Marvin Jones received his new cowboy hat in 1935 it was a not simply a symbol of an "unconquerable race," as his presenter put it, but a powerful reflection of a political culture, however brief, in which the vast majority of ordinary Texans supported revolutionary levels of big government liberalism, and often did so enthusiastically.[4]

How and why did that happen? How did political candidates in Texas—virtually all of whom were Democrats—respond to, utilize, and benefit from their support for and identification with Roosevelt and the New Deal? What did that association look like? How did voters respond? What does that response say about Texas politics during this period?

What does it say about FDR's popularity in the state and, more specifically, the state's stereotypically conservative proclivities?

This book seeks to answer those questions by exploring a sampling of state and local officials, political campaigns, and policy battles fought in Texas between 1932 and 1945—a period known to many as the "Age of FDR." It is not an exhaustive exploration of state politics, nor is it yet another history of Roosevelt and the New Deal. Rather, it aims to say something new about how state and local Democrats, including many who had previously identified themselves as conservatives (and some who would do so again in later decades) marketed themselves to Texas voters during the 1930s and early 1940s not by opposing Roosevelt's New Deal, but by embracing it. It seeks to explain Roosevelt's success in Texas not simply as a reflection of long-standing, powerful partisan loyalties, but as a somewhat surprising marker of genuine, widespread support for New Deal programs and goals and of sincere appreciation for Franklin Roosevelt as a champion for ordinary Texans and their traditional values as commonly defined at the time.[5]

As a delegate to the 1936 Democratic National Convention, Congressman George H. Mahon famously quipped that he and his fellow Texans were "Democrats first and New Dealers second." Quips like this have been used to explain FDR's popularity in the Lone Star State while, at the same time, forecasting partisan realignments that shaped Texas in later decades. Most Texans, this argument goes, supported Roosevelt because they were loyal Democrats, not because they liked the president and certainly not because they supported his New Deal. Rather, they put up with it because they had no other choice. Eventually, they rebelled. Politicians such as Mahon showed their true colors in later decades, defending segregation and states' rights, while future generations transferred their loyalties from party to ideology. This shift fractured the state Democratic Party into increasingly uncooperative and polarized conservative and liberal factions. Polarization led to mass defections and, eventually, the rise of the modern Texas Republican Party. By the end of the twentieth century, most Texans were conservatives first and Republicans second.[6]

This is a well-established narrative, for good reason. It is largely accurate and makes sense. However, it suffers from teleology. Moreover, it undervalues Roosevelt's legitimate popularity in Texas, as well as the widespread support New Deal programs enjoyed across the state, even if only briefly. During the 1930s, most Texans may very well have been

Democrats first and New Dealers second, but most of them were still New Dealers to some extent. More than a handful became true believers. Conservative anti–New Dealers often opposed the FDR White House in vocal, aggressive terms that forecast the nature of partisan politics in future decades. They decried collectivism, socialism, high taxes, growing deficits, and dependence entitlement, while warning of a Roosevelt dictatorship that would undo the Constitution and potentially America itself. At the height of the Great Depression, however, such warnings represented the politics of the minority, not the majority. Between 1932 and 1945—and particularly from 1932 to 1937—liberal Texas Democrats succeeded in campaigns not by apologizing for the president and his New Deal, nor by tugging on voters' Democratic heartstrings. Instead, candidates often won by embracing and marketing the New Deal as a set of pragmatic solutions to urgent problems. Beyond that, they also sold the New Deal as both authentically American and fully in keeping with traditional Texas values. Many Texans voting in the early 1930s had little difficulty remembering the reformist impulses of their fathers and grandfathers. As recently as 1890, for instance, Texans had backed James Stephen Hogg, among the most significant populist-progressives in state history, for governor. Hogg, among others, presided over an era theretofore unprecedented in its zeal for activism and change. Three decades later, in the shadow of global economic collapse, that sort of zeal seemed relevant once again. Still, most Texans were not looking for a revolution. Rather, they wanted sound, stable, sensible action, and they wanted it quickly. They wanted practical solutions to urgent problems. And they wanted Democrats. Beginning in 1932 and persisting until his death in 1945, Franklin Roosevelt personified almost everything that most Texas voters wanted, which also explains why so many Democratic candidates enthusiastically attached themselves to the president's coattails during this period.[7]

Ultimately, this book argues that both Roosevelt and his New Deal were far more popular in Texas than most historical narratives have acknowledged. Most Texans voted for FDR not simply because he was a Democrat, but because they appreciated his efforts on their behalf, trusted his leadership, and bought into his ideas. Roosevelt and his Texas allies sold the New Deal as little more than pragmatic, common sense. They sold Roosevelt personally as a reliable captain, navigating a troubled ship through choppy waters. Loyalty was important, but it was not decisive. If anything, Texas Democrats won more votes by blaming

Republicans for the Depression than by playing loyalty cards, though to a degree, of course, the two concepts went hand in hand. Texas Democratic politicians marketed the president, the New Deal, their party, and themselves as the voice of the "forgotten man" and of traditional values, in direct opposition to the Republican Party, corporate greed, elitist entitlement, and incompetence. This book seeks to illuminate the means and modalities by which many Democratic politicians successfully sold those messages to Texas voters.

Within this political culture of "bootstrap liberalism"—a culture that promoted the use of federal intervention as a means for reviving individual opportunity—the variables of loyalty, ideology, personality, and race deserve additional comment.

For roughly one hundred years, from Reconstruction to the 1970s, few things governed the Texas Democratic Party more fiercely than the notion of loyalty. Voters who cast a ballot in a Texas Democratic primary often did so upon pledging an oath of loyalty that they would also support the Democratic Party during the general election. A handful of exceptions notwithstanding, voting Democratic in a primary and Republican in the general election—or "bolting" as it was often called—was an unacceptable betrayal. In the words of longtime Texas newspaperman Silliman Evans, "a bolter among Democrats is about as popular as a boll weevil at a farmer's convention."[8]

The presidential election of 1928 was the most famous such betrayal in Texas history. That year, state Democrats refused to support the Catholic (and "wet") governor of New York, Al Smith, voting instead for Republican nominee Herbert Hoover. By 1932, however, circumstances had changed. Thanks to the Depression, Texans reaffirmed their Democratic loyalties, rejecting Hoover in near-record numbers while giving 88 percent of their votes to FDR. When he ran for reelection in 1936, Texans affirmed that decision, giving Roosevelt 87 percent of the vote en route to a second term. The number dropped slightly in 1940, to 81 percent, and fell again, to 71 percent, in 1944. Still, no presidential candidate since has come close to besting Roosevelt's 1944 margin in Texas. (Harry Truman's 66 percent in 1948, Ronald Reagan's 63.6 percent in 1984, and Lyndon Johnson's 63.3 percent in 1964 are easily the closest three.)

Once could argue that no state provided FDR with more political support than did Texas, just as one could argue that no state inspired more opposition.[9] Texas was just big enough to provide both. A little bit South and a little bit West—with a lot of cotton, cattle, oil, land, and money in between—the pace of social, cultural, economic, and political transformations common to the late nineteenth and early twentieth centuries accelerated during the Age of FDR. In some ways, the state evolved beyond many of its ex-Confederate leanings, though of course the incendiary passions of racial politics were never far from the surface, especially when such passions become politically useful. For a time, business-oriented progressives and pragmatic populists dominated the state, before cultural forces shifted Texans' focus during the 1920s, in some ways culminating with the Hoovercrat bolt of 1928. Historian Walter Buenger refers to this dynamic as "cultural fluidity"—a process in which voters' identities gradually shifted from regionally "Southern" to something more uniquely "Texan," the latter emerging as the miasmic vortex of rapid industrial and economic change swept the nation. This shift, coupled by a lost sense of "isolation"—the result of many factors, including population growth and communications technology—untethered Texans' political behaviors from the state's sectional past, thereby allowing for greater assimilation with the national political conversation.[10]

Erica Grieder makes a similar argument, placing the New Deal within a longstanding tradition of populist progressivism almost tailor-made for FDR. "The version of populism that flourished in Texas wasn't strictly a philosophical indictment of big business or a vote in favor of a robust public sector," Grieder says. "It was a reaction to the big business interests that already existed and were making it harder for Texas businesses to get big." Texans have traditionally welcomed government intervention to the degree that such intervention has aimed at protecting state- and locally owned business interests, usually against bigger corporations in New York or elsewhere along the East Coast. FDR and his allies succeeded in part by marketing the New Deal as a series of corrective actions against the abuses of Wall Street and other Republican elites, and perfectly in keeping with the state's Jacksonian and Jeffersonian heritages. "Most Texans were supportive of the New Deal at least to the extent that it benefited them," Grieder says, adding that it was "a kind of pragmatic (if not-quite hypocritical) self-interest that has been a recurring phenomenon in American politics to the present day."[11]

Rather than create something entirely new, therefore, the Great Depression and New Deal largely reinforced the Democratic Party's longstanding message that it was far more capable of serving ordinary Texans than was its rival. It did so, however, in a way that prioritized reform through government action. Rather than languish in a poverty not of their own making, many proud, independent Texans decided that a government of the people, by the people, and for the people could use interventionist regulation to promote regional development while at the same time protecting the "little guy" against bankers and other corporate menaces—especially those from the vilified eastern establishment. With the help of well-placed insiders (including, among others, Houston's Jesse H. Jones), boosters and civic leaders such as Fort Worth's Amon Carter (among many others) learned how to promote regional economic growth by selling Texans on the idea that infrastructural development funded by Washington would create new businesses without relying on out-of-state investment. In essence, open-minded business leaders embraced federal intervention as a pragmatic antidote for economic stagnation. Like others in the business world, Amon Carter was hardly a New Dealer at heart, but ideological misgivings did not prevent him and many others just like him from cozying up to Roosevelt when needed.[12]

Although it drew from reformist impulses common to earlier eras, the New Deal did fundamentally alter popular expectations of what the federal government owed citizens. Most Texas voters who supported FDR were not voting for ideological change, but neither were they oblivious to the New Deal's impact. Among those who did not vote for Roosevelt, however, ideology was a small but key step in forging new loyalties to the Republican Party, particularly as the GOP evolved during the decades to come. Observers during the 1930s and early 1940s frequently noted an increase in the number of right-wing reactionaries and others who were "really Republicans" just masquerading as Democrats. The story of the modern Texas Republican Party is, certainly at least in part, the story of conservative Democrats abandoning generations of partisan loyalty in the name of ideology. However, during the 1930s, most conservatives remained loyal to the party of their fathers and grandfathers. Instead of bolting, they hoped to redeem their party (again), by purging liberals from positions of influence. Sometimes they succeeded, but more often than not during the 1930s, they failed.[13]

Roosevelt, meanwhile, was one of the least ideological politicians of the twentieth century. He was rarely interested in debating ideology, though he was not above dismissing his enemies as too narrowly committed to "old ways of thinking" and therefore painfully oblivious to the realities that ordinary people were facing in the midst of the Depression. On the rare occasion that he chose to engage such conversations, FDR usually defined liberalism as "flexible" as opposed to conservatism, which he called "rigid and dogmatic." When conservatives grumbled about budget deficits and fiscal responsibility, FDR—whose level of trust with the American public far exceeded that of most Republicans— neutralized the charge by agreeing to the general concept of fiscal responsibility, before reminding listeners of Republican failures during the 1920s. He portrayed tax increases and spending bills as a means to an end—that being the restoration of a healthy economy in which ordinary Americans could thrive and in which greedy corporations would be held in check. "The object is to put capital—private as well as public—to work," Roosevelt said in 1939. "Many people have the idea that as a nation we are overburdened with debt and are spending more than we can afford. That is not so. Despite our Federal Government expenditures, the entire debt of our national economic system, public and private together, is no larger today than it was in 1929, and the interest thereon is far less than it was in 1929." Reasonable and unflappable in his delivery, Roosevelt essentially laughed off criticisms from the right while, in terms that Bill Clinton would have appreciated during the 1990s, triangulating his message by co-opting some of his opponents' concerns. Eschewing political philosophy for pragmatism, FDR reserved his passions for practical programs designed to "obtain for the people the maximum responsibility and control with respect to their economic and political affairs."[14]

Roosevelt often said that the New Deal was about restoring government "to its own people," not growing government for the sake of an ideological cause. His public statements toward liberalism and the New Deal profoundly shaped voter attitudes during the Great Depression years. When an Amarillo editorialist wrote about why he "liked the Depression"—saying flippantly, among other insensitive things, that it was "healthy" for people to eat less and wear plainer clothes—a woman in Levelland retorted that "anyone who says he likes the Depression has not had starvation staring him in the face. I don't like to see others go hungry while I have plenty, therefore, I *don't* like the Depression."[15]

Writing twenty years after he helped manage FDR's reelection campaign in 1936, Marvin Jones remarked that the New Deal succeeded because it "treated people as human beings with certain rights and privileges. It tried to make their rights, their feelings and their interests the primary consideration in the heart of all the legislation that was enacted." For Jones, the New Deal was not about pushing collectivism, but preserving individualism. The "true philosophy of the Democratic Party," he said, "is that we see that the rights of the individual are protected." Ordinary Texans, he claimed, had struggled in their fights against cronyism and corporate greed. In this view, the New Deal *was* the government and the government was "the people," striking a blow in defense of individual American dreams, such as when the New Deal used the Home Owners' Loan Corporation (HOLC) to protect individual homeowners from foreclosure by large, corporate banks. Action like this was not about ideology, Jones said; it was about helping people.[16] As Congressman Wright Patman similarly put it in 1936, the New Deal was a fight on behalf of the "the plain people of this country" who deserved "mercy" whenever possible and protection against "concentrations of wealth and power." It was also a fight against "war, monopoly, and abuse of government credited by Wall Street bankers." According to Patman, Texans had "never had a better friend in the White House than President Roosevelt."[17]

Liberals understood the value of promoting ideas as practical rather than ideological. They also understood that "collectivism" would never be as popular as "individualism," in Texas or anywhere in the United States. Meanwhile, conservatives who refused to jump aboard the New Deal bandwagon recognized that ideology was a gateway to political success, if not in the short term than in the long one. In the decades that followed FDR's death, politicians found new ways to polarize along ideological dichotomies, often associating liberalism with "socialism," usually also couched in racially tinged debates over property rights, taxes, crime, and freedom of association. Conservatives later magnified the perception of big government collectivism overwhelming American individuality in the name of civil rights and a "Great Society." However, conservatives could not win that kind of political war during the 1930s. Instead, in the Age of FDR, many Texas Democrats approached individualism from an entirely different direction, arguing that federal regulations were not a threat, a burden, or a violation of individual freedoms; they were, rather, weapons for use in the defense of individual liberty. By framing the New Deal (and liberalism, more generally) in these terms, FDR deftly reoriented the conversation in such a way as to make most Texas voters comfortable. As a result, Texas voters largely endorsed both the New Deal and the president who sold it. They believed that FDR simply wanted to make right all that had gone wrong under Republican leadership and that he wanted to restore order and opportunity and hope to their broken world. They believed that he would do this not by fomenting an ideological revolution, but through rational, pragmatic action. When Texans went to the polls to cast ballots for FDR they were, as one man from Manor, Texas, put it, putting their trust in someone who could "make things right."[18]

In a related way, Depression-era politics in Texas also reflected the persistent power of personality to shape voter behavior and identity. As would be true of Ronald Reagan under very different circumstances during the 1970s and 1980s, FDR won the hearts and minds of a majority of Texas voters in part by transcending class to connect with ordinary men and women—the "forgotten man," as he famously put it. An editorialist for the *Waco News-Tribune* put it less succinctly:

> [FDR] is not a shuffler, a dodger, a fence rider, or a hypocrite. He is a man of vision, of the highest integrity and efficiency, and ever for the constitution and the law and the rights of many. Roosevelt is neither a left-winger nor a right-winger. He is for the bill of rights all the time. He would have men of constructive minds and patriotic motives control the affairs of the Democratic Party in order that popular government be restored to the people and special privilege politicians driven from power. . . . Franklin D. Roosevelt is a builder. A Christian gentleman, he would create a little paradise here below. He would strive to make happy and content the prosperous millions of Americans who toil with hands or brains to create homes for their families and make of this republic just what its founders and fathers intended when they placed it on the map of nations more than 150 years ago. HE IS TODAY AS TRUE A TYPE OF THE JEFFERSONIAN DEMOCRAT AS THE REPUBLIC HAS KNOWN IN SEVENTY-FIVE YEARS.[19]

Perceptions of the New Deal would change over the years, but for the most part, Roosevelt connected with "common folks" without artificially transforming into someone or something he was not. He was an aristocrat but did not strike most as haughty or pretentious. Instead, Roosevelt spoke plainly and directly, often through radio, and without condescension. Scholars interested in Roosevelt-era foreign policy have frequently noted his preference for personal diplomacy and his persuasive talents in one-to-one conversations. The same was largely true of his approach to domestic politics, just as it was true of his campaign style.[20]

Speaking of campaigns, it is important to note that in a world of limited outlets, media exposure of any kind was critical to the communication of one's message, not to mention one's personality. Incumbents therefore held an enormous advantage in that media outlets considered their daily activities news. Challengers, conversely, had fewer opportunities to undermine their incumbent opponent's campaign narrative. Newspapers that ran stories about New Deal dollars pouring into local communities reinforced positive attitudes voters had toward FDR. Local officials often capitalized on FDR's good press, identifying themselves with the president and his programs whenever possible. The fact that most Americans generally trusted the media, and trusted their elected officials, made publicity all the more valuable and impactful. Political campaigns modernized rapidly during and after the 1960s, thanks to television and other advancements in direct marketing and the professionalization of public relations. Conversely, political campaigns during the 1930s were still short and simple. Most candidates promoted themselves through speeches, not artfully crafted advertisements. Speeches were typically informational rather than stylish, were usually broadcast by radio at no charge to the candidate, and often lasted thirty minutes or more. Old-fashioned stump speeches were still common, not to mention popular as a form of entertainment; only rarely did a campaign tailor messages for different audiences. Campaign season was typically short—often lasting less than a month, especially at the local level. In this environment, even minor advances in style or artistic packaging were noticeable. As James Reston once described the state's evolving political culture during this era, successful political candidates prioritized technique over substance in their pursuit of power in Texas.[21]

FDR excelled in this area. He pioneered the modern, political use of radio, and mastered it. He also utilized music and slogans, and he recognized that emotional connections were often just as critical as was specific policy. Roosevelt tried to inspire, and he tried to appeal to the best in people, prioritizing hope above fear and future opportunities above past failures. In doing so, FDR symbolized order, security, and tradition, even as his New Deal aggressively broke with tradition. In so many ways, Roosevelt established a stylistic script for political success that few effectively read again until Reagan's emergence onto the political scene more than three decades later.[22]

Finally, a word about race. Regardless of whether one defines Texas as southern or western, and regardless of how one might compare Texas with other states, it should be acknowledged clearly that race has always played a role in both state political culture and the development of specific policies. Occasionally it has played a critical or decisive role, as it has in other states, particularly those of the former Confederacy. To argue that race is not (or has rarely been) an important factor in the history of Texas politics would be counterfactual and flatly incorrect.[23] For instance, as explored in chapter 1 of this book, the Ku Klux Klan thrived in Texas during the 1920s, suggesting that bigotry and hate were powerful forces that could be awakened for political benefit when needed. And while the Klan exploited racism in explicitly repugnant ways, progressives on the left were often no less guilty of promoting variations of white supremacist thinking, whether through paternalistic moralizing about the unusually perilous dangers of alcohol consumption among Black men or the inability of Black families to persist without state intervention. In similar ways, Texas Democrats—including Senator Tom Connally and Congressman Hatton Sumners—made headlines on multiple occasions during the 1920s and 1930s by opposing antilynching laws and other proposed reforms on social justice. It goes without saying that race was critical in these moments.[24]

However, during the Age of FDR, those moments typically faded quickly, usually lost in the cacophony of debates over issues on which white Texans, at the time, disagreed; sadly, there was little disagreement among white Texans on matters of race. Voters typically assumed their candidates supported white supremacy. Accordingly, Texas candidates rarely felt the need to emphasize race during campaigns, particularly when their chief objective was to highlight differences with their opponent.[25] Additionally, the comparatively smaller percentage of African Americans in Texas (versus population ratios in other states of the former Confederacy) played a critical role in reducing the efficacy of race-baiting, as did the state's physical vastness, its widely varying levels of population density, and the complicating factor of having an atypically high Mexican American population, particularly in its southern and western regions. Beyond all that, minority voters were largely disfranchised anyway, so appealing to them was unnecessary if the goal was to win. As this book focuses on political marketing during an era in which Democrats did not need to concern themselves with minority voters, the politics of race commands comparatively less attention than do other variables. In starker terms, Texas Democrats paid virtually no attention to minority voters during the New Deal era, and neither did

FDR. Roosevelt's unwillingness to use political capital on issues related to racial equality and civil rights remains one of his greatest failings.[26]

A brief word about methodology and intended historiographical contribution: In some ways, *Bootstrap Liberalism* models a host of traditional narratives written by Texas historians, including some that date back several decades. These narratives remain invaluable to students and scholars alike.[27] At the same time, newer research has both complemented and complicated these narratives, particularly when it comes to understanding the relationship between politics and culture, and especially when it comes to understanding just how varied the state's political culture has been. For instance, few tropes are as intimately synonymous with Texas cultural mythology as the concept of the "cowboy." The image of a ruggedly individualistic cowboy knocked to the ground, only to find the internal strength to pull himself up by the bootstraps, is central to popular notions of Texas, the West, and masculine American character more broadly. And yet, as conservative as the political culture that flowed from this mythology was (and is), the history of Texas politics is replete with moments in which ordinary citizens expected their government to intervene whenever their metaphorical bootstraps broke or became too weak. In 2020, historian Gregg Cantrell argued that the origins of modern American liberalism lay in the agrarian People's Revolt of the late nineteenth century, a political movement more commonly known as "Populism." His research even suggests that no other state was as central to that movement—or to its core expectation for federal intervention on behalf of "ordinary" people—as Texas. Likewise, the aforementioned Walter Buenger has argued that government-centered progressivism thrived in various forms across Texas during the early twentieth century, another era in which many Texans expressed a willingness to work together, through government, for the betterment of all.[28]

Just as it models the more traditional narratives written during the twentieth century, *Bootstrap Liberalism* similarly models this newer scholarship in arguing that the Great Depression allowed for a moment similar to the ones described by Cantrell and Buenger—one that merged interventionist theories with a culture of political pragmatism in an effort to help struggling people pull themselves up. It also aims to advance, complement, and modernize narrative histories by assessing Texas politics and political leadership during the 1930s and early

1940s, primarily through the lens of campaign marketing, with an eye toward better understanding the dynamic interplay between political imagery, public receptivity, and the motivating power of emotion. In this way, *Bootstrap Liberalism* is more interested in political culture than political policy or impact. It explores questions about why Texas voters behaved the way they did and how political parties tried to shape that behavior. It does not seek conclusions on the success or failure of the New Deal. Rather, it is more interested in how politicians used (or failed to use) their charisma, and the charisma of others, to promote ideas and agendas. In this way, the book also hopes to contribute to conversations about Texas culture and influence, such as recent works by Erica Grieder and Lawrence Wright. Historians interested in unpacking the underappreciated nuances of "purple Texas" would do well to examine the questions raised in these highly readable books.[29]

Writers such as these have shown that everything is political, including history. At the same time, scholars can write political history in a variety of ways, using a variety of analytical lenses. With tremendous aspiration and some humility, this book was written in a similar spirit, with theoretical and methodological nods to Merrill Peterson, Daniel Boorstin, David Greenberg, and Joe McGinnis. Along these lines, it also owes a debt to Richard Slotkin's analysis of western mythology in American memory.[30]

While it is unlikely that this book will accomplish what those authors did, *Bootstrap Liberalism* similarly grants substantial space to the exploration of perceptions and images—more than it devotes to any analysis of objective reality. Yet, at the end of the day, the ballot box was the final arbiter of bootstrap liberalism's success or failure. In that sense, this is a story of manipulation from the "top down" at the same time that it affirms the power of the franchise to shape history from the "bottom up." Or at least that is the goal.

The meat of this book consists of six chronological chapters. Chapter 1 begins by exploring the variables shaping Texas political culture during the 1920s. It then looks at the Depression's early impact, showing how economic meltdown during the early 1930s upended the preceding political culture, thereby affording politicians like Roosevelt the opportunity to usher in something different. Chapter 2 unpacks some of the political marketing associated with FDR's first one hundred days in office, including his efforts toward agriculture reform. It also explores some of the ways in which state and local candidates pitched New Deal experiments in campaigns across Texas between 1933 and 1935, noting that, as Martin Dies once said, "Congress is merely a mirror that reflects the people."[31] Chapter 3 pushes the narrative forward by one year, examining the New Deal's full force on Texas Democratic campaign messaging, with FDR's first reelection bid serving as an important backdrop. No year better reflected the politics of bootstrap liberalism than 1936. Chapter 4 then tackles a dramatic turn of events in 1937 and 1938—the two least-successful years of Roosevelt's presidency. Thanks to several political miscalculations, anti–New Deal conservatives in Texas regained ground during the first years of FDR's second term, all while powerfully asserting the state's need to fight what would soon become the traditional bogeymen of the Republican right: "socialism," "communism," and "tyranny." Chapter 5 adds a new dimension, carrying the story through Roosevelt's unpreceded campaign for a third term, waged primarily because of the complicating politics of isolation and international upheaval, all of which coincided with an increasingly vocal anticommunist impulse among Texas conservatives. Finally, chapter 6 tackles the end of Roosevelt's presidency—the years of World War II and the most famous intraparty squabble in Texas history, that of the Texas Regulars. It was during this period that most conservative Democrats left the FDR fold for the last time, even as it was also a period in which, as FDR put it, "Dr. Win-the-War" replaced "Dr. New Deal."[32]

A handful of characters show up consistently in these chapters, including Jimmie Allred, Jessie Daniel Ames, James Buchanan, Tom Connally, Martin Dies, Clara Driscoll, Joe Eagle, Miriam and James Ferguson, John Nance Garner, Lyndon Johnson, Marvin Jones, Richard Kleberg, Thomas Love, George Mahon, Maury Maverick, W. Lee "Pappy" O'Daniel, Wright Patman, Sam Rayburn, Morris Sheppard, and Hatton Sumners. Some of these men and women were sincere New Deal liberals. Some were not. Neither were these the only politicians making waves during the 1930s and early 1940s. However, they were among the most influential. As such, their stories provide an effective mosaic for understanding Texas political culture in the Age of FDR.

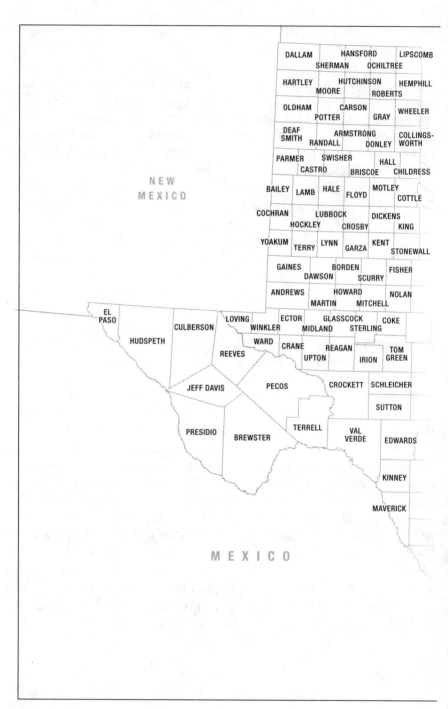

Map of Texas counties. Map by Erin Greb Cartography.

OKLAHOMA

ARKANSAS

LOUISIANA

HARDEMAN WILBARGER
FOARD WICHITA
KNOX CLAY COOKE FANNIN LAMAR RED RIVER BOWIE
BAYLOR ARCHER MONTAGUE GRAYSON
THROCK-MORTON YOUNG JACK WISE DENTON COLLIN HUNT HOPKINS WOOD CASS
HASKELL
SHACKELFORD PALO PINTO PARKER DALLAS MARION
JONES STEPHENS TARRANT KAUFMAN UPSHUR HARRISON
CALLAHAN EASTLAND HOOD JOHNSON VAN ZANDT SMITH
TAYLOR ERATH HENDERSON RUSK PANOLA
COLEMAN COMANCHE HAMILTON BOSQUE HILL NAVARRO CHEROKEE SHELBY
RUNNELS BROWN FREESTONE ANDERSON
MILLS LAMPASAS CORYELL McLENNAN LIMESTONE ANGELINA SABINE
CONCHO McCULLOCH SAN SABA FALLS LEON HOUSTON JASPER
MENARD BELL ROBERTSON MADISON TRINITY POLK NEWTON
MASON LLANO BURNET WILLIAMSON MILAM WALKER TYLER
KIMBLE BLANCO TRAVIS LEE HARDIN
GILLESPIE HAYS BASTROP ORANGE
KERR KENDALL COMAL FAYETTE LIBERTY JEFFERSON
REAL BANDERA GONZALES COLORADO HARRIS CHAMBERS
UVALDE MEDINA BEXAR WILSON DE WITT LAVACA WHARTON FORT BEND GALVESTON
ZAVALA FRIO ATASCOSA KARNES JACKSON BRAZORIA
DIMMIT LA SALLE McMULLEN LIVE OAK GOLIAD VICTORIA MATAGORDA
BEE REFUGIO CALHOUN
WEBB JIM WELLS SAN PATRICIO ARANSAS
DUVAL NUECES
KLEBERG
ZAPATA JIM HOGG BROOKS KENEDY
STARR WILLACY
HIDALGO CAMERON

1 SOMERVELL
2 ROCKWALL
3 DELTA
4 RAINS
5 FRANKLIN
6 TITUS
7 MORRIS
8 CAMP
9 GREGG
10 NACOGDOCHES
11 SAN AUGUSTINE
12 BURLESON
13 BRAZOS
14 WASHINGTON
15 GRIMES
16 AUSTIN
17 WALLER
18 MONTGOMERY
19 SAN JACINTO
20 GUADALUPE
21 CALDWELL

1 | "We Can Do No Worse"

At the height of the "roaring twenties," Thomas B. Love of Dallas was quite possibly the driest man in Texas. In 1928, he did everything he could to make his state the same way. As a Democratic state senator, Love was determined to keep the governor of New York out of the White House in Washington. Alongside legions of other prohibitionist (colloquially known as "dry") Texas Democrats, Love was a thoroughly networked political busybody, an incessant letter writer, and a Wilsonian progressive whose career stretched back to the beginning of the century. But he was not loyal to his party in 1928 and did everything he could to convince other Texans to follow suit by rejecting the candidacy of Al Smith, the antiprohibition ("wet") Democratic presidential nominee, who also happened to be the first Catholic ever nominated by a major party for the highest office in the land. That November, Love's efforts proved successful as Texas cast its lot with the Grand Old Party for the first time, thereby making a direct contribution to the election of the Republican candidate, Herbert Hoover, to the presidency of the United States.

The election of 1928 exposed the severity of sociocultural rifts in the Lone Star State, dividing Texans as few events ever had. It challenged the tenets of partisan loyalty and longstanding Democratic hegemony, and it polarized neighbors and families alike. With the wounds of this division still fresh, a Texan named Charles Berry decided to express his frustrations and hopes for healing and reunification by writing a letter to the man who would replace Al Smith as governor of New York, the newly elected chief executive of the Empire State, Franklin D. Roosevelt.[1]

Evidence in the final vote totals notwithstanding, Berry told Roosevelt that Texas voters did not actually like Herbert Hoover. Nor did they like the Republican Party. Nor, according to Berry, had Texans rejected Smith because he was Catholic, as many speculated, nor because he was a wet. Instead, the state's shift to the Republican Party was a freak occurrence—an unfortunate anomaly—the mere result of complacency and overconfidence. As Berry saw it, Texas Democrats had simply taken their state's loyalty for granted. In doing so, they had unintentionally opened the door for a small minority of disloyal radicals to usurp the people's true preference by rallying unsuspecting but otherwise well-intentioned Texans to do something he hoped they would never do again. Given a second chance, he was sure his Texas neighbors would reunite behind the Democratic Party.[2]

Charles Berry's assessment of the political realities in Texas was naïve and simplistic. In several ways, it was also flatly wrong. Texas did not swing Republican in 1928 because of complacency or overconfidence. Al Smith's Catholicism and his stand on Prohibition were directly relevant and assuredly decisive. Men like Love, Texas governor Dan Moody, and J. Frank Norris, the fiery preacher and pastor of First Baptist Church of Fort Worth, whose anti-Catholic rants had already become the stuff of local legend, made sure of that.[3] Likewise, most of Berry's neighbors were not apathetic, nor had they been duped; rather, they were widely engaged, defiant, and purposefully rebellious. The "Hoovercrat" bolt of 1928 was no accident.[4]

Still, as it turned out, Charles Berry proved to be right about at least one thing. Discouraged though he was, Berry told Roosevelt that he was optimistic that Texas Democrats would reunite behind the party's presidential nominee in 1932, especially if that nominee happened to be FDR.[5]

"Hood, Bonnet, and Little Brown Jug"

Unprecedented and surprising though it was at the time, Al Smith's loss in Texas in 1928 did not occur in a vacuum. Rather, it was, to at least some degree, a predictable reflection of broader political forces shaping the state during the 1920s. Writing in 1984, historian Norman D. Brown argued that three main issues dominated Texas politics during the so-called Roaring Twenties. Those issues were, first, the Ku Klux Klan, or "the Hood"; second, the campaigns of Miriam "Ma" Ferguson—the "Bonnet"; and third, Prohibition, or "the little brown jug." Texans paid tangential attention to other issues at the state, local, and national levels, of course, but they typically interpreted those issues through a lens that prioritized one or more of these three main forces. Any analysis of Texas politics during the age of FDR requires an accounting of the culture that preceded it.[6]

Originally conceived as a domestic terrorist vehicle for promoting Reconstruction-era white supremacy, the Ku Klux Klan existed in fits and starts, on the margins of society, or as a distant memory across the "redeemed" South throughout the final decades of the nineteenth century. Largely defunct by the early twentieth century, the Klan reorganized in 1915 and subsequently enjoyed a heyday during the 1920s. This was especially true in Texas, which became one of the Klan's banner states. A wide variety of perceived threats to the national interest inspired the Klan's rebirth and subsequent growth. The secretive organization still targeted and attacked African Americans and the agitators who dared help them. It also, however, diversified its focus to include Jews, Catholics, and political progressives who aided and abetted what the Klan perceived as the nation's steady descent toward multiculturalism. Immigration was a particularly salient source of anxiety. Klansmen and their allies believed that newcomers from southern and eastern European countries threatened their homeland's racial, ethnic, and religious status quo. They believed it was up to them to preserve and protect that status quo, which they interpreted as white and Protestant. Tapping into undercurrents of fear and anxiety, the Klan attracted sizable followings in Texas, first among elites, and later among middle- and working-class whites.[7]

Both nationally and in Texas, the Ku Klux Klan promoted a philosophy of "100 percent Americanism," arguing that the nation's moral sense of self had been lost, victimized by the onrush of modernity, manifest in racial, ethnic, and sexual permissiveness and unrest. The Klan proclaimed itself God's "instrument for restoring law and order and Victorian morality to the communities, towns and cities of the region." As interested in correcting moral failings as it was in enforcing racial segregation, the Klan attracted men and women who were concerned about the dangers of alcohol abuse and the correlated sins of adultery, domestic violence, pedophilia and child molestation, prostitution, and other forms of criminal vice. It was particularly effective in exploiting fears of black male sexual deviance and the vulnerability of white female virtue, while at the same time reifying popular assumptions about the interconnectivity of national identity, citizenship, and "whiteness."[8]

Between 1920 and 1926, the Invisible Empire grew rapidly in Texas, at one point reaching approximately 150,000 members, including most members of the state's Thirty-Eighth Legislature between 1923 and 1925.[9] This growth came in part thanks to the leadership of Hiram W. Evans, a dentist from Dallas, where popular notions of law and order, whiteness, and the perceived absence of black political influence were as deeply entrenched as anywhere in the state. Evans joined the Texas Klan in 1920; by 1922 he was the organization's Imperial Wizard, or national leader. Under Evans, the Klan prioritized political organization and engagement with all levels of government—local, state, and federal. Over the next several years, the Klan successfully strengthened its operational presence across the nation, creating well-organized local chapters that contributed directly to state and local Democratic campaigns, while also frightening more than a few locals into modifying their morally questionable behaviors. Although Evans publicly opposed the type of vigilante violence that had made the Klan famous since the late 1860s, rogue action remained a visible part of the Klan's culture and public personality. This brand of unsanctioned, vigilante "justice" was also very much in keeping with Texas's frontier history and its proclivities to see armed self-defense as a core tenet of properly patriarchal family life. Sadly, Klan violence was very common in Texas. As Walter Buenger puts it, white Texans "lynched blacks at a stunning rate and in a gruesome style" throughout the first half of the 1920s.[10]

The Texas Klan's power was on full display in 1922, when its intervention into the race for a US Senate seat proved decisive in the election of Earle Mayfield. Among other issues, Mayfield emphasized his support for Prohibition, contrasted against alcohol abuse and moral degradation more broadly. Rumors abounded that Mayfield was himself a member of the Klan, though it is more likely that he merely enjoyed the political benefits of being associated with the Hood and was not actually a full-fledged member. Mayfield largely avoided direct mention of the Klan during his campaign. The same was true among his more prominent supporters, including Texas's famously progressive United States senator, Morris Sheppard, and future Washington power broker and Klan sympathizer Congressman Hatton Sumners of Dallas, who rose to national prominence during the early 1920s, lobbying forcefully against proposed federal antilynching bills under consideration in 1920 and 1922.[11]

Regardless, Mayfield's victory was a clear reflection of the Klan's influence at the ballot box. On Mayfield's coattails, the Klan celebrated down-ballot victories across the state, most notably in Dallas, where seven such candidates won in local races. The Invisible Empire celebrated those victories with an evening parade in downtown Dallas where members marched in hoods to "Onward Christian Soldiers."[12]

Anti-Klan Democrats objected to the KKK's cultish, secretive persona, not to mention its reputation for violence. Above all, however, anti-Klan Democrats objected to the Invisible Empire's expanding political power. Strong in number, but lacking coherent organization on par with their opponents, the anti-Klan faction eventually found its leader in Miriam "Ma" Ferguson. At the time, most knew Ma Ferguson simply as the wife of former Texas governor James "Pa" Ferguson, also known colloquially as "Farmer Jim." Texas voters elected Pa to serve as governor in 1914, then reelected him for a second term in 1916. In 1917, however, the Texas House impeached Pa Ferguson over a series of scandals, including one involving academic freedom issues with the University of Texas at Austin, along with his decision to veto all appropriations to the public university in 1917. In a legally questionable attempt to skirt the implications of his impeachment, Ferguson resigned from office one day after the state's Court of Impeachment issued its conviction on the matter. Ever defiant, Ferguson continued to pursue his political career, running unsuccessfully for governor in 1918, before losing to Mayfield in the 1922 Democratic primary race for US Senate, all while the legality of his candidacies was a subject of much controversy.[13]

Refusing to go quietly into the night, Pa subsequently launched a shadow career through his wife. Together, Ma and Pa Ferguson emerged as one of the most colorful, controversial, and well-known political duos in American history. With a populist style and a penchant for the dramatic, the Fergusons offered a clear contrast to the Klan's hood, particularly on the issue of Prohibition. The Fergusons styled themselves as champions of the "forgotten man" and specifically of wets and other outsiders, shunned by the hypermoralistic. They even advocated and tried to implement a radically liberal use of gubernatorial pardoning power, releasing convicted criminals to the dismay of many and at times lending perceived credence to the Klan's criticisms of Fergusonism as an affront to law and order.[14]

Sometimes successfully, sometimes not, the Fergusons' flair for the dramatic kept them at the center of the state's political spotlight for the next two decades. Making no effort to hide their political alliance, or Pa's ongoing influence, the Fergusons ran for governor in 1924, using Ma as a front. They won, defeating the Klan-backed candidate, Felix D. Robertson. Their chief issue was the need to "unmask" and disempower the Klan. Miriam Ferguson thus became the first female governor of Texas, though Pa maintained an office in the capitol building and exerted significant control over state affairs.[15]

Thus contextualized, Al Smith's 1928 loss in Texas should not have been surprising. The Democratic Party's decision to nominate a wet Catholic for president inspired Klansmen and other similarly minded Texans to exploit commonly held bigotries, fomenting fear, anger, and backlash wherever possible. Ironically, Smith officially accepted his party's presidential nomination in Houston, which hosted the 1928 Democratic National Convention that June—the first time either national party had held its nominating convention in a southern state since the end of the Civil War. Texas newspapers covered the convention with gusto, particularly Texas governor Dan Moody's unshakable opposition to Smith, whom some opponents had taken to calling "Alcohol Smith." Dry Democrats like Moody aggressively organized support for a plank in the party's platform calling for rigid and "honest enforcement of the Constitution," specifically Prohibition. Some Texans took the opportunity to champion Moody as an alternative nominee, though that drive fizzled without gaining much traction in the national party.[16]

Throughout the rest of the summer and fall of 1928, the Ku Klux Klan promoted conspiracy theories involving Rome's alleged plan for an eventual coup in the United States, painting caricatures of Al Smith as something between a puppet and a religious wolf in sheep's clothing whose loyalty to the Vatican would overwhelm his oath to uphold the Constitution. Put more bluntly, Smith's opponents did everything they could to tar the governor of New York as un-American, exploiting narrow-minded nationalistic bigotries as blatantly as they could.[17]

Race played a similarly key role in the state's defection to Hoover in 1928, despite the issue grabbing very few headlines relative to coverage of Smith's religion or debates about alcohol. While rejecting Smith's church and his stand on alcohol, many conservatives also feared—with little cause—that he would dismantle constitutional provisions protecting states' rights, especially on issues of race. Such Democrats frequently expressed hostility to burgeoning civil rights activism, commonly describing such ideas as progressive paternalism at best, socialism and communism at worst. They insisted on holding the line. As one Houstonian told FDR in a letter just weeks before the election, Al Smith was the candidate of "the colored race" and, therefore, a "menace." Once Smith's candidacy was dead, the Houstonian hoped FDR would lead the party into the next decade, moving it away from obsession over "sumptuary" laws and the whims of the "rich and powerful," while also unequivocally rejecting federal paternalism in any form. These sentiments reflected the rampant bipolarity gripping the Texas electorate in 1928. On the one hand, Texas Democrats demanded loyalty to the party of their Confederate ancestors; on the other, they expressed considerable frustration over their growing inability to rid the party of its progressive, Northern influences. Meanwhile, as other Democrats fretted over segregation and white supremacy in the face of progressive Catholic machinations, national Republicans appeared to lose all interest in the subject and generally ignored race-related issues altogether. Beyond that, by 1928 the Party of Lincoln seemed to have become the more "lily white" of the two organizations.[18] As one observer described it to Tom Love: "The present political situation in Texas has placed many of our office seekers in a strange predicament, and they don't know where to straddle. Many of them are shouting for Governor Smith, and think they are forced to do so on account of party regularity. It is time to change horses because there is a political tornado sweeping Texas today, and many old political shells will be thrown high on the beach to dry and to bleach in our Southern sunlight."[19]

More than anything else, though, the issue of alcohol—and specifically the fear that Smith would push to repeal the Eighteenth Amendment—catalyzed bolters toward Hoover and the GOP. This was almost certainly the case for Thomas Love, who frequently told colleagues that he held "no religious prejudice whatever" and had, in fact, "been voting for Roman Catholics for forty years," adding that "some of those nearest and dearest" to him had been members of the Catholic Church.[20] Instead, Love focused on alcohol as a tool of "Tammanyites" and opponents of "good government," going so far as to label himself and his like-minded bolters the "Loyal Anti-Tammany Democrats of Texas." Earning national attention for his efforts in Texas, Love's supporters championed the state senator from Dallas for a cabinet post in the Hoover administration, while others called for Love to campaign for governor of Texas. Meanwhile, Texas Republicans capitalized on the moment, collaborating with Love, Moody, and other anti-Smith Democrats in 1928 to create pro-Hoover clubs in 249 of the state's 254 counties.[21]

Obsessed with issues of race, religion, alcohol, crime, and vigilante justice, Texans found little time for the discussion of economics. Eight years into a decade marked at the national level by slashed budgets, major tax cuts, rising stock values, and overall Republican dominance, some Texans found peace of mind in the knowledge that their state's holy trinity of economic commodities—cattle, cotton, and oil—

provided a level of stable predictability unavailable in other parts of the country. Such confidence endured even in the face of severe economic difficulties gripping Texas farmers throughout the 1920s, a precursor in some ways to the plights they would face in the decade to come. Drawing on populist attitudes that had never fully vanished, such Texans typically hated the wealthy "northeastern establishment" as they often called it, as well as the millionaires, bankers, and corporate executives they believed controlled it. Meanwhile, Herbert Hoover promoted the idea that America was "nearer to the final triumph over poverty than ever before," reflecting Americans' broader confidence in the future. Soon enough Hoover's predictions would sound quite foolhardy. Still, the state's political zeitgeist found little room for worries about the nation's economic health.[22]

All of it was simply too much for Al Smith to overcome. Having voted Democrat in every presidential election (in which it had participated) since its annexation in 1845, Texas gave Hoover 51.8 percent of the statewide popular vote in 1928. It was a scant majority, but noteworthy since, to that time, the only Republican presidential candidate to carry more than 40 percent of the Texas vote was Ulysses S. Grant in 1872—the first election in which Texas was allowed to participate since seceding from the Union in 1861. In all, just under 709,000 Texans cast a ballot for president in 1928. Four years earlier that number had been 660,453. In light of the overall increase in voter turnout, it is hard to argue that Smith lost simply because of Democratic overconfidence or apathy, as Charles Berry had perhaps wished was true. Rather, Al Smith failed to carry Texas because he was Catholic and wet. These two concerns coalesced into an ethnocultural anchor sealing Smith's fate in an otherwise loyally Democratic state. Still, Smith won 341,032 Texas votes—48.1 percent of the overall total. He won more votes than Democrat James Cox (and his running mate Franklin D. Roosevelt) had won in 1920, when Cox's 288,767 votes had been enough to carry 59.3 percent of the state. Smith also won more votes than Woodrow Wilson's 286,514 in 1916, when the president who "kept us out of war" carried 76.9 percent of the state.[23]

Clearly divided in 1928, Texas Democrats looked ahead to 1929 and the decade to come, prepared to wrestle for the future of their party along the lines of "hood, bonnet, and little brown jug." Like other Americans, however, they were not prepared for the Great Depression.

"The Supreme Need of Our Country"

Less than a year after voters elected Herbert Hoover to the presidency, the New York Stock Exchange collapsed. Whether the Great Depression began in October 1929 with the "great crash" or resulted from a far more complex interplay of numerous factors, that sudden downturn on Wall Street unquestionably accelerated a catastrophic downturn in the national and international economic order. Over the next few years, thanks to the domino effect of bank failures and related farm and housing foreclosures, it also radically transformed Texas politics, making the era of hood, bonnet, and little brown jug seem like an antiquated and rather petty environment.[24] Norman Brown's assessment of Texas politics during the 1920s reinforces the widely held view of the Lone Star State as a long-standing bastion of conservatism, or at least of social conservatism. However, as Walter Buenger and Gregg Cantrell have shown, the perception of overwhelming conservatism belies a more complicated reality, particularly when it comes to popular attitudes toward economic policy. Obviously, most Texans were against sending a Catholic to the White House in 1928. However, given the success of populist and progressive candidates in state and local races during the late nineteenth and early twentieth centuries, as well as the state's move toward greater regulatory control over both banking and oil during the 1910s and 1920s, the idea that Texas might support a northern liberal in 1932 hardly seem farfetched.[25]

This became especially apparent once the collapsing economic landscape began to hit Texas homes with more force in 1930. In the months immediately following the crash, most Texan newspapers treated Wall Street's troubles as a curiosity, assuming the meltdown's fallout would not extend beyond irresponsible financiers and disdained speculators. Eventually however, the Depression began to unravel the lives of ordinary Texans. Unemployment levels soon exceeded 20 percent in most Texas cities; in Houston, the number was 23 percent. Texas cotton farmers lost 50 percent of their land under plow, and approximately $1 billion in total farm value over the next decade. Livestock values plummeted by roughly $100 million. Industrial manufacturing slowed considerably, prompting Congressman Hatton Sumners of Dallas to promote a moratorium on new patents for all machines designed to reduce the need for human labor. Oil prices dropped from $1.30 per barrel in 1930 to $0.10 in 1931, at one point reaching a low of $0.02.

Ironically, a massive oil discovery in Kilgore, Texas, contributed greatly to a surplus of crude, thereby aiding the global oil market's collapse. Banks struggled to keep up. Many failed. People starved.[26]

Franklin Roosevelt was already campaigning by then. In fact, FDR began to lay the groundwork for his 1932 campaign almost immediately after Smith's defeat in 1928, just as Charles Berry had hoped he would. Within a few weeks of Election Day, Roosevelt sent dozens of letters to Democratic officeholders across the nation, including most in Texas. Though he strategically customized aspects of each letter, offering congratulatory notes on recent victories where applicable or making other kinds of personal comments, FDR's message in each was the same—a call for partisan unity, optimism, and help. For instance, in writing to Texas congressman Marvin Jones in late November, Roosevelt suggested that the Panhandle-based Democrat refocus his activities, giving priority to national Democrats in more competitive districts, thinking ahead to the 1930 midterms. If that went well, FDR said, Jones could well play an even stronger role during the next presidential campaign of 1932. After asking Jones to recruit local Democrats back into the partisan fold, FDR extended an invitation to his own upcoming gubernatorial inauguration in Albany, New York. The future was brighter than it seemed, FDR said; circumstances were bound to change and would eventually conspire to favor the Party of Jefferson once again.[27]

Roosevelt's ambitions may not have changed much between 1928 and 1932, but thanks to the Great Depression, his political calculus did. Like most Americans, Texas Democrats did not fully understand why things had gone so horribly wrong under Hoover, nor could they agree on precisely how the country should fix the situation. But if any single individual was to blame for the mess, it had to be Herbert Hoover; on that, virtually everyone in Texas came to agree. In response to the rapidly shifting political winds, scores of Texas Hoovercrats scrambled to retether themselves to the Democratic Party and the traditional loyalties enjoyed therein. After all, in the view of Democratic loyalists quick to use hindsight, the precipitating cause of the present disaster had been bolters' misguided flirtations with the GOP. As it turned out, Thomas Love's about-face would be as dramatic as, or more so than, anyone else's in Texas. In the immediate wake of Smith's national repudiation, Love told his fellow bolters that Franklin Roosevelt would be just as unacceptable as Smith and that the national party needed to look beyond New York for its next standard-bearer. "Texas would rather see Al Smith than Franklin D. Roosevelt," Love told Winslow Porter in mid-November 1928, adding that FDR was even "more dangerous" than Smith because he "appeared" benign but was a "Tammanyite" just the same. To William Mills that same week, Love wrote that he "could not support" FDR for president in 1932 or ever, even though he considered Roosevelt his "very close friend." "I would just as soon vote for a wet Catholic as a wet Protestant," Love said. Those in Love's network largely agreed with such assessments: "I see the Tammanyites are at it already and are booming Franklin Roosevelt," a friend told Love just after the election. To him, FDR was "just as objectionable without having Smith's ability."[28] Resolute in their defiance, dry Democrats nevertheless understood that at some point they would need to rebuild their party, most likely behind an entirely new cause and an entirely new individual. Assuming that wet forces would be unable to recover from Smith's candidacy, J. A. Edgerton—vice presidential nominee for the Prohibition Party, a national but relatively small third-party movement—told Love that it was time for "progressive people in the Democratic and Prohibition Parties to get together and plan for the future."[29]

By 1932, the future was now, the issue was the economy, and for the remainder of the 1930s, Thomas Love would be among FDR's most enthusiastic supporters. The key to Love's transformation between 1928 and 1932 lay in the reality that his myopic focus on Prohibition during the late 1920s had derived not from a religious conviction or a sense of hypermoralistic traditionalism. Rather, his political animus came from a reformist spirit that embraced activist, progressive government—"good government" as he usually called it—for the betterment of the "common good." Love's affair with progressive ideas had been central to his life and career for decades. As early as 1908, he told an audience of bankers in Dallas that state governments should aim to protect "states' rights" not by opposing regulation, but by embracing the kind of proactive, liberal reform being discussed in Washington, doing as much as it could to "thoroughly and wholesomely" protect its citizens from the imbalances of industrial economies. In Love's view, governments existed "for the protection of the weak against the encroachments of the strong." Love's evolution on FDR between 1928 and 1932, undoubtedly shaped by the Great Depression, reflects well the transitions that carried reform-minded progressives into the newer world of modern liberalism, where "evangelistic" transformation of the soul took a backseat to the "power of the federal government to provide specific economic and social benefits."[30]

Put simply, in 1928, the Prohibition issue made Thomas Love among the most impassioned Hoovercrats in Texas or anywhere in America; by 1932, his goals were different, as was his perspective of the national party. As he later confessed in a personal letter to Roosevelt, Love had "put principle above party" when rejecting Al Smith in 1928. With the benefit of hindsight, he—along with "hundreds of thousands of dry Democrats"—were ready to repent and rejoin the Democratic cause.[31]

The case of Texas congressman James Buchanan offers another window into this dynamic. First elected to the US House of Representatives in 1913, Buchanan was a conservative by most definitions of the day. He advocated limited government, low taxes, and states' rights. He was also dry, shamefully sympathetic to the Ku Klux Klan, an opponent of woman suffrage, and a vocal advocate for tighter security on the Mexican border. However, Buchanan's ideological convictions did not prevent him from considering, and on multiple occasions embracing, the value of pragmatic compromise. In fact, Buchanan routinely chose pragmatism over ideological conviction. When the KKK began to collapse in 1926 under the weight of national and regional scandals, Buchanan quickly disassociated himself from the organization. He ceased all mention of it in public and, instead, recalibrated his reelection messages to mirror the basic themes of "100 percent Americanism" without referring specifically to the hooded menace. Refusing to defend the Klan by name, Buchanan simply called himself "a Democrat from every standpoint" and a representative "mindful of the people's rights and interests."[32]

Meanwhile, Buchanan's brand of conservatism often took a backseat to his efforts on behalf of the less-fortunate citizens of his Tenth District in the Texas Hill Country. For instance, he frequently argued in favor of steeper, more graduated income taxes, saying that richer Americans should carry disproportionately higher tax burdens in order to help those less fortunate. He also supported federal action to help farmers and ranchers. In some of the more impassioned moments of his career, Buchanan argued that state governments did not have the financial resources or the infrastructure to deal with natural disasters. In one specific case involving a pink bollworm infestation, Buchanan—with a notable sense of urgency—called for direct, immediate action from Washington. He asked for $4 million in direct federal payments to southern farmers in order to protect the region's "monopoly in cotton production," which to one national reporter he exaggeratedly called "one of the greatest gifts that God ever bestowed upon our nation."

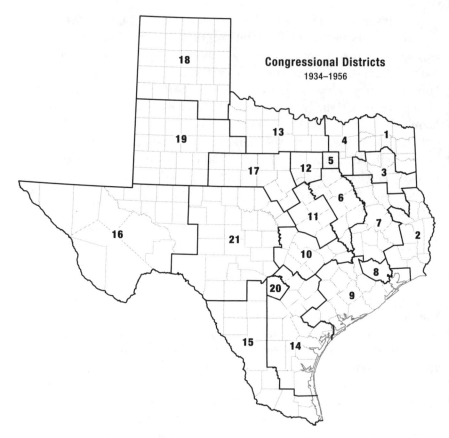

Texas congressional districts during the "Age of FDR." Map by Erin Greb Cartography.

The former Klan-sympathizing conservative that he may have been, Buchanan nevertheless supported Al Smith for president in 1928; he was many things, but he was not a bolter.[33]

By 1930, with the Depression breaching economic levees across the state, Buchanan focused his congressional reelection campaign squarely on the twin pillars of partisan loyalty and pragmatic populism. He emphasized Hoover's incompetence and the dangers of voting Republican. He also referred to himself as a "man of action" and a "Democrat of the old school." Contradicting his 1928 support for federal agriculture relief, in 1930 Buchanan said, "Local self-government is essential to the preservation and perpetuation of our representative democracy," while continuing to brand himself as a resolute defender of states' rights, defined by newspapers in his district as opposition to the "centralizing and destructive tendency to regulate everything through Federal Bureaus." At the same time, and without any sense of irony, Buchanan also backed labor unions seeking collective bargaining rights. He also attacked Republicans for allying with Wall Street corporations and banks rather than workers and farmers like the people of his home district, whom he called the embodiment of hard work, integrity, and American virtue. Editorialists described Buchanan as someone who "believes in and supports party organization, abides by the will of the majority, and votes and supports all nominees of the Democratic Party."[34]

In many ways, Buchanan was a typical Texas Democrat. He was generically conservative on everyday issues, but pragmatic enough to earn a reputation as a dealmaker. He had a reputation for being principled but willing to negotiate common-sense solutions for the common man (assuming those men were white). When push came to shove, constituents trusted him to resist ideological pressures. He held retrograde opinions about race and ethnicity, but when race receded as an issue during the 1930s, those opinions faded from the limelight. He could speak about core values and Americanism while debating minutia with any policy wonk. More than anything, Buchanan sold himself as a reliable party loyalist and advocate for hard-working white Texans who needed help overcoming Republican-made mistakes. Texas was a Democratic state by tradition, he argued, and needed to unite behind that party to defeat Republicans who did not have the average Texan's best interests in mind. Conservative in some areas, populist in others, and loyal to his party, Buchanan easily won reelection in 1930.[35]

Buchanan's brand of populist Democratic politics was common, but it did not hold a complete monopoly. Progressives remained a strong minority in Texas and played a key role in balancing the Democratic Party at the state level, especially in its operational governing culture. Wright Patman was a great example of this. In 1928, Patman defeated the incumbent, Eugene Black, for a congressional seat representing the state's First District in East Texas along both the Oklahoma and Arkansas borders. Black had served the district since 1915, but found himself increasingly out of step with the region's economic and cultural shifts, opposing government intervention on economic matters while endorsing federal crackdowns on communists and other social dissidents during the 1920s. Patman, on the other hand, promoted progressive reforms and regulatory measures, particularly for Wall Street, while identifying with—as Walter Buenger has described it—the "heroic nature of local plain people and the importance of Texas symbols," factors of increasing importance to the state's political culture as it evolved beyond its ex-Confederate moorings. Patman's populist campaign emphasized support for "plain people" in the fight against "government favoritism" to the wealthy. He argued that stronger cooperation with the federal government would aid economic modernization and provide greater opportunities for both his district and state. Along these lines, Patman advocated currency reform (as he would continue to do in varying ways for the rest of his career) and warned against the emergence of national chain stores, establishing a reputation as a friend to entrepreneurialism and locally owned small businesses. He also courted unions, including the American Federation of Labor, and lambasted Black as an ally of the Ku Klux Klan. Patman also promoted a policy for increased compensation and better overall care for military veterans. He won the election in 1928 by roughly three thousand votes and continued to represent the district until retiring in 1976.[36]

The state's best-known progressive—and one of the most visible and influential in the entire country—was Morris Sheppard. A congressman from 1903 to 1913 and a United States senator since 1913, Sheppard authored the Eighteenth Amendment that created Prohibition, advocated woman suffrage and protective legislation for children, and remains one of the least-appreciated actors shaping Texas politics during the first four decades of the twentieth century. A friend and disciple of William Jennings Bryan, Sheppard was Texas's most articulate, if at times melodramatic, champion of Democratic virtues. He also frequently condemned Republican "evils," which is the term he most often used. His oratorical elegance and devout moralism earned him national regard, and his use of religious imagery was particularly noteworthy considering he routinely applied these motifs to attacks on corporate greed. He called on his fellow Texas Democrats to support political leaders who resisted the consolidation of wealth, an act he once defined as the "lifeblood of Christian citizenship." He often said that religion was the "basis of society" and consistently contextualized his progressive attitudes within the context of his faith.[37]

Despite being somewhat of an anachronism, Sheppard's moralist progressivism blended nicely with the evolving style that would come to define modern liberalism. Sheppard expressed an unwavering commitment to the idea of government as a positive good, existing entirely to serve, protect, and defend the American Dream for any individual rugged enough to fight for it. Using his standing in the US Senate to reinforce the virtues of partisan loyalty and good government of the people, Sheppard was a bulwark against antigovernment voices in Texas, offering many who were perhaps uncomfortable with the notion of a powerful central government a cloak of moral justification. In this way, Morris Sheppard was a bridge connecting working- and middle-class whites to what would eventually be the New Deal. He even went so far as to identify progressive liberalism as "Christian" because of its commitment to protecting families, the "core unit," as he said, of healthy American democracy.[38]

By 1930, Sheppard was actively evangelizing Texas Hoovercrats, calling them to repentance and service to the party of their fathers, an act he called the "supreme need of our country." To one audience he said that "the solution of this Republic" was available only "in the legislation of the Democratic Party," adding that "for 60 of the last 68 years, the Republican Party has been in chaos, and what has been the result? The vast majority of the American people have been transformed from owners to tenants and employees." Sheppard warned Texans about the closing "channels of opportunity" that Republicans had threatened to annihilate, thus creating a "permanent dependence on all master classes for the employment that means life itself." In another speech, he called the GOP "faithless" and "inefficient." He then prophesied the woes of unchecked Republican authority:

> The danger is that a few more years of Republican supremacy may make it impossible to restore justice to agriculture and the people. . . . Nothing stands out more clearly against the backdrop of the last 60 years than the alliance of the Republican Party with concentrated financial power and all the forces of reaction . . . [the Democratic Party] will not die till liberty dies and the last aspiration for freedom shall have forever faded from the human heart.[39]

Maury Maverick shared Morris Sheppard's view of Republicans. He also shared his passion. His style, however, was less William Jennings Bryan and more Eugene V. Debs, the famed socialist agitator who once campaigned for the White House from a prison cell. The grandson of Samuel Maverick—whose refusal to brand his cattle resulted in the name "Maverick" becoming synonymous with free-spirited, rebellious

independence—Maury Maverick emerged as a key player in state politics in 1929 when he, along with a group of other prominent San Antonio business leaders, organized the Citizens League of San Antonio.
The Citizens League was a direct response to local Republican Harry
Wurzbach's controversial and disputed reelection to Congress in 1929,
after a thirteen-month legal fight against Democrat Augustus McCloskey. Maverick railed against Wurzbach's reelection and voiced concerns
that an established "machine" had rigged local politics against the will
of the people. Between 1929 and 1931, Maverick used his position as
Bexar County tax collector to build a base of grassroots backers most
notable for their animosity against Wurzbach, Herbert Hoover, and the
conservative establishments controlling, as he saw it, both the Texas
Democratic Party and the national GOP. Throughout the 1930s, few
Texans agitated more aggressively for direct state and federal relief from
the Depression's ill effects than did Maury Maverick.[40]

Men like Love, Buchanan, Patman, Sheppard, and Maverick represented overlapping varieties within the factional (and oft-fractured)
framework of the Texas Democratic Party. Divided in so many ways,
Texas Democrats unified behind Herbert Hoover's unpopularity, perceptions of the Republican Party as evil and incompetent," and the
related call to all Texans to vote Democrat as their "forefathers" had.
Above all else, they were pragmatic populists who promised to fight for
those who could not fight for themselves.

Meanwhile, the economy kept getting worse. Conditions deteriorated throughout 1930, 1931, and 1932, exacerbated by the disastrous
effects of the ill-designed Hawley-Smoot Tariff, passed by Congress and
signed into law by Hoover during the summer of 1930. Only two of
eighteen members of the House delegation from Texas voted in favor,
one of those being the lone Texas Republican, Harry Wurzbach, who
would be dead within the year. Hawley-Smoot imposed protective tariffs
on foreign imports to the United States in an effort to encourage consumers to buy American and thus save manufacturing jobs in the heavily
industrialized states of the Northeast and Midwest. Instead, the bill just
made the economic hole deeper. So did Hoover's push to raise marginal income tax rates, a decision reversing a decade of precedent in the
hopes of balancing the federal budget without cutting federal stimulus
programs, such as the newly created Reconstruction Finance Corporation (RFC). Importantly, the RFC was led chiefly by the internationally renowned shipbuilder and solidly Texan Jesse H. Jones of Houston.

Jones's participation notwithstanding, by early 1932 incredulous Texas business leaders and voters were increasingly impatient for new leadership. Some Texans even began to dream about promoting one of their own to the highest office in the land.[41]

"A Fresh Approach"

On January 7, 1932, members of the Houston Chamber of Commerce gathered to hear from William L. Clayton, by then one of the world's most influential international cotton merchants. A native of Mississippi, Clayton relocated to Houston in 1916, bringing his company's headquarters with him. Before the decade was out, Clayton's company would be the largest of its kind. If anyone had any good ideas for solving the current economic mess, surely, these leaders thought, Clayton would. Taking cues from those around him, Clayton used his speech to vilify national Republicans, Hoover specifically. Referencing Hawley-Smoot, he blamed Republicans for initiating a "rising tide of taxation" and rapped his fellow business leaders for failing to recognize that "national and international conditions" had a direct impact on their bottom lines. Not surprisingly, he called for a strictly free-market response to the global depression. As Clayton saw it, local business leaders needed to involve themselves directly in the political process, with an aim toward limiting the growth of the federal government. Even more specifically, Democrats needed to take charge of the federal budget to cut "wasteful" public spending. If possible, they needed to cut taxes as well. "Do you realize that the cost of government—federal, state, municipal—in the United States in 1931 absorbed one out of every five days of labor of every man, woman, and child who produced anything in the United States that year?" Clayton asked. "Can anyone deny that this borders dangerously on the beginning of economic disintegration? The federal treasury has surrendered to the world's greatest racket. What are we going to do about it?" Like most other Texas Democrats of the day, he spent most of his time pointing out Republican mistakes, not promoting Democratic solutions. Clearly, Clayton was among friends at the Houston Chamber of Commerce. There was little risk in publicly suggesting that Hoover was a failure or that Republicans had made things worse by promoting wasteful, tax-raising, market-interrupting failures. Government was supposed to work with business, not against it, he said. It should either help or get out of the way. A turn toward sound business principles was in order.[42]

A few weeks later, the Speaker of the US House of Representatives wrote to his congressional colleagues and fellow Texans to promote precisely the same ideas Clayton had advanced in his speech before the Houston Chamber of Commerce. In a mass-distributed letter, John Nance Garner said that it was time for Washington to cut taxes, deregulate private businesses, cut spending, and balance the federal budget. Hoover's incursions into public works and deficit spending were counterproductive and unwelcome, he asserted. Rather, the Democratic Party's success in 1932 depended on its ability to apply common-sense business practices to the management and recovery of the American economy. The Texas delegation members who received this letter almost certainly took Garner's words seriously. After all, Garner—or to many, "Cactus Jack"—was not simply the Speaker of the House; he was also quickly becoming a serious contender for the Democratic Party's presidential nomination in 1932. Widely respected by his peers, Garner became House minority leader after the 1928 elections, making him the natural heir to the speakership when Democrats took back the House in the midterm elections of 1930. By 1932, Garner seemed to be precisely the type of cool, capable, experienced Democrat the nation needed navigating the ship during uncertain times and stormy seas.[43]

Thus began the so-called Garner Boom of 1932. In 1902 voters first sent Garner, a two-term member of the Texas House of Representatives, to Congress, where he served as representative for the state's Fifteenth Congressional District along the South Texas border with Mexico. He had been born in northeast Texas, not far from the Oklahoma and Arkansas borders, but he rose to prominence in Uvalde, just west of San Antonio, and that was where he hung his hat for most of his life. A lawyer by trade, but a prototypical Texas cowboy in persona, he was a favorite subject for political cartoonists to feature. Admirers saw John Nance Garner, ever the faithful Democratic soldier, as grizzled, strong, and loyal. Supporters highlighted his resolve and stability. He held a reputation as a no-nonsense advocate for common-sense aid to Americans in need. Above all, Garner boosters promoted their hero as a consummate party man who was above the petty ideological squabbles that had been distracting voters for a decade or more.[44]

Tempered by his experiences in Washington and as pragmatic as a power-broking insider was expected to be, Garner was by most definitions a states' rights, fiscal conservative. He opposed the Eighteenth, Nineteenth, and Twentieth Amendments because, as he put it, the federal government should not "interfere" with something "states could do for themselves." He also criticized Hoover's free-spending proclivities, especially his failure to maintain a balanced budget.[45] The president had shown a willingness to experiment in 1931 and 1932, supporting various public works projects, not to mention the recently created RFC, which provided federal financing of loans to desperate banks and other private businesses. The protective tariffs passed into law through the Hawley-Smoot bill had ground global trade to a halt, and advocates of free and open markets were aghast to see Washington interfere with capitalism's purported ability to heal itself, not to mention Hoover's support for steep tax increases, passed into law that January in the Revenue Act of 1932.[46]

Like other emerging presidential candidates, Garner spent much of the spring and summer lobbying for support in Democratic circles across the country, attacking Hoover every step of the way. Beyond simply attacking Hoover's general failures to lead, most Democrats, including Roosevelt, ridiculed Hoover's fiscal strategies as unwisely experimental and excessively interventionist. "I accuse the [Hoover] Administration of being the greatest spending administration in peace times in all our history," Franklin Roosevelt said during one radio address during the earliest months of the campaign. "It is an administration that has piled bureau on bureau, commission on commission, and has failed to anticipate the dire needs and the reduced earning power of the people. Bureaucrats and bureaucrats, commissions and commissioners have been retained at the expense of the taxpayer." For a time, it seemed that Democrats would base the substance of their anti-Hooverism squarely on the need to reembrace more fiscally conservative policies.[47]

The lack of major differences among national candidates notwithstanding, most members of the Texas congressional delegation directly supported Garner's campaign, or at the very least offered it their endorsement. Marvin Jones was among those in the former category. Jones had represented the Texas Panhandle in Congress since 1917. A traditionalist, he was factionalized along Prohibition lines during the 1920s, but remained faithful to his party when push came to shove, especially in 1928. Campaigning for reelection that year, Jones openly supported both farm organization and looser credit for farmers in dire need. He also briefly touched on the need for border security and stricter im-

migration laws, as well as his support for Prohibition. These latter platform points mattered to Jones, but less so than did the farmers in his
district, most of whom were already in the throes of economic turmoil
by 1928 and were not, therefore, in a mood to experiment with partisan
disloyalty on the basis of cultural issues. Privately, Smith's nomination
appalled Jones, who told one colleague that it had been a "travesty."
Publicly, however, Jones supported Smith, saying he was obliged to support "all Democrats." He remained unflappably loyal to his party; Marvin Jones was no bolter.[48]

A states'-rights conservative in the mold of many southern Democrats, Jones campaigned for reelection throughout the 1920s telling his
constituents that most forms of government control, other than those
of the local or municipal variety, were unwanted and unhelpful. He
criticized state officials in Austin just as frequently as he did federal officials in Washington. For Jones, local tax dollars should always remain
local, state and federal spending should be as limited as possible, and
Congress should always be looking to slash budgets, not expand them.
In 1931, he attacked Hoover during a speech in Haskell, saying that
there "has been too much centralization in government. It is growing
top heavy. It is too expensive. These expenses must be cut. Bureaus
must be eliminated. There must be a revival of old-fashioned economy
all along the line."[49]

In 1931, however, Jones began to recognize that his constituents
wanted certain protections from moneyed power, corporations, banks,
and other elites most responsible for forgetting the "forgotten man."
"The decentralization of business as well as of government," Jones said
in 1931, "must be brought about." He advocated the restoration of "individual business opportunity" and "the entire revamping of the money
system so as to do away with the control and dictation of a few men,"
calling such strategies the "sheet anchor of our Republic." Like many of
his fellow Texas Democrats, Jones was as much a pragmatist as he was
a conservative. He believed that negotiated compromise was at the very
core of what made a representative democracy work. He espoused conservative ideas and traditionalist virtues with a conviction rivaling anyone in Congress. Yet at the same time, he was also unafraid of meeting
a political opponent somewhere in the middle to get things done. Jones
was a free-market capitalist, but frequently spoke about government's
foundational obligation to protect its citizens from injustice and danger:
"It is the primary function of government, any government, to hold the

scales of justice evenly balanced and open the doors of opportunity for people to do things for themselves and work out their own salvation."[50]

For Jones and many other Texas Democrats, Jack Garner was the right choice at the right time. On February 23, the *San Antonio Evening News* endorsed Garner's potential candidacy, saying it was "high time that the people awaken, and that we send to Washington a man whose heart is with the toiling millions, and who cannot be lulled to sleep by the subtle perfume of Wall Street . . . John Nance Garner is that man." Concurrent with that endorsement, Texas Democrats gathered for a pro-Garner rally at the San Antonio Municipal Auditorium. A litany of speakers praised Garner, calling him a "great statesman" and the only candidate who would unflinchingly commit to the promise of "Thou Shalt Not Tax!" On the accurate assumption that those in attendance needed little convincing of Garner's presidential bona fides, most speakers spent the bulk of their allotted time condemning Republicans for their various failures and foibles, undercutting any notion that a bolt to Hoover in 1932 would be anything other than political suicide. Referencing the Hoovercrat bolt of 1928, San Antonio mayor C. M. Chambers painted a picture of Garner as a Moses leading Texas Democrats back to the Promised Land, forebodingly adding:

> For eight years our taxes have been increased while we were chasing the Republican rainbow of hope—and as long as Mr. Hoover is our shepherd, we shall be in want. He has fired more blank cartridges, appointed more committees, and has done less for the people than any President the nation has ever had. America's car of progress has been wrecked, and the Republican full dinner pail has vanished from the earth. . . . I am informed that the Republican Party has changed its party emblem from the elephant to the wolf, because there is a wolf at nearly every citizen's door.[51]

While many Texas Democrats pinned their party's presidential hopes on John Nance Garner, there were other viable candidates, including of course Roosevelt, who enjoyed the strategic support of former Woodrow Wilson advisor and once-prominent Texas business leader Edward M. House. In fact, House's pro-FDR lobbying in other Southern states that spring directly subverted his fellow Texas Democrats' efforts on behalf of Garner. House's political influence within the Democratic Party had long been stronger at the national level than at the state level and would remain so for the rest of his life. Still, his efforts on behalf of Roosevelt throughout the spring and early summer of 1932 proved critical as Garner and others within the party positioned themselves for the nominating fight scheduled for the national convention in Chicago that June.[52]

Meanwhile, officials within the Democratic National Committee worried that a split convention would reignite tensions over the lingering though seemingly less relevant sociocultural issues that had destroyed Al Smith's campaign nationally and in Texas four years earlier. As one anonymous Texas delegate put it to a DNC official on the eve of the convention, the Lone Star State was still "fanatically dry" in 1932, adding that if the national party dared nominate Al Smith or any other "wet Catholic," he and his fellow delegates could very well bolt to the GOP once again. Such threats were hollow, however, and did not reflect the sentiments shared by most other Texas delegates, most of whom recognized that their political world had changed dramatically since 1928. "This state clearly needs education on the principles of democracy," said a different delegate. "Many have forgotten why they were ever Democrats. They are simply wet or dry, Catholic or anti-Catholic." Dogmatically lingering on the issues of alcohol and religion, this individual said, left the nation vulnerable to unwise policies and ineffective leadership.[53]

The Democratic National Convention officially opened in Chicago on June 27, 1932. Roosevelt entered as the favorite. Al Smith, basing his candidacy for renomination on little more than his fierce opposition to Roosevelt, carried the second most delegates through the first, second, and third ballots, arguing that FDR was a "demagogue" of class warfare. (Once allies, Smith and Roosevelt developed a surprisingly heated rivalry in the aftermath of 1928, as FDR replaced Smith as governor of New York and proceeded to move state policy in new directions, without consulting Smith as often as Smith had assumed would be the case. Roosevelt also replaced Smith as New York's most prominent Democratic power broker, which Smith clearly resented.[54]) Meanwhile, some liberals also opposed Roosevelt, calling him a political "lightweight" and a "trimmer" when it came to budgets. For three ballots, the convention seemed deadlocked, with FDR commanding a clear lead that fell just short of the number necessary to achieve two-thirds of the overall total. Smith and Garner remained second and third respectively.[55]

Then came a deal. On July 1, Garner—whose own bid for the nomination had reached a standstill—cooperated (thanks in part to urgings from Senator Tom Connally), to release his delegates (primarily from California and Texas) to FDR. The apparent show of unity and partisan loyalty then prompted a wave of similar defections from other states.

Fearing a deadlocked convention similar to the one that had plagued the party in 1924, and worried that a compromise candidate might not be able to unify the party, Garner cooperated with others in relinquishing his roughly 100 delegates to Roosevelt before the fourth ballot, thereby allowing FDR to surpass the 770 votes needed to secure the nomination. With the nomination assured, Roosevelt, who did not attend the first several days of the convention, took the then-unprecedented step of flying to Chicago to deliver his acceptance speech in person. In that speech, he spoke of a "new deal" for the first time in front of a mass audience, using a phrase that reminded many of the "square deal" his cousin Theodore had once similarly championed for the American people.[56]

Garner's decision (or reluctant willingness, depending on the witness) to release his delegates to Roosevelt was, ultimately, a tremendous nod toward the goal of Democratic unity in pursuit of Hoover's ouster. Selfless though it was on some levels, Garner likely would not have agreed to the shift without securing a place on the ticket. How exactly this happened remains a matter of some historical debate. But, at the very least, FDR campaign manager and chair of the New York Democratic Party, James (Jim) Farley, played a key role by negotiating directly with Texas congressman, Garner protégé, and future Washington giant Sam Rayburn. (Rayburn would play a very similar role in Lyndon Johnson's nomination as John F. Kennedy's running mate in 1960.) Regardless of how it happened, Texas Democrats were pleased to see one of their own on the ticket. Garner's selection mollified establishment conservatives, party loyalists, and the few southerners who were not already in line behind FDR. It also all but guaranteed that Texas would return to the Democratic fold in the general election. Populists trusted Garner to work with Roosevelt to foment a "restoration of government back to the people," while establishment conservatives hoped the Texan would use the vice presidency to help FDR dismantle Hoover's excessive expansions of government.[57]

FDR's top priority upon leaving Chicago was to unify the state party machines that would implement his campaign's strategy at the local level. He deputized that task to his longtime and closest advisor, Louis Howe. FDR trusted Howe, with whom he had been working since his earliest days in the New York State Legislature. In strategizing for Texas, Howe directed Democrats to avoid discussing the Prohibition issue at all costs, seeing it as a losing issue for FDR and down-ballot candidates alike. Instead, Howe encouraged state and local Democrats to adopt messages consistent with FDR's. In other words, the strategy was to prioritize economic issues above all other concerns, contextualized within a discussion of failed leadership. Howe encouraged Texas Democrats to cast FDR's style as in the mold of Andrew Jackson and Woodrow Wilson. He further directed Texas Democrats to highlight the importance of partisan loyalty and tradition and to contrast everything against Hoover's calamitous failures. When possible, Howe also emphasized the importance of projecting confidence and optimism, reminding Democrats to remind voters that FDR's victory was "certain," and that loyal Democrats should not hesitate to jump on board the "FDR train."[58]

Texas Democrats largely complied with these directives, especially when it came to connecting FDR and Wilson. The national campaign also succeeded in purging virtually all references to Prohibition or Al Smith. In Texas, Howe orchestrated a series of public endorsements from conservative Democrats, including many former Hoovercrats. Focusing on the nation's desperate need for new leadership and fresh ideas, Howe staggered FDR endorsements from Tom Connally, Governor Ross Sterling, and former governors Dan Moody, Pat Neff, and others, thus creating a parade of repentant Hoovercrats. Howe wanted drys to be FDR's most prominent backers in Texas. Conversely, he encouraged wets—"the Smith crowd" as he put it—to work in the background, thus inoculating FDR against bad memories from 1928 or a possible backlash related to Prohibition. As one local strategist said, "The wets can work under cover without publicity and can then come out in the open after the drys have committed themselves. All of the wets with whom I talked and all of the Smith men, except very few, were entirely agreeable to such a plan." Texas drys who agreed that Roosevelt was their best hope for victory in November embraced this strategy, though some encouraged Howe to prevent wets from ever entering the campaign, lest he risk another fracture. Those expressing such sentiment included Dallas's Thomas Love, who justified his support for Roosevelt by saying that FDR was a "dry at heart," but had "gone Wet [in previous years] for political purposes." Love later described himself as "one of several million Democrats who are voting for Roosevelt not because of the dripping Wet Plank in the Chicago platform, but in spite of it."[59]

Love's loyalty to FDR during the 1932 campaign was a gateway to renewed influence at the national level, limited and somewhat unwelcome though it may have at times been. During the first days of the Garner boom earlier that year, Love tried to force Garner to commit to Prohibition as the unshakeable law of the land, saying he was "not interested in nominating any Wet candidate for President."[60] Garner refused to comply, telling Love that he would not commit to anything that was not currently an issue under consideration on the floor of the House of Representatives.[61] Dissatisfied with Garner's response, Love—who was virtually addicted to correspondence—began to write more frequently to Roosevelt during the spring and early summer of 1932, sometimes as often as twice per week. Over the next several years, he offered FDR an almost unending stream of unsolicited advice. Occasionally, FDR indulged him with a response. More rarely, Roosevelt deputized Love to work for the administration as a sort of spy, reporting on conditions in the Dallas area, as if FDR needed more eyes and ears. Like most of FDR's relationships, the affection traveled in primarily one direction. Tom Love wanted to feel important, and FDR—as was his greatest political skill—cheerfully obliged when he could.[62]

While orchestrating endorsements from repentant Hoovercrats like Love, Howe simultaneously entrusted dry party loyalists like Marvin Jones with the responsibility for communicating the national campaign's message as frequently as possible. On cue, Jones spoke on the House floor on July 13, delivering a stump speech that he would repeat often in the coming months. Jones attacked Hoover for "broken promises," especially to farmers, and accused the GOP of conspiring to concentrate wealth in the hands of elitist "robber barons." He described his state as "proud" to have Jack Garner running alongside Roosevelt in a quest to overhaul government politics, a process he described as replacing "barnacles" with "modernization" and "energy." Jones also praised FDR's "fresh approach" and emphasized his historical commitment to balanced budgets. Jones even suggested that fiscal responsibility would be a cornerstone of the new administration. Garner, meanwhile, received a hero's welcome in Dallas on July 18, where local radio station WFAA broadcast the vice presidential nominee's remarks upon arriving at the Union railroad terminal.[63]

Other than their perspectives on the degree of Hoover's failure, the official Republican and Democratic platforms were remarkably similar, as historian William Leuchtenburg has noted. Roosevelt promised action, hope, and change, but rarely did he reveal specific details about his so-called New Deal. The strategic beauty of Roosevelt's appeal in 1932 was that progressives, populists, and establishment conservatives were all able to identify their own goals within aspects of the national campaign,

Presidential candidate Franklin D. Roosevelt, with John Nance Garner, campaigning in Peekskill, New York, August 14, 1932. Courtesy of Franklin D. Roosevelt Presidential Library & Museum.

particularly since Hoover's unpopularity was a stronger motivator than even FDR's optimistic charisma. Conservatives appreciated arguments that Hoover's failures revolved, at least in part, around his recklessness and financial mismanagement. Progressives, on the other hand, pined for new ideas and reforms, quickly embracing the New Deal as exactly the type of fresh start the country needed. Populists loved the forgotten-man theme, believing they would have an advocate in Washington who was willing to fight for their interests against Wall Street bankers and corporate elites. Maintaining this coalition of disparate interests necessitated a campaign message noteworthy for its articulate vagueness. Even radicals hoping for a more dramatic turn to the far left projected some optimism onto the Roosevelt campaign. Surprisingly, they did so without tarring that campaign with the tinge of "un-Americanism" as would happen more frequently during the coming decades. This articulate vagueness worked well in that it allowed hopeful Democrats the freedom to project their own beliefs onto the national campaign confident that FDR would be open to new ideas. Younger Texans hopeful for an economically secure future were often more willing to embrace experimentation than were old-line conservatives, many of whom believed that adherence to the tried and true principles of fiscal responsibility was the soundest course of action. Those younger voters could see in Roosevelt a progressive ally who might help them unseat the "minority clique" of establishment conservatives who resisted change. Morris Sheppard similarly told his fellow progressives that Hoover's failures had everything to do with his Republican worldview, which he characterized as elitist, immoral, and insensitive to the needs of average citizens. Ultimately, the less Roosevelt revealed about the precise nature of his New Deal, the more voters already predisposed to supporting anyone but Hoover could rationalize their support for FDR on the mere basis of "change." As Leuchtenburg describes it: "If Roosevelt's program lacked substance, his blithe spirit—his infectious smile, his warm, mellow voice, his obvious ease with crowds—contrasted sharply with Hoover's glumness. While Roosevelt reflected the job of a campaigner winging to victory, Hoover projected defeat."[64]

Texans would have voted for FDR in 1932 regardless of his running mate, but they were especially enthused by Garner's place on the ticket. Ironically, though, Garner's actual role in the campaign turned out to be rather limited. Garner was not a natural campaigner, nor was he comfortable trying to replicate FDR's style. Personality conflicts soon erupted between Garner, Garner's allies, and the Roosevelt team, which also undermined the Texan's influence on behind-the-scenes strategizing and policy formation. Garner rarely spoke about the "new deal" in terms that would suggest anything close to a "crusade," as Roosevelt had. Having assumed that his role on the campaign trail would be that of attack dog, Garner was further discouraged when, on August 1, Roosevelt insisted he soften his attacks against Hoover, saying that the current occupant of the White House was "flat and we can safely leave him there." Garner was a pragmatic party loyalist who was willing to experiment with new ideas, but FDR found his excessively harsh criticisms of Hoover off-script given the "new deal spirit" the campaign was hoping to project, not to mention's FDR's goal for appearing above the fray and statesmanlike. Garner replied by saying that he did not know how else to campaign other than to "give Republicans hell."[65]

Garner's frustrations did not go away. It did not help matters that some members of the national press (inaccurately) portrayed Garner as a backwoods radical who was friendly to the Klan. Garner's frustrations worsened when rumors began to circulate that he had been a closeted Hoovercrat in 1928, an allegation he denied even more vehemently than he did the others. Sensing the need to show unity, Roosevelt flew Garner to Albany for a "conference." Upon arrival, the vice presidential nominee told reporters that FDR was "the boss, the leader of the ticket, and I want to know what he wants me to do."[66]

Soon after, FDR's national campaign manager, James Farley—a close friend of Garner's—appointed Sam Rayburn to run Garner's vice presidential campaign, though Rayburn remained subordinate to Farley's wishes, and Howe's. Garner reluctantly acquiesced to the reduced role, telling Howe that he did not want to "controvert" Roosevelt and that he supposed the only way to do that was to "keep a low profile." Ultimately, Garner spent much of the campaign fishing at his home in Uvalde. Reporters soon took to mocking Garner, writing that the Speaker was "apparently more interested in fishing than politics for the time being," to which Garner retorted that he had "no news to share" other than that "the fish have been biting fine."[67]

Despite such behind-the-scenes drama, there was never any real doubt that the Roosevelt-Garner ticket would carry Texas. Just a month after the convention in Chicago, Sam Rayburn told reporters that victory in November was guaranteed, predicting the Democratic ticket would easily carry his home state while winning nationally by at least ten million votes.[68] Rayburn's optimism made perfect sense given Hoover's unpopularity, the horrendous economy, and the state's Democratic traditions. Clearly, Rayburn was not worried that voters might read his publicly expressed confidence in the assurance of FDR's election as an excuse to stay home from the polls. But with Texas all but in the bag for Roosevelt and Garner, the national campaign chose not to spend much time or capital there.[69]

"We Will Vote for a New Man"

Despite the fact that Roosevelt spent very little time campaigning in Texas—and despite his Harvard education, patrician accent, membership in one of the most famous families in the country, and relatively little interest in directly engaging the state—something about Franklin Roosevelt made him seem approachable. Throughout the fall of 1932, citizens across Texas felt comfortable writing their party's new nominee directly, sometimes to offer encouragement, sometimes advice, but more often than not it just seemed to fulfill a person's intrinsic need to be heard. Roosevelt's campaign was adept at managing the high volume of letters and responded to almost all of them. FDR relied on a variety of form-letter templates, though his staff was adept at writing canned responses with a tone that could easily be mistaken as unscripted, especially by the standards of the day. In keeping with FDR's reputation as an approachable and empathetic leader, the campaign included a high-quality facsimile of Roosevelt's personal signature on each letter, giving the candidate's response a remarkable semblance of authenticity.[70]

Without much understanding of Roosevelt's forthcoming New Deal agenda, and with Hoover's support in the state virtually nonexistent, the overwhelming majority of Texas voters lined up behind their party's ticket blindly, but optimistically, without demanding fidelity to any single ideological persuasion. From Waxahachie, Ed McElory told Roosevelt to focus his efforts on reforming agriculture, saying that FDR could establish credibility in the state by reminding Texans that Democrats were the party of farmers and "the South," while Republicans were for the "industrial North." From Bowie, E. R. Mangum told FDR the most important issue he faced was "the high rate of taxation." "This country is composed strictly of farmers and cattle raisers," Mangum said, "and we feel that the Democratic Party has the greatest opportunity to take charge of our national government since the beginning of the government. In fact, in our particular district, Hoover's administration has meant Sherman's interpretation of war." From Post, E. I. Meador told Roosevelt that he and his neighbors were "ready to tack their banner to any man that could lead them out of the wilderness, and they think you are the man," adding that Hoover's "pace of change" had been far too slow for his tastes. Grover Mitchell, chairman of the Motley County Democratic Party, expressed his good wishes to FDR, saying that he was "exceedingly glad that the Chicago convention selected you, and our own John N. Garner, as the Democratic standard bearers." Mitchell added that he and his neighbors "confidently believe that the good of the country is bound up on the supremacy of Democratic principles" and that the people of his county would give the Democratic ticket a "99 percent majority" on Election Day.[71]

Mitchell's predictions turned out to be shockingly accurate. On November 8, 1932, American voters elected Franklin D. Roosevelt to the office of president of the United States. Nationally, the Democratic ticket won 57.4 percent of the popular vote, compiling 472 electoral votes along the way. In Texas, Roosevelt and Garner won a staggering 88 percent, or 760,348 votes to be precise. By comparison, in 1928, Hoover won 367,036 votes in Texas, for a 51.7 percent majority; four years later, only 97,959 Texans—11.4 percent of the total—were bold enough to back the incumbent Republican. Grover Mitchell's Motley County delivered 96 percent of its votes to FDR, joining all 253 other counties in the state by backing the Democratic ticket; Roosevelt secured at least 80 percent of the vote in 239 of those counties. Hoover's 1932 vote total in Texas was the smallest for a Republican since Charles Evans Hughes failed to unseat Woodrow Wilson in 1916, though Hughes's percentage of the Texas vote that year had been 17.5 percent. All told, Roosevelt's landslide victory was nothing short of a national mandate for immediate change and aggressive leadership in Washington.[72]

Meanwhile, as Roosevelt waltzed to an easy victory both nationally and in Texas, state Democrats battled in down-ballot races fought along more traditional lines. No such contest was more visible or divisive than the race for governor. The incumbent, Ross Sterling, was an original founder of the Humble Oil Company—later Exxon Mobil. He won the governorship in 1930, defeating Thomas Love and Ma Ferguson in the Democratic primary. Like most other leaders of the time, Sterling struggled to respond effectively to the economic downturn, the full severity of which unfurled throughout 1930 and 1931. In his first address to the Texas State Legislature, Sterling said that his primary goal was to bring "harmony to Texas public life." He then outlined a relatively progressive agenda that included tax cuts for farmers and homeowners, education reform, the expansion of educational opportunities to prisons, the enlargement and modernization of state hospitals, better conservation of natural resources, relief to cotton farmers, an eight-hour day for all public workers, stricter enforcement of antitrust laws, and mass improvements to the state highway system.[73]

In the throes of economic collapse, however, Sterling failed to rally support for his agenda apart from passing a handful of small and somewhat idiosyncratic tax increases, none of which resulted in significantly more revenue flowing into the state's coffers. Initially, the state's economic commodities diversification shielded it from some of the more common effects of the national depression. However, the shrinking value of cattle, cotton, and oil soon caused havoc. Instead of spending more in support of his progressive agenda, Sterling vetoed $3 million in new state appropriations, most of which had been originally earmarked for public education. This miasma of misfortune effectively killed any hope Sterling had for a second term. When voters cast ballots in the Democratic primary on July 23, 1932, the incumbent governor won a paltry 30 percent of the vote, far behind Ma Ferguson's 42 percent, which led a crowded field of challengers. The subsequent runoff was much closer, with Ma narrowly winning the nomination by 3,798 votes out of 951,490 cast. The anti-Ferguson crowd alleged voter fraud in several key counties, though nothing came of the charges other than frustration and division. Ferguson tied herself to FDR during the coming months, simply saying that the time had come for a wave of new leadership both nationally and in Texas. She subsequently dispatched Republican nominee Orville Bullington in the general election that November.[74]

Bullington's campaign, however, deserves comment. A Wichita Falls attorney, Bullington touted himself as a loyal Democrat essentially running as a Republican-in-name-only. In reality, Bullington was a player in both political parties throughout the 1920s, even serving as a delegate to the Republican National Conventions in 1924, 1928, and 1932. In the wake of Sterling's defeat in the primary, Bullington convinced the beleaguered Texas Republican Party to support his candidacy, which meant dumping their previous presumptive nominee, John F. Grant of Houston. This created a momentary rift in the Texas GOP, but Bullington convinced Republicans to back his candidacy on the ground that his relationship with state Democrats gave anti-Ferguson voters a more realistic place to go in the general election. Impotent and without an attractive alternative, the GOP agreed.[75]

Ross Sterling quickly bought into the idea and publicized his own support for Bullington, saying it was his "duty to the people of Texas . . . to leave nothing undone, and make any sacrifice within [his] power to prevent the return of Fergusonism to the control of our State Government." Bullington organized his campaign against Ferguson through the newly created Roosevelt-Garner-Bullington Club, the first chapter of which was created in Fort Worth, with local civic activist Webb Walker serving as chair. With branches in most major Texas cities, the Roosevelt-Garner-Bullington Club served a dual purpose. First, the organization eagerly promoted Roosevelt's presidential campaign at a time when the national Democratic Party had almost completely pulled out of the state, considering it a lock. The club urged all Texans to support the Democratic Party in every race other than the one for governor. Second, the club attacked Ma and Pa Ferguson as unethical and reiterated allegations of voter fraud during the recent Democratic primary, while consistently referring to both as "bullies." In his opening address to the club that bore his name, Bullington said, "I am a Texan first and a party man afterword. I would despise myself if I allowed any consideration of personal or partisan advantage to influence my course in the crisis now confronting our state. My sole desire is to save Texas from the calamity which threatens it, and I am ready to make any sacrifice to that end." The politics of "hood, bonnet, and little brown jug" had virtually no impact on the presidential contest of 1932, but the bonnet, at least, continued to shape state politics even as Texans began to feel the full force of the Great Depression. Ferguson carried just under 62 percent of the vote against Bullington in the general election, claiming 237,953 fewer votes than Roosevelt won in Texas in his race against Hoover on the same day.[76]

Meanwhile, neither of the state's senators—Morris Sheppard and Tom Connally—was up for reelection in 1932, meaning both could support the national FDR-Garner ticket without having to take a stand on specific issues in their own campaigns. Texas voters sent twenty-one men to the US House of Representatives that November—each a Democrat. Pragmatic party loyalists who openly supported Roosevelt dominated the new delegation, though most simultaneously leaned conservative on issues related to federal spending and fiscal policy. This was true for instance in the Texas Panhandle, where voters enthusiastically reelected Marvin Jones. Jones pulled no punches when it came to denouncing Herbert Hoover and made no attempt to temper his enthusiasm for Roosevelt and Garner. He also embraced the idea of reform, though like FDR, he did so without advocating many specifics. He called for greater "grassroots activism," while telling the people in his home district about the importance of restoring higher prices for farm commodities. Without getting into the ideological weeds, newspapers in his home district reflected on Jones's commitment to the people of Texas: "If public service were as precious to the hearts of all our national officials as it is to Marvin Jones," the *Scurry County Times* editorialized, "there is little doubt but that the plight of these United States would be considerably less advanced."[77]

Similarly, voters in the Tenth District reelected James Buchanan. Buchanan had briefly considered retiring before the 1932 Texas Democratic primary rather than partake in the massive change heading Washington's way. "The greatest single factor in the campaign is dissatisfaction with existing conditions," a discouraged Buchanan told Brenham's T. A. Low. "Many voters will state that we can do no worse, so we will vote for a new man, for a new deal. If this slogan is properly started, it will be hard to stop." Low was one of Buchanan's most loyal supporters, and one of the more influential boosters in the district. He urged Buchanan against retirement, arguing that experienced Democrats would have far more power under a "Garner-Roosevelt" administration than they had at any point during the Republican-dominated 1920s. Of course, this meant supporting some ideas that most establishment conservatives considered radical. Compromise was a two-way street, Low argued, but Buchanan and the rest of the Texas delegation might be in a stronger position to shape national policy than ever before. Low's encouragement worked. Buchanan ran for reelection, framing his campaign around the predictable themes of Republican failure, partisan loyalty, and pragmatic fiscal conservatism. "I believe in balancing the budget by reducing governmental expenditures so far as possible," Buchanan told constituents during the campaign. "The tax burden resting upon the citizens is entirely too heavy, and we will not recover from this tragic depression until we radically reduce appropriations, expenditures, and taxes of the Federal, State, County, and Municipal Governments." He also routinely referred to the notion of a balanced budget as a "patriotic duty" and emphasized his "conviction" that American democracy functioned best in a two-party system and that his "loyalty" to the Democratic Party and "willingness to abide by the majority at all times" was of paramount importance.[78]

"For more than a decade the Republican Party has dominated and misgoverned the Federal Government with a control of the Presidency and Congress," Buchanan said during one of his more commonly used stump speeches. "Political sentiments have radically changed. It is evidence that the Democratic Party will win the Presidency and a majority in both houses of Congress in the next election. If such a blessing descends upon the country and I am returned to Congress, I will be among the leaders who will prescribe the policies and direct the destinies of the Nation. Under such conditions, I sincerely hope for my reelection in order that I may have a real chance to give the people real constructive service under the wise and just policies of a Democratic Administration." At the end of the day, Buchanan was a party loyalist and a pragmatist who believed he could work for Roosevelt so long as he could also continue to work with other Texas Democrats whose political sensibilities were similar to his own.[79]

Typical of the time, Buchanan's main competition came during the Democratic primary, not the general election. His opponent, Merton L. Harris, ran on the slogan "We Need New Blood in Congress"—a desire to tap into the broadly held sentiment for change that permeated the state and national political culture in 1932. Indicative of the national and state mood for something different, Harris tried to connect Buchanan to "Hooverism" and "runaway government spending" in Washington and argued that Buchanan was too committed to working with liberals. Harris told prospective voters that Buchanan had shifted blame to Republicans rather than accepting ownership for the broader failure of the "Washington establishment." In effect, Harris attempted to unseat Buchanan by being more fiscally conservative and by reframing Hoover's failures as "Washington's." Cutting taxes and balancing the budget were popular ideas, but Buchanan's experience and reputation as a loyal, populist Democrat with sensible mainstream Texas principles carried the day.[80]

With nods to Jones and Buchanan, no single individual reflected the collective personality of the Texas congressional delegation elected in 1932 more accurately or consistently than Sam Rayburn. A Confederate-sympathizing populist to his core, Rayburn rarely missed an opportunity to regale listeners with stories of his father's service to the South in the War between the States. He proudly and prominently displayed a portrait of Robert E. Lee in his office, and no doubt also saw himself as a defender of southern honor. His antipathy for Republicans was also the stuff of legend on Capitol Hill. "As long as I honor the memory of the Confederate dead and revere the gallant devotion of my Confederate father to the Southland," Rayburn once said, "I will never vote for electors of a party which sent the carpetbagger and the scalawag to prostrate the South with saber and sword."[81]

Yet as much as Rayburn wore gray and hated Republicans, he was also known for his hatred of railroads, banks, and utility companies, all of which he believed took advantage of poor farmers like the ones in his Fourth District in North Texas. Speaking of the Fourth District, Rayburn won his own reelection contest in 1932, carrying 95.2 percent of the vote against his Republican opponent that November—an impressive total, but hardly remarkable by Texas standards in 1932. Of the twenty-one men elected to the House of Representatives that year, excluding three who were elected to the soon-to-be-eliminated at large districts, all either ran unopposed or secured more than 90 percent of the final vote. The only exception was John Nance Garner, who carried a mere 85.8 percent of the vote in his campaign for reelection in the Fifteenth District.[82]

Like most of his colleagues in the Texas delegation, Rayburn adapted to the Roosevelt era in relatively short order. Soon, he was among FDR's most faithful, unapologetic supporters, consistently advocating and voting for liberal experimentation and reform. He was nothing if not a faithful soldier. Historians debate the sincerity of Rayburn's apparently liberal leanings during the era, just as they do for many southern Democrats. Whether Rayburn became a true believer or was simply a pragmatic politician doing whatever it took to win elections, he clearly detected the shifting political winds in Washington and willingly contributed to the reformation of a political culture in Texas that, for a time, was most notable for its enthusiastic support for Franklin Roosevelt and the New Deal legislation he proposed. In the years to come, time and again, with very few exceptions, Sam Rayburn backed FDR and the New Deal. In doing so, he and the many colleagues who came to follow his lead helped reshape the very meaning of modern American liberalism. Phrased another way, the presidential election of 1932, and the New Deal administration that came to Washington as a result, changed the course of American political history. It also launched a brief but important period in which political candidates and voters in Texas frequently aligned themselves with big-government liberals in Washington.[83]

But that was not necessarily the original goal. Rather, most political candidates in Texas backed Roosevelt and Garner out of loyalty, hoping to restore partisan order in the aftermath of four fractious, difficult years. Voters, meanwhile, backed Roosevelt and Garner primarily hoping for relief, recovery, and reform, not revolution. They were desperate. They wanted to defeat the Great Depression and they wanted to do so as quickly as possible. They voted for Roosevelt because he was a Democrat, but also because they believed he would do whatever it took to bring about quick, decisive healing. Ballots cast in Texas that

November were for hope and change, as well as for restoration. Despite its reputation as a bastion of conservatism and drama, Texas political history before (and for at least a few decades after) the Age of Roosevelt reflects an electoral culture premised on rather bland, predictable, and largely nonideological values, sometimes significantly affected by the politics of personality. Texans expected their leaders to govern wisely and to use their resources efficiently. And they expected their leaders to maintain a level head in times of trouble. Texans often saw themselves, on the other hand, as the keepers of rugged individualism and independence. In many cases, they expected their local, state, and national government to protect their interests in the battle against banks, railroads, and other corporate interests. Texans wanted to pull themselves up by their bootstraps but needed advocates in Washington to secure those bootstraps and to make them strong. Over the next several years, more than a minority of Texans would find the politics of American liberalism surprisingly attractive. The fact that Roosevelt seemed exceedingly likeable in contrast to Hoover was a major bonus.

2 | "Conservative Progressive Constructive Legislation"

On March 4, 1933, Franklin Roosevelt told Americans that he was prepared to use "broad Executive power to wage a war" against the Great Depression, adding that this power would be "as great as the power that would be given to [him] if [the nation] were in fact invaded by a foreign foe." He blamed "unscrupulous money changers" for the world's deteriorating economic condition, vowed to restore "ancient truths" to the "temple of our civilization," spoke in unmistakably moral and religious terms, and prayed for God's blessing on his administration's efforts to restore public confidence through direct federal action.[1] Roosevelt's first inaugural address touched on virtually every fear, frustration, and hope common to the American electorate in early 1933. It was arguably one of the best speeches ever given by an American president. Martin Dies later recalled having "sat on the platform only a few feet away" when Roosevelt delivered his first inaugural address. "I recall looking out upon the seas of faces and everybody had despondency written on his face," Dies said. "This country was gripped by fear everywhere . . . that speech did a great deal to restore confidence to the American people. The president . . . was a man that was needed at that particular time."[2]

Having won the presidency in a landslide the previous November, Roosevelt entered the White House with a decidedly Democratic Congress that included establishment Texas conservatives who, under less dire economic circumstances, might very well have resisted the earliest phase of FDR's New Deal on ideological grounds. The spring of 1933, however, was a not a time for taking ideological stands; it was a time for solving problems. Texas voters did not cast ballots for radical change in 1932, nor was their overwhelming support for the Roosevelt-Garner ticket a reflection of a larger ideological shift to the left. It was, however, part of a national mandate for action. Texas voters went to the polls in November 1932 to reject the Republican Party and to embrace change. Most Texans may have been socially, culturally, and fiscally conservative, but they were also pragmatic realists who, for the most part, recognized the severity of the economic crisis before them. Texans expected their Democratic representatives in Washington to work hard, to work quickly, and to help Roosevelt's New Deal succeed.

"Rehabilitation of the Unemployed"

Throughout much of the 1930s, Henry Pomeroy ("Roy") Miller was one of the most powerful men in Texas, and possibly in America. A mover and a shaker of the highest order, Miller was a one-time owner and editor of the *Corpus Christi Caller* newspaper, the thrice-elected mayor of Corpus Christi, and—far more importantly—a long-time lobbyist for the Texas Gulf Sulphur Company, one of the largest sulfur mining companies in the world. With significant ambition and personal initiative, Miller parleyed that background into influence peddling of the highest order. He maintained a regular presence in the US Capitol Building, dined with political leaders from all over the country, and occupied an office in southeast Texas through which he lobbied Texas congressional leaders toward support for unregulated markets, smaller government, states' rights, and a host of other conservative positions. A friend of John Nance Garner's, Miller was also a former business associate of Richard Kleberg, the representative from Texas's Fourteenth Congressional District, which included Miller's Corpus Christi. Kleberg's reputation in Washington had less to do with his ideological convictions or, for that matter, any real interest in policy making. Rather, the real passion for Kleberg, who had already inherited his fortune as a member of the King family, the namesake of the famed King Ranch of South Texas, was for the lifestyle afforded to congressmen in Washington, DC.[3]

Miller worked behind closed doors, often literally in a smoke-filled room, with other Texas representatives, including Kleberg, Martin Dies Jr. of Orange (Second Congressional District), and Hatton W. Sumners of Dallas (Fifth Congressional District). By 1940, most knew the "Miller Group" for its hostility to the "socialistic" New Deal—as they often called it—and to Roosevelt personally. However, from FDR's first campaign in 1932 until at least 1935 (and arguably later), Miller—like most Texas Democrats, including those in his group—largely supported the New Deal and compliantly fell in line behind Roosevelt. It might even be possible to say that Miller and most of his friends saw the earliest iterations of FDR's New Deal as a necessary and even helpful set of programs and interventions collectively designed to fix the disastrous set of messes left by the previous Republican administration. At the very least, thanks to politically astute aides such as Kleberg's young secretary, Lyndon Johnson, these men understood that backing the New Deal was good politics, a reflection of Roosevelt's popularity across the state. Historians such as Robert Caro have referred to Miller and his friends as "ultraconservatives." In many ways, particularly during Roosevelt's second term, they were. However, they were not fierce ideologues during FDR's first term, especially his first two years in office. Rather, they were business-oriented pragmatists willing to work within the new system, as long as they could see opportunities for themselves within that system. As such, they reflected the general impressions of Roosevelt and the New Deal shared by the vast majority of voting Texans during the early 1930s.[4]

Along with Garner, Kleberg, Dies, and Sumners, Miller's inner circle also included James Buchanan. Like Miller and the other members of Miller's group, Buchanan spent Roosevelt's first years in office largely subordinating his ideological convictions in order to play New Deal politics more effectively. He recognized that the Great Depression was a game changer, at least for a time. Desperate times called for desperate measures. Given the severity of the economic downturn, Texans, like most Americans, were ready to try just about anything to make ends meet. Accordingly, Buchanan crafted speeches in 1933 and 1934 similar to those used by FDR and other New Dealers. While restating his preference for small government, individualism, and self-help, he also recognized that the men and women of his state were struggling and scared. In an effort to connect with voters on an emotional level, Buchanan acknowledged the fears and uncertainties that plagued ordinary people. With empathy on the one hand, Buchanan used the other to foment anger. He blamed Republicans and told voters to do the same. Above all, he backed FDR's call for action, telling constituents to have confidence that Democrats were on the job. Through it all, Buchanan supported New Deal reforms, setting right—he said—what had gone wrong during the "Republican '20s," leveling playing fields along the way. Buchanan was so intent on paralleling FDR's message that he bounced ideas off FDR's noted "brain-truster," Harry Hopkins. Hopkins helped Buchanan craft phrases like "rehabilitation of the unemployed," all while avoiding terms like "federal subsidies" or phrases like "competition with the private sector."[5] This is precisely, for instance, how Buchanan framed his support for the so-called Bonus Bill involving expedited federal payments to American military veterans of the Great War. At the time, most conservatives opposed the bill on simple grounds that the government did not have the money, adding that federal spending was already reaching dangerously high levels. Buchanan largely agreed with that perception, but also recognized that Herbert Hoover's refusal to work with the veterans in 1932, and his subsequent decision to use tear gas in order to drive those veterans (and their families) out of Washington, had been the nail in his political coffin. Buchanan made the safe play to support FDR as often as possible, and to help those in need whenever possible—especially veterans. In similar situations across the state and nation, reluctant New Dealers strategically reframed progressive theories and populist ideas in circulation since the late nineteenth century as little more than commonsense pragmatism appropriated in direct support of ordinary Americans, such as veterans trying to feed their families in a world without jobs.[6]

Nowhere was this strategy more obviously employed than in the world of agriculture. Most Texas farmers of the early 1930 were intimately familiar with the populist agitators who had shaped the state's politics during the late nineteenth century. Mary Elizabeth Lease's famous battle cry to "raise less corn and more hell" had influenced their fathers and grandfathers, and the idea that cooperation, with federal support, could be a good thing for them and for the country was hardly a novel idea. Wall Street was the "them" in the battle of "us against them."[7] By the time FDR took office, Texas farmers—landowners and tenants both— had been struggling for more than a decade, suffering in the wake of the Great War's end, when the federal government stopped feeding and clothing hundreds of thousands of soldiers engaged in immediate combat. Having patriotically stripped their lands of the natural grasses that kept dirt from flying to raise crops that supported the war effort, Texas farmers subsequently saw the value of their land and labor decrease. For those in the northwest Texas panhandle, things got much worse when it basically stopped raining in 1930. Desperate farmers, especially in the state's Dust Bowl region, pushed their political representatives for relief. The need to feed one's family took precedence over all other concerns, including pride.[8]

Instead of fretting over the possibility of an ideological shift to the left, many Texas farmers worried that FDR might not push his New Deal reforms far enough. "Mr. Roosevelt, please do your level best to give the forgotten man a square deal when you get to Washington," one Texan wrote to FDR prior to his inauguration.[9] Dust Bowl farmers also feared that Roosevelt—being a New Yorker—might pay more attention to Wall Street than he would to them. Some speculated that FDR would simply offer a "repackaged Hooverism" that was doomed to fall short of expectations and promises. There fears were not unfounded. During the campaign of 1932, Roosevelt made it clear that he believed in hard currency and balanced budgets. The message reassured conservatives, but worried debt-ridden farmers who preferred inflationary measures that would put more money in circulation, making it easier to pay down debts and secure much-needed capital for the coming years. "Free silver" populism struck Texas farmers as common sense in 1933, as it had during the 1890s.[10]

Few Texas Democrats became more inextricably tied to farmers' fears and fortunes than Marvin Jones. In December 1932, Jones told the *Amarillo Sunday News and Globe* that he was committed to putting "agriculture on a basis of equality with industry," confidently adding that Roosevelt was prepared to work with both parties to enact "economic remedies" to accomplish that equity. Pragmatic though he was, Jones had been a reliable fiscal conservative throughout his political career to that point. Roosevelt's presidency, however, propelled Jones toward a legacy that would forever connect him to the New Deal.[11] Jones actively sold his constituents on the idea that Roosevelt was sincerely committed to agricultural reform and would prioritize direct relief to struggling farmers as soon as he took office. In January, he spoke to a national radio audience about the president's commitment, as well as his own expectations for direct action. Roosevelt's public discussion of the New Deal remained vague during the early months of 1933, as had been the case during his campaign against Hoover the previous fall. Roosevelt did not want to commit himself to any specific policies before he had to, and he certainly wanted to avoid helping Hoover, much to the president's chagrin and resentment. As such, it was up to Democrats like Jones to give the New Deal its baby teeth. Whereas FDR preferred inspiring platitudes, Jones preferred straightforward specifics. Stylistically, the pairing worked well.[12]

The earliest and best example of this concerns what, at the time, was known simply as FDR's "domestic allotment plan," the details of which began to leak in early 1933. As those details leaked, Democratic allies like Marvin Jones proactively worked to shape popular perceptions of

President-elect Roosevelt with Congressman Marvin Jones, January 21, 1933.
Courtesy of Southwest Collection/Special Collections Archive, Texas Tech
University, Lubbock, TX.

the idea ahead of predictable Republican, and in some cases conservative Democratic, resistance. The basic thrust of the domestic allotment plan was for the federal government to pay farmers not to farm, thereby reducing production, creating scarcity, and raising commodity prices. Before taking office, FDR tapped Jones—long viewed as among the most fervent, open-minded, and cutting-edge legislators when it came to anything related to agriculture—to assist in authoring the specific proposal. Jones agreed, and he and other New Dealers marketed the controversial plan as a simple solution to a sticky problem. "We are face to face with grim facts," Jones told a reporter in January. The "farm allotment bill" would solve a short-term "emergency." Traditional ideas about farming had to be temporarily "discarded." Jones tried to reassure anyone who would listen that government would—in due time—reestablish the "time-honored and proven principles" farmers had known and practiced for generations. The momentary economic crisis, however, necessitated a momentary change to those practices and traditions. It would not be easy, but Jones said it would work.[13]

"The beginning of the new Administration is a turning point in our country's history," Jones told another radio audience in March, two weeks after Roosevelt's inauguration. "After passing through a trial by fire, the American people are getting the national viewpoint. Selfish forms are being discarded and individuals are beginning to realize that their own interests are bound up with the nation's welfare." Like Buchanan, Jones was a conservative at heart. Also like Buchanan, however, Jones adjusted his understanding of rugged individualism to fit a New Deal paradigm, essentially arguing that farmers could not pull themselves up by bootstraps they did not possess. The New Deal was going to provide the forgotten man with new bootstraps, and the domestic allotment plan was a major part of the strategy for doing that.[14]

Jones and other Texas Democrats sold constituents, and perhaps themselves, on the efficacy of this and related New Deal ideas in part by frequently referring to FDR's electoral mandate for change and pragmatic experimentation, often discussed in tandem with near-hagiographic descriptions of Roosevelt himself. People wanted to trust Washington again. They wanted to trust their leaders and believe that democracy would work to their benefit. Hope for the future was a more powerful motivator than were fear and frustration. Roosevelt convinced people that he was actively pursuing concrete solutions to real problems and that he and the Democratic Party would not rest until they succeeded.

Supporters like Jones were critical to those efforts. "I am glad we have a man in the White House who is unafraid, who is willing to assume responsibility, and who has a program," Jones wrote in a widely published editorial that April. "The American people are thrilling with a new hope under his leadership." Calling FDR a "man of action," Jones further encouraged his farming constituents by speaking openly and optimistically about inflationary monetary policy as a "common sense" approach to getting farmers the help "they deserve."[15]

Thanks to Jones and the support of an overwhelmingly Democratic Congress, domestic allotment became law through the Agricultural Adjustment Act (AAA), signed by the president on May 12, 1933. Jones was among 315 representatives to vote in support of the AAA, a total that included eighteen yeas (against only three nays) cast by members of the Texas delegation to the House. In the Senate, both Tom Connally and Morris Sheppard also supported the bill.[16]

Vote totals in Congress belie the intensity of Congress's debate over the AAA. To say that political leaders in Washington hesitated on the matter, or that some constituents in Texas expressed discomfort with the AAA's central premise, would be a gross understatement. Federal intervention on the scale called for by the provisions of the AAA unsettled many, especially conservatives, including some in the Texas delegation who eventually ended up supporting the bill. Federal intervention into the agricultural commodities market sounded eerily similar to "collectivism," "socialism," and even "Russian communism."[17] Creating a planned economy that required farmers to cut production in order to create scarcity seemed un-American. The idea that farmers would receive subsidies to do this, and that the government would fund those subsidies through a tax levied on agricultural processors, also seemed dangerous. Some critics argued that the AAA would put up to eighty thousand tenant farmers out of work and that because nearly a quarter of all tenant farmers were black, the result would be a spike in crime across the state. FDR only added to this anxiety when he told a group of reporters on April 19 that the United States had abandoned the gold standard in an effort to stabilize prices for both American manufacturers and agricultural producers.[18]

Controversial actions notwithstanding, New Dealers continued to market the AAA and other reform measures as clear signs that the president would not stand idly by and let farmers, or their families, starve. "It is generally conceded today that [FDR] is doing more for the people of Texas than any member of Congress from the Lone Star State," suggested one editorialist in Amarillo, who also mentioned having "great pride" in the role Marvin Jones was playing in the new administration.[19] Thanks in part to consistently favorable coverage in the press, farmers in the Texas Panhandle praised Roosevelt's actions. They also appreciated the role their very own Marvin Jones played in pushing reforms such as the AAA through the system and into law. Jones enjoyed the attention and understood the political benefit of connecting himself to the White House. He rarely missed an opportunity to recount stories of his personal interaction with Roosevelt. On July 20, Jones spoke to a crowd of supporters in Pampa. He used the occasion to celebrate the AAA's early success, citing anecdotal reports from local producers as well as data coming out of the Department of Agriculture, all of which indicated higher prices for farm commodities. While acknowledging that the AAA was hardly in keeping with conservative traditions for individual self-help, Jones insisted that the New Deal was not about ideology, but rather about results and the promotion of, as he put it, "ordered liberty." He credited Roosevelt's action for the higher prices and for area farmers' improving overall economic prospects.[20]

Ten days later, the *Amarillo Daily News* published a photograph of a local farmer, George Morris, proudly holding a check from FDR for $517. The newspaper captioned the photo: "A trickle in a flood of $100,000,000 which the government is pouring upon southern farmers who cut cotton acreage." Marvin Jones was among those also in the photograph.[21] "More money, cheaper interest, $1 wheat, and 10-cent cotton—mixed thoroughly with a generous portion of faith in FDR—these are the essential ingredients of the 'new deal' for the American masses," Jones told another local reporter that summer. "They comprise the remedy which is curing the farm belt of an illness which six months ago had all the earmarks of a fatal epidemic. The New Deal isn't an idle promise; it's really a new day and a new economic order for the American people."[22]

Reflecting on the New Deal during an interview conducted in 1952, Jones argued that West Texas farmers supported the AAA because it democratized national agricultural production by giving farmers a voice in the decision-making process. By that time, arguments that the New Deal collectivized the agriculture industry and weakened farmers' autonomy had become mainstream orthodoxy on the conservative right. Nevertheless, Jones persisted in his defense of the New Deal as a "great deal" for his constituents. The key, according to Jones, was trust. Farmers trusted Roosevelt even when they disagreed with him. "I think a great majority of the farmers of Texas thought that Mr. Roosevelt was honestly trying to work for the good of the country," Jones said, adding that, if nothing else, the New Deal's innovations on soil conservation and farm credit alone warranted farmers' unwavering loyalty. Eager to capitalize on the AAA's momentum, New Dealers proposed another agricultural reform bill during the spring of 1934. First introduced as an amendment to the AAA, the new bill called for tax penalties on farmers failing to cooperate with the AAA provisions requiring production cutbacks. Under the original AAA, farmers' participation in such programs was largely voluntarily; incentives for compliance were minimal. By early 1934, it was clear that some farmers were simply disregarding much of the new law while simultaneously benefiting from the improving market. New Dealers, led by South Carolina representative William Bankhead, decided to take a calculated risk in proposing new tax penalties on farmers who refused to cooperate with the New Deal's bigger picture. The resulting legislation came into being as the Bankhead Cotton Control Act of 1934—or "Bankhead Bill" for short.[23]

The Bankhead Bill reignited arguments over the acceptable extent of federal intervention into economic matters. Managing markets was one thing, but penalizing individuals for not cooperating was quite another. Conservatives viewed the Bankhead Bill as an unjust tax increase and an affront to Jeffersonian principles of independence. Even Henry Wallace—secretary of agriculture and among the New Deal's most progressive voices—initially opposed the Bankhead plan.[24] Most pragmatists, however, saw it as part of the New Deal's vision for relief, recovery, and reform for hardworking families who were suffering through no fault of their own. Wallace himself polled cotton farmers across the South and was surprised to learn that 80 percent supported the plan, with only 2 percent expressing clear opposition. It seemed that cotton farmers were ready to buy into the plan as a possible solution to their problems. This is precisely how FDR framed the measure during his public statement upon signing the bill into law: "I am advised that the overwhelming majority of the South's cotton producers desire the enactment of legislation now embodied in the Bankhead Bill. It aims to prevent that very small minority which has refused to cooperate with their neighbors and the government from impairing the effectiveness of the current cotton production program which now includes ninety-two percent of

the cotton acreage." Emphasizing the idea of cooperation and neigh-
borliness, Roosevelt further justified the measure by comparing it to
similar taxes imposed by the Confederacy on cotton farmers during the
Civil War, adding that a "democratic government has consented" to the
widespread outcry for federal assistance.[25]

Having been one of the original AAA's most fervent champions,
Marvin Jones supported the Bankhead Bill in a series of speeches that
spring. Narrowly avoiding a tone of condescension, Jones taught his audiences in simple, straightforward language why the New Deal's agricultural reforms made sense. More importantly, he exhorted his listeners
that it was critical for all farmers to participate. By stressing meaningful
partnerships, logical organization, and sensible cooperation between
government and farmers, Jones convinced farmers that they could stabilize prices by working together. Washington was not collectivizing their
industry; it was simply creating a system through which farmers would
cooperate successfully. Jones emphasized the commonsense pragmatism of New Deal reforms like the Bankhead Bill, but he was not above
rhetorical flourish. He typically peppered his homespun catechisms on
agriculture with idealism, saying, for instance, that farmers were the
"last great American individualist" and should be proud of the heritage
they had formed as the backbone of American self-discipline. The New
Deal was not about charity, he said. It was about equal opportunity and
fair play. It was about correcting the abuses of Republican corruptions
on Wall Street. It was about restoring farmers to their rightful place
as a "symbol of America" itself. According to Jones, Roosevelt believed
that farmers "must be protected" against Republican schemes, adding
that farmers were fighters who in almost any other set of circumstances
"would not need anyone's help." These, however, were extraordinary
circumstances.[26]

Thomas Love used similar phrases to promote the New Deal's agricultural policies in Dallas. On January 2, 1934, Love proudly telegrammed the president to report on a speech he had just delivered
before a gathering of business leaders in Dallas. During that speech,
Love told his audience: "Whatever else has happened, Franklin D. Roosevelt has done more for the farmer—has put more money in the farmer's pocket . . . has saved more farmers' homes from loss by foreclosure,
and has made it possible for more farmers to become owners of their
homes—than any other president or statesman in any country."[27] Two
months later, during a speech to the Dallas Agricultural Club, Love told

the agribusiness leaders that FDR had "done some enormously valuable things for the people, especially for the forgotten man." Rejecting charges that New Deal agriculture policy was undemocratic, Love confidently proclaimed that, were he alive, Thomas Jefferson would have supported the Bankhead Bill. Jefferson, according to Love, considered "the encouragement of agriculture and of commerce" to be one of the "essential principles of our government." Unable to avoid hyperbole, Love declared the bill to be the "greatest service ever rendered" to cotton farmers, adding for good measure his opinion that "in a very real sense, this new Bankhead Bill is a declaration of independence for the cotton farmers of the South."[28]

Although Love spent most of his time rationalizing his support for the Bankhead Bill, he also used his platform to praise FDR and his administration, including the much-celebrated Brain Trust. He specifically singled out Henry Wallace, as well as Wallace's under secretary, famed Columbia University economist Rex Tugwell. Love's willingness to praise Wallace and Tugwell before a group of Dallas agribusiness leaders speaks to the unusual openness and malleability of Texas political culture during FDR's first term. Wallace and Tugwell were both controversial appointments, often inciting less than warm feelings from business leaders across the country, many of whom saw them as advocates for socialist interventions and federal overreach. Nevertheless, Love praised Wallace and Tugwell for making the Bankhead Bill a reality, further exhorting that "every citizen of Dallas and of Texas ought to be celebrating."[29]

Two months after his speech to the Dallas Agricultural Club, Love again telegrammed FDR, this time to offer his "heartiest congratulations" for the "unprecedented record of conservative progressive constructive legislation" successfully passed during the previous year. His use of the term "conservative progressive constructive legislation" did not exactly catch on in the mainstream political culture but did reflect the often disorienting effects that New Deal programs had in a world unfamiliar with such levels of intervention. Love singled out the Reciprocal Tariff Act in his telegram, calling the recently enacted measure—lauded by some as a major step toward liberalized free trade—"the best tariff law ever enacted by American Congress." He then optimistically added that the new tariff law was "the largest contribution to human welfare ever made by any parliament in history." Shortly thereafter, Love proudly informed John Nance Garner of another glorious resolution, adopted unanimously by the Dallas County Democratic Convention in August, affirming North Texas's enthusiastic support for the "unparalleled program of economic recovery and human welfare achieved . . . under the matchless leadership" of FDR and the New Deal on behalf of "the forgotten man."[30]

Meanwhile, Love launched a political offensive against his old foe, Jim Ferguson. Not one to sit quietly on the sidelines while others soaked up the limelight, Ferguson had been making headlines that summer by publicly opposing various New Deal reforms he considered oppositional to the state's growing oil and banking industries. Love disagreed with Ferguson. He not only supported the reforms, but also called them "the constitutional duty of the federal government." Defending Roosevelt, Love rebuffed Ferguson by saying that "any State agency for oil regulation which does not enthusiastically welcome and cooperate with the efforts of the federal government . . . carries the suspicion of insincerity and sham."[31]

By 1935, it was clear that Love's support for federal cooperation with Texas oil interests was the far better (and far more lucrative) way to go. A Supreme Court ruling in January weakened federal regulatory authority over interstate commerce, including the production and shipment of crude oil. Concurrently, the Texas Railroad Commission (TRC) struggled to enforce state-mandated crude production caps, the frequent (and flagrant) violation of which threatened to flood markets with "hot oil" and weaken prices. In response, Congress—led by Tom Connally, with FDR's support and Harold Ickes's leadership—reestablished jurisdiction over the transportation of oil across state lines, thereby undercutting rogue producers, particularly common in East Texas. In the process, policy makers strengthened the TRC's power to protect Texas wildcatters' efforts to compete with the nation's major oil companies. Enshrined as the Connally Hot Oil Act of 1935, his brand of pragmatic populism reflected New Deal marketing at its best. Connally helped establish a cooperative partnership in which local businesses worked with federal agencies to protect production, preserve prices, and make more Texans rich.[32]

The fact that these businesses were oil businesses made the partnership especially important. As Bryan Burrough has described it, "The spigot of cash Texas Oil opened in the early 1930s ranks among the greatest periods of wealth generation in American history, in size perhaps the largest creation of individual wealth between the Gilded Age and the Internet boom of the 1990s." Burrough, however, emphasizes that this boom took place not "despite the Depression" but "because of" it. Major oil companies across the country were fully aware that discoveries in East Texas were massive. However, they lacked the capital necessary to invest, thereby opening the door to local wildcatters, including men like H. L. Hunt—at one time later in life the richest man in the world—to take advantage. As Burrough explains: "The Depression hit oil companies hard, and it was their wholesale retreat from exploration that allowed men like Hunt to amass fantastic oil reserves. More than any other single factor, it was the major oil companies' retreat that created the fortunes that came to define Texas." The fact that these wildcatters found friends in the New Deal only strengthened the alliance and the partners' economic and political successes. At the same time, however, partnerships between the New Deal White House and the Texas oil industry remained fragile. By the end of the decade, no sector of the state's business community was more fiercely opposed to Roosevelt than the oil industry. Nevertheless, the two needed one another in 1934 and 1935 and formed an alliance profitable for all parties involved.[33]

Thomas Love's support for Roosevelt remained constant during the summer of 1934, bordering on obsessive. It was not, however, radically out of step with the president's support levels among most Texans at the time. Love made headlines in Dallas by championing virtually every New Deal measure under consideration at the time. A man deeply invested in the Texas banking industry, Love delivered speeches and gave interviews praising the new Federal Deposit Insurance Corporation (FDIC), saying that FDR's efforts would "protect depositors and stockholders" alike.[34] In August, his sycophancy produced a resolution to the Dallas County Democratic Convention that simply endorsed FDR's New Deal recovery programs en masse. To his credit, the convention adopted Love's resolution unanimously. Love wrote of his efforts in yet another letter to FDR, and when he did not get a personal reply on the matter, telegrammed Louis Howe to make sure the president received a complete briefing on Love's efforts and successful foot-soldiering. Though it is easy to mock the frequency of his correspondence with the president, the reality is that Thomas Love was, in fact, an important ally to Roosevelt's efforts to sell the New Deal in Texas, just as he had been for Woodrow Wilson's efforts to sell progressive ideas two decades earlier. Love's support for Wilson—particularly during the elections of 1912 and 1916—provided national Democrats with a passionately loyal voice on the ground with access to key inner circles across Texas. In some ways, Love was a critical bridge connecting Progressive Era Wilsonian Democrats to FDR and New Deal liberalism in the 1930s and 1940s.[35]

Among Roosevelt's political skills, few were as useful as his ability to recognize and then mitigate potential areas of weaknesses by enlisting unlikely allies into the New Deal cause. As annoying as Love's frequent letters to the White House may have been to White House staffers at the time, the president needed more men like Thomas Love speaking on his behalf. Sensing that his connection to business leaders—and specifically to bankers—was an area of potential weakness, Roosevelt promoted Houston's Jesse H. Jones to the chairmanship of the Reconstruction Finance Corporation (RFC). Jones had served on the RFC's board under Hoover, but FDR's decision to promote Jones in 1933 was a turning point in Texas history. Nationally, Jones was another bridge connecting business leaders and bankers to Roosevelt. In Texas, Jones used the RFC to diversity the state's economic interests. The RFC shored up Texas bank holdings and distributed federal loans and subsidies to agribusinesses and oil companies, simultaneously catalyzing new business development in areas like petrochemical production and steel. As William Leuchtenburg described it, Jones "represented the southwestern boomers' desire for expansion," adding that he also "spoke for businessmen less interested in protecting existing holdings than in fresh ventures."[36]

For the rest of the decade, Jones was arguably the nation's most powerful financier. He oversaw vast elements of the New Deal, including aspects of the FDIC, which had been modeled after a plan Jones implemented in Houston while on the RFC's board of directors in 1932. By decade's close, he was also in control of the Federal Housing Administration (FHA) and the Home Owners Loan Corporation (HOLC), both of which played a critical role in connecting the New Deal to "unregulated private markets." Such connections—widely promoted as "partnerships"—provided New Dealers with a defense against charges of socialism, while at the same time bequeathing responsibility for the preservation of home ownership and, just as critical, new home development and construction, to forces that would prioritize white prosperity and comfort for decades to come. As one of the nation's foremost economic developers and capitalist minds, Jones was critical to FDR's behind-the-scenes relationship with business leaders, particularly those in southern and western states, Texas included, where conservatives controlled much of the political apparatus. Arguably as much as or more than anyone else, Jesse Jones used the New Deal to accelerate the growth of an industrialized, metropolitan, economically diversified, Sunbelt version of modern Texas.[37]

With nods to Marvin Jones, James Buchanan, Thomas Love, Jesse Jones, and the countless others who jumped aboard the New Deal train in 1933 and 1934, no Texan advocated for Roosevelt's ideas more artfully or sincerely during these years than the state's preeminent bona fide progressive, Senator Morris Sheppard. At the 1934 Texas Democratic Convention in Galveston, Sheppard used his allotted time at the podium to recount, in excruciatingly long detail, the travails wrought by Hoover and the Republicans prior to Roosevelt's victory in 1932. Calling his speech a "tribute of loyalty and support to Franklin Roosevelt, John Garner, and the New Deal," Sheppard spouted the national administration's chief message, that the New Deal was a "rescue operation" targeting the "forgotten Americans" unjustly victimized by Republican greed. Convention-goers subsequently adopted into the state party's platform a resolution that wholly and unequivocally endorsed FDR and the New Deal, characterizing both as essential to Texas's renewal and happy recovery. The resolution even went so far as to "condemn those who for partisan purposes would thwart [FDR and the New Deal] and turn a recovering nation back to the chaos which reigned prior to [FDR's] inauguration."[38]

Sheppard was a talented and prolific orator—a throwback to the nineteenth century. He delivered numerous orations throughout 1933 and 1934, including many before civic clubs like Kiwanis and Rotary. Regardless of the audience, he took advantage of his listeners' assumed affinities for nostalgia and patriotism. In many cases, he framed his speeches around a rhetorical device that centralized Thomas Jefferson and the Founding Fathers as the New Deal's progenitors. During one speech to the Texarkana Rotary Club, Sheppard delivered a dramatic retelling of Jefferson's authorship of the Declaration of Independence, connecting it to "American individualism" and the "obligation of the American government to take every necessary and desirable step within constitutional limitation and procedure to preserve these rights and this individualism." According to Sheppard, the New Deal was, at its core, an attempt to preserve the fundamental principles of Jeffersonian democracy, or in his mind, the very soul of America. The success of the New Deal would "mean a resounding triumph for American individualism because . . . there is no room beneath the American flag for Bolshevism, communism, socialism, anarchism, or any other school of conduct or philosophy which would destroy individual freedom or individual achievement and aspiration."[39]

Sheppard's defense of the New Deal as profoundly important to the defeat of communist tyranny was an important facet of his salesmanship throughout Texas during most of the 1930s. Instead of flippantly dismissing conservative charges that the New Deal was socialism cloaked in the American flag, Sheppard appropriated the battle against communism as liberalism's own, while at the same time reconfiguring public attitudes toward the New Deal, communicating Roosevelt's programs as a bulwark against such radicalism. "There can be no greater example of the opposite of socialism, communism, and atrocity," Sheppard said in 1934, "than that of the man whose chief objective is the advancement through the New Deal of the widest possible individual ownership, individual well-being, and individual independence in America . . . [who] believes in the unrestricted right of opinion, criticism, comment, and political alignment—Franklin Delano Roosevelt."[40]

Sheppard was particularly adept at addressing charges that FDR's New Deal had thrust unwanted levels of red tape and bureaucratic control upon the American people. "They tell us that the New Deal means regimentation of the American people," Sheppard said in another speech that year. "I would rather see the American people regimented into a condition of individual economic independence than in the condition of permanent poverty and distress which threatened them prior to March 4, 1933." On a separate occasion, he defended FDR's Brain Trust, saying that he "would rather have a brain trust in Washington composed of men devoted entirely to the common good, pooling their intellectual resources for the general benefit of the people, unconnected with any special interest, laying proposals before the President for his approval or rejection, than to have the steel trust, the oil trust, the power trust, and similar trusts represented in our government."[41]

Whether he was aggressively attacking Republicans or artfully defending his own party, Sheppard was remarkably consistent and effective in selling Texans on the virtues of the New Deal. Like his mentor William Jennings Bryan, Sheppard was a living bridge between the oratorical styles of Victorian romanticism and the crisper, more direct approach of the modern era. Spellbinding, if a tad longwinded, Sheppard was perhaps most impressive in his ability to turn conservative criticisms on their head, essentially triangulating issues the way Bill Clinton would at the end of the century. Sheppard sold his vision of the New Deal as a defensive bulwark protecting religious virtue, independence, individual liberty, and democratic prosperity—in other words, the very fulfillment of Thomas Jefferson's populist vision for an ideal American way of life. In doing so, Sheppard melded all of the various emotional thrusts commonly employed by Roosevelt and his followers during the era—morality and Christian virtue, reverence for the nation's founders (Jefferson above all others), anti-Republican animus, and plain-spoken advocacy for, as they saw, common sense.[42]

Limited skepticism and lingering fears notwithstanding, most Texas Democrats bought into the New Deal's big picture in 1933 and 1934. They trusted Roosevelt and gave him a chance to enact new ideas. They also applauded and appreciated action. Nothing, however, enhanced Roosevelt's popularity in Texas more than his decision to prioritize farmers in 1933 and 1934. Those efforts established a foundation for ongoing cooperation between Texas Democrats and the White House and strengthened voters' trust in the federal government. Local political leaders such as James Buchanan, Marvin Jones, Thomas Love, and Morris Sheppard modeled their rhetoric after FDR's, or at the very least went out of their way to praise him as often as possible. Ma Ferguson often referred to Roosevelt and the New Deal in grand terms, noting the "broad spirit of humanity which has brought about the cooperating powers of the government." "Forgotten" Texans increasingly believed they had an ally in the White House who understood their problems and was committed to fighting for them. Even Texas business leaders, recognizing that unhealthy farm markets infected all economic sectors, generally supported the AAA and other New Deal measures during the first two years of Roosevelt's presidency. These common interests formed the backbone of an emerging New Deal rhetoric that championed historically conservative talking points on taxation, property rights, and small government as long-term ideals the New Deal hoped to restore through a series of short-term federal interventions. New Dealers embraced concepts like balanced budgets and free markets while, at the same time, condemning greedy Republicans and Wall Street financiers for taking advantage of the "little guy." Only a democratic government of the people, by the people, and for the people could restore Jefferson's vision for a nation of landowning individualists beholden to none.[43]

FDR and his Democratic allies sold the New Deal as a pragmatic machine built with only one goal in mind—the restoration of America's soul. As FDR previously stated during his acceptance speech at the 1932 Democratic National Convention, the New Deal would be part of a larger "crusade to restore America to its own people."[44] Establishment conservatives like Jack Garner often bristled at the thought of a New Deal crusade and struggled internally over the prospects of an increasingly liberal Democratic Party. But even Garner typically fell in line "for the good of the party," as he often put it. Garner's friendship with DNC chair Jim Farley, and Farley's willingness to work with Garner to make sure that the DNC and the White House gave Texas the attention he felt it deserved, contributed to the vice president's willingness to play ball. As for the public relations of it all, Garner rarely campaigned publicly for anyone or anything during the 1930s. He was, however, willing to make public appearances on occasion, particularly when accompanied by Farley, who made a series of visits to Texas in October 1933, ostensibly to sell the New Deal to Texas voters, though more honestly in an effort to heal factional divisions between Garner and the Governors Ferguson.[45]

"The People, the Party, and the President"

Less than two years into the Age of FDR, voters were given an opportunity to let their voices be heard. With limited exceptions, the 1934 midterms functioned as a collection of referendums on the New Deal. In Texas, voters overwhelmingly affirmed Washington's efforts, prompting Democratic National Committee chairman James Farley to declare: "Never before scarcely in the history of the American people has there been such an apparently unanimous spirit of friendliness to a national administration. The people recognize that at last the government is definitely in the hands of one who will not disabuse the people's trust."[46]

In Texas, the most high-profile race of 1934 was the one waged for governor. Among others, it featured James Allred, a longtime lawyer from Wichita Falls and the state's attorney general since 1931. Allred's 1934 campaign for governor proved significant for a variety of reasons, not the least of which is that, upon winning, he would become one of FDR's most vocal and reliable supporters. Running as a Democrat in a relatively sparse field that did not include the sitting governor Ma Ferguson, Allred waged an energetic, highly stylized campaign noted for its originality and entertainment value. As one of his speechwriters put it, Allred spoke with the talent of an "evangelist" and the stage presence of an "actor." Allred tied his bid for governor directly to FDR's bid to help the nation's "forgotten men" in their fight against "special interests." "The campaign slogan of Franklin D. Roosevelt was 'A new Deal for the Forgotten Man,'" Allred told the Waco Junior Chamber of Commerce in March. "Unlike most candidates for public office, our great president after his election did not overlook his pledges to the people. Apparently, his promise of a 'New Deal' and to the 'Forgotten Man' was no mere phrase-making," Allred went on. "It is therefore but fitting at this annual observance of the birth of the Waco Junior Chamber of Commerce that it should be combined with the general thanksgiving spirit for the leadership of Franklin D. Roosevelt."[47] To those gathered at the Mount Auburn Christians' Banquet that same week, Allred asserted that "there has never been a President of whom more was expected or who has more completely fulfilled the hopes of the people," adding: "Four outstanding characteristics have dominated his every official act during the first year. The man is sincere, honest, frank, [and] courageous."[48] A few days later, he told a crowd in Houston that he favored a "liberal interpretation of the law" and that "liberalism" was the best way to protect both "liberty and justice."[49]

Throughout his campaign, Allred remained consistent in associating the spirit of his campaign with that of Roosevelt's White House. Decrying what he described as a "campaign of misinformation" and "propaganda," Allred waged war against "corporate interests" in Texas, which, he said, were blinding the public to their "practices of greed." As Allred put it, his administration in Austin would be a true representative "of the people," just as FDR's was in Washington. "No matter how obscured by false issues or how camouflaged by outward respectability," Allred told an audience in Fort Worth in April, "there has always been a privileged enemy in some form to prey upon the rights of a sleeping people." Speaking with force about those who wish "to extend their domains of greed and power," Allred connected his campaign to both the spirit of the New Deal and that of the populists of yesteryear:

> If democracy is not to perish from the earth, we must give renewed life and vigor to those forms. We must revive the spirit of simple honesty and fair play. We must do our part here in Texas to help throttle those gigantic forces which for thirty years have been sapping the lifeblood of democracy

the world over. In short, we must rebuild a true democracy where 'equality of opportunity for all and special privileges for none' is more than a tawdry slogan for self-seeking demagogues. . . . A hundred and fifty years ago, Thomas Jefferson called the legions of democracy to war against special privilege. Fifty years ago, in Texas, John H. Reagan and Jim Hogg were fighting the battles of democracy against unscrupulous pirates of railway finance. Thirty years later, Woodrow Wilson was holding the citadel against the vicious and insidious attacks of the Wall Street money trust. Today, the banners of democracy are hold high by our peerless President, Franklin Delano Roosevelt. . . . So long as the government grants special privileges to the favored few, so long will those favored few use every means in their power to retain and enlarge those privileges.[50]

Allred's platform, however, was relatively less dramatic. Like most of his opponents in the Democratic primary, Allred promoted ideas consistent with the New Deal's general strategy for creating planning boards to create and implement solutions to economic problems.[51] For instance, he supported the expanded use of the Texas Planning Board, as well as the creation of a statewide commission on public utilities. He spoke frequently about the need to improve the state's collection of property taxes and was opposed to new and increased sales taxes, including one that Ferguson had previously supported in 1933. He also asked for funding to help modernize police departments across the state, spoke passionately about the need to fight excessive influence from lobbyists, and openly aligned himself with FDR in supporting "the will of the people" on Prohibition, by this point an issue far less relevant nationally than it had been before the Depression hit. After winning his party's nomination, Allred sailed to victory, winning the first of two terms as governor with a staggering 96.4 percent of the vote.[52]

If Allred's race for governor was not the state's most visible contest in 1934, Tom Connally's bid for reelection to the United States Senate was. Historians have tended to remember Connally as a stalwart southern conservative, particularly because of his attitudes on race, which manifest most visibly near the end of his career in the early 1950s. In 1934, however, he was a reliable New Dealer who rarely missed an opportunity to praise Roosevelt and his programs for relief, recovery, and reform. Speaking on the Senate floor in early April, Connally defended the New Deal against Republican charges that it was an unwanted "revolution" by saying that "there has been no revolution except the revolution from ruin to recovery." In a speech frequently interrupted by Republican senator Lester Dickinson of Iowa, Connally mocked Republicans for having created "the mess" in the first place, and then proceeded to paint FDR as nothing short of the national economy's savior. "The hungry have been fed, the naked have been clothed, [and] the unemployed are again busy with the implements of their toil at gainful occupations. Business is reviving. Corporations' dividends are increasing. The American people are becoming happy and prosperous once again." Connally's portrayal of economic life in the country was dramatic—and inaccurate on several levels. New Deal programs were popular and, in many cases, helping. But the overall economy was not yet booming. Nevertheless, with optimism on the rise, even establishment Democrats like Connally understood that political fortunes were, at least for the moment, intricately connected to the New Deal. "There is no revolution except the revolution from a sense of despair," Connally said, "from a sense of suffering back yonder prior to March 4, 1933, to a sense of confidence in government, confidence in President Franklin D. Roosevelt, who is leading us, and confidence in Congress, confidence that, through their efforts, America will soon come into its own again. If that be revolution—make the most of it."[53]

Connally's reelection strategy in 1934 was to align himself as tightly to Roosevelt as he possibly could. His only significant challenger came in the Democratic primary in the form of Joseph Weldon Bailey Jr., son of the former two-term US senator from Texas of the same name. The senior Bailey had been known for his hard-line conservatism on issues such as Prohibition and race and was a noted champion of all things states' rights. Elected to Congress in 1932, the junior Bailey was less strident and made few efforts to hide his personal admiration for FDR. In his bid to unseat Connally, Bailey even made a few attempts to outflank Connally on his left, advocating classic populist issues such as the free coinage of silver, stronger antitrust legislation, and collective bargaining rights for organized labor. Bailey also tried to undermine Connally's connections with FDR, saying on numerous occasions that the incumbent senator was simply trying to "ride FDR's coattails" and was not in fact sincerely representing the people of his state. Unable to make a dent in Connally's support, Bailey then tried a different strategy, attempting to drive a wedge between farmers and Connally not by attacking FDR directly but by criticizing Connally's support for the Bankhead Bill, which Bailey now began to label as dangerous "regimentation." That message fell flat, for the most part, because Connally enthusiastically spent his time on the campaign trail not simply justifying his vote record, but championing the Bankhead Bill for raising cotton prices by more than 30 percent, while also crediting the HOLC and the Farm Credit Bill for saving "thousands of Texas homes." Connally also reminded voters of the rampant fraud and mismanagement on Wall Street, crediting Roosevelt and the new Securities and Exchange Commission for finally "bringing the stock market under government control."[54]

Confident and unthreatened, Connally largely ignored Bailey during most of his campaign speeches in 1934, rarely even acknowledging that he had an opponent in the race. Bailey countered by charging Connally with "pussyfooting." The Texas press generally favored Connally's approach, praising the incumbent's style as "an excellent example" of how someone could run for public office without "slinging mud." Desperate, Bailey tried to resurrect the Prohibition issue, proudly telling voters that he was an "FDR wet," while Connally was a dry, a strategy indicating just how far popular opinion might have shifted in Texas as a result of Roosevelt's standing with voters. To his credit, Connally refused to take the bait. Instead, he simply told audiences that the matter was "settled" and that he supported the president.[55]

Bailey never seriously threatened Connally's incumbency. Nevertheless, Connally opportunistically and wisely used the campaign to promote himself as an ally to the national leadership. In one transparently rigged gimmick, Connally arranged for the "accidental public release" of an ostensibly private letter written by John Nance Garner to former attorney general W. A. Keeling. In the letter, Garner referred to Connally in glowing terms, noting that Connally had quickly risen to the ranks of the Senate's "most important" members, as evinced by his leadership on the Senate Committee on Foreign Affairs and the Senate Finance Committee. Garner added that Connally "had the confidence and regard of the President" while also telling Keeling (and an audience of millions) "it would be a great misfortune to fail to return Tom Connally to the Senate." Texas voters listened, easily reelecting Connally to a second term in Washington. Connally took just under 60 percent of the vote in the Democratic primary before crushing his hapless GOP challenger in the general election, winning 97 percent of the vote.[56]

As Allred and Connally sailed to victory in statewide raises, voters in the Panhandle overwhelmingly reelected Marvin Jones, and did so largely on his emergence as one of the nation's strongest advocates for

Congressman George H.
Mahon, circa 1937. Courtesy
of Southwest Collection/
Special Collections Archive,
Texas Tech University,
Lubbock, TX.

the national administration in Washington. The fact that Henry Wallace
referred to Jones as "good counsel" and asked him to aid FDR in his
"ardent fight" to help "solve the problems of agriculture" appealed to a
constituent base that appreciated being included as a player at the national level.[57] West Texas farmers also rallied behind George H. Mahon
in 1934, electing the thirty-three-year-old district attorney from Mitchell County as representative of the newly created Nineteenth Congressional District, of which the largest city was Lubbock. Mahon won the
Democratic primary in a runoff on August 1, defeating two other candidates, though his main competition was District Judge Clark Mullican
of Lubbock. Mullican managed to carry Lubbock County in the runoff,
but Mahon's ability to consolidate the district's rural vote allowed him to
claim an easy victory, winning 50 percent of the overall vote in a three-
way race. As would be the case throughout most of his career, Mahon
ran unopposed in the general election.[58]

Mahon's win, despite Mullican's consolidation of the vote in Lubbock, was a testament to his reputation as a friend of the farmer. Mullican focused his campaign on a contrast of experience, claiming Mahon
was too young for the job. Failing to connect his candidacy to anything
happening at the national level, Mullican underestimated the Great Depression's impact on voters' mindsets. Relying simply on the endorsement of a handful of influential Lubbockites, Mullican failed to capture
his district's attention.[59] In contrast, Mahon ran as a "loyal Democrat"
and as a champion of the New Deal, though at the end of his career he
would shy away from such associations. Nevertheless, Mahon benefited
from numerous campaign testimonials, which described him as "a man
who has been down the cotton row as a barefooted boy in this district,
who has felt the sting of the maize chaff and the prick of the cotton
burr" and who was an "active church layman." Campaign brochures connected Mahon's commitment to farmers with a phrase straight out of
the Democratic Party's 1932 platform—"special privileges to none."[60]
"He is a Christian gentleman," wrote the *Scurry County Times*. "George is
neither religious nor a gentleman for political reasons. He was born that
way, reared that way, and lives that way."[61]

Mahon strategically balanced his connections to Roosevelt, the
Democratic Party, and New Deal farm programs with a vague but firm
commitment to long-term fiscal responsibility and lower taxes. "Mahon
believes in reducing taxes wherever possible," according to a 1934 campaign flier, "but he declares the redistribution of the burden of taxation
is even more important." Emphasizing fairness for farmers above ideological concerns, Mahon's campaign championed their candidate as a
"commoner" who believed in "fair play to the powerful interests, but de-
nounces the policy of special privilege, which he says has largely brought
about the inequalities among our people." Mahon also frequently ex-
plained in speeches that he was not opposed to taxation, so long as
the "super-rich" were taxed fairly and equally, referring to "special tax
breaks for the wealthy" as a form of "discrimination" against farmers and
other workers. Reflecting the most obvious themes still popular among
Texas Democrats, Mahon's campaign billed their candidate as "for the
home, the children, the churches, the schools" adding: "Our people
cannot live on the platitudes of political candidates. George Mahon is a
man of action; who stands for the people, the party, and the President.
The people will win when George Mahon wins."[62]

In its endorsement, the *Abilene Daily Reporter* connected Mahon to a new wave of "fresh faces in Congress," and hinted that Mahon had the makings of a future senator. "The rise of the younger generation in politics has been rapid and sure. The New Deal is essentially a young man's movement. Most of the men President Roosevelt has chosen to bear the brunt of the recovery effort are of the new generation in politics. They are characterized chiefly by eagerness, social-mindedness, and courage." Mahon also made sure that most of his campaign literature included the phrase "a staunch and constant Democrat, active in the affairs of the party," a line no doubt effective in large part because of the fresh memories still lingering from the Hoovercrat bolt of 1928. Mahon campaigned for the elimination of tax exemptions on bonds and securities, the "equalization" of government benefits, an end to all "entangling alliances" between members of Congress and Wall Street. He also came out in favor of government intervention on behalf of labor, old-age pensions, a universal military draft, and the immediate payment of bonuses for all veterans of the Great War. Mahon even came out against pornography and in favor of stronger law enforcement, as if such stances needed verbalizing. In short, Mahon left no rhetorical stones unturned in his bid for Congress in 1934, with the results proving such efforts successful.[63]

Few candidates for public office in Texas were more definitive in their support for FDR and the New Deal than San Antonio's Maury Maverick. Despite a vicious primary struggle against multiple candidates, including a runoff campaign against San Antonio mayor C. K. Quin, Maverick won a seat representing the state's Twentieth Congressional District. Quin's primary strategy was to allege that Maverick had communist sympathies. It was a strategy well suited for the early Cold War 1950s but proved less effective at the height of New Deal popularity in 1934. Quin emphasized Maverick's membership in the ACLU as evidence of socialist radicalism and made much of Maverick's efforts in 1928 to secure a speaking engagement in Texas for the vice president of the Communist Party USA, Benjamin Gitlow. But Quin's attacks could not overcome Maverick's support among local progressives, most of whom shared the former San Antonio tax collector's opposition to establishment "machine rule." Maverick defeated Quin by more than three thousand votes in the August runoff election and sailed to victory against another hapless local Republican in the general election that November.[64]

Despite his opponents' efforts to brand him as a communist, Maverick ably packaged his background for maximum appeal to Texas voters. Taking his namesake to heart, Maverick fostered a public reputation for independence and tenacity. Noting that his grandfather, Samuel, had been an original Texas revolutionary in the 1830s, Maverick highlighted his military service in Europe during the Great War, and especially highlighted his personal experience fighting against gas warfare in October 1918. At the same time, Maverick branded himself a progressive liberal and a thoroughgoing New Dealer. He emphasized his role in securing the Texas Regional Labor Board, along with "many large federal appropriations for army and public construction in Bexar County." In doing so, Maverick positioned himself as a man of the people. His campaign also liked to tell a story about how Maverick disguised himself as a "tramp" in 1932, joining state representative Pat Jefferson on a train-hopping and hitchhiking tour across Texas, with a goal of gaining an intimate understanding of how transients and "hobos" were experiencing the Depression. Maverick directly referenced this experience when proposing state and federal laws designed to ease burdens on, as he put it, "the little guys." Calling himself a "wet since the cradle," Maverick supported Roosevelt's push to repeal Prohibition laws, adamantly opposed state sales taxes, organized his own Bonus Army community in San Antonio, and generally supported FDR's efforts to use the full force of the federal government to improve life for the forgotten man.[65]

Maverick promised San Antonio voters that they would immediately benefit from New Deal appropriations, went out of his way to befriend the military by promising additional funds for new buildings at Kelly and Brooks air fields, and pushed the HOLC to liberalize its appraisal policies in order to ease credit. The *Washington Post* ran a feature on Maverick before the general election in October, introducing the soon-to-be-congressman from San Antonio to a national audience by noting that Theodore Roosevelt Jr. had called FDR a "maverick" in 1932 and that the real-life Maverick from Texas would undoubtedly be a force in support of the New Deal. "Maury Maverick . . . will come to Washington with some of the same spirit that his grandfather took to the Congress of the Republic of Texas," the *Post* wrote. "He is progressively liberal. He follows to fundamental rules, a belief in the bill of rights and the freedom of speech. He is a staunch advocate of all that President Roosevelt has done." In praising Maverick's campaign, the *Post* also noted that Maverick had "out-machined the bosses" in San Antonio, no doubt a compliment that Maverick particularly relished.[66]

In all, Texans sent twenty-one men to Congress in 1934, each one a Democrat. Seventeen were reelected, including notables Wright Patman, Hatton Sumners, James Buchanan, Marvin Jones, Fritz Lanham, and Richard Kleberg. Four won their first term, including Mahon, Maverick, and Nat Patton, who would soon find a seat at Roy Miller's table alongside Sumners, Kleberg, Dies, and Buchanan. Sam Rayburn was also reelected, notable in view of Rayburn's invaluable advocacy for two major pieces of New Deal legislation, the Truth in Securities Act of 1933 and the Securities Exchange Act of 1934. Both bills carried Rayburn's name; the former represented the culmination of a twenty-year struggle by Rayburn to provide some measure of federally backed insurance to defrauded investors, and the latter added an additional layer of federal oversight with the creation of the new Securities and Exchange Commission. Rayburn's efforts, in tandem with Roosevelt's appreciative support, drew considerable ire from business leaders across the country, including some in Texas who discussed financing an opponent to challenge Rayburn in the 1934 Democratic primary, though nothing came of such efforts. Every Texas Democrat elected to Congress in 1934 did so unopposed; not a single Democrat faced a Republican challenger in the general election.[67]

The Texas Republican Party's decision to avoid challenging Democrats in the general election that November was likely based on the pathetic turnout in GOP primaries that summer. It was only the second time in state history the GOP had even attempted to stage such elections. The first time, in 1926, the state GOP attracted participation from more than 15,000 voters; the second time, in 1934, it attracted a puny 1,554. For all intents and purposes, the Texas Republican Party was moribund as FDR finished his first two years in the White House. Nationally, in what was largely seen as a referendum on Roosevelt and the New Deal, Democrats picked up nine seats in the House to go along with nine in the Senate, making 1934 the first time since the Civil War that the sitting president's party gained seats in both chambers during a first-term midterm election. It marked the lowest percentage of Republican representation on Capitol Hill ever. It also meant that Roosevelt would have an even more liberal Congress to work with in 1935. The 1934 midterms reflected the public's faith in and support for the New Deal, but it also reflected Roosevelt's personal popularity with the electorate. Washington was ready for another round of aggressive reform.[68]

"Civilization Begins with the Plow"

Few politicians have ever been more popular in the United States than Franklin Roosevelt was in late 1934 and early 1935. Americans still suffering under the weight of economic hardship supported the administration's efforts to legislate relief, recovery, and reform. That support coalesced into a powerful new bloc—the New Deal Coalition. Merging progressive intellectuals, white southerners, urban labor, and most minorities, the New Deal Coalition was big-tent Democratic politics at its height. Subordinate and pliable, Democrats took advantage of the unprecedented majorities rendered to their party in 1934 to launch a new wave of initiatives on Capitol Hill, at almost all times following FDR's lead. The New Deal Coalition would continue to dominate national politics for the next three decades, though never more so than in 1935 and 1936. Supportive of the New Deal's penchant for constant activity, Americans trusted FDR the president, but they also trusted FDR the man—the ever-smiling, gregarious, optimistic, stamp collector whose plainspokenness somehow communicated an intimate grasp of relevant complexities without projecting condescension or even the slightest pretention.[69]

On January 4, 1935, Roosevelt delivered his annual State of the Union address before a joint session of Congress. As was his nature, he spoke confidently and optimistically about the abundant progress his administration had made since taking office in 1933. At the same time, however, he admitted that much of the work remained unfinished. Specifically, he asked Congress for assistance in better managing the nation's natural resources, providing some form of a financial security program for citizens in old age, and creating new agencies charged with reducing unemployment, homelessness, and home foreclosures. Congress listened, and they subsequently embarked on a renewed flurry of legislation that historians would later call the "Second New Deal."[70]

Less than two weeks later, Jimmie Allred delivered a speech of his own, this one upon the occasion of his inauguration as governor of Texas. Within the first minute of his speech, Allred—calling FDR's 1933 inauguration speech a "model of brevity and frankness"—declared his intent to model his own leadership after the president he claimed had given "us a new deal in words and speeches as well as in ideals and statecraft." "We Texans may properly say that no other state has ever more intelligently followed two such great leaders as Wilson and Roosevelt. I pledge you that this administration will continue to go forward with President Roosevelt," Allred told the gathered crowd in Austin. Importantly, Allred went out of his way to distinguish "New Deal liberalism" from the "grosser liberalism of a New York, a Chicago, or a New Orleans" where "gangsters, bandits, thugs, and thieves" ran roughshod over an underfunded law enforcement. The rest of Allred's speech outlined a plan for relief, recovery, and reform, complete with new committees, new regulations, new programs, and, particularly noteworthy, a new plan for creating old-age pensions.[71]

For congressional newcomers George Mahon and Maury Maverick, the overwhelming Democratic majorities opened wide the doors of opportunity. Open doors made it easier to fulfill campaign promises quickly, thereby strengthening connections and deepening trust with local constituents. In West Texas, Mahon spent his first few months in office trying to emulate FDR in both word and deed. He moved fast, preferring quick, aggressive action to equivocation and debate. He gave the appearance of engagement and accessibility and did not shy away from advancing specific proposals, including plans for a new VA hospital in West Texas. He also called for increased AAA funding to farmers for feed livestock loans, asked for an additional $60 million in emergency relief through the Farm Loan Package, and requested $100,000 in federal funding—in cooperation with the Bureau of Reclamation—for a geological study of water and irrigation on the Texas High Plains. These efforts were widely publicized. Mahon spoke frequently and supported the president with enthusiasm. He advocated increased federal aid to public schools across Texas and promised to secure better funding for new libraries and more teachers. Perhaps most significantly, Mahon enthusiastically supported the enormous Emergency Relief Appropriation Act of 1935. That bill essentially created a massive new wave of alphabet soup programs, including among others, the Works Progress Administration (WPA), the Rural Electrification Administration (REA), and the National Youth Administration (NYA). Mahon's district fared particularly well with WPA-sponsored projects, and he celebrated each one with press releases, public appearances, and speeches. He also championed federal funds for highway development and better roads across his district, particularly those that connected the rural countryside with urban centers and markets. At the height of this activity, Mahon accepted an invitation to dine with FDR at the White House, joining a host of other young New Dealers. After dinner, Mahon—radiant as any new politician would be after such an occasion—extolled the president's excellent health and vibrant personality before inquiring reporters.[72]

Mahon's coziness with the New Deal reached great heights that spring but found its limit that summer when the White House announced plans to place a Negro Civilian Conservation Corps (CCC) camp in Dawson County. Knowing the pervasively racist sentiments of his district well, Mahon vigorously and publicly protested the plan. Soon thereafter, in July, the *Dawson County Courier* published a letter from Henry Wallace to George Mahon, in which Wallace announced that Dawson County's CCC camp would be for whites only. White locals celebrated the decision, hailing Mahon as a hero with surprising influence. The freshman congressman had secured the county a valuable, federally funded camp, while simultaneously preserving the region's white supremacy. Race tested the limits of New Deal liberalism in many other parts of the ex-Confederacy, where results were typically similar. Accepting federal dollars rarely demanded anything close to desegregation or racial conciliation. The White House did not push the matter. The New Deal Coalition could not survive without southern Democrats, and FDR had no desire to spend political capital on issues related to race or civil rights.[73]

Meanwhile, as Mahon spent the early months of 1935 pursuing pragmatic solutions to economic problems in his home district, Maury Maverick quickly earned a reputation as one of Congress's most aggressive representatives and an ally to progressives across the country. By March he had successfully organized a cohort of thirty-five like-minded members in the House, establishing a powerful voting bloc on a wide array of legislative initiatives, including bills mandating shorter work hours, guaranteed farm prices, cheaper farm mortgage financing, prohibitions on tax-exempt securities, extended public works programs, and guaranteed collective bargaining for organized labor. The San Antonio renegade even collaborated with New York's notoriously controversial Vito Marcantonio on a plan to establish a new tax on all corporate profits generated through war- and defense-related contracts. Maverick's partnership with Marcantonio prompted the *Philadelphia Record* newspaper to praise the freshman congressman from Texas as a true "left-winger." The national press soon dubbed the congressional voting bloc "Mavericks."[74]

Mahon and Maverick may have taken different paths on the road to supporting FDR and the New Deal, but they eventually ended up in the same place, at least during their first terms. Throughout the spring and summer of 1935, politicians and ordinary Texans alike were on safe ground in publicly supporting Roosevelt and the New Deal. Sam Rayburn, for instance, followed up his efforts in 1933 and 1934 to regulate securities more effectively by cosponsoring the Public Utility Holding Company Act of 1935, which authorized the SEC to "control and regulate" electric companies failing to operate in the best interests of the communities they served. In discussing the act before a gaggle of reporters on Capitol Hill, Rayburn affirmed his New Deal bona fides, saying that he believed control was being "restored to the government and the people, and taken out of the hands of a few, and that the American people will have cause to believe that [FDR] is trying and is establishing a government of the people, by the people, and for the people." Shortly thereafter, upon a visit home to Bonham, Rayburn began to display a photograph of Franklin D. Roosevelt in his office where, previously, the only such political iconography on display was a prominently placed portrait of Robert E. Lee.[75]

FDR inspired engagement and political activism on a scale that had been largely absent from American life for a generation. Colleges and universities reported significant increases in students majoring in political science, government, public policy, and other fields that pointed them toward a career in the Brain Trust.[76] Meanwhile, when the Women's Division of the Democratic National Committee launched efforts to redesign its outreach and engagement operations at the state and local levels across the country, many white Texas women rallied to the cause. DNC records indicate that most Texas women engaged in local politics first around the theme of loyalty and second around the theme of protecting families. Fidelity was of paramount importance. Loyal Democrats were more likely to be loyal husbands and loyal fathers, and the New Deal helped men provide for their families. This was "breadwinner liberalism" at its finest, reinforcing gendered notions that associated work with masculinity and childcare with femininity, attitudes common across the country, though particularly resonant in the South. It also offered New Dealers a bridge connecting traditionalist and progressive women voters in Texas and nationally.[77]

Whether they were marketing policies to women or men, New Dealers were intent on combatting suggestions that Roosevelt's programs fostered unhealthy levels of dependency on the government. Paychecks were better than relief checks, advocates argued, even when the paychecks came from Uncle Sam. Work was better than welfare, though the opposition to relief programs was consistently more prevalent among men than among women. Political candidates were relatively sensitive to the influence of the female vote, but consistently messaged most New Deal programs in a way that would not undermine conceptions of patriarchy. The WPA issued just such a press release in August 1935, promoting additional job opportunities in San Antonio while emphasizing that districts across Texas were "cooperating happily" in an effort to "take every employable off relief rolls." The WPA said it was committed to putting people to work; it was not distributing "handouts." Such a message worked well in Texas, where citizens hesitated to compromise their ideological principles, but also understood the importance of such programs and opportunities.[78]

Like other New Deal organizations, the WPA marketed itself very carefully. New Deal politics depended on successful public relations. The WPA rarely missed an opportunity to celebrate its achievements, providing local newspapers with ready-made stories that championed the president, his ideas, and the practical application of federal moneys for the betterment of area citizens. By late 1935, Texans undoubtedly knew that the WPA was infusing millions of dollars across each of the state's 254 counties; over the course of five years, the WPA would spend more than $80 million in Texas, while employing tens of thousands— as many as 120,000 at one point in 1936—including teachers, artists, and writers. Gambling that its significant reach into ordinary Texans' lives would mitigate any ideological resentment stemming from antigovernment conservatives, the WPA enjoyed widespread popularity. Other New Deal agencies followed suit, including the CCC, which celebrated a new camp in Lockhart, Texas, on August 21. The next day, the local *Lockhart Post-Register* devoted its entire front page to the story, including a decidedly pro-FDR history of the CCC's creation, while also directly associating the camp's organization with American military traditions and the need to protect young men and families, thereby protecting the nation's future.[79]

Texans justified their support for the New Deal in a variety of ways. Some saw it as a pragmatic but temporary necessity. Others saw it as a bulwark for family values and a model for better government. As he had during Roosevelt's first two years in office, Morris Sheppard continued to sell the New Deal as the modern manifestation of national core convictions—a heritage of democratic individualism. The New Deal, he said, was nothing short of "the people" standing together, arms locked, in defiance of "the tyranny of an elite majority." For Sheppard, FDR's

New Deal was American individualism's great protector, while the Democratic Party was "imperishable because it rests on . . . the doctrine of equal rights for all and no special privileges for any man." In Jasper, Texas, local civic leader Walter P. Smith echoed Sheppard, telling a crowd of listeners that if "civilization begins with the plow," then FDR was most inarguably Texas civilization's "Savior."[80]

While Texans supported Roosevelt and the New Deal in varying degrees and for various reasons, dissenters—few though they were—remained vocal. Most Texans appreciated Roosevelt's charm; some, however, saw a beguiling figure on a quick descent toward tyranny. Critics saw radicalism in the cabinet. Rather than accept the New Deal as a set of pragmatic solutions to immediate economic problems, these conservatives viewed the White House as the progenitor of ideological realignment and socialist regimentation. "While I have always been a Democrat, I cannot say that I am very enthusiastic over a good deal of the New Deal, although I do not feel bitterly about it like a good many of my friends in both New York and Texas do," one man wrote to Sam Rayburn in early 1935. "It does seem unfortunate however that the President has surrounded himself with advisers of the type of Wallace, Tugwell, and others who are leading him and the party toward disaster."[81]

Few concerns roiled conservatives more than rising taxes. Recalling fears that harkened back to Reconstruction, conservative whites associated federal spending with higher taxes, wealth redistribution, and welfare subsidization to the indigent and undeserving. Roosevelt was adamant that, at its best, the New Deal stimulated job creation, not dependency. Conservatives countered by associating the New Deal not simply with growing dependency, but with criminality and a breakdown in the basic concepts of self-help and communal morality. Conservatives attacked the New Deal as a purveyor of dependence and un-Americanism, charged Roosevelt with tyranny and dictatorship, and lamented higher taxes and criminal deviance. Party stalwarts like Jack Garner opposed various aspects of Roosevelt's agenda, especially the Wagner Act (National Labor Relations Act of 1935), which Garner described as an "unnecessary" threat to the party's relationship with business leaders. As was typical for Garner and others, however, he largely kept his concerns private before dutifully falling into line, while sincerer New Dealers like Congressman Joe Eagle of Houston made his support for the Wagner Act public, saying that he supported the bill "unreservedly" and that the bill did little more than protect "the proper rights of those who toil."[82]

Conservatives also worried about debt. Some deficit hawks were less concerned about rising taxes than some of their conservative brethren, instead focusing their debates on questions about the types of new taxes that were needed to prevent spiraling levels of red ink. Deficit hawks were especially vocal during national debates over old-age pensions— Social Security. Preferring a regressive sales tax to a state income tax or higher federal income taxes, conservatives in Texas challenged the New Deal's efforts to fund Social Security. Faithful to FDR, Jimmie Allred used his gubernatorial pulpit to oppose all efforts toward new and higher sales taxes, state or federal. Instead, he blamed the sales tax idea on the wealthy and specifically on Republicans and their longtime leader in Texas, R. B. Creager. Allred's opposition to new sales taxes manifest in a series of passionate public speeches, during which the state's chief executive extolled federal programs, and Washington, DC, as far more competent and capable of spending taxpayer dollars wisely than anyone else, including legislators in his own state. FDR knew what he needed and knew how to spend it, Allred said. Texans should trust him.[83]

Like Allred, other New Dealers in Texas voiced support for more aggressively graduated federal tax rates that would shift the overall tax burden more heavily to the wealthy and to corporations, whose greed, they suggested, had caused the Depression in the first place. Like Allred, these individuals framed Texas farmers as a suffering minority in need of federal protection, particularly against the discriminatory designs of Republicans and Wall Street. One of these men, Judge Edwin Hawes Jr. of Wharton, Texas, said this and more during an appearance before the Senate Finance Committee on August 2, 1935, emphasizing that farmers had been the victim of "discrimination" while adding that Congress had an obligation to protect farmers while balancing the federal budget. The only way to do that, he argued, was by raising taxes on corporations, which "punished individuals" by accepting "too many tax breaks."[84]

Ideologically committed conservatives were rarely a minority in Texas. However, at the height of the New Deal—with the Great Depression still hovering over the state and nation like a never-ending thunderstorm— they were. Pragmatic populists who defined federal action as the most effective way to protect farmers—always dichotomized against Republican and corporate foils—commanded more attention and more influence than did the New Deal's opponents. By and large, Texans did not abandon their belief in rugged individualism and self-help during Roosevelt's first term. Rather, they believed the New Deal was a weapon deployed in defense of those ideas. Republicans had catered to the wealthy during the 1920s and Wall Street had jeopardized the Jeffersonian ideal for a nation of independent, land-owning yeomen. In response, Roosevelt's vision was to supply forgotten Americans with new bootstraps. As the president began to prepare for his first reelection campaign most Texans trusted their commander-in-chief and accordingly trusted the New Deal.

Disloyal to the party of secession in 1928 and repentant of that disloyalty in 1932, Texas approached another presidential election in 1936 as firmly in Roosevelt's corner as any state in America. Progressive Texans like Morris Sheppard and Maury Maverick fit into the new culture quite naturally, while establishment conservatives like Marvin Jones and James Buchanan adjusted to the new realities with unexpected ease. FDR's focus on agriculture at the outset of his administration established credibility among the state's farmers, proud and self-reliant in conviction, but pragmatic and open to experimentation when faced with calamity. Responsive to Roosevelt's request for patience and trust, Texans rallied to the incumbent administration. Aspects of the Second New Deal that were less relevant to voters across the state—reforms like the Wagner Act, for instance—were received with less enthusiasm, but failed to dampen voters' confidence in the president. Programs like the WPA seemed to be creating jobs, while the CCC put young men to work, just as the AAA was helping farmers. Those who did not join the New Deal bandwagon remained vociferously opposed to the rapid expansion of federal regulation, but failed to connect with ordinary Texans, most of whom counted themselves among FDR's forgotten Americans who had been victimized by Republican greed and incompetence.

In short, four years into the Roosevelt presidency, Texas was a New Deal state. Such enthusiasm would not last forever. But as FDR prepared for what would be the first of three reelection bids, Texas was definitely not a swing state. Hoovercrats no more, most Texans seemed to believe that happy days had indeed come again. That is certainly how one community of rural Texans living just north of Lubbock saw it. In 1935, in an undeniable show of support for FDR and his efforts as president, the school districts of Caldwell, Center, Grovesville, and Monroe decided to merge their various educational entities into one. They named the new district "New Deal."[85]

3 | "Sired by the Devil and Born in Hell"

FDR rarely missed political opportunities, and the Texas Centennial of 1936 was as golden as such opportunities came. Facing the first of what would be three presidential reelections, Roosevelt visited the Lone Star State over three days that June, hoping to associate his pending campaign with the pervasive spirit of pride and determination that had been reflected in earlier celebrations staged across Texas between November 1935 and April 1936. The White House even backed a $3 million federal appropriation in support of new construction, exhibits, and events, most of which aimed to promote Texas' ruggedly western past—(or at least the perception of such a past)—as a foundation for a prosperous future and a model for all Americans to emulate. During a series of public appearances, the president spoke to throngs of proud Texans about things stereotypical Texans loved to hear—sacrifice, perseverance, victory, freedom, and the sheer size of their beloved homeland.[1]

On June 11, at the famed San Jacinto battleground near Houston, Roosevelt retold in vivid detail the harrowing story of Texas independence, as though his audience did not already know those details by heart. He compared the "liberators of Texas" to the "colonists of 1776," adding that the "Texas Declaration of Independence, signed at Washington-on-the-Brazos, March 2, 1836, was as natural and inevitable a consequence as the earlier Declaration at Philadelphia, July 4, 1776." He even deviated from his prepared speech text to recognize and celebrate the six flags flying in front of him, one of which was Confederate.[2]

Later that day, Roosevelt journeyed to San Antonio, where he spoke before a crowd gathered at the state's most famous landmark. Referring to the Alamo as a "shrine" and the nation's "noblest exemplification of sacrifice," Roosevelt boldly compared his administration's actions combatting the Depression to those taken by Crockett, Bowie, Travis, and the others who "shed blood" in the fight against Santa Anna's Mexican army. "I hope they knew and know that the overwhelming majority

Jesse H. Jones, FDR, and Eleanor Roosevelt in Houston, June 11, 1936.
Courtesy of the Dolph Briscoe Center for American History, University of
Texas at Austin.

of Americans of 1936 are once more meeting new problems with new
courage—that we, too, are ready and willing to stand up and fight for
truth against falsehood, for freedom of the individual against license by
the few." Taking such comparisons a step further, Roosevelt added that
the heroes of the Alamo did not give up their lives for themselves only,
but rather for their neighbors, for their communities, and for their nation. "United action alone could win," FDR proclaimed. "So we, in this
latter day, are thinking and acting in terms of the whole nation, understanding deeply that our firesides, our villages, our cities, and our states
cannot long endure if the nation falls. Travis's message—'I shall never
surrender'—is a good watchword for each and every one of us today."[3]

Roosevelt's trip to the Alamo was good politics. It was also, however, a
favor to Clara Driscoll, the woman who, along with Adina De Zavala, had
by 1936 become synonymous with both the founding of the Daughters

FDR with Congressman Maury Maverick at Alamo, San Antonio, for Texas
Centennial celebrations, June 11, 1936. Courtesy of Franklin D. Roosevelt
Presidential Library.

of the Republic of Texas and its chief organizing purpose, the restoration of the Alamo and, more broadly, the veneration of Texas history
as they saw it. Driscoll spent most of her career as an independently
wealthy philanthropist, promoting a vision of the Alamo as a shrine—
just as FDR called it when he visited in 1936. From 1922 to 1938, she was
also the Democratic Party's national committeewoman from Texas and
a staunch fundraising ally to Jack Garner and other stalwarts in the state
party. Driscoll no doubt rejoiced when reporters noted that a previously
fatigued Roosevelt emerged from his visit inside the Alamo appearing
noticeably reinvigorated, as though he "had communed with the spirits
of the 182 heroes who died" there.[4]

Upon leaving San Antonio, the president repeated similar sentiments in speeches in Austin, Dallas, Fort Worth, and Denison, seventy-
five miles north of Dallas and just south of the Red River. At every turn,
he gushed over Texas's courage and tenacity, its indomitable spirit, and

FDR at Alamo, San Antonio, for Texas Centennial celebrations, June 11, 1936. Courtesy *San Antonio Express-News*/ZUMA Press, and the University of Texas at San Antonio Libraries, Special Collections.

its "unmatched" ability to persevere in the face of hardship. Clearly, Roosevelt understood his audience. Without missing a beat, he also used the occasion to rally constituents toward the New Deal, connecting his administration's efforts to defeat economic catastrophe to those of patriots a century before, facing tyranny of another form. On June 12, he visited the locus of centennial activity in Fair Park, Dallas, which won the rights to host the event—formally the Texas Centennial Exposition—after a stiff competition with the cities of Houston, Austin, and San Antonio. Dallasites beamed with pride as the president toured the recently completed grounds, including the extraordinarily grand Hall of State, one of the largest art deco structures ever built in Texas, featuring an abundance of WPA architecture and artwork. Then, before an estimated crowd of fifty thousand at the nearby Cotton Bowl, Roosevelt spoke about "democracy of opportunity," delivering a speech as progressively partisan as it was celebratory or reverent. Later that day, he attended the unveiling of a new memorial dedicated to Robert E. Lee and called the legendary Confederate general "one of our greatest American Christians and greatest American gentlemen."[5]

The president's trip to Texas that June captivated journalists across the state and nation. The stories those journalists reported cemented Roosevelt's image as a gifted leader who was fully capable of guiding the country out of the Great Depression. More than that, Roosevelt reassured Texans—or, at least, most of them—that he knew how to connect on an emotional level. He respectfully empathized with specific local problems while simultaneously bridging a nostalgic reverence for the past with his progressive optimism for the future. As FDR told it, the New Deal was hardly radical, nor was it out of step with Texas traditions or Jeffersonian ideals. Rather, it was an expression of resolve consistent with Americanism itself. Beyond that, Roosevelt asserted that his New Deal would have seemed "familiar" to both the nation's and the state's founders, essentially suggesting their posthumous endorsement. Bold as ever, FDR and the New Deal were enjoying high tide during the spring and summer of 1936. Most Texans eagerly welcomed them ashore.[6]

"Gospel of Brotherhood"

Roosevelt peppered his well-publicized trip to Texas in June 1936 with a brand of rhetorical flourish and hyperbole that some might have considered native to the Lone Star State. At each stop, he compared his platform for relief, recovery, and reform with the state's most mythic features. FDR was not a Texan, nor did he pretend to be one. Yet in styling the New Deal as part of an enduring American fight for freedom and democracy, the president undercut arguments designed to foment resistance to his programs on ideological and patriotic grounds. In other words, FDR and his strategic handlers campaigned with a style that conservative Republicans would have appreciated in later decades. They turned the New Deal into a clear choice between freedom and tyranny, right and wrong, good and evil.[7]

While FDR and his New Deal allies in Texas frequently integrated their speeches with tales of heroism and religiosity, direct comments on race were few and far between. Despite widespread agreement in the Texas State Legislature that a centennial celebration would be good for the state's morale, legislators failed to agree on a budget appropriation for the event through 1934 and most of 1935, largely because of disagreements over how (or whether) to highlight African American contributions to state history during the events. (One citizen urged Ma Ferguson to lend her support in 1934, saying that doing so would "give a new emphasis to the name of Miriam leading the children of Texas through the Red Sea of doubt and distrust into the Promised Land given us by the pioneer men and women who made Texas.") Religious hyperbole notwithstanding, FDR refused to intervene in those debates, staying relatively silent on the matter even after the federal government provided its own appropriation. With great effort, Black advocates (primarily but not exclusively led by the Dallas Negro Chamber of Commerce) secured supplemental funding for the project, which, when coupled with federal dollars, enabled the construction of what came to be called the Hall of Negro Life. A tremendous showcase, the Hall of Negro Life received far too little attention as the nation turned its eyes to Texas in 1936. Sadly, Roosevelt also failed to challenge the Texas Centennial Commission's attempts to excise Black (and Hispanic) contributions to the state's history. In fact, Roosevelt's comments both at San Jacinto and at the dedication of Dallas's new Robert E. Lee statue that June were widely seen as a tacit endorsement of "Lost Cause" mythology. FDR's subtle and passive promotion of white supremacist narratives strengthened conservative power brokers in Texas who were committed to the fiction of statewide racial harmony grounded in the segregationist status quo. If anything, the president's Texas hosts celebrated the state's allegedly "remarkable" record for racial harmony even as it frequently obstructed Black Democrats from full participation in the statewide celebration. The prohibition on Black male participation in centennial gatherings included their exclusion from several unofficial "social events" hosted at strip clubs in Dallas, Houston, and San Antonio, perhaps the most reflective example of hypocrisy at its finest in 1936. The leering gaze of a Black man upon the naked body of a white woman was, and would long remain, entirely unacceptable.[8]

Silent on the issues of race and civil rights, but eager to embrace Roosevelt and the New Deal, Texas Democrats used the centennial celebrations that spring as a springboard to election season that summer. In Bosque County, Democrats passed a resolution reiterating their support for FDR, Garner, and the New Deal. Simple in design and purpose, the resolution conveyed images of sin, repentance, redemption, and fidelity:

Like a bow of promise, a light dawning in the east, came the new administration . . . with Franklin D. Roosevelt standing like a stone wall facing the
storms of adversity, unknown to defeat. Backed by the democracy of the
nation and its wise leaders in the legislative halls, we have decisively routed
the forces of depression; restored hope to the people; renewed life to the
financial and economic structures of the nation . . . [and] lifted from labor's
bleeding brow the 'crown of thorns' placed there by the unwise policies of
the Republican Party.[9]

A few weeks later, Sam Rayburn—preparing for his own congressional reelection bid—appeared to draw from the same rhetorical well
when he spoke to an audience of partisans upon accepting the chairmanship of the State Democratic Convention in San Antonio: "At no
time in my life would I have deemed it a higher privilege to have come
before a convention of Texas Democrats than now, because I come to
you not with apology, but as a representative of a proud, militant, and
victorious Democracy." Recounting a nearly exhaustive list of American crises—including the Revolutions of 1776, 1836, and even the Civil
War—Rayburn opined that "the most serious, far-reaching and dangerous crisis that ever threatened this country were the years from 1929
until March 4, 1933." According to Rayburn:

> People had lost the faith of their childhood in governments and in men and
> had done it to such an extent that we stood upon the verge of disaster. After
> March 4, 1933, the mist began to clear and small rays of sunshine could be
> seen, because a leader had appeared upon the scene who had a program
> and the courage and the ability to carry it out. From the hour of his inaugu-
> ration, the people took heart.

With one eye on his own reelection campaign and another on future
leadership opportunities in the US House, Rayburn left no doubt as to
where he stood. "In my opinion," Rayburn said, "the most heartening
utterance that has been delivered in America since the Declaration of
Independence fell from the trenchant pen of Thomas Jefferson was the
Inaugural Address of Franklin D. Roosevelt. In my opinion, Franklin D.
Roosevelt and John N. Garner are the greatest team that ever served in
the high positions of President and Vice President of the United States."
In this and other speeches, Rayburn evoked religious phrases such as
"Christian charity" when commenting on the impact of various New
Deal programs. He also often described the people of Texas as "high

class," "noble," and "Christianlike" for their partisan faith. Condemning the "lies coming from the far right," Rayburn painted an almost apocalyptic picture of the nation's political culture, proclaiming: "If the men who would circulate slander on the great and good man now in the White House were sired by the Devil and born in Hell they would be a disgrace to the country of their birth."[10]

On June 24, the *Dallas Journal* ran an editorial endorsing Sam Rayburn's reelection, suggesting that Rayburn's loyalty—both to FDR and to his district—reflected the virtue of a man whose rising influence Texans should applaud.[11] Rayburn never hesitated when asked about his support for the White House. Neither did he shy away from trumpeting his own role in moving New Deal bills through the House of Representatives. Rayburn promoted himself as a proud ally to the White House and a friend to both Roosevelt and Garner, though his friendship with Garner was obviously older and deeper. Still, Rayburn purposefully reinforced an image of faithful partnership in an attempt to bridge ideological divides if not obliterate them entirely. In July, he somewhat oddly defended Garner as "a help and not a hindrance" to FDR and the New Deal, adding rather bluntly that the vice president "has known his place and has kept it."[12] Rayburn also knew his place and, while allowing his colleagues in the Texas delegation to promote his candidacy for the House speakership when Joseph Burns of Tennessee died suddenly that June, he backed off the intraparty contest just enough to allow Alabama's William Bankhead to claim the seat without much controversy. Bankhead became Speaker of the House, but Rayburn knew he was next in next.[13]

As Rayburn climbed the ladder in Washington, Thomas Love used the New Deal to stay in the spotlight in Dallas, sometimes to the chagrin of both FDR and his White House advisors. Love was a longtime player in the world of Texas politics, but his time in the sun was beginning to fade by 1936. As it did, the frequency of Love's self-directed insertions into state and national political debates grew, sometimes much to the frustration of White House strategists, who preferred to direct such surrogates, and much to the detriment of his own reputation. In one particularly infuriating moment, Love lobbied (but failed to convince) the *Dallas Morning News* to print an article he had written about the benefits of New Deal cotton and oil regulations. Love styled the article as a news piece, but it was clearly nothing more than a vapid self-promotional item, which turned off the newspaper. Thwarted, he paid for the article's publication anyway, not realizing it would then appear as a clearly marked "paid advertisement," which colored the entire enterprise with a cloak of insincerity. Ever the strategist and never one to mince words, Louis Howe subsequently told White House press secretary Stephen Early that he wanted to "boil" Love "in oil" for his "stupidity."[14]

Such episodes notwithstanding, Thomas Love was undoubtedly one of Roosevelt's most enthusiastic Texas boosters. Considered a brown-noser by some and an irritant to others, Love publicly championed Roosevelt by painting verbal portraits that blended images of Thomas Jefferson—the patrician-populist champion of individual liberty—with images of Andrew Jackson, the battler of big banks and hated Eastern establishments. The connections to Jackson were particularly helpful among Texas voters for whom the populism of the late-nineteenth century has persisted either through familial ties or occupational ones. For such as these, New Deal regulations over the private sector (especially banking) were not necessary evils one had to cope with on the path toward proving one's partisan loyalty; rather, they were positive goods reflecting the heart and soul of Roosevelt's promise to restore America to its people.[15] As one *Dallas Times Herald* editorial phrased it, FDR, Jack Garner, Sam Rayburn, and the entire New Deal agenda represented the will of "the people," while Republicans remained subservient to incompetent Wall Street lawyers and the even more incompetent Herbert Hoover.[16]

Comparisons with Jefferson were even more common and typically even more effective. Arguably, no icon was more commonly evoked to justify one's opinion of FDR and the New Deal than Thomas Jefferson. In addition to citing Jefferson's writings and philosophies, New Dealers also commonly cited Jefferson's aggressive use of the federal government for the purposes of national expansion (namely the Louisiana Purchase) and for the economic betterment of ordinary citizens. Particularly effective were comparisons that drew direct parallels between the master of Monticello's affinity for yeoman agriculture and the New Deal's support for farmers, be it through the AAA, SCS, REA, or some other agency. Anti–New Deal conservatives, meanwhile, often countered New Deal appropriations by trying to quote Jefferson as saying, "The government that governs best governs least." After doing some research at the Library of Congress, liberals effectively undercut that argument by reminding voters that Jefferson had never actually said that. Undeterred, conservatives also argued that while FDR might have been a "Jeffersonian" during his stint as governor of New York—when he had advocated for balanced budgets and lower taxes—the New Deal revealed his true contempt for small government, voiding the comparison to Jefferson as no longer apt.[17]

As pro- and anti–New Dealers argued about how Thomas Jefferson would have felt about the state of American politics in 1936, Morris Sheppard decided to employ a mix of religiosity and Jeffersonian imagery as the cornerstone of his own reelection campaign, promoting his own platform as virtually synonymous with the New Deal's and Jefferson's. Speaking in Corsicana on the Fourth of July, he called the New Deal a "gospel of brotherhood," before praising that "gospel" as the most "constructive and efficient" set of legislative accomplishments ever enacted on "behalf of the people." "New Deal legislation has taken this country from the brink of collapse and placed it on foundations of new hope and strength," Sheppard declared, before referring to Texas farmers as the "backbone" of America. For Sheppard, the choice was simple: Democrats were for the people; Republicans were not. As much as conservatives might object, Roosevelt was a true heir to the traditions of Jeffersonian populism; Republicans were not. The New Deal was the people's defense against elitism and corporate greed—nothing short of a bulwark protecting both the American and Texas revolutions, as Roosevelt himself alluded during his visit a few weeks earlier. Announcing a multipoint platform for reelection, Sheppard promised to provide—as the *Dallas Morning News* put it—"the largest opportunity for economic independence and security of the average individual, including proper care of those unavoidably disabled by old age." He also spoke about the need to "repress" monopolies before saying that a "grave" had already been prepared for the doomed Republican presidential ticket that year.[18]

Two weeks later, Sheppard lauded Roosevelt and the New Deal for more than an hour before an estimated four thousand people at the Confederate Veterans' and Old Settlers' Picnic in McKinney, north of Dallas. "The chief contributions of Franklin Roosevelt to history and to human welfare may be said to be the extent to which he suggested the use of the people's credit and the people's power as expressed in a people's government in the people's interested in a crisis involving the very existence of the Republic," Sheppard said. He then spoke of the various virtues of the RFC, HOLC, and the Tennessee Valley Authority (TVA), which Sheppard said was "performing a function specified as a proper attribute of government in the first inaugural address of Jefferson 136 years ago, namely the diffusion of information" as enabled by mass electrification. In other words, what Jefferson had decreed in 1800, Roosevelt had enabled in 1936, thanks to the New Deal. Though he focused primarily on national politics, Sheppard easily won renomination, carrying 65 percent of the vote in a six-way race in which the second-place candidate managed only 14 percent. It was a sign of things to come.[19]

"To Represent without Special Privilege All the People"

Texas Democrats willing to align themselves to FDR and the New Deal during the primaries of 1936 almost universally experienced success similar to (or greater than) Sheppard's. Loyalist candidates across the state easily won local and district primaries by hitching their wagons to Roosevelt and his program for relief, recovery, and reform, thereby paving the way for a general election season in which state and local Democrats were rarely confronted with state or local issues. Instead, the chief issue of the day, and the main topic of conversation in most campaigns, was the president himself—his leadership and his agenda.[20]

Frankly, Roosevelt's popularity in 1936 made any play other than partisan fidelity seem foolish. Like Sheppard, incumbent governor Jimmie Allred also happily tied his fortunes to Roosevelt in bidding for a second term. As Raymond Brookes of the small periodical *West Texas Today* put it: "[Allred] favors a New Deal for Texas—a new deal from a new deck, with some new dealers in the game," adding that the governor "knows where he is going," "has FDR's support and ear," and had been "instrumental" in thwarting the power of the "Ferguson machine."[21] The seemingly ever-present opposition of marginalized conservatives notwithstanding, Allred was a popular governor whose reelection prospects were never in doubt. During his first term, Allred received the Outstanding Young Man of America award from the Junior Chamber of Commerce of the United States and was a frequent guest of the president's in Washington. Roosevelt's inner circle welcomed him into their confidence on numerous occasions. A nationally reputed New Dealer, Allred also earned a reputation as a law and order governor, thanks primarily to his leadership in creating the new Texas Department of Public Safety, an initiative undoubtedly inspired by the New Deal zeitgeist for proactive reform via new bureaucracies. Allred used the new department and other powers at his disposal to crack down on illegal gambling outfits in Texas, thereby undermining the state's reputation as the "end of the Crime Corridor," as he put it. Texas was a "purer" place, Allred said, thanks to the New Deal and the new governmental entities in place that were protecting ordinary Texans from malfeasance of all varieties, from Wall Street to the notorious bank-robbing duo of Bonnie and Clyde.[22]

When given the chance to speak about FDR and the New Deal, Allred usually emphasized the importance of maintaining "harmony" with the national administration and national Democratic Party. At the state convention that May, he said that Texas was "unusually harmonious" because of Roosevelt's relationship with Vice President Garner. "I know it is a source of genuine joy and satisfaction to the people of Texas to know that for once, and more than ever in before in the history of this country, Texas has come into its own in the matter of recognition in Washington," Allred said.[23] The Democratic National Committee subsequently honored Allred with the privilege of renominating Garner for vice president at the 1936 Democratic National Convention in Philadelphia. "The Vice President of the United States is just as seasoned, rugged, and individualistic as the giant cactus of the Southwest," Allred said. "The Vice President possesses an additional characteristic common to the cactus. He can stand transplanting. He survived the blighting, deadening, 'three long eras' of the Republican 'F.F.F.'—folly, fatuity, and failure."[24] Allred left Philadelphia for a campaign rally in Waxahachie, just south of Dallas. There, taking cues from Roosevelt's own remarkably progressive acceptance speech, he compared the fight for "liberal and progressive government" to the Battle of the Alamo, analogizing conservative anti–New Dealism with "the wildest premises of scheming politics" thrust upon the Texian revolutionaries a century before.[25]

A nationally recognizable New Dealer by the summer of 1936, Allred was also highly regarded across Texas, where he earned a litany of endorsements from newspapers representing towns big and small. The *Longview Daily News* praised Allred's leadership, comparing him to Stephen F. Austin, William Barret Travis, and Sam Houston, also calling him "a man of wisdom" who "fills their highest office with dignity and devotion" and a "steadfastness to ideals which all might imitate." The *El Campo News* described Allred as a "champion of the people" whose opponents were limited to "representatives of entrenched wealth." The *Alice News* described Allred as "the soundest and sanest chief executive

Texas has had in many, many years," adding that voters should want to reelect him "even were he making for a third term." And the *Cisco Daily Press* praised Allred for his fiscal wisdom, spending money where most needed, while never wasting anything or being too quick to raise taxes.[26] Allred's campaign also promoted endorsements from the *Dalhart Daily Texan, Gonzales Inquirer, Houston Post, Amarillo News, El Paso Times, Floyd County Hesperian, Southwest Railway Journal, Houston Chronicle, Dallas Dispatch, Houston Press, Athens Weekly Review, Gainesville Daily Register, Caddo Mills Monitor,* and the United Press, among others. The United Press endorsement also featured an endorsement from Jack Garner. The listing appeared in one of Allred's most popular campaign pieces, a pamphlet entitled "The Press Reviews. . . . The Steady March of James V. Allred to a Second Term as Governor and the Completion of an Enlightened and Progressive Program for Texas."[27]

Facing little serious competition, Allred avoided a runoff, carrying a clear majority of the votes in the July 25 primary. Similarly, incumbent Democrats carried eighteen of the state's twenty-one congressional districts, two of the exceptions being Oliver Cross out of the Eleventh Congressional District and Houston's Joe Eagle of the Eighth. Cross retired, while Eagle left his seat to launch what became a failed bid for the United States Senate. A longtime populist, Eagle had been a particularly reliable New Dealer during his second stint in Congress from 1933 to 1937, having previously served from 1913 to 1921 before leaving office to fight the Ku Klux Klan as an attorney. He backed virtually all of Roosevelt's first-term initiatives, including those on collective bargaining, minimum wage laws, child labor, public works programs, agriculture, and even a proposal for higher corporate, inheritance, and personal income taxes.[28] (Eagle was replaced by Albert Thomas, who soon became another reliable New Dealer and, eventually, a reliable Great Society liberal until retiring in 1966.) Thomas L. Blanton was the third exception; the once censured and relatively inactive Blanton of Albany, Texas (just northeast of Abilene) lost his bid for reelection in the Seventeenth District to Clyde Garrett, whose principal strategy was to align as carefully and as closely as possible with Roosevelt and the New Deal. Democrats subsequently swept each of the twenty-one district races in the general election that November to maintain a unanimous grip on the Texas congressional delegation in Washington.[29]

The list of reelected incumbent Democrats returned to the Texas congressional delegation included Hatton Sumners of Dallas, whose career was on the brink of taking a dramatic turn thanks to the Supreme Court's decision of January 6, 1936, in which the widely popular AAA was ruled unconstitutional in the case *United States v. Butler.* Reaction to the decision was immediate and visceral. It also sent the White House scrambling in search of potential solutions, legal and legislative, and soon pushed Sumners into the center of a political storm. Hatton Sumners was, by 1936, a Democratic stalwart. Possessing a first-rate legal and political mind, Sumners won his first congressional election in 1912, taking an at-large seat before winning the Fifth District seat in 1914. Sooner than expected, he became an established member of the Texas Democratic establishment, not to mention one of the nation's foremost orators on the subject of checks and balances, the virtue of "separation of powers," and the "consequences of consolidated power." He was also an ardent segregationist, as was reflected in his fervent opposition to antilynching bills in 1920 and 1922. Trusted by fellow Southerners, he quickly rose through the party's ranks, becoming chairman of the House Judiciary Committee in 1932. Rumors circulated that his ultimate ambition was for a seat on the United States Supreme Court. As such, he was a politically astute and well-mannered (if perhaps tempered) New Dealer throughout Roosevelt's first term in office.[30]

The Supreme Court's ruling of the AAA as unconstitutional brought Sumners a host of headaches, none of which was more persistent than the appeals of his old friend and fellow Dallasite, Thomas Love. Love was already on record denouncing the Supreme Court's 1935 ruling that the National Recovery Act (NRA) was unconstitutional, having told reporters that the Court had unjustly struck down "the greatest piece of legislation ever offered to a congress of the United States."[31] Losing the NRA was disappointing, but in Love's mind, losing the AAA was intolerable and unacceptable. Toying with a variety of political strategies, he eventually put all of his eggs into one basket, proposing to Sumners and other friends on Capitol Hill a new constitutional amendment aimed at protecting the relationship between government and agriculture. Love distributed copies of his proposal far and wide, though he relied most heavily on old friendships among established Democrats such as the ones he had long maintained with Morris Sheppard, Sumners, and John Nance Garner. Garner agreed with Love that the Court's ruling ran counter to "common sense," but told Love that "the Boss" was not keen on pursuing the idea of a constitutional amendment to fix the situation; instead, Roosevelt had other ideas.[32]

Garner's discouragement did not dissuade Love from pressuring Sumners on the same proposal. The two shared one lengthy conversation on the subject during a meeting at the Dallas County Agriculture Club, and subsequently they dialogued by letter for the next several weeks. Love tried to convince Sumners that local business leaders were unified with Texas farmers in expressing "outrage" over the decision and that any "smart" representative would do whatever he could to secure protection for farmers, even if that meant a constitutional amendment.[33] Love's persistent appeals notwithstanding, it was soon clear that Sumners did not see things the same way. He refused to "correct the record," as Love requested, on the question of whether Sumners had originally believed the AAA had been unconstitutional when it was first passed in 1933. Refusing to take no for an answer, Love again pleaded with Sumners to back his proposal for a new constitutional amendment, calling it "good politics" while pointedly adding that those who did not support the idea were "not good politicians." At one point, he admitted that he was "pestering" Sumners, but said he was doing so for what he considered a good reason: "I want to do everything possible both of omission and commission to help the Roosevelt administration."[34]

After failing to persuade his congressman, Love's tone turned more contentious. He warned his "old friend" that failure to support the president would result in a challenge to his congressional seat, specifically mentioning rumors that state senator Claude Westerfield was preparing to make a run at Sumners for control of the Fifth District. Love assured Sumners that he would back him, but also said that Westerfield had been making important inroads with like-minded New Dealers and that Sumners was more vulnerable than he realized. Dallas needed a representative who would support the president as strongly as possible and as often as possible, Love told Sumners. Failure to do so was a risk he should avoid taking.[35]

Sumners was widely viewed as a man of deep conviction, however immoral some of those convictions were in retrospect. At the same time, however, he was also politically calculating and reasonable, and while he did not overreact to Love's warnings, neither did he dismiss them out of hand. When Sumners opened his 1936 bid for reelection in Garland on July 4, former state senator John Davis overstated the reality, introducing Sumners as FDR's "right-hand man." Sumners then sounded a New Deal note, praising FDR for "recognizing" that agriculture was "a business" that needed protection from the "captains of industry," who also needed to realize that "they must share their responsibility" to help ordinary Americans get off the dole and "earn their living." He also bragged that Roosevelt had privately endorsed his reelection. However, Sumners also made it clear that he was not a "yes man" and would encourage the White House toward a more conservative second term. For instance, he told audiences that he intended to push for a balanced federal budget in 1937, saying that America had "jazzed off into the jungle" in pursuit of "broad boulevards paved with $200 bills." He then criticized several other "fantastic schemes" coming out of Washington, though he did so without blaming the president specifically. Sumners admitted that his criticisms "may not get me any votes," but committed himself to full transparency. "I've never lied to you and I won't tonight," Sumners said. Forebodingly, Sumners then warned his audience that the country was on a dangerous path toward entitlement, comparing the New Deal to political theories in Europe, which he called "a disease . . . causing the people to lose the power to govern." Sumners won his reelection bid with relative ease, though the challenges he faced from Westerfield—and passive-aggressively from Love—would grow stronger in the coming years.[36]

George Mahon was similarly reelected in 1936, though his campaign strategy differed from both Sumners's in Dallas and Sheppard's statewide. While maintaining a degree of levelheaded moderation, Mahon chose to emphasize the Supreme Court's ruling on the AAA, aggressively criticizing the decision before audiences throughout the Nineteenth District. Mahon empathized with the anger his farming constituents shared over the AAA's nullification and wisely capitalized on the issue during public appearances and speeches. He affirmed the New Deal's "common sense" pragmatism as reflected in programs such as the AAA and lauded the president's desire to assist the nation's agricultural "backbone." The messages clearly resonated with farmers in his district, many of whom began to share similar ideas in cooperative meetings across the region. Farmers also frequently shared news of such events with Mahon directly, parroting their representative's own words or the words of other political advocates in West Texas, including Marvin Jones of Amarillo. "Without government regulation, our farmers will be forced into poverty," one frustrated farmer lamented. "It is a sad state of affairs when a few men in this great country can block any legislation that will help all people, just to satisfy their own greed and selfishness and build up great fortunes for their heirs to full and quarrel over after they are dead." Another told Mahon that "farmers in West Texas, as well as other parts of the country, wish to express our gratitude to you boys in Washington who have so faithfully stood by Agriculture during these hard times we have just gone through." He further encouraged Mahon and his fellow Democrats to show "guts and backbone" in standing up to the Supreme Court. Another wrote: "We farmers of Hockley County are determined that as long as the manufacturing industries of our country are operating under an excessive tariff, we must have some kind of protection that will assure us an equal and just share of the national income."[37]

West Texas farmers were not oblivious to debates over the pros and cons of "government intervention," but as they engaged with Mahon, Jones, and other political representatives, the farmers more frequently asked for help, particularly in trying to survive the catastrophic environmental challenges of the Dust Bowl. The result of uncontrollable drought and decades of poor planning, roughly one hundred million acres of land in the northwest Texas Panhandle, eastern New Mexico, southeastern Colorado, and western Kansas and Oklahoma languished from 1930 to 1935, before New Deal programs such as the Soil Conservation and Soil Erosion Services coordinated with local farmers to preserve the land. Although the drought continued for the rest of the decade, federal efforts and local ingenuity succeeded in reducing the size of the Dust Bowl to just more the twenty million acres by 1940. Nevertheless, with so-called black blizzard dust storms raging across the plains, some observers suggested that rather than pour state or federal resources into an isolated and semiarid region, the New Deal should instead encourage resettlement to other parts of the country, where nature was a more consistent ally. While more than a third of farmers in this affected area would eventually pick up the pieces of their shattered lives and move, often to California—a process immortalized by John Steinbeck in his novel *The Grapes of Wrath*—the remaining two-thirds of the population stayed.[38] Committed to persevering, many South Plains and Panhandle farmers placed their hopes for a better tomorrow on the ability of their political representatives to fight for them at the national level. A native of the area, Mahon understood the depths of this resolve. In a speech on the House floor, he delivered a passionate plea for help, rejecting arguments that his region was "uninhabitable" or that it should be depopulated and abandoned. No, Mahon, said, West Texas should not be abandoned. Rather, it needed help from the New Deal and, specifically, a new AAA, a stronger SCS, and a friendlier Supreme Court. Reporters covering the speech referred to Mahon as a "champion of the people of West Texas."[39]

Mahon's decision to prioritize farmers in his bid for reelection made perfect sense, as did his related support for Roosevelt and the New Deal more broadly. Though he was later known as an establishment Democrat who leaned conservative, Mahon's actions in Congress throughout the 1930s were largely in accord with the Roosevelt agenda. Running for reelection in 1936, Mahon expressed passionate support for a wide variety of New Deal initiatives, including the CCC, and specifically for the maintenance of the newly established CCC camp in Lubbock's Mackenzie Park. He also supported the HOLC, which he praised for having "saved" 1,400 homes in his district alone, and praised Roosevelt for the "improvement in the condition of the banks." Calling his constituents "thoughtful and grateful," Mahon told supporters that Roosevelt's efforts on their behalf would "never be forgotten."[40]

Unlike Sheppard or Love, Mahon occasionally tempered his enthusiasm for the New Deal by criticizing specific policies or decisions less directly relevant to the voters of his district. In doing so, he enhanced his reputation as a straight shooter whose credibility was beyond question, while at the same time making his support for most of the New Deal seem even more sincere. The FDR "administration is not without fault," he told a reporter in Abilene, adding that "mistakes have been made. They were inevitable in a program so far-reaching as the program this administration has made." Still, Mahon admitted that "the people throughout the nation realize and appreciate that definite steps toward recovery have been made and that a change in leadership right now might mean national disaster."[41] Later that day, he told reporters in Lubbock that the New Deal was quickly on the path toward "normality" and that FDR's hopes were for it to "aid in the march of business." The New Deal was not perfect, but it was moving the nation toward a new era of "sustained prosperity." On the issues of greatest importance, and on questions of leadership, Mahon's praise for FDR was typically unqualified and strong; on smaller issues, he was willing to take more risks in criticizing Washington, usually by saying that "much work remains." His moderate voice fostered trust and gave him stronger legs to stand on when it came to supporting the president and certain New Deal programs that may have been less relevant to the constituents in his home district and, therefore, less popular. Like Roosevelt, Rayburn, Sheppard, and others, Mahon also understood the importance of framing the New Deal in religious tones. For instance, Mahon described the Social Security Act as a substantial and "harmful" tax increase, but also admitted that the government should do what it could to "protect orphans and widows." He feared that the new Social Security program would allow "unscrupulous" Wall Street financiers—those who had "caused" the Depression in the first place—to "escape responsibility." Yet Mahon only took his objections so far before falling in line as a party loyalist and FDR booster. As he told one constituent, "I do not agree with all of Mr. Roosevelt's policies. But he is, in my opinion, the most delightful and admirable person in national politics."[42]

Mahon's opponents in the 1936 Democratic primary tried and failed to use the Social Security issue as a wedge, not by flanking to Mahon's right, but rather by moving to Mahon's left, arguing that the Nineteenth District needed a representative even more consistently pro–New Deal than Mahon had been during his first term. Voters were unpersuaded. Mahon avoided conflating his hesitance on something like old-age pensions—which Texas voters had been debating at the state level for many years—with his broader support for FDR and the New Deal. Throughout the primary, Mahon stayed on the offensive by focusing on farmers and agriculture, while at the same time reiterating national Democratic messaging about how FDR had saved the country by helping ordinary citizens at the expense of "economic royalists." When the Republican National Committee tried to recruit Mahon's support for their party's nominee, Alf Landon, referring to the New Deal as a "betrayal" and FDR as a "dictator" set on replacing "constitutional" government with "autocratic bureaucracy," Mahon's campaign responded by distributing leaflets produced by the "All-Party Roosevelt Agricultural Committee." Under the headline "You Can Know a Man by the Enemies He Has Made," the leaflet established Roosevelt's populist bona fides (and by extension, Mahon's) by "revealing" a "list of enemies" that included "Loan Sharks, Grain Gamblers, Money Changers, Stock Speculators, Power Trusts, Packing Trusts, Crooked Politicians, Tariff Pirates, [and] Munitions Makers." Such messages were clear; Roosevelt—like Mahon—was a man of the people, not elites. The president had turned the tide of economic depression and was steering the nation in the right direction. Mahon freely acknowledged that not all of Roosevelt's policies worked or even made sense. Some, he admitted, ran dramatically against the grain. However, desperate times called for desperate measures. Like Roosevelt, Mahon earned voters' trust by demonstrating a willingness to experiment.[43]

While Mahon's path to reelection in the South Plains was relatively easy, Maury Maverick's in San Antonio was anything but. Having made it to Congress in 1934 as an uncompromisingly progressive New Dealer ready to disrupt the Washington establishment, Maverick riled Texas conservatives by moving further to the left during his first term than even his harshest critics had thought possible, often doing so in a clear effort to win time in the national spotlight. Maverick's enemies in and around the Twentieth District launched one of the most expensive and controversial congressional campaigns of 1936, in Texas or anywhere else. On June 1, Maverick unwittingly played into their hands by writing an angry letter to Stewart McDonald, the chief administrator for the FHA in Washington, alleging that Richard Tullis—director of the FHA's division in San Antonio—was conspiring with anti–New Deal conservatives to defeat Maverick in the upcoming Democratic primary that July. Maverick also claimed that Tullis was using his position within the FHA to conspire with anti–New Dealers against FDR's upcoming reelection bid in Texas that November.[44] The allegations did not sit well with John Nance Garner, who, upon hearing of Maverick's claim, made it clear that he considered Tullis a friend and that he expected Roosevelt to back him. Garner's rage only intensified when Roosevelt subsequently (and passively) refused to intervene in Tullis's defense.[45]

Maverick then took his complaints about Tullis to Tommy Corcoran, the Brain Truster and notorious Washington insider known for having FDR's ear on important matters. Maverick repeated the same allegations to Corcoran, in addition to complaining about rumors by then circulating throughout the district that FDR privately wanted Maverick to lose his race, preferring to work with a more traditional Texas Democrat in Garner's mold—someone exactly like Lamar Seeligson, the conservative establishment's candidate against Maverick that year. Seeligson came from a family steeped in oil, gas, and ranching fortunes similar to those common among the wealthiest Texans then and later. (Future congressional representative and conservative Republican Lamar Smith also descended from Seeligson's family.) Maverick blamed Tullis for the rumors of FDR's preference for Seeligson, believed the Seeligson campaign was nothing short of an anti-FDR front, and expressed rage at the un-American label his enemies were using against him in campaign propaganda. Frustrated and impatient, Maverick next took his concerns to Secretary of the Interior Harold Ickes, begging Ickes for an audience with the president. Ickes responded by saying that FDR's personal policy was to not get involved in local Democratic primaries, a response Maverick found less than acceptable, particularly given the political overtones that had framed FDR's participation in Texas Centennial celebrations a few weeks earlier.[46]

Maverick finally seemed to get his way on the afternoon of July 6 when he received a telegram from Corcoran saying that Tullis had resigned his post as director of San Antonio's FHA earlier that morning. A more formal notification arrived from Stewart McDonald shortly thereafter. Meanwhile, Garner was outraged by the entire situation, believing the problem could have been prevented had Roosevelt simply shown loyalty to Tullis back in June when Maverick first expressed his concerns to McDonald. Maverick, meanwhile, wired his appreciation to McDonald, saying that it was essential to replace Tullis with someone "friendly to the New Deal." "The result is that if an enemy of the New Deal should be appointed, as has been done in the past, he would take it all out on me because of my friendship with the Administration," Maverick said. The next day, Ickes apologized to Maverick for FDR's unwillingness to "lift a finger" in support of the congressman's reelection bid, which he claimed the president did in fact support. Maverick, who at this point believed Garner was also interfering on Seeligson's behalf, was pacified only briefly, while Garner—who previously considered Maverick a friend—lost all trust in the San Antonio New Dealer. Two days later, the FHA announced W. E. Lilly as Tullis's replacement in the San Antonio office, an appointment Maverick found unacceptable on the grounds that Lilly was even more openly oppositional to Maverick and the New Deal than Tullis had been.[47]

The Tullis affair soon faded from the public eye, though Maverick continued to stew over the entire situation. Seeligson may very well have had support from Garner and other establishment Democrats, but he also enjoyed significant support from the Liberty League and varying Texas oil and construction interests. Seeligson attacked Maverick as a "friend to radical communists" like Vito Marcantonio of New York and Marion Zioncheck of Seattle. "I am not opposed to [the New Deal]," Seeligson said in his campaign brochure, "but I want the American people to vote on those changes. I do not want them foisted on the American people by secret groups whose sincerity and Americanism are open to suspicion." Recognizing Roosevelt's popularity with the masses,

Seeligson hedged his anticommunist conservatism by supporting FDR on old age pensions, agricultural reform, and collective bargaining rights, thereby demonstrating the limits of anti–New Deal conservatism within the state Democratic Party in 1936.[48]

While Seeligson portrayed Maverick as a radical who would "do away with the form of Government under which we have lived since this country was founded," Maverick painted Seeligson as a tool of the same political "gang" he had been working to defeat since the late 1920s. He relied heavily on public appearances, direct mailings, and radio, with a targeted focus on securing support from labor, veterans, and religious groups, telling everyone that Seeligson was "an enemy of the Administration and the New Deal."[49] Maverick's unabashed support for New Deal programs served as a gateway for broader messages about the positive role government could play in the lives of everyday Texans. Whether discussing the need to protect civil liberties, including those for racial minorities, or the economic rights of Texas workers, Maverick defended New Deal liberalism as the very fulfillment of the same "Americanism" his opponents had accused him of betraying, thus creating a patriotic contextual narrative in which FDR's programs became the new "American way."[50]

On July 9, Maverick delivered a speech on local San Antonio station WOAI. Rather bravely, he said that terms like "'life-long Democrat' or 'life-long Republican' are silly [and] usually used to cover up stupidity and a lack of independent thought." Connecting independence and freethinking with his own last name, Maverick sold himself to voters by highlighting the New Deal programs he backed, particularly those that benefited local military interests and the "safety and security of America." Two days later, he delivered a similar speech on local station KTSA in which he called Seeligson's ideas "fash-is-stick" [sic]. Maverick delivered similar speeches via local radio stations on July 21 and 24, just before the election.[51]

Despite the angst, or the fact that Seeligson's campaign was among the most expensive in state history—costing upwards of $75,000 in what Maverick called "hot oiled money"—the incumbent New Dealer easily defeated his opponent in the July 25 primary. By Maverick's assessment, the win was a "resounding" endorsement of FDR and the New Deal. He also invoked religious metaphors similar to those common to the period, describing his win as an "act of God." To one supporter, he said, somewhat self-righteously, "If we are to have a Christian world, a world in which people live decently and act decently, they must have the necessities of life. So I'll go on fighting and doing my duty and I am sure that you'll be satisfied." By the end of 1936, Maverick—an Episcopalian with spotty church attendance—was openly convinced that the New Deal was an instrument of divine origins for use in the battle against the political and economic "machine."[52]

Despite the atypical drama surrounding the Tullis affair, Maury Maverick's reelection to Congress in 1936 also typified Democratic marketing strategies in Texas, particularly in the face of conservative resistance. "I represent no political group; not labor nor an industrial one; neither do I represent religious or other groups," Maverick told an audience during the campaign. "I attempt, as far as possible, to represent without special privilege all the people. And in doing so, I think always of the average man, the man who wants education for his children; a roof over his head; food to eat; clothes to wear; a small automobile to ride around in; an opportunity to work hard for a living; and a chance for recreation now and then." Maverick enjoyed telling audiences that he had secured as much as $120 million in New Deal funding for local projects, though the figure was arguably closer to $39 million, depending on the accounting practice used to calculate the numbers. Regardless, he proved that it was possible to sell the New Deal in Texas without hiding the growth or cost of federal bureaucracies in Washington.[53]

With his own renomination secure, Maverick spent the rest of the summer and fall campaigning for Roosevelt. In numerous radio speeches, he promoted the New Deal and attacked the national Republican ticket of Alf Landon and Frank Knox. He called the GOP "hollow and misleading," adding that Landon was a "flip-flopper" on the New Deal. He then charged Knox with recklessness, citing the vice presidential nominee's characterization of the New Deal as "socialist." "Believe me," Maverick told his radio listeners, "like Thomas Jefferson, [FDR] has bravely preserved democracy, and has never interfered with the human liberties of the people." Maverick told listeners that the New Deal had "preserved capitalism" and that business leaders across Texas would be wise to support the FDR agenda. In one speech, he claimed to quote an "old GOP boss" who, according to Maverick, once said, "If you have a weak candidate and a weak platform, wrap yourself up in the American flag and talk about the Constitution." Maverick told listeners that the Landon-Knox ticket was guilty of precisely this sort of rhetoric, but also claimed that the Republican nominee had ineffectively "wrapped himself in free beer and barbecue in a desperate ploy to attract attention."[54]

Tom Connally, Elliott Roosevelt, and Roy Miller, delegate from Texas, at Democratic National Convention, Philadelphia, Pennsylvania, June 24, 1936. Credit: Acme (photo in author's possession).

Sheppard, Allred, Sumners, Mahon, and Maverick may have taken different paths to reelection, but each supported the New Deal in varying degrees, and each reflected the power of Roosevelt's popularity in Texas through 1936. Sumners represented the least enthusiastic of the paths, but even he made sure voters understood that he supported Roosevelt and most New Deal proposals. Seeligson's campaign against Maverick in San Antonio reflected the bubbling undercurrent of conservative resistance slowly building in some quarters across the state. That undercurrent would bubble over in 1937. However, through most of 1936, virtually all state Democratic candidates who wanted to win did so by backing Roosevelt, supporting the New Deal, and enthusiastically endorsing their party's presidential ticket—none more so that Amarillo's Marvin Jones.

"Forward with Roosevelt"

The White House tapped Marvin Jones to play a vital role in the national campaign of 1936, appointing him to coordinate efforts in the West and Midwest along with Chester C. Davis of Illinois and Paul A. Porter of Missouri. Together, Jones, Davis, and Porter devised a marketing campaign that scrapped long-winded details in favor of short stump speeches, light pamphlets, quick-hitting bullet points, and widespread coverage on radio. Jones spent almost all of his political energy on Roosevelt's campaign, while managing his own reelection bid in the Thirteenth District from afar. The fact that Roosevelt tapped Jones to help run his national campaign was a major selling point to voters in that district, where time in the national spotlight was often hard to find. Facing no serious threat that year, Jones seized the opportunity to remind voters across the Texas Panhandle that a vote for him was a vote for Roosevelt and the New Deal. His campaign highlighted soil conservation, allotment plans, lower interest on farm mortgages, easier access to crop loans, the HOLC, the Social Security Act, and rural electrification—basically delivering his constituents a local slice of FDR's national strategy. Jones's role in FDR's 1936 reelection campaign was also meaningful because it provided yet another highly visible example of the central relevance Texas Democrats enjoyed within Roosevelt's inner circle. Jones, perhaps even more than Jack Garner, made Texans—especially those living in the Panhandle—feel as though they were vital to the New Deal's protection and success. Along with Garner, Rayburn, Sheppard, and Tom Connally (who was selected for the seconding speech on FDR's renomination at the Democratic National Convention in Philadelphia that summer), Jones reinforced Texas as a major player in Washington, merging—as George Authier of the Roosevelt Agriculture Committee put it—"South and West . . . in a common cause."[55]

The 1936 presidential campaign also established Jones as a first-rate political talent, a voice for the New Deal Coalition, and an indispensable asset for the emerging liberal Democratic establishment. The messages Jones communicated to prospective voters throughout the fall of 1936 epitomized the heart and soul of Roosevelt's appeal. Blending well-crafted metaphors, pragmatic common sense, inspirational hyperbole, and sharp but sparing attacks against the GOP, he cast a vision of FDR and the New Deal in contrast to the hopelessness, inequality, and greed of earlier Republican administrations. "Most people treat the farm problem as a class problem. It is not. It is a national problem," Jones said during a speech broadcast on NBC radio in October. "The most fundamental principle of this government, the most essential of all our principles, is that each citizen should stand on the same basis with every other citizen in the operation of the laws of the land." Like FDR, Jones enjoyed leading his listeners on strolls down memory lane, often reminding them of the horrid conditions FDR inherited in 1933 before painting an almost messianic portrait of the incumbent commander in chief. In one particularly memorable speech, Jones recalled the horrors of the Hoover years before saying:

> Then came Franklin D. Roosevelt. He lifted up his eyes and saw across this big, broad country. He saw that the entire nation is interrelated. He saw that the very essence of democratic freedom and liberty is equal and exact treatment for all its citizens. He saw that a reasonable farm price is better for the man in the city who has a job and can buy—is better than a lower price even for an idle hungry man who has no money with which to buy. No thinking city man wants to grind farmers' price down below a living level, because he knows that it means finally the loss of his own job. . . . The ambition of the President has been to keep America free—to save our government from the selfish few who would make of their country an economic feudalism—to save freedom and equality of opportunity for the average citizens. . . . Not since the days of Andrew Jackson and Nicholas Biddle has the issue been so clearly drawn between the folks on the one hand and the selfish on the other.[56]

With his expanded national presence, Jones won attention from reporters unaccustomed to Texas politics or its personalities. "President Roosevelt has men-lovers in America," an editorialist in Nebraska wrote of Jones for the *Columbus Tribune,*

> but none more devoted to him, none more ably promoting a great cause, in which President Roosevelt is both the heart and the brain. . . . I have been through the years privileged to hear many of the world's great orators. I shall not list Marvin Jones as among the master orators. I shall give him a better listing. He is in a class all by himself. He never attempts flights of eloquence, but he has a way of getting right close to his hearers, convincing them that he is one of them, and appealing to them as a friend appeals to a friend.

Whether he was in Amarillo, Chicago, Des Moines, or Columbus, Nebraska, Jones campaigned for President Roosevelt's reelection with an uncompromising populist gusto. Audiences frequently praised Jones's sense of humor and his ability to ridicule opponents without relying on fear or bitterness or anger.[57]

In the process, Jones put Amarillo more soundly on the national map. The largest city of the Texas Panhandle was exceedingly proud of the fact that their congressional representative played such a huge role in FDR's campaign. Area newspapers covered every speech Jones delivered and every appearance he made as if it were a local event. Headlines like "Jones Gives Stirring Speech for FDR" or "Jones Assails Landon, GOP" were daily occurrences in the local newspaper. The fact that Secretary of State Cordell Hull often appeared alongside Jones at various campaign rallies, providing an overview of the New Deal's approach to international trade while Jones concentrated on all things farming, only enhanced Amarillo's profile. Jones also recruited George Mahon, whom the Speakers Bureau of the Democratic National Committee assigned to help in the farm states of the Midwest, though Mahon also spoke at campaign stops in New Haven, Connecticut; New Brunswick, New Jersey; Pittsburgh, Pennsylvania; Danville, Virginia; and New York City. Like Jones, Mahon enjoyed the press coverage, as did the people of Mahon's district. The Roosevelt Club of Danville, Virginia, called Mahon a "silver spurred Texas orator," and newspapers across the state hailed the representative of the Nineteenth District as the "Texas Cowboy Congressman." Such coverage helped Jones and Mahon, while obviously helping Roosevelt, but also concurrently solidified Democratic messages about the New Deal's effectiveness and made ordinary Texans feel as though they were playing a vital role in the realm of national New Deal politics.[58]

All told, Democratic campaign strategies were relatively predictable and consistent in 1936, and very similar to strategies employed in 1932 and 1934. No other issue landed more powerfully with Texas voters than did those related to economic recovery and accusations of Republican "greed." Along these lines, Jones vilified Republicans just as skillfully as he defended the New Deal, equating the GOP with robber barons and corporate greed. He called Landon and other Republicans "tools" of the "du Pont Liberty League" and other special interests on Wall Street. "Big business has been the first concern of every Republican administration since the war," Jones wrote in an editorial for the *Amarillo Globe* in September. "It is, from every indication, the first concern of the present Republican leadership, which has the powerful support of the Morgans, the DuPonts, the Rockefellers, and others like them. They have fought every farm program ever demanded by farmers. They will destroy the present AAA if they can. They will block any alternative. They dominate the Republican Party. I do not want to see farmers' welfare placed in their hands."[59]

Following Jones's lead, other Texas Democrats successfully portrayed Republicans as the voice of greedy corporations and Wall Street fat cats, the very culprits most voters still believed had caused the Depression in the first place. Republicans on the other hand presented no clear or unified message. Landon was nowhere near aggressive or decisive enough on his own campaign trail, and his critiques of the New Deal did not correlate with those of the Republican minority, for whom ideological notions of Americanism and communism and socialism and the like were of vital importance, despite the lack of resonance those terms were having with ordinary voters. "The election this fall will be the most important in the history of our country," wrote RNC treasurer C. B. Goodspeed in a letter to Marvin Jones. "It transcends party lines. The American people will decide whether we are to continue to live under our democratic constitutional form of government or be ruled by the decrees of a dictator, enforced by an autocratic bureaucracy. The betrayal of the Democratic Party has made the election of Governor Landon and Colonel Knox essential for the preservation of the traditional form of our American government."[60] Virtual carbon copies of such hyperbole would serve Republicans well in the coming decades, but mostly rang hollow in 1936, overwhelmed by the common-sense populism of Democrats like Marvin Jones, not to mention Roosevelt himself.[61]

Jones also railed against Republicans for being ideologically motivated and portrayed Democrats as little more than sincere, above-the-fray advocates for common sense. In response to Republican allegations that the president was a dictator in the making, Jones and other Democrats portrayed FDR as a nonideological pragmatist, fearless and committed to waging "war against the Depression" and "war against human distress."[62] Roosevelt did not necessarily make Democrats' task easier when he accepted renomination in Philadelphia on June 27, delivering one of the most progressive speeches in American history. Couched in familiarly religious tones, FDR told convention-goers that they had a "rendezvous with destiny," while commenting on the "privileged princes of . . . new economic dynasties," adding language about economic equality and inequality that no doubt unnerved most conservatives and moderates in attendance.[63] Nevertheless, even as Roosevelt occasionally stepped onto the ledge of progressive idealism, his campaign managers insisted on staying practical. In Texas, Roosevelt's campaign team focused on the president's leadership skills and the practicality of his ideas. Opponents tried to pigeonhole New Dealers as radicals or as "wild-eyed liberals," but the FDR team largely succeeded in maintaining their boss's reputation as a man whose "record is clear and whose judgment is sound."[64]

Like any good salesman, Marvin Jones knew how to close a deal with his audience. "I am for President Roosevelt," he said in closing at most of his campaign appearances. "I shall vote for his re-election. I shall vote for him because I am a farmer, and more than that, because I am an American citizen. As a farmer, I will not desert the leader who has put agriculture on its feet. As a citizen, I shall seek to continue in office the man who has taken the United States out of the Depression into which it was plunged during the administration of Hoover."[65]

While no Texan worked harder for Roosevelt in 1936 than Marvin Jones, Sam Rayburn may have come close. Appointed to lead the Speakers Bureau of the Democratic National Committee, Rayburn told a group of Washington-based reporters on August 8 that he had lined up more than two thousand speakers for various campaign stops on behalf of FDR. This included every single member of the Texas congressional delegation, as well as Texas governor Jimmie Allred, though it did not include John Nance Garner. Still, Rayburn's message was clear. "We are going to present speakers who know the story of President Roosevelt and his record and are able to show the differences between 1932 and today," Rayburn said. "Texas is stronger for Roosevelt than it ever was. In that state they know the story of what the Democratic administration of the last four years has done, not only for Texas, but for the country. Texas business is the best in years. Businesses that began slipping into the red with the Hoover administration and all but went broke, are now showing profits and surpluses."[66]

A few weeks before the general election, the Texas House of Representatives concurred, passing a resolution formally endorsing FDR. The House resolution specifically cited the president's support for Texas farmers and all Americans living in poverty through no fault of their own. It also cited his restoration of confidence in banks and his ability to keep the United States out of war, an early acknowledgment that the geopolitical situations in Europe, Asia, and elsewhere threatened to push the world toward another global conflict. The resolution's summation lauded FDR for having "chiefly exemplified the ideals of Texans."[67] The conservative *Dallas Morning News* was slightly more reserved in its praise, noting that much of the nation's economic recovery was premised on billions of dollars of "printed" money, all borrowed on credit. Still, even the *Dallas Morning News* was quick to credit Roosevelt for "saving the banking industry," noting that deposits among banks in Texas were at an all-time high. And if the economy was improving on some levels, it was worth sustaining that momentum for another four years. Few campaigns have ever been as widely supported as FDR's 1936 bid was in Texas.[68]

On November 3 voters went to the polls and overwhelmingly reelected Franklin D. Roosevelt to the presidency of the United States, doing so in the greatest electoral landslide in the history of American presidential politics. Roosevelt carried all but two states (Maine and Vermont), racking up 523 electoral votes in the process, against Landon's 8. He won nearly 61 percent of the popular vote. In Texas, the wipeout was even more pronounced, with Roosevelt winning 734,485 votes to Landon's 103,874—an 87 percent supermajority. Upon seeing the first returns at his home in Hyde Park that evening, Roosevelt reportedly leaned back in his chair, blew a puff a smoke, and simply said, "Wow!"[69] Even state party leaders who expressed confidence throughout the campaign were speechless at the massive scale of Roosevelt's victory. Texas voters not only endorsed a second term for Roosevelt in astonishingly high numbers, they also voted to adopt five quite liberal amendments to the Texas Constitution, including salary increases for state officers, workmen's compensation for state employees, and the creation of a pension plan for public school teachers. That latter plan evolved into the permanent Teacher Retirement System of Texas.[70] Jimmie Allred also won reelection, as voters returned their New Deal governor to work with 93 percent of the vote and returned Morris Sheppard to the Senate by roughly the same margin. Still, Alf Landon won nearly twice as many votes in Texas as either of Allred's or Sheppard's GOP challengers, suggesting that roughly fifty thousand Texas voters went to the polls to vote Republican in the presidential race, while staying loyally Democratic in down-ballot races—not a huge number, but not nothing. Meanwhile, Democrats again dominated at the House level, carrying all twenty-one seats. Unlike 1934, however, each Democrat faced either a Republican or an officially "Independent" challenger in the general election, George Mahon being the lone exception. Sixteen of those twenty secured at least 90 percent of the vote against their GOP opponent, including Rayburn, who carried 97.5 percent of the vote in the Fourth District; Nat Patton, who carried 97.6 percent in the Seventh; and James Buchanan, who carried 99.5 percent in the Tenth. Only Maury Maverick failed to reach the 80 percent mark, winning a respectable but still relatively low 72 percent in a three-way general race in which the Republican carried 25 percent, the best performance by a GOP candidate in the state that year, at least among those in a major race.[71]

Nevertheless, if 1936 represented high tide for FDR and the New Deal in Texas, it soon became clear that low tide was on the horizon and approaching quickly.

4 | "Communism with a Haircut and a Shave"

Speaking to a friendly crowd in Dallas on November 22, 1936, San Antonio's Maury Maverick proclaimed the reelection of Franklin Delano Roosevelt as "the greatest revolution in the world's history," adding that it was "ten times, a hundred times more important than the original American Revolution." Articulating a vision for America premised on "science, intelligence, education, [and] research," Maverick described FDR's reelection as an affirmation that the American people, Texans included, had "come to find out that the function of business is the same as government—to give a person a way of life, a job, happiness, shelter, food."[1]

Maverick's assessment of the situation lacked balance, to say the least. However, given the circumstances and his own flare for the dramatic, Maverick's buoyancy was not surprising. Roosevelt's landslide reelection less than three weeks prior reflected a level of broad-based support virtually unmatched before or since in the annals of American politics. In Texas, Democratic voters from all corners of the state lined up to cast ballots in support of Roosevelt and the New Deal. Loyalists such as Maverick, Jimmie Allred, Morris Sheppard, Marvin Jones, Sam Rayburn, Thomas Love, and many others bathed their support for FDR in a wash of platitudinous superlatives more typically reserved for the founding fathers. Exuberant over the election results, Maverick even launched a book project focused on the Constitution's emphasis on promoting "democracy" and how the New Deal had finally "fulfilled" the founders' original intent. All told, it appeared to more than a few observers at the time that Roosevelt was as powerful and as popular as a president was likely to get.[2]

A speed bump was inevitable. In 1937 and 1938, the momentum that carried FDR to high tide in 1936 ebbed rather quickly due to the conflation of disparate forces. Labor unrest in Texas and other parts of the country worried business leaders that a revolution of rising expectations would soon devolve into a revolution of a more radical nature. Civil rights activists pushed for an antilynching bill that struck many

Texas conservatives as a threat to states' rights and white supremacy, as did voter registration drives, poll-tax fundraising efforts, and other evidences of increased political consciousness among Black people across the state, particularly in Dallas.[3] Growing pressure to balance budgets would interrupt the flow of federal dollars that had been priming the nation's economic pump for four years, resulting in a recession that many blamed on FDR. And a rare political miscalculation undermined the public's trust in Roosevelt, while at the same time encouraging conservatives to reassert with greater credibility their fear that individual liberties at home could not coexist with a growing bureaucracy in Washington. Having successfully sold himself to Americans as a de facto wartime president whose politics were above partisanship and whose calls for sacrifice reflected the supremacy of national unity above individual concerns, Roosevelt stumbled in early 1937, alienating a sizable segment of his working- and middle-class Texas base in the process.[4]

Through it all, the bubbling undercurrent of conservative discontent that had been growing slowly since 1933 rapidly grew hotter and more intense. This was true in Texas as it was true across much of the country. Enthusiasm for the New Deal and New Deal liberalism suffered in the state as a result, but it did not vanish. Likewise, Roosevelt's popularity in Texas waned briefly, but it never disappeared. Historians such as George Green have argued that modern Texas conservatism was born during these years. While the rise of the modern Texas Right links just as powerfully to the conflation of a wholly different set of circumstances during the 1960s and 1970s, it remains clear that conservative ideas about government, taxes, and the dangers of social justice gained traction during the first two years of FDR's second term. In 1937 and 1938, voices that had been loud but ineffectual during FDR's first term grew louder and stronger. Eventually, those voices came to reflect the future personality and modus operandi of the modern Texas Right. All told, this brief period was more politically combative than anything Texans had experienced between 1932 and 1936.[5]

"The Democratic Donkey Has Evolved into a Russian Jackass"

During FDR's first term, conservatives of varying stripes formed numerous organizations, most of which hoped to kill or at least slow the New

Deal's pace. The American Liberty League was one of the first. Founded in 1934, the Liberty League was as unapologetically anti-Roosevelt as it was anti–New Deal. Its leaders argued that FDR's forgotten man philosophy was bankrupting the nation and would eventually lead to a radical swing to the far left. Nationally, the Liberty League enjoyed quite a bit of early momentum. Most Texans, however, ignored the organization, as well as its regional offshoot, the Southern Liberty League, throughout its first year of existence. Though they did little to support it, anti–New Deal Texans shared much in common with the Liberty League. Concerns about tyranny, regimentation, and excessive control resonated with many. The Liberty League made some headway in Texas by recruiting farmers with the argument that the AAA was jeopardizing families by driving tenant farmers—nearly a quarter of whom were either Black or poor white—out of work. Out-of-work tenants, the League said, would resort to crime, thus reinforcing fears common to the conservative worldview that federal intervention was immoral in addition to being ineffective and irresponsible.[6]

In similar ways, organizations like the Liberty League commonly used race as a weapon in the fight against the New Deal, connecting civil rights advocacy to various iterations of radicalism on the left. Anti–New Dealers also frequently connected issues of race to the perceived "tragic loss" of the "traditional" Democratic Party. Few individuals were more comfortable with this strategic melding than Texas business leader and former state senator John Henry Kirby. In January 1936, Kirby told a meeting of the Southern Committee to Uphold the Constitution (SCUC) that FDR was a "nigger-loving communist" and that New Dealers were, generally speaking, "socialist vermin." At a meeting in Dallas later that year, the Reverend Harry Hodges of Beaumont told an audience: "The Democratic donkey has evolved into a Russian jackass and the New Deal is nothing but communism with a haircut and a shave." Significantly, Hodges also told his audience that he would be voting Republican that fall.[7]

Meanwhile, other influential pastors across the state, including J. Frank Norris of First Baptist Church of Fort Worth and John R. Rice, founder of the influential *Sword of the Lord* newsletter, joined the growing chorus of religious leaders questioning the federal government's reach as a potentially insidious challenge to traditional reliance on church and faith in times of trouble. Norris's transformation was particularly interesting, given his strident opposition to Al Smith in 1928, which was followed by his equally strident support for the New Deal during the first two years of FDR's first term. In 1933, he told one audience of anti–New Deal critics, "To hell with your socialism or whatever you want to call it. People are starving!" Norris's sentiments effectively captured the general attitude most Texans had about the New Deal throughout FDR's first term—that it was necessary, given the gravity of the economic situation. Nevertheless, by 1937, Norris and other pastors like him increasingly viewed the New Deal as a threat to church authority, or at least churches' influence with (or control of) their congregations. Most southern pastors continued to support Roosevelt and his efforts to ameliorate the worst effects of the Depression, despite perceptions that the New Deal was too friendly to Black people. Yet men like Hodges, Norris, and Rice attracted and influenced sizable audiences of people inclined to sympathize with conservative frustrations.[8]

Of course, antigovernment backlashes were hardly new to Texas. The modern American version of Texas was born, in part, because transplanted southerners revolted against Mexican centralism in 1835 and 1836. Twenty-five years later, those Texans, along with their offspring and tens of thousands of newcomers, seceded from the United States, opposed to what they saw as centralized tyranny in Washington, manifest most obviously in perceived threats to the slave economy that dominated their state and region. Throughout the decades that followed, Texas political culture blended antistatist, ex-Confederate, Lost Cause sentimentalities rooted in white supremacy with commitments to frontier living and populist individualism akin to stereotypes rooted in the so-called Wild West. This blend fostered a widespread sense of isolation and self-reliance. The state's proclivities toward gun ownership, for example, were rooted in this environment, one in which manhood was defined by the ability to provide for and protect one's family in the absence of outside assistance.[9]

The career of Joseph Weldon Bailey Sr. offers another clear example of early-twentieth-century conservative demagoguery in Texas. In the decades prior to the Great Depression, Bailey represented an ultraconservative, racist, conspiratorial faction of antiprogressives. According to historian Lewis Gould, Bailey was a reactionary populist who "styled himself as the 'Last Democrat,' defending Jeffersonian principles against those who would destroy the 'Old Republic' as the fathers had conceived it." A two-term United States senator from 1901 to 1913, Bailey pledged "allegiance" to principled resistance to "increased federal authority," by which he meant anything that threatened, according to Gould, the "customary social arrangements in the South that kept the Negro in bondage." Bailey's public declarations showed a flare for the dramatic. He once told reporters: "You might as well tell me a man is a Christian who denies the divinity of Jesus Christ as that a man is a Democrat who does not believe in State rights." Responding to the expansion of federal power that accompanied Woodrow Wilson's prosecution of the Great War in Europe from 1917 to 1918, Bailey told another audience that he would "never again vote for the candidate of any party which reduces our liberty and unnecessarily increases our taxes." For good measure, Bailey added that he was "fully persuaded" that "the Democratic Party must either repudiate President Wilson or it must embrace practically all of the Socialist doctrines."[10]

Bailey's public denunciations of Wilson and his "New Freedom" agenda sparked a quarrel with Pennsylvania congressman and future US attorney general A. Mitchell Palmer, a Democrat who later became the nation's most prominent anticommunist. In 1918, Palmer publicly challenged Bailey to leave the Democratic Party, taking like-minded anti-Wilsonites with him. In response, Bailey joined others in organizing a revolt among southern Democrats. The result was a document called "Declaration of Principles" affirming "State Rights" and denouncing woman suffrage, the League of Nations, and "socialism" in all forms. Throughout his career in state and national politics, Bailey routinely contrasted the virtues of white supremacy with the evils of progressivism and its alleged cousin, socialism. Bailey's followers were passionate, but all in all, surprisingly few in number. Though he remained a bombastic character in the Texas political panoply until his death in 1929, Bailey failed to regain any meaningful role in state politics after leaving the Senate in 1913. When he lost a gubernatorial bid in 1920, the *San Antonio Evening News* called the result "an announcement to the country that in National and State affairs, the people of Texas are progressive, not reactionary." That assessment may have been overly optimistic, as was Lewis Gould's assessment in 1973 that Bailey's defeat represented a "last stand" of "old-style" Texas conservatism. In fact, the Ku Klux Klan's revival during the early 1920s carried forward many of Bailey's ideas and opinions, as would Bailey's son. Bailey's brand of reactionary, racist conservatism was common, but it by no means reflected the attitudes of all white Texans. On this, Gould describes Texas Democrats from this period as "moderate" on race, at least as measured by "public rhetoric."

However, Gould also stressed that Democrats' "daily behavior and private writings revealed an abiding belief in Negro inferiority and a solid consensus on behalf of the segregated order." Sadly, little had changed by the time FDR entered the White House. That included a paradox common of Texas politics at the time—that white supremacy was so pervasive and unquestioned across the state, and the Black population proportionally so small, that matters of race or segregation rarely came up during campaigns.[11]

Bailey died in 1929, but reactionary racism continued to stoke the flames of antigovernment backlash throughout the 1930s. So did the emergence of a far richer and more powerful Texas oil industry. Wildcatters had been getting rich on Texas oil since the nineteenth century, but it was not until the 1930s that oil emerged as a fuel for political power in the modern sense. Whatever fleeting partnership Roosevelt struck with the Texas Railroad Commission during his first term seemed a distant memory by 1937. The New Deal's shifting attention—in the eyes of Texas oil, from saving capitalism to protecting labor—riled the newly affluent, who loathed taxes, collective bargaining, and regulations of which they were not direct beneficiaries. Banks across the state voiced similar notes of discontent, particularly as homeowners received protections against foreclosure. Traditionalist oilmen like Houston's Roy Cullen joined a chorus of those warning against "creeping socialism." Taken together, this fusion of right-wing animus against big government gave ultraconservative firebrands like John Henry Kirby and propagandist Vance Muse a platform on which they could dispense anti–New Deal messages. With the help of the SCUC, Kirby and Vance organized several organizations into a semi-united front against FDR and the New Deal. This included organizations such as the Southern Tariff Congress, the Texas Election Managers Association, the Sentinels of the Republic, the Order of American Patriots, and the Jeffersonian Democrats—each of which was designed to merge political and private business interests under the auspices of Americanism broadly defined. Thanks to the backing of Lewis Ulrey, it also included the formation of Christian Americans, an ostensibly educational nonprofit group the messaging for which was dedicated to opposing "negroes, liberals, unions, Communists, and the 'international Jewish conspiracy.'" Ulrey was particularly interested in the historical exploits of the "Jewish Illuminati," and criticized FDR for being too critical of Hitler's efforts to remodel Germany along anti-Semitic lines. In one particularly brazen move, the organization's magazine—*The Christian American*—published a full-page warning of a purported Soviet plot in the American South: "In the Carpet Bag days designing politicians promised the negroes of the South 'Forty Acres and a Mule' in exchange for their votes. The Communist Party goes the 'Carpet Bagger' one better . . . a Black Soviet Republic under negro rule when the present form of government has been overthrown in the United States."[12]

Though none of these groups proved singularly influential, they all contributed to a stream that eventually emptied into the modern Texas Right. Of these, the most significant was the Jeffersonian Democrats. Voicing a commitment to "traditional Democratic Party" values, specifically states' rights, limited federal government, low taxes, and free markets, the Jeffersonian Democrats enjoyed substantial popularity in Texas in 1936 and 1937. With the support of firebrands like Kirby and Muse and the infusion of like-minded conservatives such as J. Evetts Haley and Joseph W. Bailey Jr.—who inherited his late father's penchant for race-baiting and carried his antistatist agenda into the New Deal era— the Jeffersonian Democrats of Texas highlighted broad-based ideological disagreements with Roosevelt. They also pointed to specific issues, such as the party's abandonment of the two-thirds rule that had until Roosevelt required candidates to receive at least two-thirds of all votes in order to confirm a nomination at the national convention. Southerners predisposed to paranoia over sectional underrepresentation increasingly viewed Roosevelt's domination of the national party as a dangerous "power grab." When promoted by groups like the Jeffersonian Democrats, these fears exacerbated related concerns that the New Deal was a growing monolith that threatened the established order.[13]

Speaking on behalf of the Jeffersonian Democrats of Texas in October 1936, J. Evetts Haley claimed that Roosevelt held the Constitution "in contempt." He similarly charged that FDR held "antipathy" and "intolerance" toward "any law which conflicts with any whim of his or with his arbitrary will." When Al Smith—the former Democratic presidential nominee, governor of New York, and FDR ally—made national waves by asserting that the New Deal was little more than veiled socialism, Jeffersonian Democrats of Texas (almost all of whom had opposed Smith in 1928) shared excerpts of the speech in paid advertisements published in newspapers across the South. Smith's allegation that FDR was disguising "Marx and Lenin" under "the banner of Jefferson, Jackson, and Cleveland" made for particularly compelling reading. The Jeffersonian

Democrats utilized friends in the Texas press to distribute their messages, but also networked with churches across the state, many of which willingly printed the organization's literature in worship bulletins and newsletters. In some of those cases, Jeffersonian Democrats accused FDR of subverting the state's moral fiber by colluding with "bootleggers" and "liquor dealers" to traffic in vice.[14]

Whether or not organizations like the Jeffersonian Democrats, the Liberty League, and others active in Texas in 1936 and 1937 were successful is a matter of perspective. In the short term, they clearly failed. FDR won reelection easily in 1936, though defeating FDR had been an organizing impulse. Meanwhile, among liberals and loyalists, the Liberty League gained a reputation as a "rich man's club." Despite efforts to undo the New Deal throughout Roosevelt's second term, the Liberty League all but ceased to exist by the end of 1940. The Jeffersonian Democrats similarly disbanded in relatively short order. These organizations had money, much of it from newly rich Texas oil barons. They also had the ear of several friendly members of the Texas press. In time, such advantages would result in lasting influence. However, Roosevelt was legitimately popular with most Texas voters. With the Depression still looming over the state and nation, most Texans placed more faith in FDR than they did in ultraconservative warnings that the New Deal was an ideological slippery slope into a socialist abyss. Elements of the modern Texas Right may very well have been born during these years, but those elements clearly lacked the maturity, the cohesion, or the proper timing needed to transform from a marginalized movement on the political fringes into the mainstream of Texas political culture.[15]

"Boys, Here's Where I Cash in My Chips"

On January 20, 1937—in one of the most memorable inaugural addresses in American history, and the first ever on January 20—Franklin Roosevelt declared that the "test of our progress is not whether we add more to the abundance of those who have much; it is whether we provide enough for those who have too little." Between his acceptance speech at the Democratic National Convention the previous summer and his second inaugural in January 1937, FDR's ideological robustness—his call to aggressive action and his boldness in setting forth a second-term agenda—established a progressive standard that has rarely been matched at the national level. As it turned out, Roosevelt's second term would be far less revolutionary than his first, largely because of his own political miscalculations.[16]

Roosevelt's second term began under a cloud of labor unrest perceived by many as part of a broader advance by the radical Left. At the General Motors plant in Flint, Michigan, the nascent United Auto Workers staged a forty-day sit-down strike that ended, with the help of the Committee for Industrial Organization (the CIO would change its name to the Congress of Industrial Organizations in 1938), in the successful recognition of their union. The CIO then helped organize additional strikes; emboldened workers across the country saw in FDR's reelection a mandate to agitate for union recognition, not to mention better wages and working conditions. Texas business leaders watched the proceedings from afar, but worried that the labor-activism contagion would spread to their state sooner than later. It did, most famously in San Antonio, where close to twelve thousand pecan-shelling workers struck for better wages and conditions, walking off a job critical to roughly half of the nation's pecan supply. With the help of the CIO, the workers—most of whom were Tejano women—endured mass arrests and threats of violence long enough to negotiate a settlement. The pecan-shellers' strike garnered national attention, but the coverage it received in Texas heightened preexisting concerns in the business community that the New Deal's personality was shifting from probusiness to prounion. Those concerns were similarly magnified by the fact that labor unrest often paralleled calls for civil rights, as it had for Tejano sheep shearers who struck in West Texas in 1934, Tejano cigar manufacturers who struck in San Antonio in 1933 and 1934, and Tejano meatpackers who struck in the Rio Grande Valley in 1938. Strikes like this were common across Texas, just as they were common nationally. Some were organized by the CIO, others by the American Federation of Labor (AFL). Either way, the business community perceived labor unrest as an obvious threat, particularly as activism seemed to grow more common in 1937 and 1938.[17]

Labor unrest also contributed to the formation of the House Committee on Un-American Activities (later commonly known as HUAC), chaired by Representative Martin Dies Jr. of Texas's Second Congressional District. Until 1937, Dies had been a semicompliant supporter of most New Deal programs. In 1928, he managed Al Smith's presidential campaign in southeast Texas, and four years later he actively campaigned for Roosevelt, against John Nance Garner, in the weeks leading up to the Democratic National Convention. In 1937, however, he developed stronger ties to emerging forces on the right, including John Henry Kirby and other ultraconservative anticommunists. Soon, Dies was spending his time investigating the CIO's connections to allegedly communist-inspired labor uprisings. The CIO's interest in civil rights and racial equality added fuel to the fire, as did the actions of Texas-born civil rights activist Jessie Daniel Ames, who as secretary of the Association of Southern Women for the Prevention of Lynching championed a federal antilynching bill introduced in the House that February. Maury Maverick supported the bill, which passed the House in April, despite fervent objections from Dies and Hatton Sumners, both of whom argued that the bill was a violation of state sovereignty. As Sumners had put it two years earlier under similar circumstances, a federal law on lynching was unnecessary because "no other crime is being reduced as rapidly as this crime is being reduced under exclusive State responsibility." Texas conservatives pushed the same line of thinking in 1937.[18]

Debate over the 1937 antilynching bill contributed to the rapidly growing gulf between southern conservatives and the FDR White House. "When Southerners think straight," editorialized the *Dallas Journal* on the matter, "they will wake up to the fact that the South has already been sold down river by the President and his brain trusters. . . . We have been so dunderheaded in our loyalty to a name and a label that we have sold our birthright for a mess of fireside broadcasts."[19] Meanwhile, Ames pled with Sumners and other members of the Texas delegation for support. "The whole situation, to me, is as unfortunate as anything that has arisen since the days of Reconstruction," Ames told Sumners in confidence that March. In a surprisingly candid letter, Ames told Sumners that she supported the bill even though she also believed it would "not be enforceable." Above all else, she feared that Black citizens' trust in the system would be "definitely strained." "If the bill comes up and passes and becomes law, it is hurtful," Ames said. "If the bill comes up and fails to pass it is also hurtful." As Ames put it: "Negroes have been so worked up emotionally" over the issue as to threaten the political alliances Roosevelt needed for further New Deal action.[20]

Sumners—like most of his Democratic colleagues from the South— voted against the bill. Several African American Texans responded by writing House members like Sumners to warn of a political backlash.

"We will remember you, Mr. Sumners, on next election day," wrote one Black man a week after the vote, adding:

> Mr. Sumners, three weeks ago five CCC camp white boys ravaged a colored girl out of Navasota, Texas. What do you think we should do to those boys for that crime? Do you think they should be lynched for that crime? Tell us what to do about that crime. You know, the CCC boys are in the government's service. Until that lynching bill is passed, we will not have civilization.[21]

The antilynching bill passed the House, despite votes against by Sumners, Dies, and others. However, it failed to pass the Senate, thanks in large part to Tom Connally, who helped lead the filibuster that eventually killed the bill in the upper chamber. As Sumners had done in the House, Connally argued that lynching as a practice had become so uncommon in the South that passing a federal law to prohibit it was a waste of time, not to mention an unconstitutional infringement on states' rights. At the same time, Connally connected the measure to other forms of civil rights "agitation," including voter registration drives and poll-tax fundraising efforts. Such activism, most notably spearheaded by the Progressive Voters League in Dallas, highlighted the need for greater minority participation in the political process, while advocating social justice reforms that included the hiring of Black police officers and city employees.[22]

Such activism catalyzed a backlash among political leaders like Connally, for whom the politics of race was never far from the political surface. The term "white supremacy" or similar phrases were rarely explicitly incorporated into the state's campaign culture and remained relatively muted thanks to widespread disenfranchisement. That does not mean, however, that politicians were above exploiting race, as Hatton Sumners often did in describing "free government" as equivalent to "Anglo-Saxon Government." Sumners was also fond of blaming "recently admitted foreigners" for threatening the "parliamentary systems of government" in the United States, as they had done in other parts of the world.[23] Still, notwithstanding exceptions such as those highlighted in the fight over antilynching laws, the strategic practice of ignoring racial issues altogether—effectively an early brand of what historians have described as "colorblind conservatism"—was already alive and well in Texas throughout the first several decades of the twentieth century.[24]

Roosevelt could have endured concerns over labor unrest and lynch-

Political cartoon by C. K. Berryman, *Washington Evening Star*, January 5, 1937. "Now Ride Him, Cowboy!" Courtesy of Sam Rayburn House State Historical Site, Texas Historical Commission.

ing had those issues not coincided with the biggest political controversy of his career—one of his own making. As workers agitated for bargaining rights and better conditions, Roosevelt overconfidently launched a comprehensive federal reorganization initiative. In and of itself, reorganization was not a controversial idea. In fact, the idea of restructuring government to make it more efficient struck observers on both sides of the aisle as a sensible goal, perfectly consistent with other New Deal initiatives. The first prong in Roosevelt's reorganization plan focused on the executive branch, with an aim toward expanding the president's ability to hire additional staff. Based on the recommendations of a committee FDR had established the previous spring, the president's plan received widespread support when it was unveiled in early January 1937.

Lawmakers raised few objections, and those that did come up were either mild protests or doom-filled warnings against the ever-dreaded slippery slope of centralized power. Privately, some in Congress fretted over the possible loss of patronage and the related loss of political capital commonly used during negotiations. In the main however, Roosevelt had little trouble rallying support for executive reorganization. Ever the faithful soldier, Sam Rayburn touted executive reorganization to a national radio audience in early February, emphasizing the need to maximize governmental functionality and efficiency. Using such sensible, business-oriented terms had proven successful with other measures during FDR's first term. Reorganization seemed perfectly in keeping with the New Deal's broader zeitgeist. Modern problems necessitated creative, modern solutions, Rayburn argued. The president was overworked and needed help. With support from men like Rayburn, Roosevelt's plan to reorganize the executive branch aroused little passion among Americans, who typically paid only tangential attention to such bureaucratic maneuvers.[25]

Then, as the relatively placid debate over executive reorganization appeared to be moving forward, Roosevelt proposed a second reorganization bill, this time for the federal judiciary. Framed similarly as a simple effort to unburden the overworked, Roosevelt's proposal gave the president authority to appoint new associate justices to the United States Supreme Court at a rate of one for every sitting justice over seventy-and-a-half years of age, thereby potentially increasing the size of the Court from nine to fifteen. Roosevelt claimed his goal was to improve the Court's efficiency and break judicial logjams. Lawmakers on Capitol Hill, including many of FDR's allies in Texas, were stunned. Roosevelt had not briefed members of the Texas delegation prior to announcing the plan, which the press soon derided as a "court-packing scheme." Critics dismissed FDR's stated objectives, recognizing rather quickly that the president's true motivation was to protect New Deal legislation against unfavorable Supreme Court rulings, such as those the Court issued in 1935 and 1936 striking down the National Industrial Recovery Act and the Agricultural Adjustment Act.[26]

Stunned though many were, more than a handful of Texas Democrats reflexively jumped aboard the court-packing train, determined to put loyalty to FDR above all other factors at play, while assuming that loyalty would still be the politically wise move. Early opinion polls, in fact, showed Texans supporting the president on the issue at a 2-to-1 rate, while throngs of Texans expressed support in letters to their representatives in both Washington and Austin. In response to favorable public opinion on the matter, numerous elected officials, including Maury Maverick, Wright Patman, Morris Sheppard, William D. McFarlane, and Governor Jimmie Allred, also backed the measure. Supporting FDR had become virtually instinctive in some circles; for a moment, few batted an eye. Thomas Love also quickly announced his support for the plan, making judicial reorganization a central theme in his frequent public appearances in the Dallas area. Having fought the court's nullification of both the NRA in 1935 and the AAA in 1936, Love told audiences that he supported the plan because Texas farmers would be the greatest beneficiaries of a more efficient Supreme Court.[27] In the coming weeks, he gathered signatures from more than 160 Texas lawyers who, as he put it, were fully "signed on" to FDR's plan to expand the court. According to Love, the citizens of Dallas were "overwhelmingly in favor of the President's proposal." Love shared his assessment of the situation with the president directly.[28]

FDR loyalists and other liberals were quick to lend their support, but those whose patience with the New Deal had already grown thin used the opportunity to launch a counterattack. Within a day of the initial announcement, anti–New Dealers began to categorize "court packing" as an exercise in "collectivism" and power consolidation—a clear example of executive overreach. For the first time in his presidency, Roosevelt faced a truly significant backlash within his own party. Democrats who had been reluctant but submissive on other aspects of the New Deal took the court-packing controversy as a convenient opportunity to break with FDR. Led by state senator T. J. Holbrook, the Texas Legislature made its displeasure well known in early February. On February 6, Holbrook took a public stand against Roosevelt, saying that "there has never been, and will never be but two forms of government: one a democracy and the other a socialism." He then forecast that "when, and if, the President is permitted to change and re-vamp the court of our country, then respect for that branch of government will likewise disappear and vanish, at which time we will have one, and only one, functioning branch of the government, which will be the Executive." Closing with a most dire warning, Holbrook said, "There is nothing new in this form that our government is taking. It is not a 'New Deal,' except that the electorate has been purchased and has not, as yet, been subjected to the power of the sword by force submission and obedience. If we continue in our present course, in my opinion, that expedient will be reached in no distant time."[29]

Holbrook's words, which included a tirade against organized labor and the ongoing strikes at the General Motors plant in Flint, Michigan, lit a fire among conservatives across the state and nation. Newspapers across the country took notice, and thousands of anti–New Dealers in Texas—and hundreds of anti–New Dealers from other states—wrote Holbrook with words of encouragement and support. The implications of an expanded court struck some not simply as executive overreach, but as something far more sinister. Some were quick to associate a liberal court with a threat to white supremacy itself. "He will have the power and privilege to place upon the court men that will annul our separate marriage laws, our separate school laws, our separate coach laws," wrote one particularly angry constituent. "[FDR] will thrust Negro social equality upon the people of the South. Every white man and woman in the south ought to fight this move to the limit of his or her ability."[30]

Buoyed by his newfound fame, Holbrook led the Texas Senate in rescinding a speaking invitation to Harold Ickes, who was slated to appear before both chambers in Austin later that month. Holbrook's animus toward the New Deal had been clear for years, but court packing allowed him a fresh platform on which to communicate that opposition. Then, on February 9, he promoted a resolution to the Texas State Senate denouncing the plan. The resolution passed the senate by a vote of 22–3, but it was overwhelmingly defeated in the House 95–28, where Democrats at the local level were more cautious on the matter of breaking with Roosevelt. Although the resolution was entirely symbolic, the mere fact of its existence, and of Holbrook's leadership in bringing it to the table, made the state senator from Galveston (and Richard Kleberg's congressional district) a national celebrity.[31]

Holbrook's fifteen minutes of fame lasted for a few weeks, until better-known figures at the national level assumed command of the fight. Opposition to the court-packing plan grew rapidly. According to Love, business leaders in Dallas were especially worried that Roosevelt would pack the court with judicial activists committed to imposing excessive regulations on private enterprise. On March 2—Texas Independence Day—Tom Connally delivered a rousing denunciation of the plan during a speech at the capitol building in Austin, though he tempered his vitriol by affirming his "devoted, personal friendship" with FDR, despite their disagreement on this issue. Connally later told Love that he had no major objections to judicial reorganization in theory but would continue to publicly oppose the bill by calling it a "scheme" to consolidate power and liberalize the Court. He also suggested that his "corporate interests" opposed the plan and that it was more important to appease his well-funded supporters than to work with the president on a bill he could not see benefiting most Texans, despite Love's argument to the contrary.[32]

Former Dallas mayor Henry D. ("Hal") Lindsley agreed with Connally. Lindsley had a long history of antigovernment activism. He helped organize the American Legion in 1919 and remained a prominent voice of states' rights conservatism in the decades following. Soon after, the National Committee to Uphold Constitutional Government, a newly organized group formed for the sole purpose of directly opposing judicial reorganization, appointed Lindsley its Texas representative. Meanwhile, Love reported to FDR that Lindsley was a "friend but had been "kidnapped by Wall Street" and only spoke for a "fragmentary minority of people of Texas or of Dallas." Roosevelt rarely responded to any of Love's letters, but he did this time, asking for assistance in Dallas while essentially deputizing Love to the role of intelligence officer for perspectives on the issue across the state.[33]

Few Texans were closer to the drama than John Nance Garner. As vice president, Garner served as a go-between for Roosevelt and the Texas delegation throughout the spring and early summer of 1937. Initially, however, he did very little to broker anything resembling a compromise, even going so far as to leave Washington in the middle of negotiations, against FDR's will. Garner's decision to "go on vacation" during the heat of battle, coupled with his overall unwillingness to help Roosevelt on judicial reorganization, was among the final nails in the coffin that was their ever-worsening relationship—a fact that was increasingly obvious to anyone who was present when the two men were in the same room together. Eventually Garner helped Roosevelt by backing a substitute measure designed, as William Leuchtenburg described it, to prevent "bloodying the President's nose" too much. Regardless, the damage was done.[34] Given the opportunity, many FDR loyalists, including Morris Sheppard, abandoned the president's original plan, instead backing a watered-down bill that Sheppard claimed Roosevelt had been "agreeable" to as a compromise. In reality, it was clear that Roosevelt had simply lost the battle. Love was apoplectic at the turn of events, scolding Sheppard, saying that he was "very much disappointed" and feared a "permanent abandonment of Government by the people" to the Supreme Court.[35]

Throughout their first term together, Garner had been a relatively cooperative New Deal loyalist. Despite private misgivings, he enthusiastically championed the administration and the New Deal, which he, like almost everyone else, sold to voters as pragmatic program of solutions designed to make ordinary Americans' lives better. Garner had believed the emergency measures of the first "Hundred Days" were necessary for the country's survival; the reforms of the so-called Second New Deal, and the deficit spending entailed in those reforms, caused him more discomfort, though he rarely if ever voiced his concerns to reporters or the public. Garner's objections to the New Deal were just as frequently rooted in his concern that FDR was upending patronage networks by co-opting Republicans into the administration. In other words, Garner wanted all presidential appointments to go to Democrats, while Roosevelt believed that bipartisan appointments gave his administration an added layer of credibility. Ultimately, Roosevelt was a man of relationships, and he and Garner simply did not connect well. FDR often ignored Garner's advice, or at least ignored it more than Garner thought was acceptable. Over time, mediators such as Louis Howe and James Farley, with whom Garner enjoyed a very close relationship, served as Garner's bridge to FDR.[36]

For Garner, court packing was essentially the end of the line as far as his active support for the president and his New Deal was concerned. And when Garner broke, so did many establishment and conservative-leaning Texas Democrats like him. Given the state's widespread opposition to court packing, members of the Texas delegation—sensing a rare moment of political cover when it came to defying FDR—joined the chorus of defiance. None played a more important role in judicial reorganization's eventual defeat than Hatton Sumners. Sumners had already survived one dispute with Roosevelt in 1934, when he refused to support a crime bill that FDR wanted passed. He similarly survived a political dustup in 1936 by sidestepping calls from Tom Love and others to condemn the Supreme Court's ruling against the AAA. Sumners was on Roosevelt's radar for a future Supreme Court nomination when the fight over judicial organization exploded in early 1937.[37]

Sumners shared some of FDR's concerns about the court's backlog of cases and the age of its justices. He was also frustrated that some of the court's decisions had gone too far. However, rather than solve the perceived problem by backing FDR's plan, Sumners preferred a different plan to encourage an early retirement system that would protect judges against reduced salaries and shield them against some tax liabilities upon resignation. He also hoped to create a new emeritus status for retired judges. But he found the notion of the president appointing up to six new justices anathema. "Don't let Tom Love fool you," wrote his friend Allen Wright. "The President's request for power . . . has sent a chill over the thinking members of your constituency. Some of the warmest supporters of the President feel that he has furnished evidence of the worst things his enemies have said about him and his enemies feel that he has no given conclusive proof of a thirst for absolute power and a total lack of scruples as to how he obtains it." Another man refuted Love's assertion that the legal community in Texas supported the plan, telling Sumners: "Lawyers of the Bar overwhelmingly oppose any coercion of the supreme Court or arbitrary addition to its membership." After a briefing on the plan at the White House, and in view of his read of the situation back home, Sumners reportedly told several of his congressional colleagues, "Boys, here's where I cash in my chips." News of the comment was widely published and generally seen as a major moment in the breakdown of establishment Democratic support for Roosevelt and the New Deal in Texas and beyond.[38]

After coming to believe that the president's plan was a gross overreach, Sumners committed himself to obstructing the bill's progress from that point forward. As chairman of the House Judiciary Committee, he refused to introduce the bill for consideration. Then, when Maury Maverick broke rank and introduced the bill on the House floor, Sumners stalled it in committee. He then deconstructed the bill into a variety of unpassable pieces, using every strategy he could think of to kill the proposal in the lower chamber. The climax of Sumners's public fight against court packing came on July 13, 1937, during a speech on the House floor. In what he called "good, old-fashioned horse sense," Sumners delivered an impassioned and articulate treatise on constitutionality, checks and balances, and the need to fix the court "with a surgical instrument, not a meat ax." Sumners tried to deflect his criticism away from Roosevelt personally, blaming FDR's advisors for inappropriately pressuring the president to back the ill-fated plan against the president's better judgment. After much give and take with others on the floor, Sumners concluded his remarks and received what the *Congressional Record* called a "prolonged" standing ovation.[39]

Meanwhile, Sam Rayburn—whose misgivings about the bill had increased in the months since its first introduction—remained loyal to FDR. Though he privately thought Roosevelt was barking up the wrong tree, he nevertheless convinced the president to relaunch the bill through the Senate, where, Rayburn believed, it had a better chance of making it through committee. However, between February and July, the Senate Judiciary Committee refused to move the bill to a vote, thanks largely to Tom Connally's vocal opposition. As Connally worked against the bill in the Senate and Sumners stalled it in the House, John Nance Garner worked behind the scenes in both chambers, ultimately ending any hope it may have had of passing. Eventually, on Rayburn's counsel, Roosevelt abandoned the plan and accepted a much watered-down compromise.[40]

As the court-packing dust began to settle, Rayburn began working to mitigate the damage and repair FDR's reputation. During a speech broadcast over the NBC Radio Network in August, he quelled rumors that Roosevelt was on the outs with Democratic conservatives. He told his audience that politics was a rough business sometimes. He still had faith in FDR, Rayburn affirmed—and FDR still had faith in Congress. Rayburn shifted the conversation away from court packing by reselling Texans on the New Deal through a combination of brutal honesty balanced with reminders about how various New Deal programs had made their lives better. He earned credibility by acknowledging, with regret, that government was growing bigger, as were budget deficits. In plain-spoken language, Rayburn tried to move Texans past the drama of court packing by reminding audiences that the New Deal was nothing more than a series of practicalities employed in response to the calamitous economic situation Roosevelt had inherited from his Republican predecessors. FDR was still capitalism's great savior, Rayburn said—a friend to business leaders and farmers alike, and a nonideological pragmatist who was committed to staying on the job as long as it took in order to help ordinary Texans live better lives.[41]

Soon, other loyalists followed Rayburn's lead. Marvin Jones told friends in Amarillo that while he had been against judicial reorganization, the entire issue had been blown out of proportion. "The plan did not alter my feeling toward the President at all," Jones said during an interview years later. "I had a great deal of confidence in the President. I had great admiration for him. I felt that he was like any other great man—he could make mistakes. I thought this was one that he made."[42]

During a welcome distraction that September, Jones attended a gala thrown in his honor and in celebration of "victory" over the Dust Bowl. More than two thousand locals attended the event at the Amarillo Herring Hotel's Crystal Ballroom, during which a procession of speakers praised Jones's efforts on agriculture reform, while an emcee read telegrams from Texas dignitaries such as Tom Connally and Morris Sheppard. When it was his turn to speak, Jones took the opportunity to ask Washington for an additional $60 million in funding for the continuation of soil and water conservation efforts—a request that seemed to undermine the event's claim of "victory" over the Dust Bowl, but one his audience readily cheered.[43] George Mahon made similar efforts that September, telling one local reporter that Roosevelt was "still popular with the Congress and with the majority of the American people," while reiterating the litany of assistance Roosevelt had provided to area farmers. Mahon readily acknowledged that the president had "lost some ground" due to the court-packing debacle, but added that it would be impossible for FDR to "maintain the highest peak of popularity. It is well to remember that no president has ever been extremely popular throughout eight years in the White House."[44]

Reassurances from Rayburn, Jones, Mahon, and others notwithstanding, the court-packing episode clearly damaged FDR's relationship with conservative Democrats in Texas. According to William Leuchtenburg, the controversy "destroyed the unity of the Democratic Party and greatly strengthened the bipartisan anti–New Deal coalition," adding that "an angry and divided Congress would pass few" laws for any reorganized Supreme Court to consider. When combined with the administration's response to labor unrest, the court-packing drama resulted in a trend of middle-class New Dealers who had been content with the progress made since 1933 becoming less securely tethered to FDR.[45]

In correspondence with Roosevelt that September, Texas congressman William McFarlane told the president that while many continued to support the administration in public, behind the scenes some members of the Texas delegation had grown increasingly hostile to the New Deal. According to McFarlane, a disturbing number of his colleagues were already positioning themselves for a wider break, anticipating both the midterms of 1938 and the next presidential election in 1940. McFarlane also reported that several of his colleagues were now following Hatton Sumners's lead by calling the president a "dictator." He even warned that certain agriculture-related measures would face opposition "to the last ditch" depending on the scope and nature of associated regulations. "Unfortunately, these same views are held by a large majority of the Texas delegation, along with many other delegations in the South as well as the north, all of whom call themselves Democrats," McFarlane told the president. "They all seem to feel that their first allegiance is due their reactionary friends, under whose influence they have apparently become hypnotized and who have made them subservient."[46]

Labor unrest, civil rights agitation, and the court-packing scandal weakened FDR's political gravitas in Texas in ways that would have been unimaginable just a few months earlier. Meanwhile, flashes of economic recovery evident in 1936 and early 1937 emboldened conservatives to push Roosevelt for spending cuts and a balanced budget, knowing FDR's long-standing personal preference for fiscal moderation. Unfortunately, it was too much for the still fragile economy to handle. By the fall of 1937, as Roosevelt was still licking his wounds from the court-packing scandal, the national economy nose-dived. During the next several months, the "Roosevelt Recession" saw noticeably reduced manufacturing production levels, after their having finally matched pre-1929 levels. National unemployment rose to nearly 20 percent. Congressional districts that had depended on federal funding for public works projects and jobs since 1933 struggled to survive the slashed federal budget and reduced spending programs. Conservative Texans lauded spending cuts in theory, but state and local leaders of all ideological stripes responded to the downturn by promising their worried constituents a return to New Deal money for new projects.[47]

At the same time, the Roosevelt Recession was far less pronounced in Texas than it was in other parts of the country. As George Green showed, factory payrolls were reduced by a mere 5 percent in Texas, as opposed to 27 percent nationally, while "total manufacturing establishments" declined by only 2.2 percent throughout the decade, far less than "any other southern state." In other words, Texans reacted to the Roosevelt Recession as a national problem since the state and local impact was minimal thanks to the fact that Texas was still largely rural and agrarian, with limited industrial manufacturing capacity to begin with. Liberals consistently tried to blame the recession on Hoover and the Republicans. Nevertheless, in the wake of labor unrest, court packing, and economic downturn, the ratio of New Deal loyalists to anti–New Deal opponents was shifting. In that context, the emergence of new loyalists became more important than ever.[48]

"The Incalculable Human Resource of Youth"

Lyndon Johnson's career as an elected public official more or less began when James Buchanan died on February 22, 1937, from complications related to a heart attack. Buchanan had represented Texas's Tenth Congressional District for twenty-four years. His sudden death sparked Johnson and a host of others into a lively scramble to fill the newly vacated seat. In time, LBJ's bid for Congress in 1937 would prove to be one of the most significant events in the history of Texas politics, launching a career that eventually culminated in his occupancy at the White House.[49]

The suddenness of Buchanan's death notwithstanding, Johnson's campaign for Congress in 1937 did not exactly originate ex nihilo. LBJ had grown up shadowing his father, Sam, who served as a state representative in the Texas Legislature from 1905 to 1909, then again from 1918 to 1923. LBJ later recalled the energy and excitement he felt during his days in Austin, and especially by his father's side on the campaign trail, experiences he said he sometimes wished would "last forever." A cliché, politics seemed to be in his blood at an early age. (Sam Rayburn often shared a similar memory about his own youthful interests in politics, rooted in charismatic oratory and populist fire, spewed on behalf of the Texas "plain folk"—in Johnson's case, those who lived in the Hill Country, and in Rayburn's, those who lived in North Texas.) Johnson worked on Maury Maverick's first congressional campaign in 1934 before serving as a congressional secretary for Dick Kleberg until 1935, when he left that post for the directorship of the Texas branch of the National Youth Administration (NYA). Only twenty-six years old at the time of his appointment, Johnson assumed control of the Texas NYA on Kleberg's recommendation. (Kleberg once famously described Johnson as a "tornado in pants.") Johnson also won endorsements from Maverick, Rayburn, and Martin Dies; historian Robert Caro suggests that Rayburn personally asked FDR to give Johnson the appointment, after Tom Connally's efforts to the same end failed. Johnson did not disappoint, organizing what Eleanor Roosevelt later described as "the best NYA program in all of the states."[50]

Though historians have long debated Johnson's political legacy, including the degree to which his political convictions were more liberal or conservative, there seems little doubt that in 1937 Lyndon Johnson chose to define himself as an unwavering supporter of FDR and the New

Deal. "I believe this district should have as its representative in Congress a man who is wholeheartedly committed to support of the President's entire New Deal program," Johnson said on March 11, 1937, in one of his earliest radio addresses. As Johnson told his listeners, the New Deal was not a "temporary thing," but was instead built "for an age." He may or may not have been forecasting his own legacy when he said that the "man who goes to Congress this year, or next year . . . must be capable of growing and progressing with" the New Deal. Johnson's message established a clear dichotomy not between left and right, but—as he framed it—between right and wrong, and between loyalty and disloyalty.[51]

Based on advice from Alvin Wirtz and others, Johnson remained unflinchingly subordinate to FDR throughout the campaign, appealing directly to farmers, labor, merchants, teachers, and others likely to be sympathetic to New Deal initiatives. Wirtz also encouraged Johnson to differentiate himself from other candidates not simply by coming out "one-hundred percent for Roosevelt" on the New Deal, by also by aggressively supporting the president's plan for judicial reorganization. A career politician and political insider, Wirtz quickly became one of Johnson's most reliable campaign advisors, not to mention a bridge connecting Johnson to powerful interests in the Texas business community.[52]

Like Roosevelt, Johnson was a master at translating abstract ideologies into practical, commonsense solutions. Reporting on a Johnson campaign rally on March 30, 1937, the *Austin American-Statesman* highlighted the candidate's support for the New Deal, including judicial reorganization. The Austin press also emphasized Johnson's blistering condemnation of "radicals" on the right, which he associated with organizations like the Liberty League and the Jeffersonian Democrats. "The candidates the Liberty League is backing are against reforming the Supreme Court," Johnson said. "That means they are against putting into effect the president's farm program, his labor program, the water and soil conservation program, and all the helpful measures President Roosevelt has proposed."[53]

Johnson's most frequently utilized campaign slogan was "For Roosevelt and Progress." Leaflets, cards, letters all promoted this message: "I stand wholeheartedly with the President on his program, and I invite the people who favor the Roosevelt program to support me." LBJ epitomized modern liberalism's optimistic, plainspoken tone. As would be true of his future campaigns, he marketed his 1937 bid as distinctly pragmatic and nonideological. He blamed Herbert Hoover and the Republican Party for being greedy and out of touch, and he praised FDR for restoring confidence through both word and deed. His speeches were noteworthy only in the sense that his style remained stilted and bland, but in one-to-one conversations with supporters, Johnson's folksy manner, his ability to read faces and look voters in the eye, won over more than enough supporters. "Don't you remember when cotton was selling at when Mr. Roosevelt went into office?" Johnson would often say. "Don't you remember when it was selling at a nickel? Don't you remember when it was cheaper to shoot your cattle than to feed them? Don't you remember when you couldn't get a loan, and the banks were going to take your land away?" Johnson colloquially and effectively shared the FDR playbook to anyone who would listen, and then enlisted others in the district to do the same thing on his behalf. As Robert Caro said, exaggerated though it may be: "No Fundamentalist preacher, thundering of fire and brimstone in one of the famed Hill Country revival meetings, had called the people of the Hill Country to the banner of Jesus Christ more fervently than Lyndon Johnson called them to the banner of Franklin Roosevelt"[54]

"A vote for Lyndon Johnson will mean these things," Judge N. T. Stubbs of Johnson City told radio listeners on April 8. "First, farmers will have an active worker in Washington to look out for their interests." Second, Stubbs told voters that Johnson would prioritize labor at the same time that he would work with "business and professional men" and connected those constituencies by referencing New Deal programs that provided employment and public works, specifically the CCC, NYA, and WPA. Stubbs specifically highlighted river projects such as those shaping the Colorado and Brazos Rivers. "Herbert Hoover was a great engineer and a great organizer, a great businessman, but the most dismal failure as a president this country has known," Stubbs said. Ostensibly speaking about Johnson's campaign, Stubbs continued: "Franklin Roosevelt is not a great engineer. He is not a great lawyer. He is not considered a great businessman, but as a public servant, as a leader, and as president, he stands out among the leaders of all the world."[55]

Stubbs was not the only local influencer tapped by the Johnson campaign for a public endorsement, and in almost every case, LBJ's primary marketing strategy was to remind voters of their affinity for President Roosevelt. One oft-repeated stump speech written for Johnson supporters began with a recounting of the early days of the Depression: "Ranch-

FDR in Galveston following a fishing trip off the Texas coast, May 11, 1937. Courtesy of Franklin D. Roosevelt Presidential Library & Museum.

men were on the rocks. Cattle weren't worth raising for meat. Neither were goats, or sheep, or hogs. Business was in an astonishing slump. Banks were crashing in every direction. Commercial failures were at their all-time peak." But FDR saved the day, LBJ said. He had done so not by applying ideological liberalism to the situation, but by being a man of action, unwilling to sit back and let the many suffer because of the sins of the few. "Will the people be permitted to say again, as they said in November: 'We want a man in Congress who will support the President, who is for him, instead of against him, who will support him actively, instead of fighting him, or hamstringing him by indifference and inaction? Will the people rule, or will the special interests?" Johnson solicited support from just about everyone but spent more time and effort campaigning on the backroads of his district than he did in Austin, where his opponents seemed to be concentrating efforts. He was particularly hopeful of support from his hometown, Johnson City in Blanco County, where the local paper, the *Record-Courier*, promoted LBJ as an "honorable and straightforward" man whose fiery work ethic would benefit citizens across the district.[56]

Following Roosevelt's lead, LBJ associated conservatism with ideo-

FDR, James Allred, and Congressman Lyndon B. Johnson in Galveston, Texas, May 11, 1937. Courtesy of Lyndon B. Johnson Presidential Library & Museum.

logical dogma and "do-nothing" obstructionism, while depicting the New Deal not as progressivism, but as a commonsense program of solutions designed to help real people with real problems. While cognizant that former Buchanan voters had not been looking for new leadership, LBJ nevertheless offered a full-throated commitment to stand with the president who had put farmers "back on their feet" and had extended assistance to laborers and families. "He must be a 100 percent supporter of Franklin Roosevelt, not a former enemy of the President and his program, who has been converted recently for political reasons," one Johnson supporter told a small gathering just before the election. "He must be one who thunders his yes, who has been a Roosevelt man from the start. He must be ready to go the whole way. He must not support the President up to an important crisis and then lie down on the job." "For Roosevelt and Progress." Johnson shared the message as consistently

FDR, James Allred, and Congressman Lyndon B. Johnson in Galveston, Texas, May 11, 1937. Courtesy of Lyndon B. Johnson Presidential Library & Museum.

and as passionately as possible, spending more money and time on radio publicity than all other candidates in the race combined, reaching voters through small local stations as well as larger ones based in San Antonio, which boasted the strongest signals in the area. The strategy worked. LBJ easily won his district's Democratic primary that April, prompting some observers—including the *Washington Post*—to speculate that Roosevelt's popularity in Texas was as strong as ever, despite the ongoing controversies over labor unrest and court packing.[57]

In later years, historians and other political observers ascribed to Johnson a unique ability to balance progressive convictions with a Machiavellian pragmatism. That skill set allowed Johnson to make deals with conservative business interests throughout his career, while vacillating on liberal commitments, depending on which way the wind was blowing at the time. Some of this was no doubt present during Johnson's first term in Congress, as scholars have chronicled. Publicly, however, Johnson rarely hedged his bets when it came to FDR. Shortly after winning the special election, Johnson joined Allred in welcoming FDR to Galveston, where the president arrived after a fishing trip through the Gulf of Mexico with his son Elliott and Texas oil barons Sid Richardson and Clint Murchison. Johnson capitalized on the opportunity, earning a photo with Roosevelt and Allred that would become among the more famous in American presidential history. Noticeably impressed, FDR invited Johnson to join his contingent on a trip to College Station, where he was scheduled to deliver a speech that afternoon. Johnson so impressed Roosevelt during their train ride together that FDR subsequently remarked to aides that Johnson was "the most remarkable young man" and may eventually become "the first Southern President." Following his speech at Texas A&M, the president traveled to Fort Worth, where he joined his friends for an evening of barbecue and cocktails at his son Elliott's ranch, engaging in several conversations that would later captivate historians' attention for unrelated reasons.[58]

Upon beginning his legislative career in Washington, Johnson delivered a radio address on January 23, 1938, that foreshadowed what he would later call a "war on poverty." "Crime, like disease, is most at home in the slums," Johnson said. "I am unwilling to close my eyes to needless suffering and deprivation which is not only a curse to the people immediately concerned but is also a cancerous blight on the whole community." Johnson also spoke about a Christmas Day stroll down Congress Avenue in Austin, during which he encountered no fewer than forty families living on the streets in "filth and misery." He recounted the heartache of those moments, punctuating his remarks by saying, "One thing I believe all of us have learned from the Roosevelt Administration is that none of us can remain prosperous long unless more of us have an opportunity to live better."[59] A few months later, Johnson added to his reputation as one of the New Deal's most impassioned defenders, telling an audience of NYA workers: "Many persons may not be fully reconciled to the idea of the government taking care of so many boys and girls, because such persons ignore the alternative to such provisions. . . . Whether this country is in the midst of a temporary condition or a profound change, the incalculable human resource of youth is being conserved by various government agencies until stability in some form finally emerges." Few, if anyone, could moralize policy as well as Lyndon Johnson. In the years to come, it was a skill that would at times serve him well, while at other times it would contribute to what journalists eventually called a "credibility gap."[60]

"100 to 1 That It Wouldn't Be Raining in Amarillo"

In a fireside chat on June 24, 1938, FDR blamed "Copperheads" in the South for failing to support him, his party, and the New Deal. He further suggested the need for what commentators soon called a "purge" of conservatives from the Democratic Party.[61] Historians have argued that Roosevelt's attempted purge of conservatives from the Democratic Party in 1938 was yet another foolhardy political move from a president whose career more frequently reflected political brilliance. In overreaching yet again, FDR—according to common analysis—accelerated partisan realignment, not by placing his party on a more securely progressive base, but by deepening cracks and accelerating the move of states like Texas toward conservatism and, eventually, the Republican Party. The situation in Texas was particularly vexing. Members of the Texas congressional delegation had chaired no fewer than nine House committees during FDR's first six years in office; by all measurements, the New Deal would not have been possible without the support and leadership of Texas Democrats in Washington. Yet, as the court-packing drama unfolded, it was also clear that Texas adversaries wielded significant influence over national affairs. Still, throughout the summer of 1938, he approached the Democratic primaries in Texas with caution, not aggression. He

FDR, with Elliott Roosevelt, Jimmy Allred, and Congressmen Maury Maverick, LBJ, W. D. McFarlane, and Fritz Lanham, Amarillo, Texas, July 11, 1938. Courtesy of Franklin D. Roosevelt Presidential Library & Museum.

aided pro–New Deal candidates when he could, usually with a kind word or a reference to "old friendships." He also lashed out at conservatives in both parties, occasionally mentioning a specific opponent for failing to support the New Deal—and "the people"—with enough verve. Privately, however, Roosevelt knew that significant ideological realignment was unlikely. Attacking incumbent Democrats would yield little return on investment and might, he conceded, cause more problems than solutions. Court packing, backlash to the CIO, and recession weakened FDR, but ballot boxes and campaign strategies nevertheless continued to reflect most Texans' ongoing fealty to the president.[62]

Three weeks after his "copperhead" speech, FDR made another much-ballyhooed trip to the Lone Star State. In speeches seen by some as an effort to mend fences, FDR supported New Deal loyalists running for reelection, but did so without going too far in condemning the state's conservative establishment. On July 10, former and future Dem-

FDR, with Ross D. Rogers, mayor of Amarillo, and Jimmy Allred, in Amarillo, Texas, July 11, 1938. Courtesy of Franklin D. Roosevelt Presidential Library & Museum.

ocratic National Committee campaign chair for Texas Myron Blalock welcomed Roosevelt, saying in a publicized telegram that the "organized Democracy of Texas—which means ALL of Texas—extends to you a most hearty welcome." Cities and towns across the state appealed for a visit, hoping to show off New Deal projects.[63] FDR disingenuously told reporters that the main reason for his visit was to reconnect with his son Elliott at his ranch in Fort Worth. Somewhat compliantly, FDR often mentioned his son when speaking about his visits to Texas, a convenient strategy by which he could identify as a sort of quasi-resident. The White House leaked several telegrams similar to Blalock's from other friends and well-wishers, each of which characterized the president's trip to Texas a sort of romanticized homecoming.[64]

John Nance Garner also welcomed FDR via telegram, though some viewed his physical absence from the traveling contingent as a slap in the White House's face. Garner, who increasingly grumbled that he believed Roosevelt was stabbing loyal Democrats in the back just for expressing the occasional misgiving, said it was "too far to walk" and, quite oddly, that he was now in Uvalde "working for a living." Newspapers reported the "snub," speculated that the rift between FDR and Garner was about FDR's desired purge, and openly speculated about FDR's plans for a third term, and where that would leave Garner.[65] Journalists speculated that FDR was most eager to eliminate "copperheads" like Richard Kleberg, Fritz Lanham, Hatton Sumners, and Martin Dies, each of whom had taken steps away from the president since 1937. Dies may have been at the top of that list, having broken with the president several times since 1936, seeing his political future along an anticommunist path rather than a New Deal one. Privately, Roosevelt referred to Dies as "Martin Fish," a comparison of sorts to the better-known Republican anticommunist, Congressman Hamilton Fish of New York.[66]

On the other hand, FDR welcomed Sam Rayburn, Lyndon Johnson, Marvin Jones, Maury Maverick, and W. D. McFarlane on various parts of his trip, referring to each as a "friend" of the administration. At the same time, he also welcomed conservatives Hatton Sumners and Tom Connally, but conspicuously diminished their importance by withholding the same affection.[67] Such snubs annoyed both men, but especially Connally, whose wound Roosevelt salted on July 11 by announcing the appointment of Jimmie Allred to a federal judgeship, an action widely perceived as a jab at Connally, who, as a member of the Senate Judiciary Committee, had nominated someone else. Roosevelt's decision to appoint Allred—who was coming to the end of his last term as governor— was likely less a strategic attack against Connally than a reward to Allred. It was also a compromise, given that Connally and Morris Sheppard had recommended two different men, neither of whom was Jimmie Allred. Still, many saw the move as a strategic favor to the state's pro–New Deal contingent.[68]

The trip's grand finale came in Amarillo on the afternoon of July 11 in a speech that quickly became part of Roosevelt lore, not so much because of what the president said, but because—in the heart of the drought-plagued Dust Bowl—Roosevelt delivered his speech in the middle of an unexpected thunderstorm. "If I had asked the newspapermen on the train what the odds were, they would have given me 100 to 1 that it wouldn't be raining in Amarillo," Roosevelt quipped with a smile. "But it is!" FDR went on to remark that it was in Amarillo that his wife Eleanor had received "the biggest bunch of flowers in all the world," continuing that the rest of the country was looking at the West Texas Panhandle in awe, seeing evidence of the government's ability to promote a well-regulated agricultural economy, significant environmental obstacles notwithstanding. According to the *Shamrock Texan*, those in attendance were undoubtedly "charmed" by the "famed Roosevelt smile," as one woman confirmed, remarking that it was "worth standing in the rain" to see FDR's "congenial" smile, adding that the entire experience was "wonderful."[69]

Despite the negativity that had plagued his second term, Roosevelt's visit was a political positive for New Dealers across the state. Voters in the Texas Panhandle affirmed their support for Marvin Jones, overwhelmingly reelecting the incumbent New Dealer just days after FDR's rain-soaked visit to Amarillo. Jones was unapologetically pro-Roosevelt and pro–New Deal in 1938, as he had been since 1932. He also benefited from public endorsements by John Nance Garner, William Bankhead, and Sam Rayburn, each of whom went out of his way to highlight Jones's unwavering loyalty to the Democratic Party. He also received special mention in the *Washington Herald*, another achievement of national recognition that was particularly flattering to Jones's home district in the oft-ignored Texas Panhandle. Jones emphasized his support for farm mortgage refinancing, rural electrification, water and soil conservation, soil payments, and a variety of other bills designed to help agriculture prosper. He spoke proudly about New Deal bills he had cosponsored and warned voters against conservative efforts to deregulate the stock market.[70] "I pledge cooperation with the national government," Jones told audiences in a standard stump speech, adding quite liberally that

> with proper cooperation between state and nation, I feel that better farm conditions can be permanently established and thus the prosperity of the state and nation assured. . . . I favor furnishing every reasonable opportunity for homeless people, both in the city and the country, to become home-owning citizens. Under the Democratic program, the farmer has been returned to the road of freedom and prosperity. I favor keeping him on that road.[71]

George Mahon's 1938 campaign similarly highlighted loyalty to the New Deal and a willingness to remain above the political fray. Mahon's reputation as an honorable man whose loyalty to the president was an asset and whose commitment to area farmers would always be a priority made his reelection a foregone conclusion. Like Jones, Mahon focused on tangible improvements to the economy and infrastructure within his district. He highlighted PWA grants in Muleshoe, WPA programs in Lubbock, New Deal initiatives that helped Dust Bowlers suffering from lack of food, clothing, and other necessities, and generally made status-quo support for the New Deal the heart and soul of his political messages. Just four years after his first election, Mahon used his overwhelming popularity in the Nineteenth District to advocate for appointment to the highly influential House Ways and Means Committee. As liberal Democrats in the north and east lobbied against the appointment of any Texan to that committee, Mahon emerged as a sort of compromise appointment. Mahon received the appointment within the year, thus launching him onto a track that eventually ended with him becoming the longest serving chairman of the House Appropriations Committee (1964–1979) in American history.[72]

While Jones and Mahon sailed to easy victories in West Texas, Wright Patman faced a more difficult fight on the other side of the state. A liberal-populist first elected in 1928, Patman represented the First Congressional District, with East Texas population centers in Texarkana, Paris, and Marshall.[73] Having assumed office before the crash of 1929 on a blended platform of states' rights (broadly defined) and a "square deal" emphasizing anti–Wall Street progressivism and the necessity of federal regulation, Patman fast-tracked his district beyond the world of wets, drys, and isolationists for one that prioritized economic reform and an actively engaged federal government. In 1932 he introduced a bill to expedite promised bonus payments to veterans of the Great War. That bill finally passed in 1936, but not before it created the famed Bonus Army debate and contributed to Herbert Hoover's final political demise in the White House.[74]

Given the political atmosphere, one might assume that any challenge to Patman's incumbency in 1938 would come from the conservative right. In fact, Patman did face a challenge, but not one from his right. George Blackburn tried to sell voters that he was a more effective, efficient New Dealer than Patman, suggesting that FDR no longer trusted Patman. "If Mr. Patman is a main cog in the New Deal," Blackburn told voters at a rally in Mount Pleasant, "no one seems to know it but him." Blackburn's campaign emphasized stories of a perceived snub, in which FDR failed to include or acknowledge Patman at any point during his trip to Texas in July. Blackburn told voters that if FDR had considered Patman essential to the New Deal, he would have reminded voters of that during his trip. Blackburn pointed out numerous cases in which

FDR endorsed someone simply by calling them a "friend," and said that failing to do so for Patman was tacit to rejection. "Patman swung with all his might and missed when the President came to Texas," Blackburn said in one speech. "Mr. Roosevelt openly endorsed four Texas Congressmen and totally ignored Mr. Patman. This rebuff shows how little our congressman, who tells us the New Deal will collapse unless he is re-elected, commands from the President."[75]

Patman should have been more secure in his standing across the district. Instead, he let Blackburn get to him. Four days after the president's speech in Amarillo, Patman telegrammed DNC chairman James Farley and pleaded for some sort of public endorsement from the White House. The next day, the president's appointments secretary, Marvin McIntyre, wired Patman, saying, "Just before sailing, the President asked me to wire you and express his regret that he could not come to Texarkana on his trip across Texas. He was sorry that he did not get to see you." Patman immediately turned the wire into a press release, with the following addendum: "The President recently invited Congressman Patman to the White House to discuss pending legislation, an honor that seldom comes to a Congressman, other than Chairmen of the most powerful committees." Not wanting to leave any doubt, Patman's press release ended by saying that "the relations between the President and Congressman Patman, both personally and politically, have always been warm and mutually cooperative."[76]

Blackburn responded to Patman's press release by doubling down on the idea that FDR did not fully trust Patman and that he would be more aggressive in challenging conservative and Republican opposition to the president.[77] Nevertheless, Patman quickly seized the upper hand. During a July 21 speech in Roxton, he proudly declared himself to have been "one of the first liberals elected to Congress" from Texas. He also depicted himself as a sort of martyr to the cause, saying he endured accusations of socialist sympathies because of his advocacy for old-age pensions and support for soldiers' bonuses:

> Up until my election, those in charge of the federal government had always contended that the people should support the federal government, but that the federal government, in no case, should use its wealth and resources to aid those in distress—the unemployed, those who were about to lose their homes on account of foreclosure, the aged, or any other class or group. . . . During my service I have seen this government transformed, and I have as-

sisted in transforming it, from a conservative government, which recognized no responsibility to its citizens whatsoever, to a liberal government, which has assisted practically every class and group. . . . At last the government has recognized its duty for the security of the people and the fundamental right to work.[78]

Wright Patman typified the success that came to Texas Democrats not in spite of Roosevelt's liberal New Deal, but because of it. He survived the perceived snub of July, won the Democratic primary fight against Blackburn, and campaigned as a "man of the people," beholden to none, "fearless, fair, able, and honest," and a champion for "economic security." Above all else, Patman branded himself as a Roosevelt man whose support for the New Deal was unquestioned. "The plain people of this country have never had a better friend in the White House than President Roosevelt," he wrote in one campaign brochure that year. "My record has encouraged the active opposition of holders of special privilege and the greedy. It has been my privilege and pleasure to cooperate with our great leader, the Honorable Franklin D. Roosevelt." Patman won reelection and continued to serve as a valued liberal member of Congress until his death in 1976.[79]

New Deal loyalists did surprisingly well in 1938, winning primaries across the state. Even state senator T. J. Holbrook, whose foray into the court-packing fight of 1937 had earned him a short-lived national spotlight as leader of the conservative anti–New Deal cause, lost to William E. Stone, who ran on a platform of stronger cooperation between Austin legislators and the White House. Stone told constituents that Holbrook's stand against Roosevelt had "pleased Republicans and Liberty Leaguers," but had not done Texas any favors, attaching to Holbrook the labels of "obstructionism" and "anti–New Dealism" throughout his bid to unseat the incumbent State Senator.[80]

Of course, not all New Dealers fared as well. In the midst of recession, once-committed liberals spoke openly about the virtues of unfettered free markets and the concurrent need to avoid "interfering with some of the natural economic laws." San Antonio reflected some of that backlash when voters ousted Maury Maverick in favor of the far more conservative Paul J. Kilday. Unlike the situation in other districts, Maverick's loyalty to the president likely contributed to his defeat, while Kilday went on to represent San Antonio's Twentieth Congressional District until 1961.[81]

To my friend of may years Mourin Jones
Hatton W Sumners

Congressman Hatton W. Sumners. Courtesy of Southwest Collection/Special Collections Archive, Texas Tech University, Lubbock, TX.

Kilday's primary strategy was to attack Maverick as a radical. On occasion, he even referred to Maverick as a "radical communist," citing Maverick's endorsement by the CIO and his support for John L. Lewis and sit-down strikes as evidence. While conservatives happily accepted endorsements from the AFL that summer, the CIO's support for Maverick became an albatross. Kilday's red-baiting forced Maverick into a defensive position very different from the one he had enjoyed two years earlier when FDR was running for a second term. "The often repeated charge of Communism and radicalism, in my opinion, is such old and grossly insincere stuff as to be unworthy of an answer," Maverick told radio listeners on July 20. Nevertheless, Maverick insisted on giving an answer, emphasized in the radio transcript in all capital letters as "I AM NOT NOW, AND HAVE NEVER BEEN A COMMUNIST; I HAVE NO SYMPATHY FOR THAT PHILOSOPHY AND DO NOT WANT SUCH

SUPPORT." Retreating from the brazen language he had used in the weeks after his reelection in 1936—including statements describing FDR's reelection as more important than the "original" American Revolution—Maverick tried to sell himself not as a radical, but as a man who believed in "constitutional democracy and free speech and press and religion." Yet, the very fact that Maverick had to defend himself against Kilday's charges of communism kept the idea front and center during the campaign. Kilday controlled the narrative. Whether trying to defend his support for "public health" as something other than a belief in "socialized medicine" or reassuring audiences that he had never "asked any man to have any ill feeling for those who have property or are rich," Maverick's footing was shaken in the weeks leading up to the Democratic primary. Nor did it help that Maverick accepted numerous invitations to speak before labor-friendly audiences in Ohio, Michigan, and Maryland, thereby removing him from Texas altogether at the height of the campaign.[82]

Still, Maverick lost by fewer than six hundred votes, a point emphasized by the *Chicago Daily Times*, which blamed Maverick's defeat—one of the most significant defeats for FDR and the New Deal that year—on the AFL's support for Kilday and Kilday's exaggeration of Maverick's connections to the CIO. Maverick clearly blamed his loss squarely on Kilday's anticommunist tactics and publicly worried that his loss was a harbinger of the New Deal's waning popularity in Texas. The truth was more likely a simple matter of Maverick's visibility among national progressives as a political leader whose leftist proclivities exceeded those promoted in most New Deal programs. Unlike other losers that July, Maverick failed to recede quietly into the background. In August, the *San Antonio Light* reported that, at Maverick's leading, the FBI was investigating voter irregularities in Bexar County. When that investigation reached a dead end, Maverick filed paperwork to wage an independent bid during the general election, promising anyone who would listen that he would support FDR and the Democratic Party from top to bottom if elected. The Texas secretary of state denied Maverick's petition.[83]

Excepting Maverick's, few elections were as tinged by the rumors of a Roosevelt-led "purge" as the one involving Hatton Sumners in Dallas. Sumners's image in conservative circles glowed in 1938 from what many viewed as a principled stand against executive overreach the previous year. However, as much as observers assumed Roosevelt would want to oust Sumners, they also reported that few incumbents were as safe as

Sumners was in Dallas. Part of Sumners's security came from efforts to mitigate the impression that Congress's leader against court packing was on the outs with FDR. Neither offered an explicit denunciation of the other in public, and the two did, in fact, remain close behind closed doors. Preparing for his reelection, Sumners assured the press that he and FDR were still on good terms, saying that FDR had endorsed him in a "private letter," while reminding reporters that he had supported the president on eleven of twelve bills sent to the Congress that year.[84]

Thomas Love, however, was not willing to forgive or forget what he ironically—given his efforts on Herbert Hoover's behalf in 1928—condemned as disloyalty to the Democratic Party. Love put his money where his mouth was by declaring his own candidacy for the Fifth District seat that July, calling himself a "Franklin D. Roosevelt New Deal Democrat" who supported the president's "unsurpassed mandate from the people of Dallas County and Texas and the Nation." He even said that he would drop out of the race if Sumners could prove that Roosevelt actually supported him. Love, who frequently corresponded with both FDR and Sumners, told reporters that FDR needed, and in fact wanted, someone who was "indispensably a New Deal ambassador to the New Deal government in Washington" and that the citizens of Dallas agreed with their president.[85] Sumners responded: "Campaign charges are being made that I have fought the President and his program. If by that they mean I have failed to support the President 100 percent in all that he has proposed, of course that is true. On the other hand, it is known that I have supported the President earnestly and, I think, effectively in the great majority of his proposals."[86] Love then pushed Roosevelt for a public endorsement, as did the third candidate for the seat, the equally pro–New Deal attorney from Dallas, Leslie Jackson, whose campaign was arguably even more pro-FDR than Love's.[87]

Perhaps a tad exasperated, and aware of the odds against unseating Sumners, Roosevelt limited his public involvement to avoid tying himself to a clear loser. Behind the scenes, he and Sumners pursued rapprochement. Sumners complained to White House press secretary Stephen Early that the perceived "feud" was a campaign liability that the president needed to correct. FDR then spoke to advisors about various political favors he could offer Sumners and his district. That discussion ended with Sumners's appointment to the House Monopoly Investigations Committee, which Sumners then highlighted in his campaign. Sumners was already on the House Judiciary Committee, and FDR—knowing that Sumners could easily highlight court packing during his reelection campaign—wanted to give Sumners an opening to celebrate the new appointment and his long-standing record in the House without rehashing FDR's weakest moment as a chief executive. If he could not defeat Sumners, FDR hoped he could accelerate the incident's movement into distant memory. The strategy worked. Sumners was hardly a New Deal loyalist, and he would continue to operate with influence among conservatives for the rest of his career. Facing reelection in 1938, however, he freely associated himself as a Roosevelt supporter, instead distancing himself from perceptions that he was a copperhead.[88]

"Blood-Warming Phrases of the Familiar Shouting Evangelist"

In a very memorable year, no political feat stood out as more spectacularly peculiar than the election of W. Lee "Pappy" O'Daniel to the governorship of Texas. A former president of the Fort Worth Chamber of Commerce who was subsequently fired from his job as a flour salesman, O'Daniel was best known as an amateur showman who helped popularize western swing music through radio programs designed to sell his new companies' products, often using the slogan "Pass the Biscuits, Pappy." In early 1938, O'Daniel read a fan letter during one of his radio broadcasts. The letter, from a man claiming to blind, praised O'Daniel as a voice of the people, and urged him to make a bid for governor. O'Daniel asked his listeners to chime in by mail, and many did; nearly 55,000 letters poured in urging Pappy to run. He agreed. In telling listeners that he was running "for them," O'Daniel used his status as a radio celebrity to run on a flamboyantly vague populist platform of the "Ten Commandments and the Golden Rule." (O'Daniel's campaign eventually came up with a more specific slogan: "Less Johnson Grass and Politicians, More Smokestacks and Businessmen.")[89]

Though he—like Hatton Sumners and most other Democrats running for office in 1938—publicly expressed fidelity to FDR, O'Daniel was critical of the New Deal, perhaps more so than any other major candidate in the state that year. He railed against government expansion, labor unions, and the Fair Labor Standards Act of 1938, which both Lyndon Johnson and Sam Rayburn publicly supported. He also vehemently opposed a proposal for a new state sales tax, promising to veto such a bill as soon as he could. At the same time, he supported a raise in state pensions (without explaining how he would pay for them), spoke optimistically about the need for government to assist in both corporate and small-business development across the state, and openly opposed the death penalty. Anyone looking for ideological consistency found little in O'Daniel's 1938 campaign. On the other hand, voters looking for a nonpolitician capable of shaking up the establishment seemed to have found their man. Rural voters were particularly enamored.[90]

O'Daniel's foray into politics was almost entirely self-made. As Seth Shepard McKay put it, O'Daniel had "no political organization of any kind, no campaign manager other than his wife, no newspaper support in the early weeks of the contest, and was totally lacking in political experience." But, as McKay also speculates, O'Daniel's lack of political background was a refreshing change of pace for many voters and likely resulted in his eventual victory.[91] In other words, O'Daniel was ahead of his time in using his celebrity as the basis for a political campaign. Before running for office, O'Daniel was most famous for writing the song "Beautiful Texas," which he quickly incorporated into all of his campaign appearances. This song, and the charisma with which he used it, reflected the power of mass culture, sentimentality, and pride to over-come a shortage of experience. For voters, "Beautiful Texas" became a sort of anthem, subtly distinguishing the state from its ex-Confederate brethren, while maintaining a level of nostalgia and patriotism common throughout the states of the Lost Cause:

> Oh, beautiful, beautiful Texas,
> where the beautiful bluebonnets grow . . .
> We're proud of our forefathers,
> who fought at the Alamo . . .
> You can live on the plains or the mountains,
> or down where the sea-breezes blow . . .
> And you're still in beautiful Texas,
> the most beautiful place that I know.[92]

Not everyone in the state was charmed, however. The *Dallas Morning News* called O'Daniel a "clown" whose entire appeal was based on his "hillbilly band" and the "blood-warming phrases of the familiar shout-ing evangelist" that successfully allowed him to "mix music and religion with politics." Critics also charged that O'Daniel's proposals lacked sub-stance or budgetary forethought. Pundits specifically lampooned his proposed pension plan as an unfunded boondoggle that would cost the state more than $45 million.[93]

O'Daniel's campaign also garnered significant national attention, almost all of it negative. Leading periodicals depicted O'Daniel as a political hack. Newspapers up and down the East Coast—most notably the *New York Post*—ridiculed O'Daniel's followers. Attentive to the narrative of Roosevelt's supposed purge, the *Post* also highlighted the survival efforts of incumbent New Dealers, including Texas's Maury Maverick. In one particularly effective cartoon that merged the two storylines, the *Post*'s cartoonist depicted an elderly Texas couple gathering around a radio in order to listen to Maury Maverick talk about "real issues," only to flee the radio in panic when a troupe of girls dancing to a nameless "Hillbilly Band" interrupted Maverick's speech. The message was clear: intelligent Texans were listening to pro–New Dealers while cheap, superficial showmanship was distracting others.[94] In the end, O'Daniel's charisma and embodiment of a fresh, antiestablishment alternative proved too much for other Democrats to overcome. The former flour salesman and country music entrepreneur won the Democratic primary easily, securing enough votes to avoid the customary runoff election. In carrying such a surprisingly large percentage of the vote in a multi-candidate race, Democrats ranging from Jimmie Allred to John Nance Garner subsequently pledged their support for the nontraditional candidate's general election campaign. O'Daniel then sailed to victory in November.[95]

Privately, conservatives and other establishment Democrats held skeptical assessments of O'Daniel's acumen for governing. Nevertheless, those connected to the oil and banking industries were pleased to have someone in office who was sympathetic to the business community's concerns about big government, labor unions, and "creeping socialism." The *Dallas Morning News* reported O'Daniel's victory as evidence of a "New Deal slaughter," also commenting that Sumners had been "marked for purge" by FDR and had won reelection anyway. Somewhat dramatic and incomplete in its coverage, the paper emphasized victories by O'Daniel and Sumners while paying less attention the widespread success New Dealers continued to enjoy in other parts of the state, not to mention the degree to which conservatives like Sumners had avoided a total break with FDR. The "purge" of 1938 was, in more ways than often realized, much ado about nothing.[96]

———

Franklin Roosevelt survived the first two years of his second term, but not without sustaining damage to his political credibility and popular standing. Even in Texas, where a record number of voters had supported FDR's reelection in 1936, anti–New Dealers were emboldened. A variety of right-wing organizations emerged and/or evolved in 1937 and 1938, taking advantage of the tumultuous circumstances surrounding labor unrest, judicial reorganization, and recession. In the process, these conservative groups deployed narrow definitions of "Americanism" as anathema to both Roosevelt and his New Deal, moving the country closer to what would later become its second major "red scare." For the time, however, such organizations remained limited in influence and reach, particularly at the ballot box. Most Democratic candidates running for office in Texas felt little pressure to abandon Roosevelt or the New Deal, at least not entirely, during the 1938 midterms. For every Roosevelt critic there was an equally vociferous Roosevelt apologist. Meanwhile, voters continued to endorse much of the New Deal's status quo, and certainly the money that poured into their communities because of it. Such voters decided to reelect FDR loyalists in municipal, county, and district races across the state. It is true that many of the tenets that later defined modern American conservatism were visible during the middle of FDR's second term; however, those tenets hardly codified into a meaningful shift in either candidate or voter behavior. All told, after two years of significant political upheaval, the New Deal Coalition remained relatively strong in Texas as 1938 gave way to 1939.

Of course, most Texans likely assumed that Roosevelt would leave office at the end of his second term, retiring quietly to the idyllic surroundings of his home and newly constructed presidential library in Hyde Park, New York. Many were no doubt similarly comfortable with the idea of Jack Garner as a replacement. Despite his relatively public break with the White House in 1937, Garner remained a popular, respected political figure, which explains FDR's persistent efforts to re-enlist the vice president's services and loyalties in November 1938, writing affectionately from Warm Springs in an effort to charm Garner into returning to Washington. "I wish very much that I could have your judgment," Roosevelt wrote, lamenting that the issues involving budgets, business recovery, and national defense demanded more than written correspondence could provide. (Garner accepted Roosevelt's invitation and the two conferred at the White House on December 8. The meeting adjourned with the two as divided as ever, particularly on the matter of the pending budget.) Nevertheless, many Texans saw "Cactus Jack" as a sort of a pragmatic bridge connecting conservatives and liberals across choppy New Deal waters. Unbeknownst to everyone at the time, however, the closing of the New Deal era was rapidly approaching, not because FDR planned to retire, or because Garner would be able to kill it, but rather because of the rapidly deteriorating state of international politics.[97]

5 | "My Very Old and Close Friend"

The Great Depression dominated the first six years of FDR's presidency, just as it dominated the lives and political interests of ordinary Texans. Across the state, most Democratic candidates framed their campaigns around economic issues. In doing so, most also prioritized partisan loyalty and the New Deal's immediate benefit to the so-called forgotten man. Persistent criticism from the conservative right notwithstanding, Texans who supported Roosevelt typically perceived New Deal liberalism as little more than commonsense pragmatism—a series of practical solutions to urgent domestic problems. However, the political tumult of 1937 and 1938 cast FDR as more ideologically driven and potentially radical than some of his most loyal supporters had wanted to believe. As a result, the president's popular standing suffered. Regardless, however, the overwhelming majority of Texas voters consistently funneled their experiences and circumstances through a national prism that conflated long-standing Democratic fidelity, historic distrust of all things Republican, and an image of Roosevelt as a reliable captain successfully navigating choppy waters. In short, from 1932 to 1938 most Texas Democrats who wanted to win elections aligned themselves to Roosevelt and the New Deal. Voters usually affirmed that strategy at the ballot box.[1]

Within this context, Texas politicians spent comparatively little time discussing foreign policy. Like most Americans, Texans by and large believed that economic recovery was more important to their immediate situation than was political instability on a different continent. Accordingly, FDR spent the bulk of his political capital on the New Deal, advocating policies favorable to farmers, workers, and the American capitalist system more broadly. Democrats across the country, including most in Texas, usually followed FDR's lead, zeroing in on domestic economic concerns while marginalizing geopolitical ones. That is not to say, however, that Roosevelt was disinterested or uninvolved in world affairs. He was, in fact, a Wilsonian internationalist at heart, having served as assistant secretary of the Navy during the Great War. Yet as president, Roosevelt's public commentary on the subject was typically subdued, limited to reassuring voters that he would keep the country out of another European war. This strategy enabled Texas Democrats to unite behind FDR and the New Deal without having to address issues of isolationism or interventionism, at least not directly.[2]

By 1939, however, the unmistakable drumbeats of war in Asia and Europe began to push foreign affairs closer to the center of Texas political debates. Officeholders and candidates who had paid only tangential attention to such troubles during the previous six years began to think and talk more openly about the pros and cons of American intervention overseas. Concerned citizens expressed their fears more frequently, writing to representatives not simply about their need for a job or their support for (or opposition to) New Deal spending programs, but about the coming war. Economics ceased to dominate the state's political culture. Rather, the New Deal competed for attention with questions about national security, neutrality, the value of FDR's experience in world affairs, and the parameters of loyalty and "true" Americanism.[3]

"And Now, As Is Usual at This Hour Each Sunday Morning . . ."

On January 17, 1939, an estimated sixty-five thousand fans filled War Memorial Stadium on the campus of the University of Texas at Austin to witness Pappy O'Daniel's inauguration as governor of Texas. Described by James Ferguson as an "imposing" celebration, the event featured extraordinary pomp and circumstance that soon gave way to one of the most notoriously turbulent administrations in the history of that office.[4]

During his first few months as governor, Pappy O'Daniel reversed course on most of his campaign pledges. Having promised to provide a monthly pension of thirty dollars to all Texans age sixty-five and older, and to do so without raising taxes, O'Daniel instead proposed a widely panned plan for a new statewide sales tax, despite having opposed such a plan during the campaign. He also responded to a revenue shortfall by slashing funds for public highways, hospitals, and law enforcement. The battle over his pension and sales tax plans was particularly embarrassing given the backlash it fomented in the state legislature, including from a cohort of anti-O'Daniel Democrats dubbed the "Rebellious 56."[5]

Along the way, O'Daniel lost most of the policy battles he waged, in part because he did not fight back, choosing instead to use his office

168 | CHAPTER 5

for patronage and self-promotion. He appointed (or tried to appoint) friends and supporters to various positions within his administration (regardless of their qualifications) and developed notoriously unfriendly relations with members of the Texas and national press, a fact he eagerly highlighted in speeches broadcast directly to the public. Little of this surprised O'Daniel's critics, just as little of it fazed O'Daniel's supporters, most of whom saw the newly elected governor as a "man of the people" whose status as a political outsider and flare for the dramatic were refreshing assets, not liabilities. As O'Daniel described it, his governorship would reflect the traditions of Jesus Christ, the American founders, and former Texas governor and noted populist Democrat James Hogg. The *Dallas Morning News* compared him to the recently assassinated "Kingfish" of Louisiana, Huey Long.[6]

O'Daniel's emergence as a preeminent voice in the world of Texas politics coincided with a nadir of FDR's political standing in the state to that time. It also paralleled (and in some ways fueled) a resurgence of antiunion attitudes, which O'Daniel and like-minded conservatives used to revitalize charges that New Deal collectivism was leading the country down a slippery slope to communism. Until 1938, O'Daniel had openly supported FDR and many New Deal reforms. However, as a candidate and then as governor, he quickly fashioned a new role representing an emboldened populist right that was both weary and wary of seemingly endless federal growth. He also rallied support from the state's business community, promoting a "Sell Texas" program designed to maximize both the state's production of natural resources and its manufacturing capacity.[7]

In one well-publicized event just weeks before officially taking office, O'Daniel met with Henry Ford and other leaders in the automotive industry about a possible relocation of synthetic rubber manufacturing from midwestern states, where some executives viewed union activism and labor strikes as a constant threat. To O'Daniel's credit, the strategy worked; Texas would become a national leader in synthetic rubber manufacturing during the next few years. Similarly, O'Daniel worked with local boosters and the RFC to secure millions of dollars in funding for new steel armament plants and blast furnaces such as those eventually constructed in 1941 near Rusk and Longview in east Texas. Successes like this emboldened O'Daniel and his supporters, who were convinced that probusiness, antiunion policies would lead directly to industrialization, jobs, and economic expansion across the state.[8]

O'Daniel was not shy about promoting his successes, nor did he hesitate to broadcast his political visions as far and as wide as he could. Though stylistically folksier and more brazen than FDR, O'Daniel nonetheless borrowed from the president's strategic playbook. Most obviously, he used radio to control (or at least influence) the news narrative and connect with Texans on a personal, emotional level. Of the roughly one hundred radio speeches he delivered in 1939 and 1940, at least a quarter focused primarily or exclusively on family, faith, and the threats he believed were facing those Texans committed to preserving "traditional values."[9]

O'Daniel delivered the vast majority of these radio addresses on Sunday mornings from 8:30 to 9:00 a.m., just as many listeners were preparing for or already on their way to church. In each, O'Daniel tried to strike a relatable tone while simultaneously embracing his reputation for showmanship. An announcer began each broadcast by saying: "And now, as is usual at this hour each Sunday morning, we switch you to the Governor's Mansion in Austin, Texas for a visit with Governor W. Lee O'Daniel. The next voice you hear will be the friendly voice of Governor W. Lee O'Daniel." Pappy would then welcome his audience: "Good morning, ladies and gentlemen, and hello there boys and girls." For the next twenty-five minutes, O'Daniel—with a team of producers—would divide the airtime into a series of sermonettes (though on at least one occasion O'Daniel simply read "inspirational" poetry). O'Daniel and his producers also mixed in Christian hymns and patriotic songs, which served as transitions from topic to topic, sermon to sermon. For instance, one of his earliest such broadcasts featured snippets from the songs "Beautiful Texas," "Jesus Savior Pilot Me," "God Bless America," "Jesus, Lover of My Soul," "Faith of Our Fathers," and "Whispering Hope."[10]

One of O'Daniel's favorite strategies was to offer his audience political nuggets in the form of a prayer request shared among close friends. In this way, O'Daniel sounded more conversational and approachable—perhaps even transparent and vulnerable—in the hopes of eliciting the kind of emotional support that would translate into political pressure on his enemies in the legislature. Based on the feedback he received from listeners, the strategy worked.[11] "I have not mentioned politics this morning because very little has transpired," O'Daniel said in his April 23 broadcast, in specific reference to the legislative battle over his doomed pension plan. "On behalf of the old folks, the dependent blind, the helpless children, and the retired school teachers of this Great State of Texas may I invite the prayers of Christian people in Texas today, and this week, that this most perplexing problem be settled in a satisfactory manner for the benefit of distressed citizens who need aid."[12] A month later, still facing resistance on the pension plan, O'Daniel complained of the "professional politicians" actively conspiring in a "diabolical plunder plot" to destroy him personally, at the expense of "the masses of the people."[13] Two weeks after that, he offered the following:

> Now to all my friends who are listening in, let me tell you that my prayers morning, noon, and night are that God will guide me right in this fight I am waging for the great masses of common citizens of Texas, but may I beg of you who believe in prayer to please plead with God in Heaven to give strength and courage to my wife and children that they will be able to withstand the untruthful criticism which they are forced to hear from day to day heaped upon the one they love.[14]

Though he remained a divisive figure, O'Daniel's use of radio was effective; he maintained a passionate following across the state, in some ways attracting the same populist base that had carried Ma and Pa Ferguson to power a generation earlier. "If you were never able to put over your program, you are worth at least a billion a day as Christ's Ambassador of Cheer and Good Will," wrote one adoring fan in December 1939, specifically to request that O'Daniel run for reelection. "I thoroughly am for you 100 percent," wrote another man that same month, for the same reason. "The workman, the man you meet at the filling station, the fellows paying their taxes on a little home, seem to be for you by a large percentage." Another wrote to proclaim O'Daniel "the greatest governor ever," comparing "Pappy" to his predecessors who were, in his words, "old cussers and irreligious men to whom we would not cite [to] our children as examples to emulate."[15] The press meanwhile spent as much time rehashing the drama surrounding O'Daniel's personality and surprising election as it did challenging the substance of his ideas or his lack of success with the legislature. Newspapers both magnified and capitalized on the buzz surrounding O'Daniel's bizarre success.[16]

Often in tandem with his focus on family and faith, O'Daniel exploited his standing as governor to raise the specter of "un-Americanism." He rebuffed reporters by questioning their patriotism, challenged his critics' loyalties, and frequently castigated opponents as "fifth columnists." In early 1940, he enlisted Texas citizens in the cause, encouraging them to report potential subversive threats across the state, a call to which many of his faithful radio listeners responded. Just north of Waco in the community of Bellmead, for instance, an anonymous informant warned O'Daniel of a high school teacher who was promoting "Hitlerism." Another anonymous informant made a similar allegation in Fort Worth, against a "Mr. Harris" who apparently criticized American foreign policy in front of his students at Arlington Heights High School. "I am proud that you have started on the rounding up of Un-Americans among us," the informant added in his letter. "They are almost at our elbow." In San Antonio, an anonymous informant wrote of a "Spanish girl from Mexico sponsored by the government" who was conspiring with Hitler on a planned invasion of Texas. "I have wanted to write you, telling you we are friends and admire, approve, and love you for your Christian character," the informant wrote. "I am furious when you are criticized." Along the South Texas border, another citizen shared stories of "fraud voting" throughout her district, alleging that politicians "get Mexicans to write their names then the politicians do the voting for them on Election Day."[17]

From 1939 to early 1941, O'Daniel conflated fascism and communism as morally equivalent forms of godless totalitarianism, stressing that while German Nazism posed a significant threat, it was no less dangerous that Soviet Communism. Encouraging his listeners to read Adolph Hitler's book, *Mein Kampf*, O'Daniel noted the "accuracy" of Hitler's "prophecies" and how similar "strikes in this country were planned by the Communist Party, and how those strikes are now working out on the schedule." In other commentaries on international affairs, O'Daniel warned against ongoing dependence on New Deal "collectivism," adding that societal dependence on the State threatened the nation's Christian underpinnings and, therefore, its democracy. That threat was particularly dire when located in growing labor unions, which he argued drew support from both communists and Nazis.[18] This was O'Daniel's core message, for instance, in May and June of 1940, when he garnered national attention by sending FDR a telegram about "fifth columnists" working against American interests in Texas. In the telegram, O'Daniel offered to have the Texas National Guard and other officers in the Department of Public Safety work with federal officials to root out both Nazi and communist sympathizers across the state. News of the telegram was widely reported, as was Roosevelt's complete dismissal of the allegation. Nevertheless, O'Daniel's message resonated with pastors and clergy of the state's Protestant establishment, many of whom increasingly saw the New Deal as a threat to the long-standing social and cultural hegemony of local churches.[19]

Using a strategy that was simultaneously ahead of its time and reminiscent of the Ku Klux Klan's golden age, O'Daniel framed his political agenda in religious trappings, suggesting that Texans faced a spiritual battle against surreptitious enemies both foreign and domestic. During one of the seemingly endless debates on how to finance state-level pensions, for instance, O'Daniel accused those who suggested Texas might consider licensing and then taxing horse racing of being "forces at work" who wanted to "undermine the state's purity" by legalizing "vice." He failed, however, to counter that proposal with an alternative solution. He then embraced the issue of vice to deepen connections with religious voters, reigniting controversies over Prohibition, the repeal of which he connected to gambling and organized crime. O'Daniel also enthusiastically supported Martin Dies and the HUAC, associating that organization's efforts with the "will of God" and the preservation of American democracy against the forces of "collectivism." He promised radio listeners that as governor he would do everything in his power to identify and stop anti-American "subversives," especially those affiliated with labor unions and the CIO. During one radio address, O'Daniel admitted that Roosevelt's New Deal had resulted in "some" economic benefit to ordinary Texans, but also warned against liberalism's challenge to religion as citizens' chief source of stability and peace. On May 26, 1940, he specifically addressed the importance of preserving "Americanism," calling the word "one of the greatest terms in our patriotic vocabulary." O'Daniel defined Americanism in broad terms, emphasizing vigilance against all "special interests" that prioritized ideology above traditional values. At the same time, O'Daniel also mentioned the importance of evangelistically extending Americanism to "every race, every class, and every creed."[20]

O'Daniel polarized the state's political culture in remarkably passionate ways. To his supporters, he was a protector of traditional values and economic opportunity. To his opponents, he was a radical farce. As one citizen-observer later commented, O'Daniel possessed "two great political talents. One for making unsuitable or wholly impossible appointments; the other for using his religion as a political asset." The usually conservative *Dallas Morning News* took its criticism a step further, calling O'Daniel a "laughingstock" while warning Texans who had not recently traveled outside the state to prepare for the "shame" that was ahead of them because of their governor's horrendous national reputation.[21]

Still, few if any of O'Daniel's critics held Roosevelt to the same standard, rarely attacking the president for his own frequent appropriation of religious imagery for political purposes. This suggests either a double standard on the issue or, more likely, a perception that O'Daniel's use of religious images in the late 1930s was more threatening to the status quo than was Roosevelt's in years prior, when the world was less obviously on the brink of war and less immediately threatened by right-wing, anti-Semitic regimes. Regardless, Pappy O'Daniel was the most prominent and influential political voice in Texas throughout 1939 and 1940, and it was his vision of Americanism that catalyzed many of the political shifts that shaped Texas in the decades to come.[22]

Within this rapidly changing context, Democrats across the state struggled to navigate political waters in their home districts. No Texas politician experienced the brunt of Pappy's war on un-Americanism more clearly than Maury Maverick. After losing in the 1938 congressional primary largely due to perceptions that he was sympathetic to the radical left, Maverick won the mayoral election in San Antonio, beginning his term in early 1939. Just a few months later, in August 1939, he permitted the local chapter of the Communist Party to meet in the city's municipal auditorium for a fee of ten dollars. San Antonio Communists met there on August 25, surrounded by anticommunist protestors. A skirmish ensued, resulting in police intervention. Less than a week later, anticommunists—led by aspiring Republican gubernatorial candidate Alexander Boynton—generated a recall petition against Maverick. Among other charges, anticommunists said that Maverick and his associates in city hall had "aligned themselves with and given aid and comfort to enemies of free institutions by allowing Communists to meet in the Municipal Auditorium contrary to the wishes of a majority of citizens." The petition further alleged that Maverick's actions had "resulted in injury to many citizens, damages to public property, as well as uncalled for shame and disgrace to the city." Others alleged that Maverick and his "fellow travelers on the WPA payrolls" were conspiring to ramp up communist indoctrination of children in the city's public schools, lamenting the effectiveness of their "babbling 'free speech' defense."[23]

Opponents had long considered Maverick a radical, often to the far left of Roosevelt in his support for the welfare state and, especially, racial equality and civil rights. As Maverick struggled to fend off the recall election, the *Christian American* began to contact state officials and business leaders to express their concern over Maverick's influence on the New Deal administration and, specifically, the question of race rights. After circulating a flyer headlined "Maury Maverick Champions Social Equality and Shatters All Southern Precedents," the chief editor of the *Christian American* reached out to Herman Brown of the famed Brown and Root construction company to complain about Maverick's agitation on the subject of civil rights. "A whispered conference was held between white Congressman Maverick and black Congressman Mitchell and out of the blending of these two colors came the revival of the Red-supported proposal to make lynching a Federal offense," Earnest Stack told Brown.[24] Stack recalled an antilynching bill that had been defeated earlier that year, thanks in large part to Tom Connally's opposition and the widely held (and disingenuous) argument that "racketeering" was a far more dangerous and common problem. "Congressman Maverick was observed vigorously bending his stubby neck in enthusiastic ascent to the colored man's demands," Stack elaborated. "The ebony countenance of the colored member was all smiles, for he had found a white champion of the anti-lynching legislation and he was not only a Southerner, but from Texas, the banner Democratic state of the Union." Maverick was a "Red Radical" according to Stack, who pressed Brown to influence the recently elected congressman of the Tenth District, Lyndon Johnson, and others in the Texas delegation toward opposition of future efforts at social equality between the races.[25]

Significant press coverage of civil rights and labor activism (especially CIO-led labor activism) in other states perpetuated the stereotype that "un-American anarchists" actively threatened the nation's security and economic stability. Meanwhile, as Maury Maverick fought anticommunist opposition in San Antonio, Marvin Jones—whose political standing was at an all-time high thanks to his leadership on FDR's reelection campaign in 1936—sounded anticommunist notes of his own in late 1938, associating CIO-led strikes in Michigan and elsewhere with vigilante mob violence. In his district newsletter, Jones compared union activism to "the use of force," adding that anyone who advocated the "violent method of changing the policies or the principles of the United States government . . . should be handled at once, and if he is not a citizen he should be deported. Any anarchist or any Communist who advocates any such methods should be deported at once." Jones was one of FDR's strongest allies in Congress and probably his most effective champion for agriculture reform. He had set a tone of cooperation with labor throughout much of the New Deal era. Yet within the context of Roosevelt's supposed purge of 1938, and a devolving world order, the trend of once-loyal New Dealers defecting from the FDR fold on issues of labor—or at least balancing their support for the New Deal with their concern about "labor radicalism"—continued for the next several years.[26]

This was also true for George Mahon, who in 1939 and 1940 increasingly balanced his support for FDR and the New Deal with calls to protect Americanism from the so-called radical left. During the summer of 1939, Mahon lobbied for New Deal dollars from the WPA, CCC, and RFC, hoping to assist the communities of Snyder and Colorado City in their efforts to recover from major storm damage. He also openly celebrated his cooperation with Secretary of Agriculture Henry Wallace, whom many conservatives viewed as a threatening symbol of the New Deal left. On occasion, Mahon even defended Wallace, repudiating charges that Wallace was a "radical socialist" as O'Daniel and others claimed. He simultaneously dismissed charges that the New Deal was a slippery slope or that Texans had become addicted to federal handouts. For Mahon, the New Deal—for all its successes and failures—was still common sense. The longer O'Daniel was in office however, the more Mahon seemed willing to dip his toes into anticommunist waters, just as Jones did in the district to Mahon's north. As Mahon promoted his ability to secure New Deal funds in cooperation with Henry Wallace in 1939, he also expressed support for Marin Dies and HUAC, inviting constituents to share concerns over "un-American" activities, just as O'Daniel would do in 1940. He subsequently received dozens of letters warning of subversions disguised as union organization, farming cooperatives, and even health-care reform. On point, the State Medical Association of Texas lobbied Mahon that March, asking him to oppose any and all union-backed legislation associated with what it freely called "socialized medicine" for the elderly.[27]

A few months later, on July 20, 1939, Mahon sided with Republicans and conservative Democrats on a resolution to establish a new committee chaired by Democratic representative Howard W. Smith of Virginia. The Smith Committee was charged with the purpose of launching an investigation into the political activities of the relatively new National Labor Relations Board (NLRB). The resolution specifically authorized the

Political cartoon by C. K. Berryman, *Washington Evening Star,* July 30, 1939. "Everything Is Harmonious Mr. President." Courtesy of Sam Rayburn House State Historical Site, Texas Historical Commission.

new committee to investigate the NLRB's internal operating practices, its connections with organized labor, and its associations with perceived radical left-wing agitators. FDR opposed the resolution, but Mahon— who had previously supported the NLRB—broke with the president and joined thirteen of his colleagues in the Texas delegation by voting in favor of establishing the new committee. Albert Thomas of Houston and Robert Thomason of El Paso were the only members of the delegation to stick with labor and Roosevelt; even Sam Rayburn and Lyndon John- son buckled under the growth of HUAC's pressure, voting "present" rather than take a public stand either way.[28]

By the summer of 1939 it seemed that a growing number of Texas Democrats had become at least slightly more comfortable with the idea of breaking with FDR along ideological lines. Just how many were willing to go rogue, however, remained unknown. A few weeks after Congress voted on the NLRB investigation resolution, the *Fort Worth Star-Telegram* examined the broader voting habits of every member of the Texas delegation—House and Senate—and found that, while breaks with the White House were becoming more regular, the vast majority of Texas congressmen remained solidly and somewhat surprisingly in FDR's corner. Focusing on the legislative session that had just ended, the *Star-Telegram* noted Rayburn, Johnson, Albert Thomas, Marvin Jones, and Robert Thomason—along with Senator Morris Sheppard—as having voted "with FDR" without exception, while George Mahon and Nat Patton of Crockett strayed from the FDR fold only once. Even Tom Connally—widely known as an emerging "anti–New Dealer"— voted against Roosevelt only four times. FDR's inability to stop the NLRB investigation indicates just how strong the push to root out "un-American" activities was in 1939 and early 1940.[29]

As was true of other once-loyal New Dealers, Mahon embraced anticommunist rhetoric more often in the years that followed. He soon joined conservative Texas Democrats in supporting a bill to curb strikes in defense industries, arguing the bill would protect "patriotic American workers" against "racketeers in labor." At the same time however, Mahon's deepening commitment to anticommunist, antilabor policies lived symbiotically with an ongoing willingness to utilize and celebrate federal funds through New Deal agencies, such as new WPA-funded airports in Lubbock and Big Spring.[30]

Neutrality questions further complicated this dynamic. Shortly after winning reelection in 1936, Mahon told constituents that he was against military intervention in Europe, plain and simple. Like many others, he did little to contradict widespread opinions that American action during the Great War had been a mistake. In 1937 and 1938, Mahon supported extensions to the Neutrality Acts, the genesis of which included cosponsorship efforts from Maury Maverick as early as 1935. Privately irritated by Maverick's efforts on neutrality, Roosevelt gambled that by accepting congressional action on the matter he would quell arguments that executive power had grown too far too fast. For Roosevelt, protecting the New Deal coalition was more important than battling with his liberal allies over foreign policy. This political calculation explains why his deepest misgivings over strict neutrality remained private and why his public statements on the matter generally aimed at reassuring Americans that he had no desire to put American soldiers in harm's way.[31]

Meanwhile, Mahon qualified his public support for neutrality with frequent comments that he would do "whatever" it took to keep the country "safe," even if that meant proactively funding military prepared-ness efforts. As a member of the House Appropriations Committee, Mahon shared the same message to Roosevelt in private, hedging his commitment to neutrality against his ongoing support for FDR and, more importantly, his ongoing desire to attract New Deal programs for his home district. Morris Sheppard similarly urged the country toward active military preparedness in 1938 and 1939, telling one group of naval reserve officers: "Nothing will contribute more effectively to . . . world peace than the maintenance by the United States of an adequate military and naval defense."[32]

In early 1939, FDR asked Congress to consider specific revisions to existing neutrality laws, hoping for greater flexibility, particularly in selling arms to potential allies in Western Europe, namely Britain and France. However, those efforts stalled in Congress, where FDR held less sway than at any point in his presidency. Sheppard's colleague in the Senate, Tom Connally, straddled the line on neutrality, at one point leading a Senate filibuster against the president's request. In a conver-sation with Connally on March 16, Roosevelt said that without revising existing arms-embargo provisions, the United States risked being "on the side of Hitler." Connally remained unconvinced, as did much of Congress, including much of the Texas delegation. Faced with what ap-peared to be an immovable resistance, Roosevelt launched a charm of-fensive. On July 18, he held a White House meeting with Vice President Garner and several influential Republican senators. FDR's visitors left the White House "unmoved"; Garner flatly told the president to give up. Roosevelt was undoubtedly frustrated, but again chose to pull back in the hopes of preserving the New Deal. However, as the conditions in Eu-rope grew hotter, a patient Roosevelt found that the situation on Capitol Hill had changed. Among others, Connally moved into the president's corner; by August, he was more or less an ally. Two days after Germany's invasion of Poland in September 1939, as even the most isolationist of Texans began to recognize the geopolitical gravity and potential threat, the conservative *Dallas Morning News* predicted an industrial boom for Texas should war engulf Europe, adding that the Texas congressional delegation was now likely to back expanded presidential authority in global affairs.[33]

With critical help from John Nance Garner and Sam Rayburn, the delegation did so. A fiery speech by Rayburn, delivered on the House floor on November 2, was particularly important and led directly to House passage of what came to be known as the "Cash and Carry" bill. Nevertheless, political leaders across Texas still struggled to strike the right balance in debates over taxation, defense funding, and ongoing advocacy for economic help through the New Deal. Did proactive efforts to win federal contracts for new defense-related construction projects commit the state's leaders to a preparedness campaign that would ultimately lead to war? Could or should isolationist Texans sincerely advocate for such economic benefits? Easy answers to these and similar questions often seemed in short supply, as elected Democrats labored to balance their commitment to peace at home with their support for the president and desire to help Texans more than a decade into the worst economic crisis of all time. Through it all, as the prospect for war increased, antiwar correspondence to congressional representatives also increased, as did comparisons between autocratic dictatorships abroad and the ever-expanding federal state at home. At the same time, the number of Texans convinced that American entry was both inevitable and necessary also increased. All such conversations complicated the relationship between Texas Democrats and the president, who despite frequently assuring the public that he was opposed to entering a war, had been vocal enough in his condemnation of Germany and in his support for Britain and her allies to worry those who were committed to neutrality.[34]

"Catastrophic Proportions of World Happenings"

In May 1940, citing the "international situation," FDR canceled plans for a "western trip" that had included Texas. Roosevelt originally planned the trip as part of an effort to build support for a third term. His decision to cancel dismayed supporters who worried that FDR's pursuit of a third term—at the time still unofficial and unannounced, but widely assumed—would alienate establishment Democrats and possibly contribute to GOP growth in the state. Nevertheless, the president's focus on global crises overwhelmed other considerations. White House strategists looking to strengthen the president's case for a third term emphasized the "catastrophic proportions of world happenings." They also contrasted Republican political ambitions against what they called

Roosevelt's "lifelong" engagement with "international affairs" and "national security."[35]

Despite winning consecutive landslides in 1932 and 1936, Roosevelt was by no means a shoo-in as the election of 1940 approached. Many Texans assumed that John Nance Garner was the party's heir apparent, despite, or perhaps because of, his increasingly frigid relationship with the White House. The possibility that Garner's ascension might not happen frustrated establishment conservatives and placed high-ranking Texas Democrats like Sam Rayburn in a very precarious position. While not exactly an ever-faithful soldier, Garner had been a unifying force within the Texas Democratic Party during most of the 1930s, offering an important bridge between conservative and liberal factions, particularly during FDR's first term. As an intermediary between Congress and the White House, Garner—despite frequent ideological misgivings over much of the New Deal—brought an important measure of stability and cohesion to Democratic campaigns in Texas. His presence in Washington also kept most establishment Democrats in the fold, despite their frequent discomfort with many New Deal policies. In doing so, Garner came to reflect a sizable portion of the Texas electorate—fiscally conservative, suspicious and fatigued of progressive legislation, but virulently anti-Republican and loyal to the core. Above all else, Garner, like his fellow Texans, respected authority, supported their president, and supported the Democratic Party.[36]

Yet Garner's relatively public break with the White House during the political troubles of 1937 and 1938 undermined his image as a bridge, particularly among national progressives. New Dealers grumbled over Garner's actions. As it became clearer that the vice president would eventually announce formal plans to seek the Democratic nomination during the summer of 1939, Roosevelt—aware of Garner's reputation for consuming large quantities of whiskey—joked to staffers that Garner had "thrown his bottle—I mean his hat—into the ring."[37]

New Dealers privately resented Garner, thinking him an obstructionist and turncoat, though in public they usually aimed their Texas-based frustrations at what they considered a right-wing conspiracy led by the "Roy Millers" of the state. Garner's allies, on the other hand, viewed the vice president's retreat from Washington as fully justified. In fact, Garner's refusal to back the president on court packing and labor reform, and his insistence on balancing the federal budget, enhanced his reputation among Texas conservatives. It also strengthened establishment

Democrats' resolve to promote Garner as the most qualified and deserving candidate, regardless of his relationship with or fidelity to FDR and the New Deal. In February, with the assistance of Clara Driscoll and E. B. Germany, the "National Garner for President Committee" was actively promoting "Cactus Jack" for the White House, distributing promotional materials designed to establish Garner as the clear favorite in the race. "The eyes of the United States are upon Texas," the committee said. "Every poll—every survey—shows John N. Garner to be the choice of the Democrats of the whole country by a ratio of more than 2 to 1. If he becomes President it will be because of his support by the AVERAGE AMERICAN who believes in plain, simple old-fashioned Americanism." Within weeks, Garner's by-then-official campaign was actively intersecting with a burgeoning "Stop Roosevelt" movement active across parts of the state and nation.[38]

Meanwhile, some questioned whether Garner's break with FDR revealed a temperamental and reactive nature unbefitting the leader of the free world during a time of global war. Speculation abounded as to whether it would be smarter to promote a different, more loyally pro-FDR Texan for the nomination, with Marvin Jones and Jesse Jones among the most frequently mentioned alternatives. Resisting the idea that any other Texan could reasonably elevate to the White House in 1940, Garner's team aggressively marketed their candidate as a favorite son, a man of the people, a grizzled veteran of Democratic politics, and an independent thinker. As had been true in 1932, political cartoonists like Clifford Berryman quickly adopted such themes, making Garner one of the most popularly drawn subjects of the era. However, while Berryman and others rarely undermined perceptions of Garner's integrity or core convictions, they frequently noted his ongoing rift with FDR, making a point to show Garner on his ranch in Texas, stubbornly noncooperative with the administration in Washington. Rather than ignore the fact that Garner was, for the most part, out of FDR's inner circle, the vice president's team embraced the rift as evidence of Garner's free spirit. It sold their candidate as a maverick, courageous and principled in his break with FDR. It was a risky strategy, given the inherent importance that partisan loyalty played in the state's overall political culture, not to mention FDR's persistent popularity with most voters.[39]

As Garner's team labored to clear its own path forward, FDR operated from a position of strength. Loyalists frequently praised FDR while reminding voters of the Democratic Party's commitment to populist principles and the New Deal's fulfillment of that commitment. "Clearly it is the purpose of the Democratic Party to establish the widest possible opportunity for the welfare and progress of the average individual in America," Morris Sheppard said in 1940. "The Democratic Party is carrying forward the principles that have made it, from the day of Jefferson to the present hour, [the] foremost champion of human rights and needs, of individual initiative, and of private enterprise." For Sheppard, the New Deal was the perfect reflection of applied democratic populism. It was the will of the people made manifest. If the people wanted to support FDR for a third term, so would Sheppard.[40]

And so would Ma and Pa Ferguson. By early 1940, the Fergusons joined the chorus of those backing a third term, advocating the idea even before Roosevelt did. While Pa worked behind the scenes to convince FDR that he would have no difficulty carrying Texas, Ma challenged Pappy O'Daniel in the Democratic primary. Though she won less than 8.5 percent of the vote, Ferguson's campaign connected itself to Roosevelt and the New Deal, at times advocating policies more liberal than those coming out of the White House, including calls for higher taxes, greater support for tenant farmers, and expanded appropriations for both secondary schools and public colleges and universities.[41]

Like Sheppard and the Fergusons, Maury Maverick also played a key role in promoting FDR's campaign for a third term. Maverick used the mayor's office in San Antonio to promote what he called "the necessity" of a third term for FDR. Soon enough, Maverick was widely acknowledged as one of the major faces of FDR's unofficial "Third Term Movement" in Texas.[42] Working in coordination with the Democratic National Committee and the Roosevelt Democrat Club of Texas, Maverick effectively shaped local precincts across the state into pro–New Deal, pro-FDR campaign organizations. Rather than attack Garner, those organizations instead attempted to sell Texans on the idea of a third term without alienating voters who might otherwise have been happy to support Garner simply on the assumption that FDR's second term would be his last. In effect, rather than attack his old friend as disloyal, Maverick characterized the entire situation as unique, portraying Garner as a good teammate who would have deserved the nomination under different circumstances. Maverick even circulated a resolution to precinct conventions across the state, aiming to thwart "Stop Roosevelt" movements by passively backing Garner while still leaving room for the third term everyone knew was inevitable:

We endorse the humanitarian and forward-looking administration of our National Government under the peerless leadership of President Franklin D. Roosevelt and our distinguished Texan, Vice-President John Nance Garner. We vote for our native son, Vice-President John N. Garner, as nominee for President. We condemn the stop-Roosevelt movement and our delegates are instructed and shall pledge themselves that they shall never become a party thereto. We instruct our delegates to the county convention, state convention, and national convention, insofar as this resolution is concerned, to vote as a unit.[43]

An obvious ploy, the resolution went nowhere at the precinct conventions. Garner supporters knew that adopting the resolution would kill their candidate's campaign as soon as FDR announced, which everyone believed he would. Garnerites were willing to endorse the president's first two terms. They were also willing to give Garner credit for supporting those terms. However, they were unwilling to promise anything other than an unwavering commitment to Garner, regardless of what FDR eventually decided to do. Nevertheless, Maverick's resolution formed the basis for FDR's marketing strategy for the next several months.[44]

Maverick next recruited Lyndon Johnson (whose support for FDR, whether based on ideological accord or Machiavellian strategy, was unwavering) and Karl Crowley, a longtime FDR loyalist from Fort Worth, to help with the cause. Importantly, they also enlisted support from longtime Texas insider, LBJ advisor, and former under secretary of the Treasury Alvin Wirtz. Together, Maverick, Crowley, Johnson, and Wirtz recruited other loyalists in implementing plans to keep Texas in the FDR column at the Democratic National Convention that summer. Among other strategies, they aggressively assisted down-ballot Democrats who remained pro-FDR. Winning those primary races would add a layer of protection for FDR when things heated up during convention season that summer. They also hoped to force down-ballot candidates to choose sides sooner rather than later, confident that most would hitch their wagons to Roosevelt as the safer bet. The group also hoped to create a bridge that would enable the easy return of Garner backers into the New Deal fold after the DNC in July. Confident that FDR would carry the convention with ease, Maverick's team—which behind the scenes evolved into Johnson's team—paid nominal lip service to Garner, hailing him statewide as a hero at the same time they pledged fidelity to FDR. In doing so, they hoped to model a balanced political position that would enable undecided Texans to straddle the fence and come back to the fold when Roosevelt faced his Republican challenger in the general election that November.[45]

Once Maverick, Johnson, and their combined allies settled on a strategy for dealing with Garner, they turned their attention to repackaging Roosevelt as more than just the architect of the New Deal. Instead, they used radio to focus attention on the war in Europe and the desperate need for American vigilance. When Maverick spoke about the New Deal, he did so by connecting democracy's fragility to the importance of maintaining an activist welfare state, such as that afforded by the New Deal. He also highlighted the unraveling of democracy abroad as evidence of that fragility. While Maverick continued to emphasize the importance of domestic concerns, such as rising poverty rates in Texas, he connected local plights to international ones and purposely used the term "conservative Nazis" when discussing political opposition to the New Deal. In short, Maverick told listeners that FDR would be a source of security in an otherwise insecure world.[46]

The Garner/Roosevelt split in the state Democratic Party reached a critical moment in April when Lyndon Johnson took the lead in mediating an increasingly contentious rift between Wirtz and Myron Blalock, who, along with E. B. Germany, was the de facto leader of the Garner boom in Texas. For the party's sake, those efforts succeeded. With great fanfare, Johnson, with Sam Rayburn as a torn and somewhat reluctant cosigner, won important concessions from Blalock.[47] Those concessions included a promise that Garner would not directly oppose a third term once FDR went public with his intentions, nor would Garner's supporters do anything but applaud when the New Deal was mentioned during the first state convention in May. (The Texas Democratic Party typically held two conventions during presidential election years, the first in May, to elect delegates to the national convention, and the second in September, to finalize a platform.) It was essentially a buy-in on Maverick's resolution to precinct conventions a few weeks earlier. In exchange for these concessions, Wirtz agreed to stay out of Garner's way in Texas, thereby conceding the upcoming state convention to the vice president. The compromise allowed Garner supporters to express their support for new leadership and new policies, while simultaneously leaving the door open for their return to the FDR fold after the national convention in July. It also cemented Lyndon Johnson's position as one of FDR's most important allies in Texas, which Robert Caro argues is exactly what Johnson had designed. Within days of the agreement, Garner and Roosevelt separately leaked reports of their personal support for the compromise to various press sources across the state and nation. As far as the public knew, peace seemed to be at hand.[48]

Newspapers then covered the "Texas Harmony" agreement with great gusto. Stories typically emphasized Garner's popularity in Texas, his loyalty to the New Deal, and Texans' ongoing fondness for FDR— along with FDR's support for the compromise as a sign of respect to Garner. A reluctant Rayburn and an eager Johnson covertly shaped the tone of these stories in an effort to buttress the storyline of peace and "harmony," as most papers phrased it. Reporters typically added a dose of realism to their coverage, noting for instance that the "Good-Will accord" was a "seal of defeat in the biggest efforts since Texas became a state to send a Texan to the White House." The *Dallas Morning News* added that the compromise was critical since Texas had become the "foundation" to the national anti–third term movement, adding that wounds from the Hoovercrat bolt of 1928 remained unhealed in some quarters. Privately, activists on both sides of the debate were displeased, but for different reasons. Some expressed their frustrations directly to Maverick, Johnson, or Rayburn. Others resented being "dictated to" or "interfered with." John Sargent, secretary of "Roosevelt for Third Term" in Harris County, angrily told Johnson that FDR did not need anyone's help, that Garner's support across the state was overstated, and that Roosevelt had been forced to appear weaker than he actually was.[49]

The fact that "harmony" was not the same thing in private as it was in public became even clearer at the state convention in Waco on May 28. As delegates tried to suppress their emotions in deference to the harmony accord of the previous month, Maverick made a strategic blunder. Knowing that the harmony agreement effectively prohibited Garner's supporters from publicly opposing FDR or a third term, Maverick organized an impromptu parade around the convention hotel, at one point mocking a group of Garner supporters who stood by to watch. Maverick's actions reflected overconfidence and threatened to fracture the compromise that had been keeping the opposing Democratic wings from publicly attacking each other. Things got so unruly that Waco police officers were dispatched to restore order, and in one case break up a fight between members of the two camps. Once the police left, the convention reconvened and authorized a slate of delegates to the national convention pledged to Garner, with the understanding that they would not oppose a third term for FDR once that option was officially placed on the table. It was a clear victory for Texas New Dealers. The harmony agreement between the FDR and Garner camps essentially killed whatever legitimate hopes anyone in Texas had for a Garner presidency. Predictably, most Texas Democrats soon ceased to cause much of a ruckus over the idea of a third term. Marvin Jones, Jesse Jones, and Thomas Love each celebrated the agreement, praising Garner as central to FDR's success, while also praising the president.[50]

Meanwhile, FDR continued to focus on the war. Using the bully pulpit to rally support for increased preparedness, Roosevelt delivered a message to Congress on May 16, speaking of the grave necessity to support Britain and France with the full force of American industrial might and to avoid any new restrictions that would inhibit that support. In a Fireside Chat on May 26, he spoke about America's need to be vigilant in its commitment to allies overseas, though he also struck a lighter note when dismissing certain fringe groups that were calling for a delay or suspension in the election, or for Roosevelt to invite a Republican to his ticket in the spirit of promoting total unity. "I do not share these fears," Roosevelt said, adding that he was unwilling to do anything that upended "our freedom, our ideals, our way of life," particularly "silly" ideas that were also "unconstitutional." The message was classic Roosevelt. He emphasized the importance of stable, reliable, consistent leadership, the gravity of the situation abroad, and the foolishness of counterarguments, including one proffered by famed pilot Charles Lindbergh. A week earlier, Lindbergh had suggested during a national radio address that the United States faced no urgent threats from overseas conflict and that efforts to "prepare" the country for potential attack were ludicrous and unnecessary. Privately, Roosevelt called Lindbergh's speech the stuff of "Goebbels" and referred to Lindbergh's followers as "fifth columnists." Publicly, he dismissed Lindbergh and warned of "spies" and "saboteurs" committed to undermining and weakening the nation's defenses.[51]

Roosevelt was still not an officially declared candidate for reelection when the Democratic National Convention opened in Chicago that July. Garner and former FDR campaign manager Jim Farley were the leading declared candidates going into the convention. Officially, Roosevelt was "drafted" into running because of a staged moment during a speech by Senator Alben Barkley of Kentucky. Barkley's speech included a reference to Roosevelt's desire to avoid a third term, after which delegates on the floor erupted in a "We want Roosevelt!" chant. At that point, FDR essentially feigned surprise before agreeing to run. Garner carried Texas and Virginia on the first ballot, with Farley carrying South Dakota and Nevada. Roosevelt carried forty-three of the remaining forty-four states, easily winning the nomination. Democrats left Chicago having overwhelmingly renominated the incumbent president. Two months later, party leaders in Texas gathered for their second convention, meeting this time in Mineral Wells, just west of Fort Worth. When keynote speaker Hal Collins launched into a tirade against FDR and the New Deal, the crowd turned hostile, shouting Collins down and drowning him out with a chorus of jeers. Shortly thereafter, Elliott Roosevelt turned the room around, offering a jolly endorsement of his father's leadership. Editorializing on the episode the following day, the *Dallas Morning News* sided with Collins, assessing FDR's presidency as an "orgy of spending" and an "invitation to public bankruptcy," while also repeating oft-made charges that the New Deal "bribed the electorate with federal jobs, federal charity, and federal loans," not to mention its "roughshod disregard for state rights." Nevertheless, by the time of the general election, most Texans who opposed a third term for FDR typically did so not because of any opposition to the president personally, or to the New Deal, but because they were against the very concept of a third term no matter who was running. For those holdouts, the only option was to vote Republican. In this case, that meant backing Wendell Willkie, a lifelong Democrat who switched his party affiliation just before announcing his bid for the presidency. Ironically, Willkie was probably less popular among Republicans than he was with anti-Roosevelt Democrats who saw the GOP nominee as a convenient alternative. In October, a group of anti-FDR Texans that included Joseph Bailey, E. B. Germany, Mike Hogg, John Kirby, Steve Pinckney, and John Boyle organized an official branch of "Democrats for Willkie" and then used that organization less as a means for promoting the Republican than as a mouthpiece for all things anti-Roosevelt. Rather than shy away from Willkie's recent defection, these Texas Democrats embraced it, counterintuitively marketing the newly declared Republican as a more authentic Democrat than Roosevelt.[52]

Organizations like "Democrats for Willkie" reflected a small but persistently vocal opposition to the New Deal order in Texas. State commissioner of agriculture J. E. McDonald openly supported Willkie, the most prominent public official to do so. McDonald's refusal to support

188 | CHAPTER 5

FDR in 1940 foreshadowed actions that would become more common during the coming decades. But with the world on the precipice of war, most ordinary voters backed FDR without much drama, despite bluster over Henry Wallace's addition to the ticket as Roosevelt's running mate. (Sam Rayburn seconded Wallace's vice presidential nomination at the national convention that summer. This, despite the fact that, according to Martin Dies, Garner was "heartbroken" about not being included on the ticket, believing that Roosevelt had yet again stabbed him in the back, an opinion Rayburn likely shared. Whether Dies is correct in his recollection is open to historical debate. Regardless, Rayburn's partisan loyalty ruled the day, which came in handy two months later when Rayburn was unanimously elevated to the role of Speaker of the House following the sudden death of William Bankhead.)[53]

After months of uncertainty, consternation, and drama, the Texas electorate soon settled in for a rather routine fall election. On October 11, the *Dallas Morning News* reported on a poll showing that no fewer than 80 percent of Texas voters backed FDR for president, including 83 percent of farmers—a particularly noteworthy number since Willkie's core message was that farmers had suffered rather than succeeded under New Deal programs like the AAA.[54] Roosevelt's support in Texas included men like Robert Lee Bobbitt, who had backed Garner during the spring when he served as southwestern manager for the Democrats in Texas organization, under the auspices of the state wing of the Democratic National Committee. By November, however, Bobbitt was readily back in the FDR camp. "I am proud of my Democratic Party," Bobbitt told Rayburn that fall. He added:

> I am proud of the administration; I am particularly proud of our great Democratic leaders from Texas, all members of the Congress and others who have had a part in the triumph of the past seven years. I am proud of the President, of his character, his vision, and his leadership. It is not necessary and I do not agree with him on all of the various "side shows" which have been in operation during the past seven years, but I am wholeheartedly in favor of the "main circus" which has been in operation for the past seven years, and which has preserved and extended real Democracy in this country.[55]

Bobbitt's sentiments echoed those of most Texas Democrats. One did not have to agree with every aspect of the New Deal in order to back Roosevelt as an effective leader or to see him as the best possible

John Nance Garner, Tom Connally, and Morris Sheppard share a laugh upon the opening of a new Congress, January 2, 1941. Courtesy of the Dolph Briscoe Center for American History, University of Texas at Austin.

representative of the Democratic Party in the United States. Ideologues opposed to big government were growing in number, but they were not growing fast enough to do any significant damage to Roosevelt's popularity in Texas in the fall of 1940. On November 5, Franklin D. Roosevelt won an unprecedented third term as president of the United States. He carried only 55 percent of the national vote, but won 85 percent of the electoral votes, including twenty-three from Texas, which once again delivered the incumbent Democrat an overwhelming landslide—81 percent of the vote, to Willkie's 19 percent. It is worth noting that while Roosevelt carried Texas by larger margins in 1932 and 1936—winning 88 percent and 87 percent respectively—his overall vote total in Texas actually increased from 1936 to 1940, from just under 740,000 to just under 910,000.[56]

Two days after the election, E. B. Germany told reporters that Roosevelt "would heal all sores and bring complete unity and harmony" to Texas by removing Harold Ickes and Frances Perkins from his cabinet, while naming his just-defeated Republican opponent, Wendell Willkie, as the new "head of the National Defense Commission." (Roosevelt did none of these things.) Nevertheless, as if there was any doubt that he and like-minded conservatives were not yet ready to refold into the New Deal camp, Germany added that he hoped FDR would rapidly "clean out the Socialists, Communists, Nazis, and Republicans and give the nation a real Democratic administration the next four years." Thomas Love responded, saying that the overwhelming majority of Texas voters disagreed with Germany's sentiments. Clearly, harmony was not yet a widespread reality in state Democratic circles.[57]

The anguish of anti-Roosevelt conservatives notwithstanding, the outcome of the 1940 presidential election was predictable. Similarly, state and local races offered few surprises. With little to worry about in their home districts, Lyndon Johnson and Sam Rayburn—with significant help from Johnson's new staffer and future Texas political giant John Connally—circumvented the official Congressional Campaign Committee in 1940, led by Victor "Cap" Harding. (According to Connally, Harding was "a nice guy, but basically lacking in imagination.") With Roosevelt's blessing, Johnson, Rayburn, and Connally created an ad hoc committee that assumed all behind-the-scenes efforts for Democrats across the country, in the process raising significant resources, particularly from donors in Texas, California, and New York. With Johnson's increasingly liquid resources in the world of Texas oil, the 1940 campaigns were among the most heavily funded in American history, establishing a precedent and a trend for the future.[58]

Meanwhile, Pappy O'Daniel was easily reelected to a second term as governor and Tom Connally was reelected to the Senate, winning 94 percent of the vote in the general election after taking 85 percent in the Democratic primary. Nineteen of Texas's twenty-one incumbent Democratic congressional representatives were also reelected. Of the two incumbents not reelected, only one, Clyde Garrett in the Seventeenth District, actually lost in a Democratic primary. All twenty-one seats remained Democratic. Thirteen of those ran unopposed in the general election, including George Mahon, who was easily reelected in the Nineteenth District. Mahon's campaign differed little from his earlier ones. He continued to mention the New Deal by name; he also emphasized the need for additional federal funding to farmers in his district, his support for increased cotton production, his support for low-interest federally backed loans, and his support for additional funding to the Soil Conservation Service. Mahon was also noticeably more open about his spirituality in 1940 than in previous elections. Before multiple audiences, Mahon shared his personal faith in "Jesus Christ as Lord and Savior" before also suggesting that much of the world's violence and political unrest could more effectively be solved through spiritual revival than through militarism or international intervention.[59]

By far the most notable change in Texas's congressional delegation came not as result of voter preference, but from FDR himself. After twenty-three years, Marvin Jones retired as representative of the state's Seventeenth District, choosing instead to accept Roosevelt's nomination to a judgeship on the US Claims Court. Though his district was relatively isolated, Jones was by the early 1940s one of the most well-respected men in the national Democratic Party. He counted both Franklin Roosevelt and Lyndon Johnson among his friends and was a confidant to Sam Rayburn. Jones's move notwithstanding, the 1940 election cycle ended in relative predictability. One of the most popular presidents in American history was easily reelected, as were the state's governor and its only senator up for reelection, while all twenty-one of the state's congressional seats remained firmly in Democratic hands, and mostly in incumbent hands. Unbeknownst to Texas voters in November 1940, however, the state's political environment was about to receive a major jolt in the form of an unexpected special election to the United States Senate.[60]

"Take Up Your Personal Problems with President Roosevelt"

On April 9, 1941, Morris Sheppard died. First elected to the United States House of Representatives in 1902, then to the Senate in 1912, Sheppard was one of the most consequential political figures in Texas for much of the first half of the twentieth century. His sudden death from a brain hemorrhage at the age of sixty-five set into motion a series of political events that would culminate in one of the most infamous elections in state history. Needing to fill Sheppard's vacant seat via special appointment, Governor O'Daniel selected Andrew Jackson Houston, then eighty-six years old. The son of Sam Houston, named for Houston's friend and the seventh president of the United States,

Andrew Jackson Houston had been living quietly in retirement since 1924. His only public responsibilities since retirement had involved the ceremonial oversight of San Jacinto State Park, where his father had earned fame in 1836 in the decisive battle with Santa Anna and the Mexican army that basically ended the Texas Revolution. Houston's most significant foray into the world of politics had come in 1892, when he waged an unsuccessful campaign for governor, running as a Republican. Possessing no qualifications beyond his famous name, Houston left the Republican Party in order to accept O'Daniel's appointment to the US Senate as a Democrat. He then promptly moved to Washington, attended one meeting, became ill, was hospitalized, and died on June 26, 1941—just five days after his eighty-seventh birthday.

O'Daniel had not necessarily expected Houston to die in office, but neither had he expected him to be a candidate for Sheppard's seat when the Democratic Party was scheduled to hold a special election on June 28. Rather, O'Daniel wanted that seat for himself. Initially, he was but one of twenty-nine men vying for Sheppard's seat. (Twenty-five of those candidates ran as Democrats, against two Republicans, one independent, and one self-proclaimed communist.) Among serious Democratic contenders, however, O'Daniel quickly became one of only four—the other three being Martin Dies, Lyndon Johnson, and Texas attorney general Gerald Mann. Mann enjoyed some early attention, thanks to his reputation as a devout Christian and a strong, sincere leader who was unflinchingly loyal to FDR without being too eager to promote all New Deal policies. Dies also drew significant early attention thanks to support from anticommunist voters who disapproved of O'Daniel's celebrity persona. Conservatives were especially supportive of Dies's blistering attacks against organized labor, the CIO, and immigrants. As one San Antonio–area business leader said, "spies" were crossing the Texas-Mexico border in order to "invade" the state with "those classes who are now causing the most murderous, uncivilized killing of innocent women and children." The same man added that the New Deal had been little more than a "series of grants to organized labor" and had opened the door to unwanted labor "radicalism." Much to the White House's dismay, Dies also won support by arguing that the Communist Party was covertly threatening national security through the leadership of New Deal agencies and was, therefore, nothing short of an illegal criminal conspiracy.[61]

Nevertheless, within weeks of Sheppard's death, it was clear that the race would come down to O'Daniel and Johnson. This was particularly

SUPPORT ROOSEVELT AND JOHNSON

An able team; help your country, yourself and your good friend ELECT LYNDON JOHNSON U.S. SENATOR.

Lyndon Johnson and Roosevelt

LBJ campaign postcard, 1941 (museum image). Courtesy of Lyndon B. Johnson Presidential Library & Museum.

evident after FDR invited Johnson to declare his candidacy at the White House on April 22 before a gathering of the national press. FDR described Johnson as an "old, old friend"—much to the amusement of the White House press corps. Without using the specific words, he then proceeded to offer Johnson a glowing endorsement for the Senate, all the while saying that it was inappropriate for him to interfere in state political contests between Democrats.[62]

Four years into his career in Congress, Johnson was widely regarded as one of Roosevelt's most loyal and ideologically compatible allies, and certainly "his man" in Texas. The White House did not want to replace Sheppard, a loyal New Dealer, with Dies, O'Daniel, or any conservative likely to oppose FDR on the New Deal, not to mention foreign affairs. So close was LBJ to FDR in 1941 that the *Dallas Morning News* reported on Johnson's campaign announcement by saying that FDR had "picked" Johnson himself. Other Texas newspapers, many of which were far more loyal to FDR than the *Dallas Morning News*, quickly endorsed LBJ's candidacy as "right for Texas," emphasizing Johnson's "experience, his youth, his energy, his proven ability, and his 'entrée' to New Deal councils." John Connally's courtship of national newspaper mag-

LBJ campaign material, 1941 (museum image). Courtesy of Lyndon B. Johnson Presidential Library & Museum.

nate Charles Marsh was especially important to the Johnson campaign, which focused most of its efforts on Houston and small towns. The *Waco News-Tribune, San Marcos Record,* and *Abilene Reporter-News* each endorsed Johnson, as did papers in Corpus Christi and San Antonio. All praised LBJ as a loyal "patriot" and future "general" who would champion Texas interests from his seat in the United States Senate.[63]

With FDR's support, Johnson's approach to the 1941 Senate race was relatively simple. Paying virtually no public attention to his opponents, Johnson cast himself as a thoroughgoing party loyalist who would bridge gaps with the Texas establishment and heal the wounds that remained from 1940, thus reuniting Democrats under a bi-ideological, but unwaveringly pro-Roosevelt, banner. Employing slogans like "Roosevelt and Unity" and "He Gets the Job Done," LBJ marketed himself as competent, energetic, and loyal, and as someone with the president's ear. He unapologetically credited the New Deal for strengthening the state's economy and vowed to continue Sheppard's legacy by supporting progressive legislation and a well-organized, optimistic future for all Texans.[64]

"My intimate associations with our great Chief Executive have been most helpful," LBJ wrote in one widely distributed form letter to constituents. "It has been my happy privilege to be one of the men who has been steadfast in his support of the President. When I was elected to Congress it was on the promise that I would give him my loyal and continued support. I am vain enough to say that I have kept the faith and my

Lyndon B. Johnson during 1941 US Senate campaign, with Mrs. Mattie Malone (age seventy-seven), May 29, 1941. Courtesy of the *Austin American-Statesman*.

record along these lines in unquestioned." In other letters, and in most of his speeches, Johnson promoted himself as Sheppard's heir, reverently recalling the recently deceased senator's support for the New Deal: "Sheppard gave unqualified support to the President," Johnson would say, adding that he too had "never wavered in [his] fidelity." Johnson exhorted Texans to "Keep in Washington a person who can and will take up your personal problems with President Roosevelt and get results."[65]

It is possible that Johnson's 1941 Senate campaign is the clearest, best example of a candidate attempting to capitalize on Roosevelt's popularity in Texas. Photos of Roosevelt peppered Johnson's campaign literature, and references to FDR and the New Deal were ubiquitous throughout the campaign. Bumper stickers were widely distributed, and campaign flyers bore headlines like "Friends of Roosevelt" and used images of the president to draw crowds for LBJ rallies. One widely distributed postcard included a captioned FDR quote, saying of Johnson: "He is my very old and close friend." Another, similar postcard—as if to preempt charges of photographic manipulation—added the description: "Actual picture of Roosevelt shaking hands with his 'old and close friend' Lyndon Johnson, the candidate Roosevelt wants to pick up where Morris Sheppard left off."[66]

Johnson's strategy was so blatant that many of his opponents, particularly Mann and liberals like him, argued that Johnson had no ideas of his own. FDR's endorsement overshadowed such concerns. Johnson's first campaign rally in Texas came on May 3 in San Marcos, just south of Austin, where he had attended college. Johnson opened by focusing on Roosevelt's leadership on the world stage, the dangers of onrushing war in other parts of the globe, and the potential perils of less than full support for the commander in chief. He also proposed full parity pricing for all farm products, expansion of the national Social Security system, the promotion of "industrial hygiene" for corporations, and the efficient conservation of natural resources, including oil. Johnson also touted the benefits of strong state leadership for the oil industry writ large, the expansion of federally funded maternity leave and childcare options for women, and the equal "encouragement of all creeds." As part of that discussion, Johnson also frequently dropped FDR's name, mentioning the president as his "friend" while also drawing on his experience in the NYA and REA.[67]

In the following weeks, Johnson ran a campaign dedicated almost solely to the Roosevelt agenda. He cited a litany of New Deal initiatives designed to support Texas farmers and released a telegram from FDR in which the president confirmed his support for a Johnson proposal to provide farmers with full parity pricing by 1942. He also frequently referred to farmers as the nation's "real first line of defense" while proclaiming that FDR had "done more in solving world problems, especially those that effect [sic] the agricultural industry, than any man who has served as Chief Executive of the nation." Johnson clearly hoped to undercut O'Daniel's popularity among rural voters. To that end, Johnson

Rally opening Lyndon B. Johnson's 1941 US Senate campaign in San Marcos, Texas, May 3, 1941. Courtesy of the *Austin American-Statesman*.

also benefited from allies, Alvin Wirtz and Roy Miller in particular, who privately lobbied state legislators to stay in session as long as possible in order to prevent O'Daniel from campaigning at all. Miller's support was particularly important in this regard, not simply because it came with substantial amounts of money, but because it helped unite anti-Roosevelt figures behind a pro-Roosevelt candidate on the simple hopes of regaining entrée to the White House through Johnson, with the ultimate hope of preserving the unregulated flow of Texas oil and the money that resulted.[68]

Johnson also cast dire warnings about international dangers and domestic threats. While framing himself as a friend of the New Deal, he tugged on Texans' patriotic heartstrings, foreshadowing themes of duty and sacrifice, a bold strategy given the persistence of isolationist sentiment in the nation at that time.[69] "When I am elected to the United States Senate," Johnson said in one letter, "I will be in a more strategic position to be of service to you in your efforts for national defense and in many other ways." Not content to leave this as clear evidence of his loyalty, Johnson doubled down by adding: "I am obsessed with the sentiment 'Roosevelt and Unity and National Defense' and I am dedicating my life to rendering any possible assistance that I can give in this connection." "We are in a national emergency," Johnson warned in another letter. "When I opened my campaign for the United States Senate I said I was all out for President Roosevelt and his foreign policy. No other candidate can say that. Now, more than ever, we realize the absolute necessity of unity. Will you help me to help Roosevelt?"[70]

Campaign ads called Johnson a "Champion Rough-Rider in Congress for President Roosevelt's Foreign Policy" and a "Champion of all-out defense of America, now, wherever necessary."[71] On another occasion, Johnson passionately urged vigilance against "fifth columnists, foreign agents, communists, fascists, proponents of every ism but Americanism," and Republicans in Congress like "Taft and Vandenberg" who insisted on neutrality and isolation in the midst of world war:

> The question you must answer is: What kind of man do you want to take up Morris Sheppard's work? Texans must determine whether their new voice will . . . ring out with Morris Sheppard's in support of Roosevelt, against appeasement, and in defiance of the dictators and everything for which they stand. Texas has lost its pilot. Why not sign up the co-pilot, who served a four-year apprenticeship in defense with Morris Sheppard. . . . Like Winston Churchill, it may be mine to say to you: I bring you blood and sweat and tears. But if that dark day comes, I'll mingle my blood and my sweat and my tears with you to get this staggering job we all have on our hands done. We must win. With Roosevelt and Unity we can win. With our sacrifices, our hard work, our loyal spirit, we will win. All for one and one for all. Let's go down the line from this minute out.[72]

Johnson's audiences were well aware that O'Daniel was an isolationist, just as the Republicans LBJ cited during his campaign were. O'Daniel's isolationism had not been an issue during his gubernatorial reelection bid in 1940. In fact, it had given him a slight boost in most of the German counties across the state. At the same time, Johnson undoubtedly incorporated anticommunism into his interventionist messages in order to characterize himself as tough on communism, like his opponent and Dies, and yet tougher on Hitler, fascism, and all other foreign enemies of the day.[73]

Johnson's 1941 campaign was also exceptionally well organized and modern. Creating local rallies out of statewide radio broadcasts, the campaign organized "radio parties" that often included live music, refreshments, barbecue, and a live broadcast of a Johnson speech. The campaign also cultivated relationships with newspaper editors, provided backstage access and "inside" information to reporters, and "leaked" press releases to volunteers ahead of publication as a way to foster a sense of loyalty.[74] Johnson also incorporated direct targeting strategies with women, including ads purchased through the Texas Federation of Women's Clubs. Those ads typically ran in the FWC's newsletter "Federation News" and included a photograph of Johnson in full cowboy gear. One particularly striking ad included a manufactured image of LBJ roping a list of women he planned to employ once elected to the Senate.[75]

Yet for all of Johnson's efforts to establish himself as the clear front-runner, O'Daniel—whose campaign was less organized and less active—remained a formidable candidate. O'Daniel's chief strategy was to depict Johnson as little more than an FDR puppet whose friendship with the president was overstated. He also argued that his experience as governor was more valuable than Johnson's experience in Congress. Stylistically, O'Daniel shaped an agenda designed to rally discontented conservatives no longer captivated by FDR's charm. On May 25, he delivered a radio address designed to establish his bona fides on international affairs. Acknowledging the danger posed by totalitarian aggression in Europe, O'Daniel insisted that God was calling the nation to a moment of spiritual renewal. A Senator O'Daniel, he argued, would be an asset to American Christians in the face of such global unrest.[76]

Above all other considerations, however, O'Daniel marketed himself as an antiunion, probusiness deficit hawk. He told campaign audiences that he would propose a constitutional amendment to forbid deficit spending entirely, adding that he was even willing to raise taxes in order to balance the federal budget, an indication that, among conservatives, budget deficits were less popular than high taxes. O'Daniel also continued to attack Roosevelt—and LBJ by association—as far too sympathetic to labor. He compared communists in the CIO to Nazis marching across Europe and warned against all forms of anti-Christian subversion, which in his mind included organized labor strikes. By early June it was clear not only that the race would come down to Johnson and O'Daniel but that the contest reflected the liberal-conservative split in the Texas Democratic Party as clearly as any race in recent memory.[77]

Martin Dies Jr. speaking in Wooldridge Square Park, Austin, Texas, May 28, 1941. Courtesy of Austin History Center, Austin Public Library.

O'Daniel got a boost on June 5 when the *Houston Post* ran a story quoting anonymous sources suggesting that Roosevelt's support for Johnson was less sincere than publicly stated. According to the story, Roosevelt's opinion of the Texas Senate race was far more ambiguous than the Johnson campaign was saying, adding that the much-bally-hooed friendship between the two liberals was mostly one-sided and aspirational. The story clearly intended to convey the impression that Johnson was overstating his friendship with the president and that he was, in fact, out of his league in running for the Senate.[78] In a rushed response, the Johnson campaign tried to discredit the *Houston Post* by leaking word that Roosevelt was so deeply committed to LBJ's candidacy that he had personally called Mann and O'Daniel, pleading with both men to withdraw from the race and support Johnson. The strategy worked when several Texas outlets ran the story, prompting White House press secretary Stephen Early to respond that he could "neither confirm nor deny" the rumors, tacitly affirming its core truth.[79] All of this prompted LBJ-friendly newspapers to expedite their own endorsements. This included Amon Carter's *Fort Worth Star-Telegram*, which endorsed Johnson on June 15 because, it said, of Johnson's friendship with Roosevelt and his strong accord with the New Deal. Carter, whose own loyalty to FDR had seen plenty of ups and downs throughout the years, was so pleased with the editorial that he personally sent Roosevelt a clipping, along with assurances that Texas would remain solidly in the president's corner—meaning Johnson's corner—come June 28.[80]

The story of Roosevelt's intervention was fading when, a week later, O'Daniel—whose public tone toward FDR shifted in the final weeks from decidedly oppositional to reluctantly supportive—went public with a new and widely panned proposal to create an autonomous Texas army and navy as part of an overall enhancement to state-organized border security. He specifically cited the need to protect Texans against foreign invasions through Mexico. In making this proposal, O'Daniel inspired headlines about national defense that Roosevelt felt obliged to answer. Roosevelt privately denounced the plan as "preposterous" before telling reporters that he would "take the plan under advisement." Reporters misconstrued the comment, thinking it more favorable than it was, prompting the White House to leak Roosevelt's actual response— "preposterous"—in time for morning headlines on Election Day. At the same time, the White House leaked yet another telegram from Roosevelt to Johnson reiterating the president's absolute support.[81]

Johnson ended his campaign—the most expensive in Texas history to that point—on the night of June 27 with a radio address that again emphasized the critical value that his relationship with FDR would bring Texans:

> What every one of you has been saying is: Yes, Mr. President, we know you're right. Your foreign policy is right. Your heart and mind and strength are with us in everything. And we are with you. So we're sending Lyndon Johnson. He has worked with you. You know him as an old and dependable friend. He can work with our Congress and the cabinet and all the federal government, for us and for all. He is a trained, experienced foot-soldier in our defense program. We have no other choice.[82]

The next day voters went to the polls. In one of the most controversial elections in American history, Pappy O'Daniel defeated Lyndon Johnson by a scant 1,300 votes, or less than one-quarter of one percent of the total. The final tally reflected the nip-and-tuck nature of the campaign. O'Daniel won 175,590 votes to Johnson's 174,279. Mann, the other pro-FDR candidate, who refused to back out of the race and endorse his fellow liberal, finished third with 140,807 votes. The other viable conservative, Martin Dies, finished fourth, with 80,551. Assuming that most of Mann's voters would have landed in Johnson's camp had Mann withdrawn, the pro-FDR vote in Texas was a clear majority. Mann, however, took a different tack in the final week of the campaign. Rather than attack O'Daniel or Dies, Mann angrily denounced LBJ's "obvious attempts to take advantage of our love and affection for Franklin D. Roosevelt."[83]

Mann's last-minute effort to win over LBJ voters may have cost Johnson the election. Early returns had shown LBJ to be the winner. But as the days went on, O'Daniel's vote total increased enough—just barely enough—to win the election. Historians have effectively chronicled the allegations of voter fraud in this race. Evidence seems clear that the O'Daniel camp stole the election thanks in part to well-placed friends, but thanks even more to well-placed foes whose efforts to rig precinct returns in East Texas were motivated not by a desire to get O'Daniel to Washington but simply to get him out of Austin. Seven years later, in 1948, Johnson applied the hard lessons of his 1941 loss by stealing the same Senate seat in a race against then-governor Coke Stevenson.[84]

All controversies notwithstanding, some pundits believed O'Daniel's win had more to do with Roosevelt than with voting irregularities. According to that argument, anti-LBJ Texans resented the level of FDR's intrusion into state affairs and voted for O'Daniel out of spite. According to one critic, the president used "command, money, threat, coercion, and power" to try force people to elect Johnson. Texans, he argued, would not submit to that kind of pressure. Others argued that Roosevelt's intrusion had cost Gerald Mann—who finished third in the race, some 35,000 votes shy of O'Daniel—the support of moderates and liberals. Whether or not Roosevelt's decision to involve himself in the race worked in Johnson's favor or O'Daniel's likely depends on the voter.[85] Nevertheless, after the special election, O'Daniel's opponents refused to support their new senator, complaining that Pappy was not the kind of "statesman" the country needed, particularly given the degenerating condition of world affairs. O'Daniel was "naïve," some said, in boiling all of the world's problems down to one: collective "falling away" from religion. "It now appears to be a sad fact that we in Texas have a man who thinks mostly of advertising himself, and who cares little and knows less about the serious things confronting us," wrote one citizen in a letter to the editor published by the *Dallas Morning News*. "He deceived us, making us think that he was a good boy talking about the Sabbath, Mother's

Day, and the Bible. Now we know him for what he is, a pranking, hillbilly show-off, all at the expense of the taxpayer."[86]

Pappy O'Daniel did not waste much time grabbing headlines. Just weeks after his victory in the special election, he complained to a statewide radio audience that FDR had not yet invited him to the White House for conference, as was often customary for newly elected members of the upper chamber. According to O'Daniel, the president was trying to "avoid" the meeting on the excuse that he was "going fishing." As it turned out, FDR was not "fishing" per se, but rather meeting with Winston Churchill in the middle of the Atlantic Ocean—negotiating the Atlantic Charter, as it was soon known. In response, Texas Democratic Party chairman E. B. Germany censored O'Daniel's ridiculous comments from published transcripts of the speech, a controversial move that Germany justified by saying O'Daniel "was only jesting." Yet, during the same speech, O'Daniel also went out of his way to promise Texans that he would oppose FDR whenever needed. He also criticized his pro–New Deal colleagues as "rubber stamps," mocked Congress as "delicate," and contrasted himself to the entire establishment, saying he was "his own man"—muscular, Christian anticommunism at its finest.[87]

Three days later, upon returning from his "fishing trip," FDR did in fact invite O'Daniel to the White House. The conversation focused on O'Daniel's plan to introduce an antistrike law to the Senate. Roosevelt expressed concern that the bill would significantly reduce labor rights. Nevertheless, after the meeting O'Daniel told reporters he had convinced Roosevelt of the bill's merits. He had not, and the bill quickly went down to an overwhelming defeat. Still, for the time being, O'Daniel found it politically useful to balance his outspoken independence with at least some evidence that he was capable of working with the commander in chief, whom he described to reporters after the meeting as "confident" and "in command." O'Daniel also tried to boost his own stature by telling reporters that FDR had given him a private, confidential briefing on foreign relations and the war situation overseas, though Roosevelt's comments on the subject had been little more than cursory, essentially repeating information he had already given to reporters earlier in the day.[88]

Several weeks later, O'Daniel resumed his attacks on the president, telling a radio audience in October that the devolving state of world affairs had little to do with realities on the ground and was, instead, a result of spiritual failings in Washington, which were the result of a failure of moral leadership. "This world upheaval is, without dispute, caused by the vast majority of the people who dwell in the United States getting too far away from the true practice of religious principles." Many of O'Daniel's listeners agreed, and they continued to express their misgivings over the potentiality of American involvement, flooding congressional offices with letters of opposition to the repeal or reform of any existing law, the adjustment of which would expand the president's authority to deploy American forces into any combat zone.[89]

And then everything changed on December 7, 1941, when Japan launched a surprise attack on US naval forces stationed at Pearl Harbor in Hawaii. FDR asked Congress for a declaration of war the next day, as Texans grappled with the harsh realities of sending their fathers, husbands, sons, and brothers into combat half a world away. Texans also quickly recognized the possibility that the president some had opposed when he ran for a third term might very well run for a fourth.

6 | "A Closer Connection with Our Federal Government"

By the time Franklin Roosevelt began his third term, some might have struggled to recall a time when the grandfatherly patrician of Hyde Park was not guiding the nation through some sort of crisis. Among establishment politicos in Texas, FDR's popularity had diminished since his last reelection. Expressed fears of "creeping socialism" and "tyranny" had grown louder during those years, factional divides wider. For some, Roosevelt's third term smacked of American totalitarianism akin to what had developed in antagonistic regimes overseas. For many others, however, Roosevelt personified America at its best: rational, optimistic, and actively engaged. In reflecting these qualities, the president defined modern liberalism at *its* best. Few speeches captured FDR's vision for modern liberalism more effectively than his 1941 State of the Union address. Distilling Rooseveltian liberalism into "four freedoms"—freedom of speech, freedom of worship, freedom from fear, and freedom from want—the president laid a foundation upon which he and others would eventually explain the significance of US involvement in both World War II and the coming Cold War.[1]

On a more practical level, World War II forced FDR to shift his attention from domestic to foreign affairs. In doing so, the bread-and-butter connections he had forged in states like Texas throughout the previous decade weakened, as the pragmatic bootstrap liberalism of the New Deal began to appear more ideological and global. And yet, as different as the demands of his office were by 1942, his approach—and the approach of many loyal New Dealers in Texas—remained remarkably consistent with the one he introduced to Washington in 1933, at the height of the Great Depression. In his first inaugural address, Roosevelt asked for "broad Executive power to wage a war against the [economic] emergency, as great as the power that would be given [to him] if we were in fact invaded by a foreign foe." Less than a decade later, he adapted that same message to the international emergency. In doing so, the president promoted a vision for national sacrifice and global engagement framed around a combination of New Deal liberalism and Wilsonian internationalism, much of which had roots in the transatlantic progressivism born from sociopolitical reactions to industrial excesses during the late nineteenth and early twentieth centuries. As they had been faithfully doing for years, FDR's allies promoted the same basic message. Most Texas voters continued to respond positively, even as the force of anti-FDR conservatism grew concurrently stronger and more successful.[2]

From the standpoint of practical governance, World War II became, in some ways, an even bigger obstacle to conservatives' resistance to big government than the New Deal had been. Howls of slippery slopes resonated, but New Dealers and moderate Democratic loyalists still won more battles than they lost, usually by sounding the voice of simple, necessary, pragmatic sacrifice, with the goal of winning the war as quickly as possible, thereby saving as many lives as possible. Conservatives warned against regulations and dependence, government-based entitlements and welfare; liberals rejected those fears as shortsighted, insisting that winning the war required unprecedented mobilization, and that the only sure way to preserve freedom and, ultimately, the American Dream itself was to win the war. In the decades to come, ideological factionalism paid significant dividends for the Texas right. Even between 1942 and 1945, the state's conservative establishment regained some of the ground it lost during the 1930s. Some once-loyal New Dealers even abandoned FDR entirely, taking major steps toward the Republican Party in the process. However, as the lives of roughly sixteen million sons, husbands, brothers, and fathers seemed threatened, most Texas voters remained deferential to the longest-serving commander in chief in American history and to the New Deal Democrats who stood by his side.

"Skunks, Buzzards, Wolves, Thugs, Termites, Pirates, and Racketeers"

The debate over neutrality ended when Japan attacked Pearl Harbor, Hawaii, on December 7, 1941. For years FDR had been warning Americans that the evolving global conflict—particularly but not exclusively the one in Europe—threatened not just US interests, but "Christian civilization" itself. While promising not to send "boys" to their death in a needless war, Roosevelt also emphasized the importance of preparedness. This, coupled with his call to international vigilance, prompted a counterwave of isolationism, perhaps most visible in the "America First" movements that, in the spirit of preserving neutrality, often dismissed FDR's warnings about the dangers posed by totalitarian regimes in Germany and Japan. But after December 7, the calculus changed. The question was no longer whether Americans should fight, but how they should do it. The United States was at war.[3]

In this new wartime context, allegations of un-Americanism grew as potent as ever. During the next few years, a political culture that questioned one's patriotism along ideological lines festered in Texas, reducing complicated policy questions into a polarized dichotomy that forced political candidates to choose between pro- and antigovernment camps. Few groups felt more pressure to prove their patriotic Americanness than labor organizers. The argument that labor unions bred corruption and interrupted free enterprise had been around for decades, particularly in states like Texas. After Pearl Harbor, however, conservatives increasingly argued that organized labor threatened the war effort and that, specifically, labor strikes put American lives at risk by interrupting wartime production. Business leaders and their elected allies appropriated the values of service, sacrifice, and patriotism to their own cause. Two months after Pearl Harbor, Congress launched an investigation into the activities of organized labor in relation to the awarding of federal defense contracts. Conservatives used the investigation to conflate "racketeering" and government "corruption," rising taxes, and what they argued was the New Deal's legacy of "unchecked" bureaucratic growth. As union leaders sought protection by reaffirming their loyalty to Roosevelt, conservatives doubled down on their allegation that liberals' coziness with the left was threatening national security.[4]

Texas conservatives were soon on the front lines of this fight against organized labor, with Pappy O'Daniel among those leading the charge in the US Senate, while Martin Dies did so from the House. Over the next few years, few Texans would be more overtly anti-Roosevelt or anti-labor than O'Daniel and Dies, both of whom alleged that "racketeers" in the CIO were attempting to foment radicalism and revolution by manipulating the White House, an act they viewed as not simply un-American but illegal. O'Daniel, Dies, and others argued that socialist radicals in Washington were "taking advantage" of the widespread "disorder" in the hopes of maximizing the federal government's interference with the private sector. The rapidly growing wartime economy—fueled in part by defense contracts for expanding industries such as steel, rubber, aviation, and of course oil and petroleum—amplified the perceived danger, particularly in Texas. No other state except California benefited more from these growing industries and the wartime contracts that enabled them than did Texas, making the debate over organized labor's role in shaping local economies all the more urgent.[5]

Right-wing anticommunists like O'Daniel and Dies may have been the state's most vocal antiunion voices, but they did not hold a monopoly on the issue. For instance, George Mahon spent more time discussing the labor issue in the months after Pearl Harbor than at any other point in his career. Mahon refused to blame Roosevelt for labor stoppages, telling constituents that he and the president still shared a commitment to the common man. However, in a series of editorials published across his West Texas district during the first three months of 1942, Mahon made it clear that his top priority on behalf of the war effort was the fight against "racketeering in defense industries." Like others, he saved his harshest attacks for the CIO and its former president, John L. Lewis, whom he accused of "treason." Mahon's editorials resonated with voters in his district. A group of citizens in Terry County responded to Mahon's editorials by sending a petition directly to FDR demanding immediate action against anyone caught jeopardizing national security by "ringleading" strikes. When the president failed to respond, one of the citizens told the local newspaper that FDR was "right with a bunch of Reds."[6]

As Texans paid more attention to organized labor and the problem of union-led strikes, they also paid more attention to rising taxes, particularly in view of the perception that the federal government was using tax dollars to support union radicalism. "Certainly every true American will not object to a proportionate increase in taxes if he knows the money is going to be spent in a sensible and business-like manner to WIN THIS WAR," one man told Mahon. "But, sooner or later, the average voter is going to resent every mention of new taxes if the money is spent on boondoggling, crack-pot ideas, and for the interests of a special group." Another of Mahon's constituents said he was willing to "pay his fair share" of taxes for the war effort, but lamented that "bureaucracy" was fast replacing "democracy" as the nation's overarching organizational principle.[7]

Elsewhere in Texas, New Deal loyalists insisted on backing Roosevelt, even if that meant supporting both organized labor and higher taxes.[8]

"Labor should not be forced to protect itself by striking or demanding a 40-hour week or time and a half overtime," Lyndon Johnson said at one point during the investigation that spring. "It is a duty and responsibility of the Government to see that an equalization is brought about between Capital and Labor which is just and fair." Acknowledging the "fragility" of the war effort at that time, Johnson wanted more federal protections for labor, not fewer. At the same time, he argued that forward-thinking politicians like himself should be working on a compromise to solve the matter and preserve national security by eliminating unions' need to strike in the first place. "In no event should the Government tolerate the actions of any individual or group of individuals which directly or indirectly hinders the progress of the war effort," Johnson told Sam Rayburn privately. "During the unlimited national emergency and state of war, there are no individual 'rights' or 'privileges' provided for or guaranteed by the Common Law or the Constitution when the exercise of those 'rights' and 'privileges' would be a detriment to the national welfare."[9]

Wright Patman also supported the president's general thinking on labor, saying publicly that he was entirely committed to protecting "the working man," even during a time of war. Beyond supporting FDR and collective bargaining rights, Patman was vocal on consumer advocacy issues, and also supported the creation of a national system of federal credit unions, which he and others believed would help farmers and laborers by creating a competitive alternative to traditional banks.[10] Patman's public support for Roosevelt and labor rights was unwavering, but privately he expressed concerns over how the politics of labor activism might shape the 1942 midterms. On one occasion, Patman asked FDR to visit his home district to talk about the issue, suggesting that if anyone could quell the people's anxieties, it was Roosevelt. Texas business leaders feared the "intolerable boss dictatorship of politically organized unions" and the "bureaucratic control" of their industries by the federal government, Patman told FDR. These concerns posed a significant threat to liberal Democrats in Texas, Patman said, adding that Roosevelt's standing in the state was still strong enough that a personal appearance to discuss the situation would go a long way toward resolving the concerns once and for all.[11]

Patman's assessment of the political situation in his First District was accurate. Unfortunately for Patman, however, Roosevelt had bigger fish to fry than the antiliberal ones in East Texas. Meanwhile, a growing number Texas conservatives attached themselves to the fight against organized labor, painting that fight as a battle to protect national security against un-American radicalism. Ordinary workers found themselves caught in the middle, subjugated to the whims of union bosses on one side, reviled by private-sector management on the other. The debate grew still hotter as women and minorities made up an increasingly large percentage of the wartime workforce, hired into defense-manufacturing jobs vacated by white men moving into the armed services. Meanwhile, Roosevelt's wartime efforts to normalize the Soviet Union as an ally in the fight against Nazi fascism also inflamed conservatives like O'Daniel and Dies, who were inclined to see liberalism as socialism's naïve cousin and, therefore, communism's gateway into the hearts and minds of vulnerable Americans.[12]

It was within this context during the spring and summer of 1942 that Texas Democrats fought each other in political campaigns across the state, with questions of labor, patriotism, and wartime regulations dominating the conversation in almost every case. The year's highest-profile contest was O'Daniel's campaign for a full term to the United States Senate. In the months following his special election victory against Lyndon Johnson in 1941, O'Daniel solidified his reputation as an anticommunist conservative, frequently voting with Republicans as he tried to position himself as a national authority on the "dangers of big government." He also often referred to himself as a "victim" of "communists in the press" whose sole objective was to "destroy" his political career. He asked Texans to pray for his victory against such enemies and for a national "spiritual healing." He insisted that the most pressing threat to the United States was not enemies abroad, but "labor racketeers" and "Communistic labor influencers" conspiring against him. Editorialists and cartoonists mocked O'Daniel's assessment of the global "communist threat," in one case depicting him as a hysterically laughing guitarist, oblivious to the graves of Texas soldiers dying in combat. Still, as the Democratic primary approached, O'Daniel was clearly the state's most vocal and well-known anticommunist. A divisive character who inspired passionate feelings on both sides, O'Daniel had supporters as loyal in 1942 as at any point in his four years on the political stage.[13]

Conversely, liberals struggled to coalesce behind any single candidate. Given his controversial loss a year earlier, many assumed Lyndon Johnson would make another run. Johnson considered it, but the outbreak of war changed his mind. A lieutenant commander in the US Naval Reserve, Johnson was called into active duty three days after Pearl

Harbor. By the spring, he was in the Pacific under the command of General Douglas MacArthur, without a clear understanding of how soon he would be able to return to Texas. Johnson spent much of his time in the South Pacific with John Connally, who was also on a naval deployment in that theater. The two spent significant time discussing politics on the home front, though Johnson was briefly engaged in combat in New Guinea, an experience for which MacArthur awarded him what was later described as the "most talked-about and least deserved medal in U.S. military history."[14]

LBJ was released from active duty on July 16, shortly after Roosevelt signed a law requiring elected officials on deployment to either resign their office or return to the States. His return to Texas preserved his seat in Congress but came too late for a Senate bid in the state Democratic primary, scheduled for July 25. Instead, Johnson used the opportunity to solidify his relationship with the White House, corresponding with the president and his advisors about the political landscape in Texas. Johnson joined Wright Patman in telling FDR that Texans would respond well to a visit and joined Harold Ickes in pressuring the president to take a stronger stand on primaries across the state. Initially, Roosevelt disagreed, insisting that direct involvement in state-level Democratic politics was "out of bounds" in a wartime environment. FDR was also sensitive to allegations that he had been too involved in the O'Daniel-Johnson fight a year earlier. Ickes, however, warned Roosevelt that states like Texas were too critical to the administration's ongoing agenda to ignore and that the president needed allies from the Lone Star State to advance his policies on both the home and battle fronts. Roosevelt slowly acquiesced to such urgings, using Ickes, Johnson, and Sam Rayburn as surrogates for greater involvement.[15]

While the White House had interest in congressional elections across the state, no Texas race commanded Roosevelt's attention more than O'Daniel's. New Dealers agreed that defeating O'Daniel was a top priority, but with Johnson's candidacy off the table, they struggled to identify a viable challenger. Eventually, they landed on former governor Jimmie Allred. Roosevelt quietly broached the subject with Allred that February, after determining that Johnson was not an option. The president assured Allred that his New Deal bona fides were beyond question and that he would have his support if he chose to run. Not everyone in the anti-O'Daniel camp was as excited about Allred's candidacy. Some feared that Allred was too widely perceived as being in FDR's back pocket. Sensing vulnerability, the O'Daniel campaign spread rumors that FDR had bribed Allred into running by offering the former governor a federal judgeship as potential consolation prize. The rumors paid political dividends, in addition to being true.[16]

Other than Allred, only Dan Moody managed inroads strong enough to disrupt what would eventually become a two-horse race. Moody tried to angle his insurgent candidacy toward anti-Pappy moderates he hoped were ready to pull back from the New Deal but not ready to abandon the White House completely, particularly in the middle of a war. As the primary approached, most Texas newspapers made it clear that they were against O'Daniel, but endorsements typically varied between Allred and Moody. In response to the unfavorable press coverage of his campaign, O'Daniel alleged—as historian George Green has described it—a "vast conspiracy among Moody, Allred, the professional politicians, the politically controlled newspapers, and, of course, the 'Communistic labor leader racketeers.'" Green once called O'Daniel's allegation against the Texas press the "dirtiest campaign misrepresentation in Texas history," while J. Frank Dobie soon noted that the vastness of O'Daniel's allegation seemed odd given that, in 1940, the Communist Party had polled a scant 260 votes out of more than one million cast.[17]

O'Daniel won 475,541 votes on Election Day—not a majority, but clearly more than Allred's 317,501 votes or Moody's 178,471. Analysts attributed O'Daniel's large margin to his strength with older voters, while younger voters simply failed to turn out. Still, as historian Seth Shepard McKay observed, O'Daniel's success in 1942 was as much a reflection of the anticommunist chords he struck by using words like "regimentation," "bureaucracy," and "interference" as it was a reflection of anything else. The drama surrounding perceived labor unrest, as well as the accusations of "communist conspiracy," also catalyzed voters on the right. Some also admitted voting for O'Daniel simply because they wanted someone to resist the New Deal establishment and did not believe that Allred or Moody could or would do that.[18] Still, without a majority, O'Daniel still faced an August 22 runoff with Allred. With Moody out of the picture, newspapers overwhelmingly endorsed Allred, and many predicted his victory. Allred capitalized on a solid relationship with reporters across the state, granting as many interviews as he could, in the process reestablishing a reputation as helpful and transparent.[19] Unfortunately for Allred, press coverage took an unintended turn for the worse when the very conservative *Houston Post* ran a detailed interview with Allred, in which the New Deal loyalist unwisely shifted his attacks from O'Daniel to O'Daniel's supporters:

> I do not say that everyone who votes for my opponent is a Republican, but I do say that every Republican who enters the Democratic primary will vote against me. I don't say that everyone who votes for my opponent is a Roosevelt hater, but I do say that everyone who hates Roosevelt first and Hitler second will vote against Jimmie Allred. I don't say that everyone who votes for my opponent is a Nazi sympathizer, but I do say that every Nazi sympathizer in Texas will vote against Jimmie Allred.[20]

A liberal Texas Democrat attempting to play the loyalty card by comparing his conservative opponent to a Republican was far from unusual. Comparing one's opponent to a Nazi, or even coming close to that, was something far different. Allred had been too casual with his words, and the *Houston Post*'s reporting on the matter opened the door for O'Daniel to once again charge the Texas press as complicit in the "New Deal's attacks" on Texas free enterprise, reviving earlier allegations of a "conspiracy" within the press. Recognizing the salience of such attacks, O'Daniel spent more time in the final days of the campaign attacking journalists than he spent attacking Allred. At one event he called Texas newspaper reporters "skunks, buzzards, wolves, thugs, termites, pirates, and racketeers." So effective were O'Daniel's assaults on the press that the Democratic National Committee (DNC) upped its surveillance of the journalistic landscape in Texas, curious to see if O'Daniel's allegations had any merit, while also wondering if the press coverage he was receiving had more to do with conservative news outlets than it did with liberal ones. Over the course of the next year, the DNC began to warn Texas Democrats about granting interviews to certain newspapers in Texas, particularly the *Houston Post*, which it described as a "reactionary" weapon of anticommunist radicals like Oveta Culp Hobby, the *Post*'s editor and president, who it said was obsessed with undermining White House initiatives as aggressively as possible. Somewhat on cue, a *Post* editorial shortly thereafter encouraged conservative Democrats to make a permanent defection to the GOP.[21]

In the end, O'Daniel successfully turned the press's perceived bias into the most impactful issue of the race. The backlash against Allred for his use of the word "Nazi" to describe O'Daniel voters pushed the New Dealer into a defensive position and distracted voters from O'Daniel's own penchant for verbal intemperance. When coupled with the earlier rumors about his "secret" judgeship deal with FDR, the bad press quickly scuttled Allred's momentum. O'Daniel won the runoff with 51 percent of the vote. Postelection analysis from the *Dallas Morning News* suggested that Allred's relationship with FDR had been too cozy for most voters' liking. At the same time, the paper's analysis also suggested—somewhat obviously—that voter behavior was utterly complicated, varied, and unpredictable. In fact, it even noted that an exit poll of rural O'Daniel voters suggested that those backing the conservative incumbent actually believed that stories of O'Daniel's poor relationship with FDR were untrue and that O'Daniel would be an important ally to the president, particularly on the question of helping, not hurting, labor unions. Defining such voters as confused was certainly easier than doing so along liberal or conservative lines.[22]

The only other 1942 race to garner as much attention as O'Daniel's was Coke Stevenson's bid for a full term as governor. An establishment Democrat, Stevenson entered office far more qualified and prepared to serve than his predecessor. Newspapers reporting on the O'Daniel governorship often described Stevenson as a behind-the-scenes source of stability and competence. "It is not a secret around the Capitol that Stevenson is called into almost daily conference with O'Daniel," the *Dallas Morning News* reported in May 1939. "The recent statesmanlike messages and utterances emanating from the politically inexperienced chief executive had their inception in the advice given by [Stevenson], who is regarded as one of the most astute politicians in Texas. Friends say he is getting in practice and will be ready to occupy the Governor's chair." Stevenson typically promoted himself as a man of "balance." He also identified as a "common old cowboy" from the "hills of West Texas" and as a "self-made man" and supporter of at least some New Deal programs, including Social Security. At campaign rallies, he calmly criticized his opponents as too deeply connected to corporations and said that he personally "hated taxes" but also lamented the often "reasonable necessity" for some tax increases. Unlike O'Daniel, whose political appeal depended on flamboyance, Stevenson struck a more even tone.[23]

Over the next several years, voters straddling the ideological divide responded positively to Stevenson's campaigns. "While I am a native Texan, and certainly a local self-government Democratic," a man from Pampa told Stevenson in 1941, continuing:

I believe Texas has needed for some time past a closer connection with our Federal Government directly from the governor's office. I know you are the very man who can accomplish this happy medium or middle ground of having and keeping close contact for our State with the Federal administration and yet at the same time allowing no man or set of men to dictate from Washington the course that Texas shall take within our own boundaries.[24]

Stevenson—or "Calculating Coke" as some called him—held retrograde opinions on race that were common across the state and South at the time. But he was also a fiscal moderate who compromised with liberals in Austin and Washington. He often connected state business leaders and legislators in productive dialogue and tolerated the New Deal, rarely demonizing it as "un-American" or dangerous as O'Daniel liked to do. He often criticized Washington's handling of various issues but did not go out of his way to identify with the conservative right, at times qualifying his criticism of Washington with praise for Roosevelt's leadership. As governor, Stevenson oversaw dramatic improvements to the state's highway system, increased salaries for public school teachers, approved several expansions at the University of Texas at Austin, and supported farm bills with special attention to soil conservation.[25]

Hal Collins, famous for his anti-FDR speech at the state Democratic convention in Mineral Wells two years earlier, challenged Stevenson in the 1942 primary. This time, however, both candidates emphasized patriotism and support for the war, minimizing criticism of FDR and the New Deal in the process. Collins's primary message to voters was an awkward blend of praise for FDR and moralistic calls to rid the state of vices like alcohol and gambling. He argued that Stevenson was a man of corporations, not the people. The message flopped and Stevenson won the primary, carrying 68.5 percent of the vote to Collins's 28.6. Stevenson then dispatched his Republican opponent, C. K. McDowell, carrying an impressive 96.8 percent of the general election vote.[26]

In reelecting both O'Daniel and Stevenson, Texans chose incumbent stability over change. The same was true at the congressional level, where twenty of the state's twenty-one Democratic incumbents won reelection. Of those, sixteen eventually ran unopposed in the general election. Of the four incumbent Democrats who eventually faced a Republican challenger, only one—Paul Kilday—failed to win at least 97 percent of the vote. (Kilday won reelection out of San Antonio with 82 percent of the

FDR with John N. Garner, Uvalde, Texas, September 27, 1942. Courtesy of
Franklin D. Roosevelt Presidential Library & Museum.

vote, compared to his GOP challenger's 18 percent.) In Dallas, Hatton
Sumners overcame objections to his prewar stand on neutrality, defeating both Bill Bowen and Harry Hines. Bowen contrasted himself to Sumners by saying that he was "for all-out war against the Axis" and for doing
his "utmost to aid President Roosevelt, irrespective of creed, prejudices,
or political viewpoint." Hines pursued a different strategy, alleging that
Sumners had grown disinterested in the job and was no longer capable
of lobbying for defense contracts on Dallas's behalf. Both arguments
resonated with voters, but not nearly enough; Sumners campaigned on
"experience" and "trust." He won easily.[27]

Meanwhile, Roosevelt's only visible foray into state politics that fall
came at the tail end of an inspection tour out West in which he was able
to see, firsthand, the American war machine cranking out the planes,
tanks, and guns he had been calling for since at least 1940 if not earlier. On September 27, Roosevelt's train detoured to Uvalde, where the

FDR with Elliott's family, at Elliott's ranch, near Fort Worth, Texas, September 28, 1942. Courtesy of Franklin D. Roosevelt Presidential Library & Museum.

president—perhaps aware that his standing in Texas was weaker than it had been in previous elections—hoped to bury the hatchet with his former running mate, Jack Garner. It was a wonderful photo opportunity for both men, but especially for Roosevelt, whom Garner at one point patted on the head while saying, "God bless you, Boss."[28]

Whether it was out of loyalty to their party or to their country, most Texas voters chose not to rock many boats in 1942. Incumbent Texas Democrats survived the 1942 midterms relatively unscathed. Nationally, however, Republicans made historic gains, picking up forty-seven seats in the House of Representatives and nine in the Senate. Texas Democrats initially dismissed the Republican gains as little more than a "friendly refresher." However, the conservative backlash against labor activism and perceived "regimentation" and "bureaucracy" did not fade, nationally or in Texas, and became an important weapon in the Republican political arsenal. A few weeks after the midterms that November, a coalition of West Texas farmers made headlines by denouncing federal rationing measures as un-American, objecting specifically to gas rationing mandates they said would "cripple" their ability to produce for their families, let alone the war effort. West Texas was a land of "wide open spaces," one farmer said; either Washington did not know that, or it did not care. How could farmers, especially those living in the "cradle of American agriculture," produce the commodities necessary for the war effort without having full access to fuel and, therefore, the ability to drive from farm to market? One farmer even warned that gas-rationing measures had forced him to question his Democratic loyalties, though he tempered his complaints by expressing appreciation for all the New Deal had done to help him and his family during the previous decade. Still, if Roosevelt wanted to act like a "dictator," perhaps it was time to give the Republican Party a fresh look.[29]

Like labor unrest, rationing mandates inspired backlash across the state and soon became the newest hot issue in the fight against big government and the slippery slope to socialism. In December, Hatton Sumners again won national attention for himself, giving a speech on the House floor in which he decried rationing measures such as those on gasoline as too cumbersome and contrary to the tenets of a "free government." An admirer from Hereford wrote to Sumners: "None of us wants to be disloyal to our President or to our government, but our president is not infallible, and in a time like this it is hard to comply with all the decrees. The taking away of our experienced farm help to the Army and the gas rationing is going to cause the greatest world famine that has ever been recorded."[30]

Pappy O'Daniel called rationing of any kind "a Communistic, totalitarian measure designed to beat the people of the U.S. into submitting to the edicts of an autocratic, bureaucratic dictatorship," adding that the FDR administration had planted "parasitic government snoopers" in every corner of the nation. While O'Daniel's colleagues in the Senate almost invariably distanced themselves from their Texas colleague's excessive extremism, many also recognized that antigovernment animus was, potentially, a strategic pathway to renewed conservative influence in Austin and Washington. An improving wartime economy only made this strategy easier. As the war persisted on two fronts, the economy improved, and as the economy improved, the relevance of New Deal dollars declined. One-time New Deal liberals began to speak more frequently about "wasteful spending." Few Texans batted an eye when the

CCC disbanded in 1942, and fewer complained with the WPA and NYA both ceased to operate in 1943, the same year Roosevelt began telling reporters to stop using the term "New Deal," adding that the wartime economy was in the process of "restoring the country to its own people once again."[31]

Ironically, popular discontent with wartime regulations coincided with an economic boom in Texas rooted in federal defense contracts. In short, war—paid for in federal dollars—was good for the Texas economy. New jobs flooded emerging industrial centers in the Dallas–Fort Worth Metroplex, Houston, San Antonio, and Austin, accelerating the evolution of those cities into metropolises soon identified with the postwar Sunbelt and the "military-industrial complex" of the later Cold War.[32] Few such contracts were as lucrative as the famed "Big Inch" and "Little Inch" pipelines, which connected Texas oil to defense manufacturing operations in Pennsylvania, New Jersey, and, by extension, the world. Jesse Jones and J. R. Parten were among the Texas links in the ever-stronger chain that connected federal outlays to economic diversification across the emerging Sunbelt. Other construction and manufacturing projects proved critical as well, while accelerating the relationship between politics and corporate dollars. With a nod to Jesse Jones, the most important player in that acceleration was Lyndon Johnson, whose relationship with Brown and Root (later a subsidiary of Halliburton) revolutionized the integration of corporate funding and campaign finance. Johnson's financial holdings diversified greatly during the early 1940s. He maintained political fingers in a number of pies, including radio, much to Elliott Roosevelt's chagrin and entrepreneurial detriment. (Elliott had his own hopes of starting a political radio network in Texas and saw Johnson's foray into the industry as a threat.) LBJ's wife "Lady Bird" purchased the couple's first radio station in 1942, KTBC-Austin (later renamed "KLBJ"), at a cost of $17,500. Johnson, meanwhile, brokered his media influence into a network of political partnerships and quid pro quos that have been well documented as among the most extensive in American history. Two decades later, KLBJ was valued at $7 million, with profits of roughly $10,000 per week. That, coupled with his other radio stations and financial ventures, made LBJ one of the richest politicians in the United States.[33]

Wartime patriotism promoted an atmosphere of unity through much of 1943. However, as the calendar turned to another election year, anti-government factionalism grew heated again, particularly as questions over whether FDR would run for a fourth term grew more relevant. In January, national organizations such as the Committee for Constitutional Government (CCG), which had been leading anti-FDR efforts since 1937, began massive fundraising efforts aimed at unseating the president and his supporters, including many in Texas. Using the term "New Deal Nazis," CCG raised roughly $250,000 in January and February 1944, half of that amount coming from conservatives in the Texas oil industry. While a DNC poll conducted in February 1944 showed that 65 percent of Texan Democrats planned to support a fourth term for FDR, 10 percent were already planning to bolt for the presumptive Republican nominee, Thomas Dewey of New York, while the remaining 25 percent were torn.[34]

A few weeks later, Pappy O'Daniel launched what would essentially be the opening salvo in what would be a quasi–civil war within the Texas Democratic Party. On March 23, 1944, O'Daniel delivered one of the most famous speeches of his career, ripping FDR for befriending "radical foreign elements" and wondering aloud whether Texas conservatives should rethink their Democratic loyalties altogether. O'Daniel ally and longtime anticommunist agitator Vance Muse also upped his game that spring, promoting articles that called FDR "un-American." US District Attorney Clyde O. Eastus, a longtime Democratic insider, told a friend that Pappy's partnership with Muse would make him "dead to the party." Regardless, O'Daniel repeated the message several times in April and May, telling anyone who would listen that Texans—"except those on the federal payroll"—no longer supported the president, let alone the idea of a fourth term. With "Stop-Roosevelt" movements springing up around the country, conservative Democrats prepared for one of the most famous intraparty squabbles in American history.[35]

"Voluntarily Surrendering Our Constitutionally Protected Rights"

On May 23, 1944, precisely two months after O'Daniel's "radical" speech, the national "Elect Roosevelt Committee" ran a double-full-page political advertisement in the *Austin American-Statesman* with the headline, "On the Eve of Invasion, Support your Commander-in-Chief!" The two-page spread featured an image of the president with accompanying instructions to support FDR's "war leadership." It also tried to assure readers that Roosevelt was "carrying America and her allies to ultimate victory." The ad was a call to unity, cloaked in patriotism, contextualized by the impending cross-channel invasion of France that Americans and their allies had been waiting for since the war began and had been told to expect at any moment. The timing of the ad, however, had far more to do with state politics than with D-Day; the Texas Democratic Party was scheduled to open its convention in Austin that same day.[36]

The impending fracture in the Texas Democratic Party was a long time in the making. Some conservatives had been distancing themselves from Roosevelt since 1937. Still more threatened to bolt in 1940 before the famous "harmony" accords strengthened party loyalties. But Roosevelt's decision to replace Garner on the 1940 ticket with Henry Wallace horrified establishment conservatives, while segregationists feared that the next phase of unimpeded New Deal liberalism was a plan to impose a variety of racial amalgamations on the South. Those fears grew more palpable on April 3, 1944, when the United States Supreme Court ruled the Texas Democratic Party's all-white primary unconstitutional in its famed ruling, *Smith v. Allwright*, a case originating out of Houston. Former state party chair E. B. Germany, in consultation with the party's new chair, George Butler, called the Texas Democratic Executive Committee into session, determined to find a way around the ruling. Among the most popular alternatives discussed came from Dan Moody, who recommended a total elimination of all primaries and the reestablishment of an intraparty nomination process that excluded voters entirely. *Smith v. Allwright* ultimately thwarted most Democratic workarounds, and the court's ruling remained a significant source of agitation among Texas conservatives for years to come.[37]

One month after the Supreme Court's ruling on the Texas Democratic Party's white primary, Tyler Democrats demanded that the state party be free to send an "uninstructed" delegation to the national convention in Chicago that summer. On paper at least, an uninstructed delegation would be free to support Roosevelt. Everyone knew, however, that an "uninstructed delegation" was code for one that would be under conservative control and, therefore, immovably anti-FDR. What happened in Tyler did not stay in Tyler. Two days later, a precinct convention in Dallas voted 2–1 against any pledge that would commit a Democratic delegate to support FDR at the national convention. That Dallas precinct went so far as to suggest alternatives they might be willing to support instead. It also called on FDR to cut Henry Wallace from his ticket and to replace him with Sam Rayburn. The precinct further suggested that Texas consider boycotting the national convention altogether rather than pledge its support to a fourth term for Roosevelt. However, no "unified action" organized because local precincts under conservative control still faced pressure from pro-Roosevelt constituents and Democratic operatives loyal to the White House.[38]

It was a recipe for chaos. On May 23, as the state convention proceeded through its agenda in the state capitol building in downtown Austin, Alvin Wirtz pushed the convention for a final answer on the question of whether the Texas delegation would be uninstructed or, as tradition held, obligated to support the national nominee, even if that nominee was Roosevelt. As predicted, conservatives lobbied for an uninstructed delegation. Some said they would be willing to back Roosevelt if, and only if, the Democratic Party restored the so-called two-thirds rule, in which the national party could not formalize a presidential nomination if fewer than two-thirds of the national delegates failed to rally behind a single nominee. The two-thirds rule was meaningful for traditionalists, given that its origins stretched back to the days of Andrew Jackson. More importantly, the rule also applied to the adoption of platform planks just as it applied to the nomination of candidates. Without this check—which had been eliminated in 1936 much to the consternation of conservatives—segregationists feared not simply a fourth Roosevelt term, but also the inclusion of a stronger plank on Black civil rights.[39]

Liberals countered by saying that it was essential, particularly in wartime, that the state and national parties unify behind Roosevelt. They added that Texas voters—who had overwhelmingly backed FDR in three previous elections—should expect nothing less than a delegation unwavering in its commitment to the president. Eventually a resolution designed to require that commitment was motioned to the leadership for consideration. However, the leadership, clearly under conservative control, denied the motion and overruled additional attempts to bring the proposed mandate to the floor. At this point, several conservative delegates turned to Lyndon Johnson, yelling, "Throw Roosevelt's pinup boy out of there!" It was clear the convention was at an impasse. Then, a faction of roughly 250–400 pro-FDR Democrats—led by Lyndon Johnson, Alvin Wirtz, and others—marched out of the state senate chamber and moved across the hall to the house chamber, where they quickly reconvened, all while singing "The Eyes of Texas."[40] Following the walkout, two competing conventions were seemingly underway,

Political cartoon by C. K. Berryman, *Washington Evening Star*, May 25, 1944. "Bolting Donkeys." Courtesy of the Dolph Briscoe Center for American History, University of Texas at Austin.

though neither recognized the other as legitimate. Not surprisingly, the conservatives who remained in the senate chamber elected a slate of uninstructed delegates to the party's upcoming national convention. They also passed a resolution denouncing the federal government's usurpation of state sovereignty for the purpose of increased regulation and control by Washington.[41] Meanwhile, pro-FDR loyalists in the house chamber referred to the ongoing meeting in the senate chamber as an unauthorized coup of "Republican sympathizers" who did not represent the wishes of Texas voters.[42]

By day's end, it was unclear whether the Texas Democratic Party had actually concluded its convention and elected a slate of delegates or not. What was clear to observers across both the state and the nation was that the Texas Democratic Party was unraveling. Conservatives claimed that their meeting on May 23 had been the "regular" meeting of the party and that the liberals who bolted were simply upset that they did not have a majority in the hall and subsequently refused to abide by basic democratic rules of procedure. Many "Regulars"—as they soon were known—denied allegations that they were Republicans "in disguise." They also denied that "uninstructed" was code for opposition to Roosevelt, claiming a willingness to back FDR in exchange for restoration of the two-thirds rule. However, the Regular message quickly expanded beyond that one issue, with many saying the movement was nothing less than a commitment to stop "voluntarily surrendering constitutionally protected rights to the federal government." Regulars also began to highlight the term "states' rights" with far greater frequency.[43]

In the coming weeks, the rhetoric only grew more heated. Pappy O'Daniel called for the absolute "defeat of the New Deal" and end of the "Roosevelt Dynasty." In July, his personal newspaper, which claimed to promote "the truth and nothing but the truth about the national government" while also "giving facts which are withheld by a partisan-controlled press," published the "Texas Regular Platform," which specifically called for the return "of state rights which have been destroyed by the Communist-controlled New Deal." As if any confusion remained, the Texas Regulars also made it clear that they advocated the "restoration of the supremacy of the white race."[44]

Liberals predictably disagreed with the Regular assessment of the situation. They insisted that their decision to leave the May 23 meeting had resulted from undemocratic and surreptitious efforts by the conservative leadership to pass resolutions during the convention without the knowledge of the entire body. Conservatives had been deceptive and deliberately noncommunicative in an effort to "ram decisions down the convention's throat," they argued. LBJ told a reporter that Regulars were making a "deliberate attempt to create fear in the hearts of citizens." Jesse Jones said the anti-Roosevelt faction was attempting to "deprive Texans of the right to vote for FDR," while adding that the vast majority of voters in the state remained firmly and faithfully in the president's corner. Jones added that he agreed with the Regulars' position on the two-thirds rule but predicted that Roosevelt would easily win renomination and that fighting of the issue would not get the party—or the state of Texas—anywhere. He also reminded reporters that FDR had carried Texas in 1940 by a wider margin than in any other state in the nation and predicated that he would do so again in 1944, with or without Regular support.[45]

Pro-Roosevelt Democrats subsequently adopted a resolution unequivocally denouncing the Regulars as "enemies of democracy," while emphasizing that the conservatives were nothing more than "Republicans masquerading as Democrats." The resolution committed the pro-Roosevelt faction to opposing "manipulation of the party machinery" and to supporting the nominee of the Democratic National Convention, while warning that failure to do so would "result in the loss of freedom and democracy across the world."[46]

In the view of at least one liberal, "the so-called regular Democrat delegates to the national convention should be kicked out and branded as Tories." Others stressed the importance of loyalty to the Democratic Party, regardless of differences over issues and ideologies. Another stressed that the "real" Democrats were the ones who had countered the Regular forces in order to hold a truly "democratic" convention. "We felt that after the monied interests of our state had bought Dallas, Fort Worth, Houston, and San Antonio with Republican money and stacked it with Republicans, Willkieites, Hoovercrats and Roosevelt haters, that we shouldn't continue to sit in the convention," the participant said.[47]

The controversy surrounding the May 23 convention and the subsequent Texas Regular movement of 1944 foreshadowed the partisan realignments of later decades. Liberals insisted that no virtue was more important than loyalty and that loyalty to the Democratic Party meant, in this case, loyalty to both the president of the United States and his policies. Not missing an opportunity, they also magnified the wartime context, emphasizing themes of patriotism, duty, and honor in contrast to selfishness, greed, and tyranny. As FDR loyalists called Regulars "traitors," Regulars worked equally hard to convince voters that they were in fact the "real" Democrats of Texas, defined by ideology, not allegiance to one man. Regulars marketed themselves as defenders of "Constitutional Government of the People," adding that FDR and the New Deal represented the will of elitist bureaucrats in Washington, not the average citizen.[48] Editorialists friendly to the Regular movement called the New Deal "a pile of economic contradictions" and "a rubble of half-baked ideas and decayed ideals." Others revived connections between the New Deal and racketeering. Still others rekindled memories of Roosevelt's efforts to pack the Supreme Court in 1937. Some also spoke ominously about Washington's growing support for racial equality and the inherent dangers therein, vastly overstating the degree to which the New Deal had used federal tax dollars to redistribute wealth into African American hands.[49] In the Regular world, there was a clear connection between the New Deal and an unspoken war against white supremacy, often framed as a war against "constitutional liberties." The Texas political culture was particularly interesting in this regard, as Mexican workers, under an agreement between the United States and Mexico (commonly known as the Bracero Program), filled jobs across the state vacated by men who were off fighting the war. Job competition among the races reignited racial discord and reminded conservative segregationists of the threat class-consciousness and organized labor presented to white supremacy. Conversely, racialized conversations about workers' rights and labor organizing tinged American rhetoric about liberty and equality with an unmistakable air of hypocrisy.[50]

With the Democratic National Convention scheduled for July, the DNC pushed for a compromise in which it would seat both Texas delegations and give each a one-half vote. The deal allowed the Regulars to sit in front, with pro-FDR loyalists sitting behind. However, once the convention began, the Regulars quickly realized that things would not go their way and, in an ironic twist, simply got up from their seats and left the hall. The remaining pro-FDR delegates quickly filled the seats, making it clear that what was left of the Texas delegation was firmly in FDR's corner. The convention quickly renominated FDR for a fourth term as president of the United States.[51]

With the national convention over, pro-FDR delegates returned to their home precincts in Texas to begin work on the fall campaign, while Regulars like Pappy O'Daniel mounted a two-pronged attack on the status quo. First, the Regulars pursued a legal battle aimed at having two slates of Democratic electors added to the November ballot, one pro-FDR and one uninstructed. They also waged a public relations campaign designed to brand their rebellion as a success, citing Missouri senator Harry Truman's replacement of Henry Wallace as running mate as direct evidence of their influence with the national party. Meanwhile, loyalists focused their energy on the upcoming state convention in September, hoping to undo the damage from the May convention. Led this time by Jimmie Allred, the loyalists largely succeeded, narrowly winning an 803–774 vote on the question of offering voters a choice between two slates of electors—one for Roosevelt and one uninstructed. That vote, and a state supreme court ruling on the matter, eliminated any prospect that two Democratic slates would appear on the ballot that November.[52]

After the state supreme court's decision, the Regulars—led by O'Daniel, Martin Dies, Dan Moody, Oveta Culp Hobby, E. B. Germany, and a slew of oilmen and other conservative business leaders—announced the formation of a new political party, simply calling themselves the Texas Regulars. In their opening statement, the Texas Regulars cited the need to combat "state socialism" and "Bronx Negro politicians, the Communists, the CIO Political Action Committee, and the big-city machine politicians." They subsequently filed the appropriate paperwork necessary to register as a third party in the state of Texas and succeeded in getting an uninstructed slate of electors added to the November ballot under the name Texas Regulars. Their official party platform highlighted virtually every grievance the conservative right had held against the New Deal since its inception, but also, again, added specific lines about the need to preserve white supremacy and fight communism.[53]

"I Cannot Agree with the President . . . But"

Lyndon Johnson highlighted his opposition to the Regulars in his 1944 bid for reelection to Congress. Johnson's opponent in the Tenth District primary was Buck Taylor—a pro-O'Daniel Regular who was also the editor of a small Austin newspaper called the *Middle-Buster*.[54] Taylor painted Johnson as a rubber stamp for the New Deal and chief cause of the Democratic factionalism more broadly. He accused Johnson of undermining party traditions and alienating himself from "true and tried Democrats" and of "ruling out" anyone who dared suggest that the party reestablish the two-thirds rule for nominations at the national convention. "Do you or do you not agree with the Regular Democrats that the tendency of the states to surrender powers to the Federal government in return for financial aid is an evil which should be checked?" one Taylor advertisement read. The ad continued: "And Lyndon, please tell us. . . . Did you or did you not join hands with supporters of the CIO political action committee in bringing about the convention 'Bolt' in Austin?" Taylor contrasted himself to Johnson as an antiunion fiscal conservative who would "get our boys back home," "prevent the reckless spending of taxpayers' money," "cut out all useless boards and bureaus" in Washing-

228 I CHAPTER 6

ton, and wage war against labor "racketeers" and professional "bureau-crats" who did not have America's best interests at heart.[55]

Taylor's message resonated with conservatives, and his campaign against FDR's "good friend" from Texas drew more attention than most congressional primaries across the state that year. One editorial out of Henderson, Texas, accused Johnson of forcing Texans to "surrender their rights and swallow the New Deal program, hide and hair, without a murmur." "Lyndon, in case, you've forgotten," the editorialist contin-ued, "is the man the White House sought to ram down the throats of Texans in the race for United States Senator." Calling Johnson a "mis-sionary for the administration that seeks to undo all we in the South fought and bled for in the sixties and before," the newspaper closed by declaring that "Washington is against the South, any way you look at it. To see a Texan like Lyndon Johnson and others you know fall in line and help accomplish this end is nothing short of disgusting."[56]

Despite the vitriol and widespread attention his campaign received, Buck Taylor was never a serious threat to unseat Lyndon Johnson, just as the Regulars were not a serious threat to damage FDR's reelection bid. Johnson eventually defeated Taylor in the Democratic primary, win-ning nearly 70 percent of the final vote. However, Taylor's challenge did force Johnson to go out of his way to prove that he was not a "rub-ber stamp" as Taylor and conservatives increasingly believed. For the first time in his political career, Johnson distanced himself from FDR, though only barely. He highlighted examples of legislative proposals he had opposed, despite Roosevelt's support, in his speeches and cam-paign advertisements. He also spent time decrying "excessive wartime bureaucracy" and "excessive regulation" and promised constituents that he would work to abolish various agencies that existed only because of the war and would no longer be relevant once the war inevitably con-cluded. He also said that a "silver lining of the war" was that it had taught Texans about what the future could look like if it chose to develop and channel its natural resources toward industrial growth.[57]

Some historians have seen Buck Taylor's challenge to LBJ in the 1944 Democratic primary as a "sign of things to come"—in effect, a harbinger of a growing conservatism that would challenge liberals in the decades to come. Indeed, nascent organizations like the CCA backed anti–New Deal candidates like Taylor in races across the state in 1944. Conservative success, however, was limited. Whether out of loyalty, ide-ological accord, or patriotism, most Democratic candidates remained in the president's corner, as did most voters. "I cannot agree with the President in many of his views," said one Texan, "but I do not doubt the sincerity of his efforts to better the nation." In essence, it was FDR him-self—his persona, his record of leadership, and the trust that came with it—that most Texans continued to support, even as many increasingly disagreed with the brand of liberalism he helped to create. Beyond that, minor disagreements still paled in comparison to the thought of voting Republican.[58]

Within this political context, FDR loyalists painted the Regular move-ment as a partisan betrayal akin to the Hoovercrat bolt of 1928. Pro-FDR Texans associated O'Daniel with "Hoover's party," while rallying populist ire against big business in all forms. One advertisement even listed the names of business leaders and companies who had "plotted" to foment Republican growth in the state and linked those leaders with O'Daniel and other perceived "traitors" to the party. Another sarcasti-cally referred to the Regulars as having been "born in sin" while suffer-ing from "Hooveritis." They also minimized anticommunist sentiment within a context of support for America's Soviet ally against Hitler and insisted on patriotic unity until the "boys were home."[59]

As Sam Rayburn put it, "real Democrats" kept their promises. "I'm supporting all Democratic nominees from Roosevelt and Truman down," Rayburn told one crowd in Abilene, while also calling the Regu-lars "political tricksters who represent big cities and big money." Ray-burn highlighted popular New Deal programs, especially those related to soil conservation and agriculture. He also attacked Regulars and Re-publicans, questioning their loyalty, honor, and patriotism. In one par-ticularly bold and unfair moment, Rayburn even blamed the GOP for enabling Pearl Harbor on the grounds that they had failed to cooperate with the president's preparedness efforts in 1940 and 1941.[60] Thanks to the deep pockets of Houston oil mogul Roy Cullen, Rayburn faced a rare primary challenger that year. Like his protégé from the Tenth District, Rayburn survived the challenge and was reelected. In response to Cullen's effort to unseat him, Rayburn commented of conservatives: "All they do is hate."[61]

Running for reelection in the Nineteenth District, George Mahon emphasized his support for the president more clearly than he had two years earlier. He prioritized the war effort and called Roosevelt a trust-worthy "ally" to area farmers, billing himself an "original supporter of the Rural Electrification Program and the Soil Conservation program."

Mahon also devoted significant time in speeches to the value of FDR's foreign policy and wartime leadership, and highlighted his own role as member of the Military Appropriations Committee, which he argued was crucial to the sustenance of the overall war effort. To that end, Mahon promoted a photo of himself shaking hands with the chief of staff of the United States Army, General George C. Marshall. For the most part, Mahon distanced himself from the Texas Regulars, but he also balanced his commitment to FDR and New Deal agriculture policy by sharing frustrations over growing budget deficits, higher taxes, and "waste" in Washington, as he often put it. He spoke against "lavish Washington parties" and "bureaucrats" appointed by the president who were misusing government funds while the people suffered through rationing of basic goods. He told constituents that taxes were too high. At one point he said that his "first loyalty" was to his country, not his party. In each case, however, Mahon avoided pinning FDR with the blame for such developments. Instead, the blame rested with "appointed bureaucrats" and "radicals." "Things may not be perfect," Mahon said in one stump speech, "but unity and victory are most important." He spoke about standing "for less regimentation of the people and the abandonment of governmental interference with private business after the war," though he was always careful to say that farmers were an exception and that farmers should, and would, continue to partner with Washington. Mahon also told voters that labor strikes had "hurt morale and the war effort more than any one thing" and that he would continue to speak out against "wartime strikes and profiteers," adding proudly that he was likely on "John L. Lewis's blacklist."[62]

Mahon related well to his West Texas constituents, was widely admired, and maintained trust within important intra–White House circles. He cooperated with the press, learned how to give a safe interview, and presented himself as a reasonable, balanced leader, without appearing beholden to any faction or special interest. He was a participant in the 1944 Dumbarton Oaks Conference that laid the groundwork for the United Nations, and Mahon's support for international cooperation garnered national praise, including one letter from Archibald MacLeish, the famed poet, librarian of Congress, and future assistant secretary of state for foreign affairs.[63] In many ways, George Mahon's political evolution—slow and steady though it was—reflected the changes in his district, state, and nation. Having come to politics as a faithful Democrat, willing to prioritize and promote pragmatic solutions to immediate problems, Mahon had conservative impulses that began to re-surface more powerfully during the war, as loyalty to the nation and to the war effort slowly supplanted loyalty to Roosevelt and the Democratic Party. The *Lubbock Avalanche-Journal* described Mahon's approach this way:

> [Mahon] has no desire to beat around the bush, or to leave the false impres-sion. . . . He is among the ranks of those who would like to see the President quit playing politics; quit being dominated by pressure groups in general and by organized labor in particular. Like many other citizens, this writer would like to see Mr. Roosevelt clean out a lot of his crack-pot advisors and send in the "first team," regardless of political slants. Yet, bewailing as we do . . . we believe Mr. Mahon, in going down the line with most of the Roosevelt policies, has been following the wishes of his West Texas constituents. The majority likes FDR's ideas on social security [and] his cleanup of the finan-cial front in the early part of his tenure.

The editorial continued:

> Not every one of Mr. Roosevelt's 19th Texas district's voters approves all the President's policies. On the other hand, the overwhelming majority of West Texans believe with good reason that Mr. Roosevelt's handling of the vast international aspects of his job has been very good indeed. The prosecution of the war on the fighting front under the Roosevelt administration has to date been all we could ask for, and more than most of us hoped for. Since the vote totals of 1932, 1936, and 1940 prove beyond doubt that 75 percent or more of the people of the 19th Texas Congressional District approves of the President and his broad policies, what surer mandate could any repre-sentative of that district have from his constituency?[64]

Mahon's opponent in the 1944 Democratic primary was C. L. Har-ris. Harris's campaign highlighted several aspects of the Roosevelt ad-ministration that were particularly intolerable to those in the Regular movement, including the usual dog whistles designed to attract white su-premacist voters. "One of the greatest protections we have from the dan-gers of dictatorship is that of states' rights," Harris told the *Borden County Sun* in February, adding that he "would guard them most jealously here in Texas." Harris spoke in favor of the "rights of organized labor," but qualified that support by saying that he was opposed to the "labor rack-eteer" and that "there should be no strikes on the home front" during the war.[65] Conservative though he was, Harris was not entirely anti-

Roosevelt. Instead, he sought to bridge a middle ground between Regulars and loyalists. "I would cooperate with the President when I thought he was right and for the best interest of people in the district," Harris said during the campaign, "and I would oppose him when I thought he was wrong." Charging Mahon with "inaction," Harris marketed himself as a supporter of the "free American business enterprise" and a promoter of "freedom from bureaucratic meddlers." "Free enterprise made this country great and its greatness will be perpetuated only by the slashing of red tape and the elimination of bureaucratic snoopers," one campaign brochure read. "I propose to carry the flight to the halls of Congress to bring about the changes necessary that the small businessman may pursue his business efforts un-annoyed by constant regulations." In addition to emphasizing the evils of "red tape" and "bureaucratic meddling," Harris's campaign employed numerous clichés, including his support for "constitutional government," "free American enterprise," and "strong economic, military, and spiritual stands." He argued that under Mahon and Roosevelt, farmers had received a "poor deal" and that better-adjusted price ceilings were long overdue. Finally, Harris sold his candidacy as healthy for democracy, saying that "frequent change" was good. In the end, Harris's efforts were not enough. Mahon easily won reelection, defeating his opponent nearly two to one.[66]

Elsewhere, Hatton Sumners barely survived the 1944 primary. Facing a staunch Regular in the primary whose campaign prioritized ideological conviction ahead of pragmatic politics, Sumners employed a starkly anticommunist message. "It will probably be determined during the next Congress whether we will move back toward Constitutional government, tested through the centuries, or toward the socialistic, communistic philosophy of government which the CIO Political Action Committee is trying to force upon the United States," Sumners said in his opening campaign speech, delivered to a primetime audience via KRLD radio in Dallas. Sumners linked communist threats abroad to labor activism locally, at one point mixing his metaphors to compare the CIO's efforts to "penetrate government" to "a time when Confederate soldiers were disfranchised and federal bayonets protected brutal and corrupt government which pillaged our people." Though he mitigated his denunciation of the CIO by saying that the "rank and file" members of the union were "generally . . . fine, upstanding citizens," it was clear that Sumners was drawing a line in the sand in which those on the side of labor rights would be castigated as un-American and, therefore, alien to the values traditional Texans held dear.[67] Sumners gave the same speech on KGKO and WFAA radio stations several times throughout the campaign. Surrogates delivered similar messages via the same means, painting Sumners as a victim of the CIO and other "communistic labor radicals" who were "seeking to destroy" the congressman and his values.[68] Sumners won the primary, and then defeated his Republican challenger in the general election, winning 71 percent of the vote—by far the worst showing of his career. Dejected, Sumners retired rather than run for reelection again in 1946.[69]

In south Texas, Richard Kleberg's 1944 reelection campaign reflected a different aspect of the state's evolving political dynamics. Like Sumners, Kleberg was a longtime member of the influential Miller Group and an oft reluctant but typically reliable team player throughout most of the 1930s. However, Kleberg's break from the Roosevelt fold was total by 1944, particularly on the labor front. His image in the Fourteenth District hinged strongly on antiunion sentiment, usually conflated with messages about patriotism and anticommunism. Like O'Daniel and his colleague Martin Dies in the nearby Second District, Kleberg helped popularize "un-American" as a political pejorative. He reveled in the CIO's attacks against him in 1942 and 1944, taking special care to name CIO organizer Sidney Hillman as one of his enemies while simultaneously reminding constituents that his paternal grandfather had fought with Sam Houston at the Battle of San Jacinto in 1836. "Dick Kleberg is an independent Democrat," read one paid political advertisement titled "Americanism beyond Challenge." "He is just a plain, courageous American. He refuses, as a matter of habit, to surrender to pressure groups." Recognizing the demographics of his south Texas district, Kleberg distributed these advertisements in both English and Spanish.[70]

A relatively unknown figure at the national level for most of his career, Kleberg emerged as one of the nation's foremost critics of New Deal liberalism in 1943, popularizing connections between progressivism in Washington and "socialistic totalitarianism," "intellectual dishonesty," and "Europeanism." He spoke to audiences across the country about mounting federal deficits, the "surrendering of states' rights," and "conspiracies to abolish our Constitution and Bill of Rights." A hero to some, Kleberg drew fierce condemnation from party loyalists.[71] His most rousing such speech came in March before a meeting of the Texas and Southwest Cattle Raisers Association. "We Americans . . . have been far too careless in permitting the inculcation of foreign ideologies and isms which have crept into this great system of ours," Kleberg said. "This laxity has brought the ravaging enemy of confusion into our midst." He blasted FDR and Henry Wallace for "ignoring" the Constitution, characterized federal subsidies as enemies of "the American way of life," and specifically criticized the president for refusing to "abdicate" his office. While he grudgingly pledged loyalty to his "Commander-in-Chief" during wartime, he also spoke hopefully of the day when "real Democrats" would restore "individual initiative" and "freedom of enterprise" to the nation, as Texas's "founding fathers" had intended. It was a patriotic but clearly anti-Roosevelt speech, and it drew hundreds of support letters from conservatives both in and out of Texas.[72]

Kleberg used his speech with the Texas and Southwest Cattle Raisers Association to launch his reelection campaign in earnest. Over the next two months, he told audiences that he was lifting his "voice against those in the executive branch of the government who . . . seek to destroy the Constitution and establish a world order under which Americans would lose their freedom." "I would not surrender one iota of American freedom for all the Four Freedoms of the Atlantic Charter," Kleberg said during one speech that May. "It is time now, not when the war is over, to see to it by legislative action that we do not lose the right of exercising our own self-determination." Kleberg's campaign depicted him as a leader in the "rising indication among Democratic members, particularly in the South and West, against the dictatorial trends of the [FDR] Administration." If any confusion remained, Kleberg also told audiences that Americans had "surrendered our legislative, constitutional powers under the emergency which has been proclaimed since 1933." To the degree that he was among the earliest Texas Democrats to argue that partisan fidelity should take a backseat to ideological conviction—or that conservatism was synonymous with true Americanism— Dick Kleberg could be a considered a pioneer who foreshadowed the Texas Republican ascendancy of later decades.[73]

However, to the degree that voters in his district were ready to listen to such rhetoric in 1944, he is a better example of voters' enduring fidelity to FDR and partisan loyalty. Richard Kleberg lost his reelection bid in 1944. In ousting Kleberg, voters in Fourteenth District turned to John Lyle, a younger man and military veteran virtually handpicked by county boss George Parr to restore a measure of order to Parr's famed Duval County machine. Lyle premised his campaign on his status as a hero of invasion of Italy in 1943. He alleged that Kleberg had voted against a pay increase for soldiers and paired the charge with broader concerns about Kleberg's opposition to FDR. Kleberg ineffectively retaliated against the war hero by playing up his image as a sort of "cowboy congressman" and ranch owner. Voters chose the war hero. Unfettered by the demands of reelection, Kleberg promptly endorsed the Republican Thomas E. Dewey of New York for president of the United States. Then, in his farewell speech on the House floor, Kleberg railed against the New Deal for an hour, at various times connecting CPUSA chairman Earl Browder, Sidney Hillman, the CIO, and Felix Frankfurter to "communist infiltrations" in the White House and "Marxist schemes to fasten totalitarianism" by establishing an "international Gestapo" to destroy American sovereignty in foreign affairs.[74] As one admiring observer noted in a letter to Kleberg the following day:

> I sincerely hope, and truly believe, that your address was the tinder which will ignite the flame of Americanism lain smoldering these many years. It would be to our party's credit if some member of Congress would raise his voice to carry where you left off. I won't limit this thought to one party, but rather to both parties since it is all too evident that the candle burns low and American's destiny rides the flames.[75]

Kleberg was not the only Texas Regular to lose his congressional seat in 1944. That list included Martin Dies, who retired in May rather than face the prospect of defeat in the Democratic primary, where labor organizers in the heavily unionized city of Orange were grooming an anti-Dies campaign. Retirement gave Dies the freedom to participate as fully and as aggressively as he wanted on behalf of anti-Roosevelt conservatives. However, those actions came at the cost of a public denunciation in his home county of Orange, where a strong union presence rebuked Dies for his attacks against labor and his unqualified red-baiting efforts in Washington. With the CIO's help, Democrats in the Second District nominated a county judge named Jesse Combs to fill Dies's seat. Combs ran a bland campaign, but represented the interests of all who opposed Dies and the rest of the Regular movement. Combs went on to serve that district until his retirement in 1953. Jack Brooks subsequently filled the seat, remaining in Congress until 1995, after he was defeated in the 1994 midterms by a "Contract with America" Republican. Like Dies and Kleberg, the conservative Miller Group member Nat Patton also failed to win reelection in 1944, losing in the Seventh District Democratic primary to Tom Pickett, a district attorney who contrasted himself to Patton by affirming the importance of Democratic loyalty and support for Franklin Roosevelt, public works projects, and conservation.[76]

Despite the setbacks, Texas Regulars encouraged voters across Texas to rethink their Democratic loyalties. In October, Pappy O'Daniel—who was not running for election that year—reunited his Hillbilly Band in what essentially became a personal effort to defeat Roosevelt. Through it all, O'Daniel insisted that his actions were "nonpolitical" in nature and that he was simply fighting to protect American values against hostile "forces." He told audiences that Roosevelt had chosen "radical labor" over the "safety and security" of US soldiers overseas, often couching his criticism as requests for "prayer" for the future of the country. While he lobbied for the uninstructed slate of Regular electors, calling the New Deal "collectivist tyranny," he just as frequently lauded the Republican candidacy of Thomas Dewey as an equally viable alternative.[77] National Republicans took notice of the surging anticommunism in Texas, with some—most notably Dewey's running mate, Ohio governor John Bricker—making personal visits to the Lone Star State in the hopes of rallying disaffected conservative Democrats into a more permanent relationship with the GOP.[78]

None of the rallies held by either the GOP or their Regular surrogates was as eventful as the one O'Daniel staged in Houston on November 2. Thanks largely to the emotional instability of a crowd that included both Regulars and protesting FDR loyalists, a riot broke out, necessitating police intervention and multiple arrests. Witnesses recalled seeing punches, eggs, and tomatoes thrown, the latter lobbed most commonly at O'Daniel, who surveilled the incident safely from his stage. Later that day, Pappy predictably told reporters that he blamed the incident on "communistic labor racketeers, New Deal fellow travelers, and lawless elements which constitute the principal backing of the New Deal party." He even claimed that the riot had been "prearranged, presumably on orders from Washington." At another rally the following day, O'Daniel quite dramatically told his audience that the episode had been "ordered from the gang of Communists close to the throne of Franklin the Fourth in Washington."[79]

O'Daniel's campaign against Roosevelt helped crystalize conservatives' antiliberal rhetoric in ways that would certainly prove useful in the coming years and decades. However, despite the fanfare, most Texans remained loyal, creating a coalition of liberals, moderates, progressives, and pragmatists easily large enough to offset Regular inroads across the state. Sam Rayburn actively campaigned for FDR that fall, as did Wright Patman, Jimmie Allred, and Lyndon Johnson. Myron Blalock, the one-time leader of the "Stop Roosevelt" movement of 1940, also came around, as did one-time Regular Tom Connally, who by the end of the campaign was a particularly aggressive voice against Dewey and the Republican Party. Connally's anti-Republican messages helped normalize the election for many voters, as did his willingness to praise Roosevelt's wartime leadership and vast experience during campaign speeches across Texas that October.[80]

The drama ended on November 7 when Franklin D. Roosevelt won an unprecedented fourth term as president of the United States, carrying 432 electoral votes nationally, including 23 from Texas, where he won more than 71 percent of the vote. It was his weakest showing in four elections, but still a landslide by almost any definition, and certainly an overwhelming vote of confidence from both the nation and Texas, which gave Dewey a mere 17 percent of the vote; the Regulars won just under 12 percent. In addition to backing Roosevelt for the fourth consecutive election, Texas voters once again filled all twenty-one congressional seats with Democrats, eighteen of them incumbents. The only three incumbents not returned to the House of Representatives in Washington were Kleberg, Dies, and Patton.[81] The next day, Lyndon Johnson took a victory lap of sorts, ridiculing Pappy O'Daniel and his Regular allies before an audience of reporters while eulogizing the year's conservative uprising as a soon-to-be-distant memory:

> With all their ballyhoo, the best this tight little oligarchy could do was run third in a three-man race, and you can't run lower than that. It should be written in the book of political experience that the people do not like turncoats who run for the United States Senate on a platform of supporting the administration and after the election take money from the Administration's enemies. The vote also repudiates the Junior Senator from Texas, Wilbert Lee O'Daniel and his traveling sideshow.[82]

Elsewhere, an unnamed Regular was purported to have remarked to his colleagues: "Gentlemen, the yokels have discovered that they can outvote us." Such a comment not simply revealed a less-than-sanguine attitude toward the virtues of democracy, but also a recognition that conservatives would need to convert more "yokels" to their cause if they hoped to win elections in the age of FDR, or the future to follow.[83]

New Dealers and other Democratic loyalists across the state and nation had reason to gloat over the outcome of elections in 1944, but few if any others were as proud as was Johnson. After he ascended from the Hill Country to Capitol Hill by associating as closely with FDR as possible, Johnson's career path eventually took him to the White House, where he served as president of the United States from 1963 to 1969. With FDR's portrait on prominent display in his Oval Office, President Johnson championed the "Great Society"—a liberal program of federally funded public works projects and other initiatives that, he said, would fulfill everything the New Deal had left unfinished more than two decades earlier. As it turned out, however, LBJ's commitment to big government liberalism—coupled with his inability to win a war overseas or even maintain the peace at home—killed not only his presidency, but also the New Deal Coalition upon which he and other liberal Democrats had built their careers since 1932.[84]

But that is another story. At the time of his death on April 12, 1945, FDR—as measured by the collective will of its voting electorate—was among the most popular politicians in Texas history, having guided the state through the worst economic crisis of its history, not through austerity, but through one of the most popular government initiatives of all time: the New Deal. Inevitably however, Roosevelt's aura as a national grandfather faded, as did the appeal of New Deal liberalism in Texas. In the decades that followed, establishment conservatives came out of "hibernation," as one Texan put it—regaining control of the state, often by using the same religious overtones once applied to the New Deal to shape support for smaller government, unregulated private markets, and states' rights.[85] What did not fade, however, was the New Deal's enduring legacy across Texas—not just its political legacy, but perhaps more importantly, its physical one. Conservatives may very well have dominated state politics in the decades following FDR's death. But during those same decades, as Texans of all races, religions, creeds, and persuasions gazed upon the San Jacinto Monument, snacked on deepfried delicacies at Fair Park in Dallas, strolled the Riverwalk and El Mercado Farmer's Market in San Antonio, stood in silence at Dealey Plaza in Dallas, challenged municipal policies at city hall in Houston, swam in the regionally renowned freshwater pool at Balmorhea State Park in the deserts of far west Texas, or studied in any of the dozens of schools and libraries built by the New Deal, they (often unknowingly) celebrated communal experiences and opportunities now deeply embedded in the state's culture—all of which would not have existed without the New Deal. Future generations will undoubtedly celebrate such things, even if they fail to recognize their origins.[86]

Conclusion
"The Forgotten Man"

Texas politics changed in several dramatic ways following FDR's death in 1945. For a time, Democrats managed to maintain control of the state's levers of power, mitigating the impact of its increasingly contentious intraparty factionalism—the divide between conservatives and liberals that had, in some ways, crystalized during debates over FDR and the New Deal. Eventually, however, those ideological fissures grew too pronounced for any one party to manage. As the Texas Democratic Party fractured along ideological lines, the state's nascent Republican Party made significant inroads, attracting conservative converts from within the state while, at the same time, benefiting from the Rustbelt-to-Sunbelt migration that made the 1960s and 1970s one of the most economically and culturally dynamic eras in Texas history. By the 1980s and 1990s, conservative Republicans had transformed Texas into a battleground state. By 2004, the Lone Star GOP had clearly won that battle, taking 100 percent of statewide elected offices and clear majorities in both houses of the Texas Legislature. They even controlled the White House, as former Texas governor George W. Bush won his second term as president of the United States.[1]

Sixteen years and numerous defeats later, Democrats waged a spirited (and expensive) presidential campaign for Joe Biden in 2020, hoping to "turn Texas blue" for the first time since Jimmy Carter carried the state in 1976. Biden ran a relatively moderate campaign, aimed at middle-class voters and independents, many of whom had voted for Donald Trump four years earlier. Biden won the presidency and came within 5.5 percentage points of winning Texas, closer than any Democratic presidential nominee since Carter. Still, Trump kept Texas "red." Meanwhile, Democratic efforts to upend Republican control in the Texas Legislature also came up short in 2020, just as Beto O'Rourke's progressive campaign to unseat Republican Ted Cruz from the US Senate came up 3 points short in 2018. Conservative Republicans continue to win in part because of widespread popular opposition to what some on the right decried as the "radical socialist agenda" of progressives like Alexandria Ocasio-Cortez of New York, who, after winning election to Congress in 2018, championed ideas for big government programs, including one environmental initiative called the "Green New Deal." The message fell flat, or at least flatter than was needed to win in the Lone Star State. Texas Democrats ended 2020 optimistic about the future, but Texas Republicans still held most of the cards.

And yet, as much as things changed in the decades following FDR's death, many of the characteristics that defined Texas political culture during the 1930s and early 1940s—the "Age of FDR"—remained the same. Most notable in this regard was the state's affinity for pragmatic populism, marketed to voters within a campaign culture that prioritized the preservation of "bootstrap" individualism for the "forgotten man." At the height of the Great Depression, New Deal Democrats in Texas spoke to voters who were angry at elitists on the East Coast—Wall Street bankers and "establishment" power brokers—who monopolized wealth at the expense of the farmer, the ordinary worker, the traditional family. FDR's "New Deal" was sold as a promise to restore individual opportunity to ordinary citizens whose pursuit of the American Dream had been unjustly obstructed by those power brokers—"economic royalists," as FDR called them. Several decades later, Texas Republicans promoted a political worldview that utilized a very similar message about elitist power on the East Coast. In that worldview, however, the vilified "eastern establishment" had—through a combination of arrogance, ignorance, and ambivalence for the values of the "forgotten man"—bred a culture of lawlessness, moral degradation, and economic exploitation through high taxes and wasteful spending. FDR found his enemies on Wall Street; conservative Republicans of the late twentieth and early twenty-first centuries found theirs on Capitol Hill. Government was no longer the solution to anyone's problems; government *was* the problem. And the "forgotten man" was now the "Silent Majority."[2]

The politics of exclusion takes many forms. Donald Trump won the presidency in 2016 thanks in part to his campaign slogan, "Make America Great Again." Like any good slogan, the phrase's meaning varied from person to person. This one, however, seemed to resonate most potently with white voters in the rural South and the Rustbelt regions of the Midwest, where a combination of economic stagnation and backlash to perceived political correctness—"wokeness," in the parlance of the day—and activist movements like Black Lives Matter contributed to a political climate notable for its perpetuation of fear, anger, and resentment. In Trump's world, the blame rested on liberals and bureaucrats in Washington—the "swamp," as he put it. Trump's proposed solution? "Drain the swamp" and "make America great again."

Arlie Russell Hochschild explored this kind of dynamic in her book, *Strangers in Their Own Land,* a sociological study that, though based on research conducted between 2010 and 2014, all but predicted the rise of Trump and "MAGA" in 2016. Hochschild chronicled her five-year immersion into a largely impoverished community in the Louisiana bayou, with an eye on understanding the relationship between white, rural southerners and the "reactionary Right"—the "Tea Party" as it was commonly known for a time during the early 2010s. In explaining how this cross section of the country interpreted the rapidly changing world around them, Hochschild imagines a long line stretching end-lessly uphill in which ordinary (usually white) citizens wait patiently for their piece of the American Dream. As they wait, however, they see women, immigrants, and minorities "cutting in line," aided and abet-ted in this unjust malfeasance by liberal politicians hoping to promote dependence on the state and, eventually, "socialism." In Hochschild's allegory, the longer people wait in line, the more frustrated they grow. Eventually, they begin to question the Dream's existence at all. The re-sulting frustrations form an "empathy wall" in which those in line refuse to acknowledge the plight of those they see "cutting in line." The equal but opposite reaction from the left is to dismiss the frustrations of those who feel like they are being cheated and "left behind" as intolerance, racism, ignorance, or some other "deplorable" shortcoming. The eco-nomic realities on the ground matter little in this scenario, and neither does any fair analysis of the policies that created those realities. Rather, what matters to self-perceived "forgotten" men and women who never quite reach the American Dream, despite playing by all the rules, is that someone somewhere stand up to fight on their behalf. To the politician willing to stand up and fight goes an undying loyalty. J. D. Vance made similar observations in his national bestseller, *Hillbilly Elegy,* also pub-lished in 2016, as did Robert Wuthnow in *Left Behind: Decline and Rage in Small Town America* (2019). Other have grappled with these dynam-ics, particularly as emotions, perceptions, and misperceptions tangle in a world filled with social media apps, niche websites, and "fake news" all algorithmically designed to maximize echo chambers and reinforce preexisting opinions and emotions.[3]

As dysfunctional and disruptive as all that may sound, Trump's campaigns in 2016 and 2020 were framed, at least in part, by the same kind of "forgotten man" politics that other presidential candidates have been utilizing in various forms for decades. Bill Clinton, Ronald Reagan, Jimmy Carter, and Richard Nixon each won the White House by iterating a slogan about "restoring" America to some sense of former greatness; all but Clinton carried Texas at least once. Ronald Reagan's 1980 campaign even used the phrase "Let's Make America Great Again," as did Clinton's in 1992, though only briefly. Contexts matter, of course, as does tone. Barack Obama, for instance, styled the optimism and hopefulness of his 2008 campaign on Reagan's 1980 bid, while Clinton spoke of "a place called hope" in 1992, then repeated references to "making America great again" while campaigning for his wife, against Obama, in the 2008 Democratic primaries. Regardless, to many observers, Trump's utilization of "Make America Great Again" in 2016 sounded notes quite similar to the ones that George Wallace rung in his "Stand Up For America" third-party presidential campaign of 1968, not to mention those from Nixon's "This time, vote like your whole world depends on it" campaign of the same year.[4]

Interestingly, Trump's bids for the White House also mirrored elements of Pappy O'Daniel's statewide campaigns in Texas in 1938, 1940, 1941, and 1942. Additional parallels between Trump and O'Daniel are extensive, with both claiming to be an "outsider" called into service "by the people" to do battle against "professional politicians" or, in Trump's case, "the swamp." Trump's rise from business mogul to political stardom similarly mirrored O'Daniel's, the former capitalizing on his celebrity as a television show host, the latter as a radio show host. Additionally, both cultivated an evangelical Christian base that perceived the political left as a direct threat to family values and the freedom of religion. Associations between "atheistic socialism" and American liberalism have effectively motivated voters for decades, but O'Daniel and Trump have been among the most enthusiastic promoters of that message over the course of the last century. Similarly, speaking in 2012, Franklin Graham—the evangelist son of Billy Graham (and himself a noted Trump supporter in 2016 and 2020)—blamed FDR, the New Deal, and the "federal welfare state" for intentionally turning poor people against the church and, as a result, against religion—effectively replacing society's once-common reliance on the church with a new reliance on the state. "A hundred years ago, the social safety net in the country was provided by the church," Graham said. "If you didn't have a job, you'd go to the local church and ask the pastor if he [knew] somebody that could hire him. If you were hungry, you went to the local church and told them, 'I can't feed my family.' And the church would help you. But the government took that. And it took it away from the church."[5]

With all due respect to Franklin Graham, Donald Trump, and Pappy O'Daniel—or to Bill Clinton, Ronald Reagan, Jimmy Carter, Richard Nixon, or George Wallace—the most effective effort to capitalize on the "forgotten man" at any point in the last one hundred years was Franklin Roosevelt in his first campaign for the presidency in 1932. With unprecedented millions of Americans unsure of where they would find their next meal, FDR promised hope in the face of fear, engagement in the face of defeatism, and "a new deal" for the "forgotten man at the bottom of the economic pyramid"—and he did all of it while modernizing campaign strategy and American politics in ways that have persisted ever since.[6] In promising to restore "happy days" to Americans, FDR all but promised to make America great again. It was and remains a winning message. As William Leuchtenburg puts it, Roosevelt "revolutionized the agenda of American politics" and "re-created the modern presidency," dominating American press coverage "as no President before." In this sense, the "Age of FDR" could (and perhaps should) more appropriately be known as the "Roosevelt Revolution."[7]

Notes

DBCAH   Dolph Briscoe Center for American History, University of Texas at Austin
DHS   Dallas Historical Society, Dallas, TX
DMN   *Dallas Morning News*
OF2   Official File—200: Trips of the President, Franklin D. Roosevelt Presidential Library, Hyde Park, NY
OF3   Official File—300: Democratic National Committee Franklin D. Roosevelt Presidential Library, Hyde Park, NY
FDRL   Franklin D. Roosevelt Presidential Library and Museum, Hyde Park, NY
GMP   George Mahon Papers, Southwest Collection/Special Collections Library, Texas Tech University, Lubbock
HWSP   Hatton W. Sumners Papers, Dolph Briscoe Center for American History (DBCAH) and Dallas Historical Society (DHS)
JBP   James Buchanan Papers
LBJL   Lyndon B. Johnson Presidential Library and Museum, Austin, TX
MJP   Marvin Jones Papers
MMC   Maury Maverick Sr. Collection
MSP   Morris Sheppard Papers
PPPLBJ Pre-Presidential Papers of Lyndon B. Johnson
RJVA   Records of Governor James V. Allred
RKP   Richard M. Kleberg Papers
RWLO   Records of Governor W. Lee O'Daniel
SWC   Southwest Collection/Special Collections Library, Texas Tech University, Lubbock
SRP   Sam Rayburn Papers
TBLP   Thomas B. Love Papers
TSLAC   Texas State Library and Archives Commission, Austin

Introduction

1. *DMN*, February 20, 1935; *Houston Chronicle*, March 9, 1935; *DMN*, April 14, 1935; letter from Amon Carter to Sam Rayburn, April 14, 1935, box 3R274, SRP, DBCAH; *DMN*, April 14, 1935.

2. Telegram from Bob Barker to FDR, May 11, 1935, file 2488, President's Personal File, FDRL.

3. *Amarillo Globe*, October 17, 1935; Scrapbook II, 1913–1939 (vol. 2), MJP, SWC. For more on Marvin Jones, see Irvin M. May, *Marvin Jones: The Public Life of an Agrarian Advocate* (College Station: Texas A&M University Press, 1980).

4. V. O. Key, *Southern Politics in State and Nation* (New York: Vintage, 1949), 259.

5. There is an abundance of such histories, including among many excellent others, William E. Leuchtenburg, *Franklin D. Roosevelt and the New Deal, 1932–1940* (New York: Harper & Row, 1963); H. W. Brands, *Traitor to His Class: The Privileged Life and Radical Presidency of Franklin Delano Roosevelt* (New York: Doubleday, 2008); Robert Dallek, *Franklin D. Roosevelt: A Political Life* (New York: Viking, 2017); and Anthony J. Badger, *The New Deal: The Depression Years, 1933–1940* (New York: Noonday, 1989).

6. For more on Mahon, see Janet Neugebauer, *A Witness to History: George H. Mahon, West Texas Congressman* (Lubbock: Texas Tech University Press, 2017); for more on partisan realignment in Texas during the 1960s and 1970s, see Sean P. Cunningham, *Cowboy Conservatism: Texas and the Rise of the Modern Right* (Lexington: University Press of Kentucky, 2010).

7. For more on the Populist Party, as well as populism and progressivism as movements in Texas, see Walter L. Buenger, *The Path to a Modern South: Northeast Texas between Reconstruction and the Great Depression* (Austin: University of Texas Press, 2001), 75–103; Gregg Cantrell, *The People's Revolt: Texas Populists and the Roots of American Liberalism* (New Haven, CT: Yale University Press, 2020); and Lewis Gould, *Progressives and Prohibitionists: Texas Democrats in the Wilson Era* (Austin: University of Texas Press, 1973); see also Key, *Southern Politics in State and Nation*, 262.

8. Letter from Silliman Evans to James Farley, August 25, 1933, box 31, DNC3, FDRL.

9. Miscellaneous files, 1932–1945, box 31, folders O–Z, DNC3, FDRL.

10. Buenger, *The Path to a Modern South*, xxiii–xxvi.

11. Erica Grieder, *Big, Hot, Cheap, and Right: What America Can Learn from the Strange Genius of Texas* (New York: Public Affairs, 2013), 134–136, 158.

12. Buenger, *The Path to a Modern South*, xxiii–xxvi. For more on this general narrative, see Scott M. Sosebee, "The Split in the Texas Democratic Party, 1936–1956," MA thesis, Texas Tech University, 2000; Joseph Schiller, "Don't Sell Texas Short!: Amon Carter's Cultivation and Marketing of West Texas Na-

ture," *Southwestern Historical Quarterly* 121, no. 4 (April 2018): 389–415; Patrick L. Cox, *Ralph W. Yarborough: The People's Senator* (Austin: University of Texas Press, 2001); Brian A. Cervantez, *Amon Carter: A Lone Star Life* (Norman: University of Oklahoma Press, 2019); Steven Fenberg, *Unprecedented Power: Jesse Jones, Capitalism, and the Common Good* (College Station: Texas A&M University Press, 2011). For an example of how business leaders in another state embraced New Deal liberalism when doing so was advantageous, see Kathryn S. Olmsted, *Right Out of California: The 1930s and the Big Business Roots of Modern Conservatism* (New York: New Press, 2015).

13. Miscellaneous files, 1932–1945, box 31, folders O-Z, DNC3, FDRL.

14. Speeches and Speech Material, file 1820, container 12, President's Personal File, FDRL; "Sidelights," February 13, 1939, box 24, MJP, SWC.

15. Randolph B. Campbell, *Gone to Texas: A History of the Lone Star State* (New York: Oxford University Press, 2003), 380.

16. Unpublished memoir of Marvin Jones, copyright Columbia University Press, box 16, MJP. SWC.

17. Political announcement of Wright Patman for representative in Congress (1936), box 2L48, MMC, DBCAH.

18. Speeches and speech material, file 1820, container 12, President's Personal File; letter from A. N. Ashmore (Manor, TX) to FDR, January 1, 1933; letter from G. W. Allison to FDR, February 11, 1933; general correspondence from Texas voters to FDR, box 337, Papers of the Democratic National Committee, FDRL.

19. *Waco News-Tribune* (undated newspaper clipping, circa October 1932), box 338, Papers of the Democratic National Committee, FDRL.

20. General correspondence from Texas voters to FDR, box 338, Papers of the Democratic National Committee, FDRL. For more on FDR's penchant for personal diplomacy, see Michael Fullilove, *Rendezvous with Destiny: How Franklin D. Roosevelt and Five Extraordinary Men Took America into the War and into the World* (New York: Penguin Press, 2013).

21. James Reston, *The Lone Star: The Life of John Connally* (New York: Harper & Row, 1989), 40.

22. Martin Dies Jr., interview by Dr. Ray A. Stephens, May 31, 1966, transcript, 44, University of North Texas Oral History Collection, Willis Library, Denton; unpublished memoir of Marvin Jones, copyright Columbia University Press, box 16, MJP, SWC; see also Cunningham, *Cowboy Conservatism*, 239–242.

23. For instance, see Michael Phillips, *White Metropolis: Race, Ethnicity, and Religion in Dallas, 1841–2001* (Austin: University of Texas Press, 2006).

24. William A. Link, *The Paradox of Southern Progressivism, 1880–1930* (Chapel Hill: University of North Carolina Press, 1992), 57, 71, 75, 246–247.

25. Key, *Southern Politics in State and Nation*, 260.

26. For more on the politics of race during the New Deal, and specifically the

New Deal's inattention to African Americans and issues of specific import to African American communities, see David M. P. Freund, *Colored Property: State Policy in White Racial Politics in Suburban America* (Chicago, IL: University of Chicago Press, 2007); Linda Gordon, *Pitied but Not Entitled: Single Mothers and the History of Welfare, 1890–1935* (New York: Free Press, 1994); Thomas J. Sugrue, *The Origins of the Urban Crisis: Race and Inequality in Postwar Detroit* (Princeton, NJ: Princeton University Press, 1996); and Patricia Sullivan, *Days of Hope: Race and Democracy in the New Deal Era* (Chapel Hill: University of North Carolina Press, 1996); see also Alwyn Barr, *Black Texans: A History of African Americans in Texas, 1528–1995* (Norman: University of Oklahoma Press, 1996); Glenda Elizabeth Gilmore, *Defying Dixie: The Radical Roots of Civil Rights, 1919–1950* (New York: W. W. Norton, 2008); Neil Foley, *White Scourge: Mexicans, Blacks, and Poor Whites in Texas Cotton Culture* (Berkeley: University of California Press, 1997); and Emilio Zamora, *Claiming Rights and Righting Wrongs: Mexican Workers and Job Politics in Texas during World War II* (College Station: Texas A&M University Press, 2009).

27. See, for instance, Alwyn Barr, *Reconstruction to Reform: Texas Politics, 1876–1906* (Dallas, TX: Southern Methodist University Press, 1971); Gould, *Progressives and Prohibitionists*; Norman D. Brown, *Hood, Bonnet, and Little Brown Jug: Texas Politics, 1921–1928* (College Station: Texas A&M University Press, 1984); Norman D. Brown, *Biscuits, the Dole, and Nodding Donkeys: Texas Politics, 1929–1932* (Austin: University of Texas Press, 2019); George N. Green, *The Establishment in Texas Politics: The Primitive Years, 1938–1957* (Norman: University of Oklahoma Press, 1979); Seth Shepard McKay, *Texas Politics, 1906–1944* (Lubbock: Texas Tech University Press, 1952).

28. Buenger, *The Path to a Modern South*, xxiii–xxvi; Cantrell, *The People's Revolt*, 21, 408.

29. Thomas Frank, *What's the Matter with Kansas?: How Conservatives Won the Heart of America* (New York: Henry Holt, 2004); Grieder, *Big, Hot, Cheap, and Right*; Lawrence Wright, *God Save Texas: A Journey into the Soul of the Lone Star State* (New York: Alfred A. Knopf, 2018).

30. Daniel J. Boorstin, *The Image: A Guide to Pseudo-Events in America* (New York: Vintage Books, 1961, 2012); David Greenberg, *Nixon's Shadow: The History of an Image* (New York: W. W. Norton, 2003); Joe McGinnis, *The Selling of the President 1968* (New York: Trident Press, 1969); Merrill D. Peterson, *The Jefferson Image in the American Mind* (New York: Oxford University Press, 1960); Richard Slotkin, *Gunfighter Nation: The Myth of the Frontier in Twentieth-Century America* (Norman: University of Oklahoma Press, 1998).

31. Martin Dies Jr., interview by Dr. Ray A. Stephens, May 31, 1966, transcript, 37.

32. *New York Times*, December 24, 1943.

Chapter 1. "We Can Do No Worse"

1. Letter from Charles D. Berry to FDR, December 6, 1928, box 332, Papers of the Democratic National Committee, FDRL.

2. Letter from Charles D. Berry to FDR, December 6, 1928.

3. Letter from James Ralph Bell (Gainesville, TX) to Thomas Love, September 5, 1928, box 32, Hoover Campaign 1928, folder 1, TBLP, DHS.

4. General correspondence, box 32, Hoover Campaign 1928, folders 1U–11U, 1, 2, TBLP, DHS.

5. Letter from Charles D. Berry to FDR, December 6, 1928, box 332.

6. Norman D. Brown, *Hood, Bonnet, and Little Brown Jug: Texas Politics, 1921–1928* (Texas A&M University Press, 1984). The best discussion of shifting Texas culture and its intersection with politics and economics during the first decades of the twentieth century can be found in Walter Buenger, *The Path to a Modern South: Northeast Texas between Reconstruction and the Great Depression* (Austin: University of Texas Press, 2001), and V. O. Key, *Southern Politics in State and Nation* (New York: Vintage Books, 1949), 264–265.

7. Brown, *Hood, Bonnet, and Little Brown Jug*, 49–87; For additional information on the Ku Klux Klan in Texas and the United States during the 1920s, see among others Linda Gordon, *The Second Coming of the KKK: The Ku Klux Klan of the 1920s and the American Political Tradition* (New York: W. W. Norton, 2017), and Nancy Maclean, *Behind the Mask of Chivalry: The Making of the Second Ku Klux Klan* (New York: Oxford University Press, 1994). For more on modernism and 1920s American culture broadly, see Lynn Dumenil, *The Modern Temper: American Culture and Society in the 1920s* (New York: Hill and Wang, 1995).

8. Brown, *Hood, Bonnet, and Little Brown Jug*, 56; Michael Phillips, *White Metropolis: Race, Ethnicity, and Religion in Dallas, 1841–2001* (Austin: University of Texas Press, 2006), 75–76.

9. Patrick L. Cox and Michael Phillips, *The House Will Come to Order: How the Texas Speaker Became a Power in State and National Politics* (Austin: University of Texas Press, 2010), 34.

10. Buenger, *The Path to a Modern South*, 256.

11. Phillips, *White Metropolis*, 85–102. Additional sources of information on the Texas Klan include Charles C. Alexander, *The Ku Klux Klan in the Southwest* (Lexington: University of Kentucky Press, 1965); see also Robert Wuthnow, *Rough Country: How Texas Became America's Most Powerful Bible-Belt State* (Princeton, NJ: Princeton University Press, 2014), 47–50.

12. Brown, *Hood, Bonnet, and Little Brown Jug*, 111–128; Phillips, *White Metropolis*, 85.

13. For more on the Fergusons, see Lewis L. Gould, *Progressives and Prohibitionists: Texas Democrats in the Wilson Era* (Austin: University of Texas Press, 1973); see also Brown, *Hood, Bonnet, and Little Brown Jug*, 211–296.

14. In 1930, opponents of Ma Ferguson ran an advertisement in the *Dallas Morning News* depicting a stream of "violent offenders" walking free from prisons, all "unconditionally pardoned" by "Fergusonism." The image included the word "RAPISTS" in all capital letters, though each of the prisoners depicted in the cartoon was white. Still, the image appeared under the heading, "Do Such Acts of Fergusonism Assure Your Home, Your Sister and Your Friends Safety?" Even as conversations about the Klan and Prohibition faded in view of the Depression, the potency of race, often communicated under the auspices of "law and order," continued to resonate. *DMN*, July 21, 1930, box 4ZB213, JBP, DBCAH.

15. Brown, *Hood, Bonnet, and Little Brown Jug,* 211-296.

16. *Houston Chronicle,* June 26-29, 1928; letter from Elmer Johnson to Thomas Love, September 26, 1928; letter from Thomas Love to C. M. Rork, November 17, 1928, box 32, Hoover Campaign 1928, folder 1, TBLP, DHS. For more on Moody, see Patricia Bernstein, *Ten Dollars to Hate: The Texas Man Who Fought the Klan* (College Station: Texas A&M University Press, 2017).

17. John F. Kennedy faced many of these same obstacles when he ran for president in 1960, though the power of television and an astutely managed appearance before Protestant ministers in Houston effectively mitigated the issue for him in 1960, whereas Smith had no such skill or good fortune when he ran in 1928. For more on Smith's campaign broadly, see Robert Chiles, *The Revolution of '28: Al Smith, American Progressivism, and the Coming of the New Deal* (Ithaca, NY: Cornell University Press, 2018).

18. Letters from William Henry to FDR, September 11, 21, 1928; miscellaneous letters, container 14, Campaign of 1928: General Correspondence, FDRL; Brown, *Hood, Bonnet, and Little Brown Jug,* 374-422; see also Martin Dies Jr., interview by Dr. Ray A. Stephens, May 31, 1966, transcript, 3-4, University of North Texas Oral History Collection, Willis Library, Denton.

19. Letter from Charles R. Johnson (Bellville, TX) to Thomas Love, October 13, 1928, box 31, Hoover Campaign 1928, folder 1, TBLP, DHS.

20. Letter from Thomas Love to C. M. Rork, November 17, 1928.

21. Political Campaign Files, 1927-1930; letter from Thomas Love to Winslow Porter, November 19, 1928, General Correspondence, box 32, Hoover Campaign 1928, folder 1, TBLP, DHS; letters from William Henry to FDR, September 11, 21, 1928; miscellaneous letters, Campaign of 1928: General Correspondence, FDRL; Brown, *Hood, Bonnet, and Little Brown Jug,* 374-422.

22. *Houston Chronicle,* August 12, 1928; Randolph B. Campbell, *Gone to Texas: A History of the Lone Star State* (New York: Oxford University Press, 2003), 360-395; For more on Texas cotton culture during this period, see Neil Foley, *The White Scourge: Mexicans, Blacks, and Poor Whites in Texas Cotton Culture* (Berkeley: University of California Press, 1997); and Keith J. Volanto, *Texas, Cotton, and the New Deal* (College Station: Texas A&M University Press, 2004).

23. The Texas State Historical Association's *Texas Almanac* is an excellent source for simple statistical data on Texas elections, and much of the data is available online at https://texasalmanac.com. To compare with other ex-Confederate states, Al Smith carried Alabama, Arkansas, Georgia, Louisiana, Mississippi, and South Carolina (in addition to northern states Massachusetts and Rhode Island). Among the southern states in Smith's column, Alabama gave him the smallest percentage (51.3%) while South Carolina gave him the largest (91.4%); Roger M. Olien, *From Token to Triumph: The Texas Republicans since 1920* (Dallas, TX: Southern Methodist University Press, 1982), 47; Brown, *Hood, Bonnet, and Little Brown Jug*, 374–422; Gould, *Progressives and Prohibitionists*, 281–282.

24. Gould, *Progressives and Prohibitionists*, 282. Gould argues that the "onset of the depression and the coming of the New Deal ended the era of ethnocultural controversies, returned Texans to their Democratic loyalty, and opened the modern era of state politics." See also William E. Leuchtenburg, *Franklin D. Roosevelt and the New Deal, 1932–1940* (New York: Harper & Row, 1963), 9.

25. Buenger, *The Path to a Modern South*, 237–239; Gregg Cantrell, *The People's Revolt: Texas Populists and the Roots of American Liberalism* (New Haven, CT: Yale University Press, 2020).

26. Campbell, *Gone to Texas*, 360–395; Patrick Cox, *The First Texas News Barons* (Austin: University of Texas Press, 2005), 179–184; Cox and Phillips, *The House Will Come to Order*, 36–37; William E. Leuchtenburg, *The Perils of Prosperity, 1914–1932* (Chicago: University of Chicago Press, 1958), 261.

27. Letter from FDR to Marvin Jones, November 30, 1928, box 23, MJP, SWC.

28. Letter from Thomas Love to William Mills, November 17, 1928, box 32, Hoover Campaign 1928, folder 1, TBLP, DHS.

29. Letter from J. A. Edgerton to Thomas Love, November 16, 1928; letter from Thomas Love to Winslow Porter, November 19, 1928, box 32, Hoover Campaign 1928, folder 1, TBLP, DHS.

30. Leuchtenburg, *The Perils of Prosperity, 1914–1932*, 137; McKay, *Texas Politics, 1906–1944*, 188; Olien, *From Token to Triumph*, 47; Norman D. Brown, *Biscuits, the Dole, and Nodding Donkeys: Texas Politics, 1929–1932* (Austin: University of Texas Press, 2019), 3–6.

31. Letter from Thomas B. Love to FDR, December 19, 1933, box 3E262, Franklin D. Roosevelt Letters, DBCAH.

32. "Americanism," speech by James Buchanan, *Congressional Record,* June 5, 1920, box 4Zc51; "Speeches re: Prohibition, National Women's Suffrage," box 4zb310; Campaign Pamphlet, 1926, "Buchanan's Service Outlined by Reed: Travis Chairman for Congressman Urges His Re-Election on Training," box 4zb424, JBP, DBCAH.

33. Speech by James Buchanan, March 15, 1928, box 4zb158; editorial,

Shreveport Journal, April 3, 1928; *Boston Herald*, March 20, 1928, box 4zb158; letter from John Nance Garner to James Buchanan, November 29, 1929, box 4ZC112, JBP, DBCAH. Garner and Buchanan also discussed whether the pink bollworm infestation could have been prevented by tighter security on the Mexican border and suggested that illegal transports from Mexico were likely to blame for the problem.

34. "Congressman James P. Buchanan, A Man of Action," editorial, *Brenham Banner-Press*, June 11, 1930; *Austin American-Statesman*, June 13, 1930, box 4zb310, JBP, DBCAH.

35. "Congressman James P. Buchanan, A Man of Action"; *Austin American-Statesman*, June 13, 1930.

36. Campaign newspaper—1928: "Wright Patman Opens Campaign for Congress: Announces Platforms and Arraigns Present Incumbent," box 77B, Wright Patman Papers, LBJL; Nancy Beck Young, *Wright Patman: Populism, Liberalism, and the American Dream* (Dallas: Southern Methodist University Press, 2000), 52–54, 62–72, 73–104; see also Buenger, *The Path to a Modern South*, 225, 240–252.

37. Gould, *Progressives and Prohibitionists*; see also Escal F. Duke, "The Political Career of Morris Sheppard, 1875–1941," PhD diss., University of Texas at Austin, 1958. Assorted speeches by Morris Sheppard, 1929–1932; *Texarkana Gazette*, November 24, 1930; speech by Morris Sheppard, "Our Dry United States" at the Anti-Saloon League Banquet, Washington, DC, January 19, 1932; *Congressional Record*, January 19, 1932, box 3N187, MSP, DBCAH. For more on the various ways in which religion informed progressive Texans' view of government during the 1920s and 1930s, see Wuthnow, *Rough Country*, 196–197.

38. Gould, *Progressives and Prohibitionists*; see also Duke, "The Political Career of Morris Sheppard, 1875–1941"; assorted speeches by Morris Sheppard, 1929–1932; *Texarkana Gazette*, November 24, 1930; Sheppard, "Our Dry United States"; *Congressional Record*, January 19, 1932. "Creed of the Hooverist—A.D. 1932," box 335, Papers of the Democratic National Committee, FDRL. Sheppard persisted with dramatic, rhetorical religiosity in his fight against alcohol even after FDR's election. In one speech, Sheppard warned that the "repeal of prohibition would be the beginning of the dismemberment of the soul of America." "Thirteenth Anniversary of Eighteenth Amendment—Shall America Retreat From an Ideal," speech by Morris Sheppard, *Congressional Record*, January 16, 1933, box 3N188, MSP, DBCAH; see also speech by Morris Sheppard, *Congressional Record*, August 11, 1937, box 2G198, MSP, DBCAH. For more on the concept of "breadwinner liberalism," see Robert O. Self, *All in the Family: The Realignment of American Democracy since the 1960s* (New York: Hill & Wang, 2012); and Elaine Tyler May, *Homeward Bound: American Families in the Cold War Era* (New York: Basic Books, 2008), 39–57. May does not use the term "bread-

winner liberalism," but does effectively connect political behavior to patriarchal and familial traditions, framed by religion.

39. Speech manuscript by Morris Sheppard (1929); speech by Morris Sheppard, April 30, 1929, box 3N187, MSP, DBCAH.

40. Biographical Details, MMC, DBCAH; Brown, *Biscuits, the Dole, and Nodding Donkeys*, 166–168.

41. House Vote #60, 1930 (71st Congress), To Agree to Report of Conference Committee on H.R. 2667, June 14, 1930, https://www.govtrack.us/congress/votes/71-2/h60; Olien, *From Token to Triumph*, 58–59.

42. "Facing the Facts in 1932," an address by W. L. Clayton, at the Annual Meeting, Chamber of Commerce, Houston, TX, January 7, 1932, box 4zb310, JBP, DBCAH.

43. Letter from John Nance Garner to Marvin Jones, January 23, 1932, box 21, MJP, SWC; letters from John Nance Garner to Sam Rayburn, January 23 and 27, 1932, box 3U106, SRP, DBCAH; see also Bascom N. Timmons, *Garner of Texas: A Personal History* (New York: Harper & Brothers, 1948).

44. Miscellaneous political cartoons by Clifford Berryman, boxes 2W94 and 2W95, John Nance Garner Papers, Dolph Briscoe Center for American History, University of Texas at Austin; undated editorial, "John Garner for President," by JAS. E. Ferguson, box 4zb310, JBP, DBCAH; see also Thomas T. Spencer, "For the Good of the Party: John Nance Garner, FDR, and New Deal Politics, 1933–1940." *Southwestern Historical Quarterly* 121, no. 3 (January 2018): 254–282.

45. *New York Times Magazine*, November 22, 1931, box 66, TBLP, DHS.

46. Letters from John Nance Garner to Sam Rayburn, January 23 and 27, 1932, box 3U106, SRP, DBCAH; David T. Beito, *Taxpayers in Revolt: Tax Resistance during the Great Depression* (Chapel Hill: University of North Carolina Press, 1989), 161–163. Beito argues that both Congress and the electorate remained relatively conservative during the Hoover years, 1929–1933, and did not necessarily see support for FDR as a mandate for aggressive reform. However, the American electorate did move to the left after Roosevelt assumed office, thanks to positive impressions of Roosevelt's leadership and the effect of his policies, at least through 1937; see also Robert S. McElvaine, *The Great Depression in America, 1929–1941* (New York: Times Books, 1984).

47. Letter from Edmund R. Cheesborough to Beauford Jester, May 10, 1947; "Extracts from Speeches of Franklin D. Roosevelt as to Economy in Government and Spending," box 4-14/81, Records of Governor Beauford H. Jester, TSLAC.

48. "Marvin Jones for Congress—Pamphlet," campaign brochure, 1928, box 23, MJP, SWC. For more on Jones, see Irvin M. May, *Marvin Jones: The Public Life of an Agrarian Advocate* (College Station: Texas A&M University Press, 1980).

49. "Marvin Jones for Congress—Pamphlet"; May, *Marvin Jones*. Remarks by Marvin Jones in Haskell, Texas, October 21, 1931, box 24, MJP, SWC.

50. Unpublished memoir of Marvin Jones, copyright Columbia University Press, box 16, MJP, SWC; general correspondence, box 23, MJP, SWC.

51. *San Antonio Evening News*, February 23, 1932, box 4ZC112, JBP, DBCAH.

52. H. W. Brands, *Traitor to His Class: The Privileged Life and Radical Presidency of Franklin Delano Roosevelt* (New York: Doubleday, 2008), 245–246; Brown, *Biscuits, the Dole, and Nodding Donkeys*, 211–213.

53. Pre-Convention Notes: Texas, 1932, box 332, Papers of the Democratic National Committee, FDRL. For a discussion of how these issues shaped the 1932 Democratic National Convention, see, among many good sources, Brands, *Traitor to His Class*, 245–247; see also Robert Dallek, *Franklin D. Roosevelt: A Political Life* (New York: Viking, 2017), 101–132.

54. For more, see, among others, Terry Golway, *Frank and Al: FDR, Al Smith, and the Unlikely Alliance That Created the Modern Democratic Party* (New York: St. Martin's Press, 2018).

55. Brown, *Biscuits, the Dole, and Nodding Donkeys*, 285–287; Leuchtenburg, *Franklin D. Roosevelt and the New Deal, 1932–1940*, 4–5.

56. *New York Times*, July 1, 1932; see also Anthony R. Carrozza, *The Dukes of Duval County: The Parr Family and Texas Politics* (Norman: University of Oklahoma Press, 2017), 32.

57. Seth Shepard McKay, *Texas Politics, 1906–1944* (Lubbock: Texas Tech Press, 1952), 243; Leuchtenburg, *The Perils of Prosperity, 1914–1932*, 266; Leuchtenburg, *Franklin D. Roosevelt and the New Deal, 1932–1940*, 8; general correspondence, letters to FDR from Texans, August 1932, box 333, Papers of the Democratic National Committee, FDRL; Spencer, "For the Good of the Party," 257; According to Martin Dies Jr., Garner forever regretted his decision to give up the speakership of the House in exchange for a place on FDR's ticket, calling it "the greatest mistake of my life." Martin Dies Jr., interview by Dr. Ray A. Stephens, transcript, 6.

58. Memorandum from Louis Howe, re: The Political Outlook: Texas, box 332, Papers of the Democratic National Committee, FDRL.

59. Memorandum from Louis Howe, re: The Political Outlook: Texas; letter from C. W. Amberg, County Treasurer, Fayette County, TX, to FDR, June 8, 1932; general correspondence, folder 728, box 332, Papers of the Democratic National Committee, FDRL; Political Correspondence, box 21, MJP, SWC; Olien, *From Token to Triumph*, 47–48; Gould, *Progressives and Prohibitionists*, xxvii, 25, 61, 115; Brown, *Biscuits, the Dole, and Nodding Donkeys*, 225–228, 289.

60. Letter from Thomas Love to John Nance Garner, January 14, 1932, box 66, TBLP, DHS.

61. Letter from John Nance Garner to Thomas Love, January 16, 1932, box 66, TBLP, DHS.

62. Love's letters to FDR gushed with superlatives and platitudes. White

House staff from both eras often perceived the redundant correspondence as an exercise in sycophancy. The same had been true of Love's letters to Wilson. For more, see Franklin D. Roosevelt Letters, DBCAH; letter from Thomas B. Love to FDR, December 19, 1933; general correspondence, Love to FDR, box 3E262, Franklin D. Roosevelt Letters, DBCAH.

63. Unpublished memoir of Marvin Jones, copyright Columbia University Press, 600, box 16, MJP. SWC; *DMN*, July 18, 1932.

64. Speech manuscript by Morris Sheppard, 1932, box 3N187, MSP; "Old Line Dems Work to Hold Party Lines." *Austin American-Statesman*, July 9, 1932, box 4Zc88, JBP, DBCAH; Leuchtenburg, *Franklin D. Roosevelt and the New Deal, 1932-1940*, 4-19; Leuchtenburg, *The Perils of Prosperity, 1914-1932*, 261.

65. Letters from/to FDR to/from Garner, August 1, 1932, box 335, Papers of the Democratic National Committee, FDRL.

66. *DMN*, August 9, 1932; *DMN*, August 14, 1932; Spencer, "For the Good of the Party," 254-282.

67. Spencer, "For the Good of the Party," 254-282; letter from John Nance Garner to Louis Howe, September 2, 1932, box 335, Papers of the Democratic National Committee, FDRL.

68. *DMN*, August 7, 1932; *DMN*, August 18, 1932.

69. General correspondence, 1932, boxes 335 and 336, Papers of the Democratic National Committee, FDRL.

70. General correspondence, 1932.

71. General correspondence, 1932; letter from Ed McElroy (Waxahachie, Texas) to FDR, October 1, 1932; letter from E. R. Mangum (Bowie, Texas) to FDR, October 4, 1932; letter from E. I. Meador (Post, Texas) to FDR, September 7, 1932; letter from Grover Mitchell (Motley County, Texas), October 13, 1932, box 336, Papers of the Democratic National Committee, FDRL.

72. General correspondence, 1932; letter from Herbert Spencer (San Antonio, TX) to FDR, November 15, 1932, box 340, Papers of the Democratic National Committee, FDRL.

73. McKay, *Texas Politics, 1906-1944*, 243-244.

74. McKay, 218-221, 238-244; Brown, *Biscuits, the Dole, and Nodding Donkeys*, 196-198.

75. Olien, *From Token to Triumph*, 62-63.

76. *DMN*, October 19, 1932; *DMN*, October 23, 1932; *DMN*, November 10, 1932; McKay, *Texas Politics, 1906-1944*, 243-244.

77. *Scurry County Times*, July 7, 1932; unpublished memoir of Marvin Jones, copyright Columbia University Press, box 16; general correspondence, box 23, MJP, SWC.

78. Letters from T. A. Low to James Buchanan, January 15, 1932, March 25, 1932, April 23, 1932, "Political Correspondence, T.A. Low, 1930-1935"; miscellaneous letters, "Political and Personal Correspondence, 1930-1935"; letter

from James Buchanan to Constituents, "Campaign Correspondence, 1932," box 4zb310, JBP, DBCAH.

79. "1932 Campaign Speech by Buchanan," box 4Zc88; miscellaneous letters, "Political and Personal Correspondence, 1930–1935," box 4zb310, JBP, DBCAH.

80. Newspaper clippings, pamphlets, speeches—1932 Campaign, box 4zb424; "Address of Hon. Merton L. Harris, Candidate for Congressman from the Tenth Congressional District, delivered at Taylor, Texas, City Park, Friday Evening, July 8, 1932"; Platform Statement, W. Gregory Hatcher, Candidate for Railroad Commissioner, *Austin American-Statesman*, July 9, 1932, box 4Zc88, JBP, DBCAH.

81. James Reston, *The Lone Star: The Life of John Connally* (New York: Harper & Row, 1989), 39; Robert A. Caro, *The Path to Power: The Years of Lyndon Johnson* (New York: Alfred A. Knopf, 1982), 306; Martin Dies Jr., interview by Dr. Ray A. Stephens, transcript, 14.

82. Garner's decision to run for reelection while also running on the presidential ticket served as a model for Lyndon Johnson, who did the same thing in 1960, running for vice president at the same time as running for reelection to the United States Senate.

83. Reston, *The Lone Star*, 39; Caro, *The Path to Power*, 306.

Chapter 2. "Conservative Progressive Constructive Legislation"

1. Inaugural Address of President Franklin D. Roosevelt (speech file 610), March 4, 1933, box 13, Franklin D. Roosevelt, Master Speech File, 1898–1945, FDRL. For more on the subject of FDR and religion, see Alison Collis Greene, *No Depression in Heaven: The Great Depression, the New Deal, and the Transformation of Religion in the Delta* (New York: Oxford University Press, 2016); see also Robert Wuthnow, *Rough Country: How Texas Became America's Most Powerful Bible-Belt State* (Princeton, NJ: Princeton University Press, 2014), 197–198.

2. Martin Dies Jr., interview by Dr. Ray A. Stephens, May 31, 1966, transcript, 28, University of North Texas Oral History Collection, Willis Library, Denton.

3. Robert A. Caro, *The Path to Power: The Years of Lyndon Johnson* (New York: Alfred A. Knopf, 1982), 269–277.

4. Caro, *The Path to Power*, 269–277.

5. Letter from Harry Hopkins to James Buchanan, October 29, 1934; "Retail Ledger," *Magazine of Retail Management*, October 1934, box 4zb178, JBP, DBCAH.

6. Letter from T. A. Low to James Buchanan, December 20, 1932, and letter from T. A. Lowe, president, First National Bank of Brenham, TX, to James

Buchanan (undated), "Political Correspondence, T.A. Low, 1930–1935," box 4zb310, JBP, DBCAH.

7. For more, see for instance Gregg Cantrell, *The People's Revolt: Texas Populists and the Roots of American Liberalism* (New Haven, CT: Yale University Press, 2020); Richard Hofstadter, *The Age of Reform* (New York: Vintage, 1955); Alan Trachtenberg, *The Incorporation of America: Society and Culture in the Gilded Age* (New York: Hill & Wang, 1982); Michael Kazin, *The Populist Persuasion: An American History* (New York: Basic Books, 1995); and Charles Postel, *The Populist Vision* (New York: Oxford University Press, 2007).

8. Letter from Charles D. Smith to FDR, January 1, 1933, box 339, Papers of the Democratic National Committee, FDRL.

9. Letter from Charles D. Smith to FDR, January 1, 1933.

10. William E. Leuchtenburg, *Franklin D. Roosevelt and the New Deal, 1932–1940* (New York: Harper & Row, 1963), 47–51.

11. *Amarillo Sunday News and Globe*, December 25, 1932, Scrapbook 2, 1913–1939 (vol. 2), MJP, SWC.

12. Speech by Marvin Jones, "Emergency Farm Program and Business Recovery," Columbia Radio Network, January 14, 1933, Scrapbook 2, 1913–1939 (vol. 2), MJP, SWC. For more on FDR's largely silent relationship with Hoover in the months between his election and inauguration, see, among other good sources, David M. Kennedy, *Freedom from Fear: The American People in Depression and War, 1929–1945* (New York: Oxford University Press, 1999), 104–130.

13. *Amarillo News*, January 22, 1933; *Pittsburgh Press*, "January" (undated, circa 1933), Scrapbook 2, 1913–1939 (vol. 2), MJP, SWC.

14. Speech by Marvin Jones, "The Essentials of Farm Legislation," Columbia Radio Network, March 18, 1933, Scrapbook 2, 1913–1939 (vol. 2), MJP, SWC.

15. "Sidelights" by Marvin Jones, April 20, 1933, and "Sidelights" by Marvin Jones, April 22, 1933, box 24, MJP, SWC; see also Leuchtenburg, *Franklin D. Roosevelt and the New Deal, 1932–1940*, 83; Martin Dies Jr., interview by Dr. Ray A. Stephens, May 31, 1966, transcript, 1, University of North Texas Oral History Collection, Willis Library, Denton. Even Martin Dies Jr.—the reactionary conservative who later created the House Committee on Un-American Activities—embraced similar populist measures during the debates over agricultural reform, at one point introducing his own bill to provide for the sale of farm surpluses abroad in return for a silver rate above world market prices. Dies frequently noted that the Populist Party and the populist leanings of his father, Martin Dies Sr., inspired him into politics.

16. House Vote #7 in 1933 (Seventy-Third Congress), To Pass H.R. 3835 (P.L.10), To relieve the existing national economic emergency by increasing agricultural purchasing power, to raise revenue for extraordinary expenses incurred by reason of such emergency, to provide emergency relief with respect to agricultural indebtedness, to provide for the orderly liquidation of joint-stock

land, banks, and for other purposes, March 22, 1933, https://www.govtrack.us /congress/votes/73-1/h7; Senate Vote #43 (Seventy-Third Congress), To Pass H.R. 3835, April 28, 1933, https://www.govtrack.us/congress/votes/73-1 /s43.

17. *DMN*, March 27, 1933; *DMN*, April 8, 1933; *DMN*, April 23, 1933; *DMN*, May 4, 1933; *DMN*, May 10, 1933; *DMN*, May 12, 1933.

18. Kennedy, *Freedom from Fear*, 203–204; Leuchtenburg, *Franklin D. Roosevelt and the New Deal, 1932–1940*, 47–51, Seth Shepard McKay, *Texas Politics, 1906–1944* (Lubbock: Texas Tech Press, 1952), 405.

19. Newspaper clipping, Editorial, *Amarillo Globe* (undated, circa 1933), Scrapbook 2, 1913–1939 (vol. 2), MJP, SWC.

20. *Amarillo Daily News*, July 20, 1933, Scrapbook 2, 1913–1939 (vol. 2), MJP, SWC. For more on the popularity of the AAA in Texas, see again Scott M. Sosebee, "The Split in the Texas Democratic Party, 1936–1956," MA thesis, Texas Tech University, 2000, and Keith J. Volanto, *Texas, Cotton, and the New Deal*, (College Station: Texas A&M University Press, 2004), 27–57, 88.

21. *Amarillo Daily News*, July 30, 1933, Scrapbook 2, 1913–1939 (vol. 2), MJP, SWC.

22. Newspaper clipping, "Jones Recites New Deal Cure" (undated, circa August 1933), Scrapbook 2, 1913–1939 (vol. 2), MJP, SWC.

23. Questionnaire/letter from Lionel V. Patenaude to Marvin Jones, September 28, 1952, box 19, MJP, SWC; see also Sosebee, "The Split in the Texas Democratic Party, 1936–1956"; Volanto, *Texas, Cotton, and the New Deal*, 67–84.

24. Leuchtenburg, *Franklin D. Roosevelt and the New Deal, 1932–1940*, 75.

25. Statement upon signing the Bankhead Cotton Bill (speech file 694), April 21, 1934, box 17, Franklin D. Roosevelt, Master Speech File, 1898–1945, FDRL.

26. "What the 'New Deal' Means to the Farmers of America," Remarks of the Honorable Marvin Jones of Texas in the House of Representatives, June 15, 1934, box 23; "New Agricultural Adjustment Legislation," speech by Marvin Jones, August 17, 1935, NBC Radio, box 24, MJP, SWC.

27. Telegram from Thomas B. Love to FDR, January 2, 1934, box 3E262, Franklin D. Roosevelt Letters, DBCAH.

28. "The New Bankhead Bill, the Greatest Service Ever Rendered the Cotton Farmer," speech by Thomas B. Love to Dallas Agricultural Club, April 16, 1934, box 3E262, Franklin D. Roosevelt Letters, DBCAH. Similar sentiment was expressed by farmers throughout Texas in 1933 and 1934, many attempting to defend themselves against allegations that they were either unpatriotic or "communistic" in their calls for federal intervention and assistance. Letter from Charles D. Smith to FDR, January 1, 1933, box 339, Papers of the Democratic National Committee, FDRL.

29. Leuchtenburg, *Franklin D. Roosevelt and the New Deal, 1932–1940*, 75–78.

30. Telegram from Thomas B. Love to FDR, June 19, 1934, box 3E262, Franklin D. Roosevelt Letters, DBCAH; letter from Thomas Love to John Nance Garner, August 8, 1934, box 66, TBLP, DHS.

31. Press Release, June 24, 1934, box 3E262, Franklin D. Roosevelt Letters, DBCAH.

32. Bryan Burrough, *The Big Rich: The Rise and Fall of the Greatest Texas Oil Fortunes* (New York: Penguin Press, 2009), 78; Patrick L. Cox and Michael Phillips, *The House Will Come to Order: How the Texas Speaker Became a Power in State and National Politics* (Austin: University of Texas Press, 2010), 37; Erica Grieder, *Big, Hot, Cheap, and Right: What America Can Learn from the Strange Genius of Texas* (New York: PublicAffairs, 2013), 92–93; George N. Green, *The Establishment in Texas Politics: The Primitive Years, 1938–1957* (Norman: University of Oklahoma Press, 1979), 18.

33. Burrough, *The Big Rich*, 85–87.

34. Unidentified newspaper clipping, June 1934, "Love Defends Insurance of Bank Deposits," box 3E262, Franklin D. Roosevelt Letters, DBCAH.

35. Telegram from Thomas B. Love to Louis Howe, August 8, 1934, box 3E262, Franklin D. Roosevelt Letters, DBCAH; Lewis L. Gould, *Progressives and Prohibitionists: Texas Democrats in the Wilson Era* (Austin: University of Texas Press, 1973), 77, 82, 279, 290.

36. Leuchtenburg, *Franklin D. Roosevelt and the New Deal, 1932–1940*, 71.

37. Leuchtenburg; *Houston Chronicle*, October 12, 2008; see also Lionel V. Patenaude, *Texans, Politics, and the New Deal* (New York: Garland, 1983). For more on the politics of home ownership, see David M. P. Freund, *Colored Property: State Policy and White Racial Politics in Suburban America* (Chicago: University of Chicago Press, 2010), 121, 433.

38. Morris Sheppard, speech manuscript, State Democratic Convention, Galveston, Texas, September 11, 1934, box 3N187, MSP, DBCAH; Resolution approved by Dallas County Democrats and adopted by Democratic State Convention, Galveston, Texas, September 15, 1934, box 3E262, Franklin D. Roosevelt Letters, DBCAH.

39. Morris Sheppard, speech to Rotary Club of Texarkana, August 26, 1934, box 3N187, MSP, DBCAH.

40. "Origin and Definition of the New Deal—in Comparison with Communism and Socialism," box 2G196, MSP, DBCAH.

41. Morris Sheppard, miscellaneous statements, comments, and speeches, box 2G196, MSP, DBCAH.

42. Morris Sheppard, miscellaneous statements, comments, and speeches.

43. See, for instance, letter from Miriam A. Ferguson to W. W. Heath, March 9, 1934, box 301-484, Records of Governor Miriam Amanda Ferguson, TSLAC.

44. Acceptance Speech on Receiving Nomination (speech file 483), Chi-

cago, Illinois, July 2, 1932, box 9, Franklin D. Roosevelt, Master Speech File, 1898–1945, FDRL. For more on corporate America's response to the early New Deal, see among others Kim Phillips-Fein, *Invisible Hands: The Businessmen's Crusade against the New Deal* (New York: W. W. Norton, 2009). Roosevelt was not above referencing Jefferson in defense of his own agenda, but also routinely referred to his cause, and Jefferson's, as "American" rather than simply the Democratic Party's offspring. In March 1934, Roosevelt suggested that the party's annual Jefferson Day dinner include Republicans, saying that "much as we love Thomas Jefferson, we should not celebrate him in a partisan way." Leuchtenburg, *Franklin D. Roosevelt and the New Deal, 1932–1940*, 84.

45. Thomas T. Spencer, "For the Good of the Party: John Nance Garner, FDR, and New Deal Politics, 1933–1940," *Southwestern Historical Quarterly* 121, no. 3 (January 2018): 263–268; Caro, *The Path to Power*, 557.

46. Letter from James A. Farley, chairman, Democratic National Committee, to Marvin Jones, August 24, 1934, box 21, MJP, SWC.

47. McKay, *Texas Politics, 1906–1944*, 248–256, 269; Excerpts from the Address of Attorney General James V. Allred at the Waco Junior Chamber of Commerce Banquet, March 9, 1934, box 1985/024-1, RJVA, TSLAC.

48. "Allred Outlines Forgotten Man's Rehabilitation," *DMN*, March 7, 1934, box 1985/024-1, Pre-Gubernatorial Records, RJVA, TSLAC.

49. "Allred Visions Change in Law Construction: Attorney General Tells Constables More Liberal Trend Is Likely," *Houston Post*, March 11, 1934, box 1985/024-1, Pre-Gubernatorial Records, RJVA, TSLAC.

50. Address of Attorney General James V. Allred in Fort Worth, April 20, 1934, box 1985/024-1, Pre-Gubernatorial Records, RJVA, TSLAC.

51. "The Mary Hughes Attitude." *Houston Chronicle*, May 1, 1934.

52. McKay, *Texas Politics, 1906–1944*, 248–256, 269.

53. Speech of Hon. Tom Connally of Texas, April 3, 1934, *Congressional Record*, box 32, GMP, SWC.

54. McKay, *Texas Politics, 1906–1944*, 282–288.

55. McKay.

56. McKay.

57. Speech by Marvin Jones, September 6, 1934, Amarillo, Texas, box 24; letter from Henry Wallace to Marvin Jones, November 10, 1934, box 21; letter from Julien Frient to Marvin Jones, October 1, 1934, box 21, MJP, SWC.

58. Votes and Opponents in General Elections, 1934–1968; George Mahon's Races for Congress and List of Opponents, 1934–1978; Election Returns, 1934, box 3, GMP, SWC.

59. *Lubbock Avalanche-Journal,* July 28, 1934, box 3, GMP, SWC.

60. Oral history transcript, George Mahon, folder 22; statement by U. D. Wulfjen, "Farmer-Rancher"; "George Mahon for Congress," campaign brochure, 1934, box 3, GMP, SWC.

61. *Scurry County Times*, undated editorial (c. 1934), box 580, Scrapbook 1934, GMP, SWC.

62. "George Mahon for Congress," campaign brochure, 1934.

63. "George Mahon for Congress," campaign brochure, 1934; *Abilene Daily Reporter*, undated editorial (c. 1934), box 580, Scrapbook 1934, GMP, SWC.

64. "Colorful Maury Maverick Has Had Rapid Rise in Career of Politics: Violated Political Rules," *Fort Worth Star-Telegram*, October 2, 1934, box 4K118, MMC, DBCAH. For more on Maverick, see Richard Henderson, *Maury Maverick: A Political Biography* (Austin: University of Texas Press, 1970).

65. *San Antonio Light*, September 13 and 28, 1934; "Colorful Maury Maverick Has Had Rapid Rise in Career of Politics: Violated Political Rules," *Fort Worth Star-Telegram*, October 2, 1934, box 4K118, MMC, DBCAH.

66. *San Antonio Light*, September 13 and 28, 1934; "Colorful Maury Maverick Has Had Rapid Rise in Career of Politics: Violated Political Rules"; "Maury Maverick Arrives from the 'Free State of Bexar,'" *Washington Post*, October 14, 1934, box 4K118, MMC, DBCAH.

67. Caro, *The Path to Power*, 325–328.

68. McKay, *Texas Politics, 1906–1944*, 289–290; Leuchtenburg, *Franklin D. Roosevelt and the New Deal, 1932–1940*, 116.

69. The literature on Roosevelt's image, public persona, and personality is, obviously, vast. For a concise analysis, see, among other sources, Leuchtenburg, *Franklin D. Roosevelt and the New Deal, 1932–1940*, 167–170.

70. Leuchtenburg, 162–163; Message to the Congress on the State of the Union (speech file 759), January 4, 1935, box 20, Franklin D. Roosevelt, Master Speech File, 1898–1945, FDRL.

71. Inaugural Address of Governor James V. Allred, delivered Tuesday, Noon, January 15, 1935, box 1985/024-114. RJVA, TSLAC.

72. Miscellaneous newspaper clippings, Spring 1935; *Cochran County News*, April 6, 1935; *Dawson County Register*, July 18, 1935; *Dawson County Register*, September 28, 1935, box 579, Scrapbook 1935, GMP, SWC.

73. Miscellaneous newspaper clippings, Spring 1935; *Cochran County News*, April 6, 1935; *Dawson County Register*, July 18, 1935; *Dawson County Register*, September 28, 1935, box 579, Scrapbook 1935, GMP, SWC.

74. "Maury Organizes Private Bloc: To Wear No Brands," *San Antonio Light*, March 10, 1935; "Liberals Win Fight to Tax War Profits," *Philadelphia Record*, April 6, 1935, Box 4K118, MMC, DBCAH.

75. Caro, *The Path to Power*, 325–328.

76. Leuchtenburg, *Franklin D. Roosevelt and the New Deal, 1932–1940*, 64.

77. Miscellaneous files, boxes 62 and 63, Papers of the Democratic National Committee, Women's Division, 1933–1944, FDRL; see again, Robert O. Self, *All in the Family: The Realignment of American Democracy since the 1960s* (New York:

Hill & Wang, 2012); see also Linda Gordon, *Pitied but Not Entitled: Single Mothers and the History of Welfare* (New York: Free Press, 1994), 89, 188–207. Gordon's work is particularly useful to the history of the Children's Bureau, where women exerted influence and leadership on both economic and social issues, often through New Deal agencies.

78. Press release from L. E. Harwood, WPA, San Antonio, August 26, 1935, box 4Zb164, JBP, DBCAH; see again Gordon, *Pitied but Not Entitled*, 188–207; see also Elaine Tyler May, *Homeward Bound: American Families in the Cold War Era* (New York: Basic Books, 1988), 30–48.

79. *Lockhart Post-Register*, August 22, 1935; press release from WPA, November 30, 1935, box 4zb424, JBP, DBCAH.

80. Morris Sheppard, speech manuscript, circa 1935—delivered to Texas State Senate; speech manuscript, September 1935—delivered to U.S. Senate Committee on Military Affairs, box 3N187, MSP, DBCAH; "The Birth-Right of the New Deal: The Dawn of a New Era," speech by Walter P. Smith (Jasper, TX), April 24, 1935, box 452, GMP, SWC.

81. Letter from John Dailey to Sam Rayburn, May 21, 1935, box 3R274, SRP, DBCAH.

82. Letter from F. E. Morriss, executive secretary, Texas Retail Dry Goods Association, Dallas, TX, to James Buchanan (undated), "Issue Mail, 1926, 1934–1937," box 4zb178, JBP, DBCAH; Spencer, "For the Good of the Party," 268; Cantrell, *The People's Revolt*, 420.

83. *Fort Worth Press*, "Who's Behind the Tax in Texas? Campaign Aims at Support of Writing Levy into Constitution," February 28, 1935, box 4zb178, JBP, DBCAH.

84. General correspondence; Statement of Edwin Hawes Jr. (Wharton, TX) to Senate Finance Committee, August 2, 1935, box 360, GMP, SWC.

85. Charles G. Davis, "New Deal, TX," Handbook of Texas Online, Texas State Historical Association, accessed July 28, 2021, https://www.tshaonline.org/handbook/entries/new-deal-tx.

Chapter 3. "Sired by the Devil and Born in Hell"

1. General correspondence (1936); miscellaneous press clippings, boxes 19, 20, 24, 37, 41, OF2, FDRL; Patrick L. Cox, *The First Texas News Barons* (Austin: University of Texas Press, 2005), 205. For more on the political maneuverings necessary to fund the Texas Centennial, see Kenneth B. Ragsdale, *The Year America Discovered Texas: Centennial '36* (College Station: Texas A&M University Press, 1987), 62–87.

2. San Jacinto, Texas—Address at Battlefield (speech file 865), June 11, 1936, box 25, Franklin D. Roosevelt, Master Speech File, 1898–1945, FDRL.

3. San Antonio, Texas—Address (speech file 866), June 11, 1936, box 25, Franklin D. Roosevelt, Master Speech File, 1898–1945, FDRL.

4. For more on Clara Driscoll, Adina De Zavala, and the Alamo's place in Texas mythology, see among other excellent works Randy Roberts and James S. Olson, *A Line in the Sand: The Alamo in Blood and Memory* (New York: Touchstone Books, 2001). For specific information about FDR's visit to the Alamo in 1936, see Roberts and Olson, *A Line in the Sand*, 224–225.

5. General correspondence; miscellaneous press clippings, boxes 19, 20, 24, 37, 41, OF2; Dallas, Texas—Address, Texas Centennial Exposition (speech file 868); Dallas, Texas—Remarks at Unveiling of Robert E. Lee Memorial (speech file 870), June 12, 1936, box 25, Franklin D. Roosevelt, Master Speech File, 1898–1945, FDRL; miscellaneous records, box 24, 62, 1936 Texas Centennial Commission Papers, DHS.

6. Political cartoon by Jack Patton, *Dallas Journal* (circa 1936), box 3E262, Franklin D. Roosevelt Letters, DBCAH; general correspondence (1936); miscellaneous press clippings, boxes 19, 20, 24, 37, 41, OF2, FDRL; letter from Thomas B. Love to FDR, June 13, 1936, box 3E262, Franklin D. Roosevelt Letters, DBCAH.

7. Telegram from Cullen F. Thomas to Miriam A. Ferguson, March 1, 1934, box 301-485, Records of Governor Miriam Amanda Ferguson, TSLAC; Ragsdale, *The Year America Discovered Texas*, 79; Robert Wuthnow, *Rough Country: How Texas Became America's Most Powerful Bible-Belt State* (Princeton, NJ: Princeton University Press, 2014), 154–195; Michael Phillips, *White Metropolis: Race, Ethnicity, and Religion in Dallas, 1841–2001* (Austin: University of Texas Press, 2006), 113–116.

8. Telegram from Cullen F. Thomas to Miriam A. Ferguson, March 1, 1934; Ragsdale, *The Year America Discovered Texas*, 79; Wuthnow, *Rough Country*, 154–195; Phillips, *White Metropolis*, 113–116.

9. "A Resolution Adopted by the Democratic County Convention of Bosque County, Texas"—May 5, 1936, Meridian, Texas, box 2G198, MSP, DBCAH.

10. Speech of Hon. Sam Rayburn, Accepting the Temporary Chairmanship of the Democratic State Convention at San Antonio, Texas, May 26, 1936, in Miscellaneous Speeches by Sam Rayburn, 1929–1936, box 3U92, SRP, DBCAH.

11. *Dallas Journal*, June 24, 1936, box 3R274, SRP, DBCAH.

12. *Bonham Daily Favorite*, July 18, 1936, box 3R274, SRP, DBCAH.

13. "Office, House of Representatives, Rayburn for Speaker of the House, 1936"; general correspondence (1936); letter from Charles Bindercup, Nebraska, to George Mahon, October 6, 1936, folder 19, box 92, GMP, SWC.

14. Letter from Thomas B. Love to Louis Howe, December 18, 1934; memo from Louis Howe to Steve Early, January 24, 1935, box 3E262, FDRL, DBCAH.

15. *DMN*, August 27, 1936; speeches by Thomas B. Love to Dallas Agricultural Club (January 13, 1936) and Dallas Technical Club (January 21, 1936),

box 3E262, Franklin D. Roosevelt Letters, DBCAH; see also Gregg Cantrell, *The People's Revolt: Texas Populists and the Roots of American Liberalism* (New Haven, CT: Yale University Press, 2020).

16. *Dallas Times Herald*, September 2, 1936, box 3E262, Franklin D. Roosevelt Letters, DBCAH.

17. Letter from Thomas B. Love to FDR, July 7, 1936; letter from FDR to Thomas B. Love, July 15, 1936, box 3E262, Franklin D. Roosevelt Letters, DBCAH; letter from Edmund R. Cheesborough to Beauford Jester, May 10, 1947; "Extracts from Speeches of Franklin D. Roosevelt as to Economy in Government and Spending," box 4-14/81, Records of Governor Beauford H. Jester, TSLAC. For more, see Merrill D. Peterson, *The Jefferson Image in the American Mind* (New York: Oxford University Press, 1960), 356–363, 426–431.

18. *DMN*, July 5, 1936; press release, July 5, 1936, box 2G196, MSP, DBCAH; see also Seth Shepard McKay, *Texas Politics, 1906–1944* (Lubbock: Texas Tech Press, 1952), 303.

19. *DMN*, July 24 and 27, 1936.

20. *DMN*, July 24 and 27, 1936.

21. General correspondence, box 62, Papers of the Democratic National Committee, Women's Division, 1933–1944, FDRL; Raymond Brookes, "He Knows Where He Is Going: New Dealer Program Complete, as Jas. V. Allred, Governor-Elect of Texas, Smilingly Awaits His Day," *West Texas Today*, January 1935, box 1985/024-115, RJVA, TSLAC.

22. Publicity release—"Midterm Status Report," January 15, 1936, box 1985/024-115, RJVA, TSLAC.

23. Address of Governor James V. Allred, before the State Democratic Convention—San Antonio, Texas, May 26, 1936, box 1985/024-115, RJVA, TSLAC.

24. Speech by James V. Allred, Governor of the State of Texas, Re-nominating John Nance Garner for the Vice Presidency, Democratic National Convention, 1936, box 1985/024-115, RJVA, TSLAC.

25. Speech of Governor James V. Allred in Campaign for Reelection at Waxahachie, Texas, June 30, 1936, box 1985/024-115, RJVA, TSLAC.

26. "Clippings from the Texas Press Concerning the Centennial Governor, 1936," box 1985/024-115, RJVA, TSLAC.

27. Campaign Pamphlet, "The Press Reviews . . . The Steady March of James V. Allred to a Second Term as Governor and the Completion of an Enlightened and Progressive Program for Texas," box 1985/024-115, RJVA, TSLAC.

28. Cantrell, *The People's Revolt*, 419–422.

29. *DMN*, July 26 and 27, 1936; McKay, *Texas Politics, 1906–1944*, 290–302.

30. Speech by Hatton W. Sumners, "Our Choice—Decentralization of Governmental Responsibility or Government by a Centralized Bureaucracy," February 26, 1925, box 31, folder 8.8, HWSP, DHS.

31. "Love Defends President on Regimentation," *Dallas Times Herald*, June 10, 1935, box 31, folder 8.10, HWSP, DHS.

32. *Dallas Journal*, January 14, 1936, box 31, folder 8.4, HWSP, DHS; letter from John Nance Garner to Thomas Love, January 16, 1936, box 66, TBLP, DHS.

33. Letter from Thomas Love to Hatton Sumners, November 5, 1935; letter from Thomas Love to Hatton Sumners, January 10, 1936, box 31, folder 8.2, HWSP, DHS.

34. Letters from Thomas Love to Hatton Sumners, January 18 and 28, 1936; letter from Hatton Sumners to Thomas Love, February 1, 1936, box 31, HWSP, DHS.

35. Letter from Thomas Love to Hatton Sumners, April 7, 1936, box 31, folder 8.2, HWSP, DHS.

36. *DMN*, July 5, 1936; *DMN*, July 26, 1936.

37. General correspondence, "Farm Program, 1936—Supreme Court Decision," box 257; miscellaneous newspaper clippings, box 578, Scrapbook 1936, GMP, SWC.

38. The definitive work on the Dust Bowl remains Donald Worster, *The Dust Bowl: The Southern Plains in the 1930s* (New York: Oxford University Press, 1979). Numerous scholars have contributed to Dust Bowl literature over the years. For more on the social and communal impact of the struggle, see, among others, Timothy Egan, *The Worst Hard Time: The Untold Story of Those Who Survived the Great American Dust Bowl* (New York: Houghton Mifflin, 2006).

39. Miscellaneous newspaper clippings, box 578, Scrapbook 1936, GMP, SWC.

40. Miscellaneous newspaper clippings; *Lockney Beacon*, July 10, 1936, box 578, Scrapbook 1936, GMP, SWC; see also Sarah Barwinkel, "A Legacy in Lubbock: How Three New Deal Programs Left Their Mark on the South Plains," MA thesis, Texas Tech University, 2009.

41. *Abilene Report*, July 8, 1936, box 578, Scrapbook 1936, GMP, SWC.

42. *Lubbock Avalanche-Journal*, July 10, 1936, box 578, Scrapbook 1936, GMP, SWC; letter from George Mahon to Joe Caton, July 12; letter from George Mahon to Ervin C. Clark, September 9, 1935; letter from George Mahon to John Couch, June 1, 1936; personal correspondence and general correspondence, box 29, GMP, SWC.

43. Letter from C. B. Goodspeed, treasurer for the Republican National Committee, to George Mahon, August 31, 1936; leaflet, "You Can Know a Man by the Enemies He Has Made," by All-Party Roosevelt Agriculture Committee, 1936, box 452, GMP, SWC.

44. Letter from Maury Maverick to Stewart McDonald, June 1, 1936, box 2L48, MMC, DBCAH.

45. Thomas T. Spencer, "For the Good of the Party: John Nance Garner, FDR, and New Deal Politics, 1933–1940." *Southwestern Historical Quarterly* 121,

no. 3 (January 2018): 271–273; Robert A. Caro, *The Path to Power: The Years of Lyndon Johnson* (New York: Alfred A. Knopf, 1982), 558.

46. Letter from Maury Maverick to Thomas G. Corcoran, June 18, 1936; telegram from Harold Ickes to Maury Maverick, June 29, 1936; letter from Maury Maverick to Harold Ickes, June 30, 1936, box 2L48, MMC, DBCAH.

47. Telegram from Thomas G. Corcoran to Maury Maverick, July 6, 1936; telegram from Maury Maverick to Thomas G. Corcoran, July 6, 1936; telegram from Stewart McDonald to Maury Maverick, July 6, 1936; letter from Maury Maverick to Stewart McDonald, July 6, 1936; letter from Harold Ickes to Maury Maverick, July 7, 1936; telegrams from Maury Maverick to Thomas G. Corcoran, Franklin D. Roosevelt, and Stewart McDonald, July 9, 1936, box 2L49, MMC, DBCAH.

48. "Where I Stand," 1936 campaign brochure for Lamar Seeligson, box 2L48, MMC, DBCAH.

49. Letter from Maury Maverick to Phillip Maverick, June 30, 1936, box 2L48, MMC, DBCAH.

50. General correspondence; letter from Paul V. Betters, executive director, United States Conference of Mayors, to Maury Maverick, April 9, 1936, box 2L48, MMC, DBCAH.

51. Radio addresses by Maury Maverick, July–October 1936, box 2L60, MMC, DBCAH.

52. Telegram from Maury Maverick to Stanley High, July 28, 1936; letter from Maury Maverick to George Biddle, August 1, 1936; letter from Maury Maverick to E. W. Biles, August 1, 1936, box 2L49, MMC, DBCAH.

53. Speech by Maury Maverick, July 17, 1936, Plaza Hotel, San Antonio, Texas, box 2L60, MMC, DBCAH.

54. Transcript of radio address by Maury Maverick, October 22, 1936, KTSA Radio; transcript of radio address by Maury Maverick, October 30, 1936, WOAI Radio, San Antonio, box 2L60, MMC, DBCAH.

55. McKay, *Texas Politics, 1906–1944*, 302; unpublished memoir of Marvin Jones, copyright Columbia University Press, box 16; Statement by George F. Authier, Director of Publicity, Roosevelt Agricultural Committee—October 1936, box 23; campaign ad 1936, "Marvin Jones for Congress"; miscellaneous newspaper clippings "1936," Scrapbook 2, 1913–1939 (vol. 2), MJP, SWC.

56. "The Philosophy of the Roosevelt Farm Program," radio speech, October 27, 1936, NBC Radio Network, box 23, MJP, SWC; for a similar example of such rhetoric, see speech by Morris Sheppard to Fort Worth Convention, September 1936, box 2G196, MSP, DBCAH.

57. Letter from Mrs. Alex Miller (secretary of state of Iowa) to James Farley, September 30, 1936; *Columbus* (NE) *Tribune*, October 13, 1936; scrapbook: 1936 Presidential Campaign, MJP, SWC.

58. Miscellaneous newspaper clippings, scrapbook: 1936 Presidential Campaign, MJP, SWC.

59. *Amarillo Globe*, September 24, 1936; scrapbook: 1936 Presidential Campaign; "The Philosophy of the Roosevelt Farm Program," radio speech, October 27, 1936, NBC Radio Network, box 23, MJP, SWC.

60. Letter from C. B. Goodspeed (RNC treasurer, Chicago) to Marvin Jones, August 28, 1936; Editorial, *Amarillo Globe News*, undated clipping (circa September 1936); scrapbook: 1936 Presidential Election, MJP, SWC.

61. For more on the evolution of conservative Republican campaign rhetoric during the latter decades of the twentieth century, see among many others, Sean P. Cunningham, *Cowboy Conservatism: Texas and the Rise of the Modern Right* (Lexington: University Press of Kentucky, 2010), and Lisa McGirr, *Suburban Warriors: The Origins of the New American Right* (Princeton, NJ: Princeton University Press, 2001).

62. Statement of Marvin Jones, September 23, 1936; speech by Marvin Jones, September 30, 1936; miscellaneous speeches and comments, 1936, folder 14, box 23, MJP.

63. For more on the perceived radical progressivism of FDR's acceptance speech at the 1936 Democratic National Convention, see Jefferson Cowie, *The Great Exception: The New Deal and the Limits of American Politics* (Princeton, NJ: Princeton University Press, 2016), 1-7.

64. Editorial, unidentified newspaper, July 5, box 578, Scrapbook 1936, GMP; statement of Marvin Jones, September 23, 1936; speech by Marvin Jones, September 30, 1936; miscellaneous speeches and comments, 1936, folder 14, box 23, MJP, SWC.

65. Speech by Marvin Jones, 1936 (undated), box 23, MJP, SWC.

66. *DMN*, August 9, 1936.

67. HR41, Adopted by Members of the Texas House of Representatives, October 16, 1936, file 2488, President's Personal File, FDRL.

68. *DMN*, September 13, 1936, box 3E262, Franklin D. Roosevelt Letters, DBCAH.

69. William E. Leuchtenburg, *The FDR Years: On Roosevelt and His Legacy* (New York: Columbia University Press, 1995), 145.

70. *DMN*, November 4, 1936.

71. McKay, *Texas Politics, 1906-1944*, 303.

Chapter 4. "Communism with a Haircut and a Shave"

1. Speech by Maury Maverick, November 22, 1936, Dallas, Texas, box 2L60, MMC, DBCAH.

2. Miscellaneous notes re: "Constitution," box 2L49, MMC, DBCAH; *Houston Chronicle*, November 4, 5, and 5, 1936.

3. Letter from Hatton Sumners to Senator William E. Borah, November 29, 1935, box 75, folder 8.2, HWSP, DHS.

4. William E. Leuchtenburg, *Franklin D. Roosevelt and the New Deal, 1932–1940* (New York: Harper & Row, 1963), 84, 243; Michael Phillips, *White Metropolis: Race, Ethnicity, and Religion in Dallas, 1841–2001* (Austin: University of Texas Press, 2006), 116–117.

5. George N. Green, *The Establishment in Texas Politics: The Primitive Years, 1938–1957* (Norman: University of Oklahoma Press, 1979). For a slightly different perspective, see Sean P. Cunningham, *Cowboy Conservatism: Texas and the Rise of the Modern Right* (Lexington: University Press of Kentucky, 2010); see also Norman D. Brown, *Biscuits, the Dole, and Nodding Donkeys: Texas Politics, 1929–1932* (Austin: University of Texas Press, 2019).

6. For more on the Liberty League and its opposition to the New Deal, see Kimberly Phillips-Fein, *Invisible Hands: The Businessmen's Crusade against the New Deal* (New York: W. W. Norton, 2009); see also Seth Shepard McKay, *Texas Politics, 1906–1944* (Lubbock: Texas Tech Press, 1952), 404–405.

7. McKay, *Texas Politics, 1906–1944*, 397–413.

8. Samuel K. Tullock, "'He, Being Dead, Yet Speaketh': J. Frank Norris and the Texas Religious Right at Midcentury," in *The Texas Right: The Radical Roots of Lone Star Conservatism*, ed. David Cullen and Kyle G. Wilkison (College Station: Texas A&M University Press, 2014), 51–67; Allison Collis Greene, *No Depression in Heaven: The Great Depression, the New Deal, and the Transformation of Religion in the Delta* (New York: Oxford University Press, 2016), 115, 159.

9. For more on the role of perceived isolation in shaping Texas political culture, see, among other good sources, Robert Wuthnow, *Rough Country: How Texas Became America's Most Powerful Bible-Belt State* (Princeton, NJ: Princeton University Press, 2014).

10. Lewis L. Gould, *Progressives and Prohibitionists: Texas Democrats in the Wilson Era* (Austin: University of Texas Press, 1973), 23, 172, 258–266.

11. Gould, *Progressives and Prohibitionists*, 23, 49, 172, 258–266.

12. "Soviet Republic Ruled by Blacks Proposed in South," reproduced from *Christian American*, July 1936, box 1965/111-6, Thomas Jefferson Holbrook Papers, TSLAC; Bryan Burrough, *The Big Rich: The Rise and Fall of the Greatest Texas Oil Fortunes* (New York: Penguin Press, 2009), 126–130, 135–137; Green, *The Establishment in Texas Politics*, 60–61. For more on the growth and sustenance of antigovernment and antitax organizations at the grass roots during the 1930s, see also David T. Beito, *Taxpayers in Revolt: Tax Resistance during the Great Depression* (Chapel Hill: University of North Carolina Press, 1989). Beito's study is ostensibly national in scope, though it gives primacy to cities in the North and Midwest.

13. For more on the rise of Jeffersonian Democrats in Texas, see Scott M. Sosebee, "The Split in the Texas Democratic Party, 1936–1956," MA thesis, Texas Tech University, 2000; see also McKay, *Texas Politics, 1906–1944*, 397–413; Green, *The Establishment in Texas Politics*, 60–61.

14. *New York Times*, January 26, 1936; paid advertisement by J. Evetts Haley, chairman, Jeffersonian Democrats of Texas [appearing in undated and unidentified church newsletter]; *Dallas Times Herald*, October 11, 1936, box 3E262, Franklin D. Roosevelt Letters, DBCAH.

15. Burrough, *The Big Rich*, 138; see again, Green, *The Establishment in Texas Politics*; Cunningham, *Cowboy Conservatism*; and Wuthnow, *Rough Country*.

16. Inaugural Address of President Franklin D. Roosevelt (speech file 1030), January 20, 1937, box 31, Franklin D. Roosevelt, Master Speech File, 1898–1945, FDRL. For more on the radical tone of FDR's acceptance speech at the 1936 Democratic National Convention, see Jefferson Cowie, *The Great Exception: The New Deal and the Limits of American Politics* (Princeton, NJ: Princeton University Press, 2016), 1–7; "Sidelights," February 4, 1937, box 24, MJP, SWC.

17. Arnoldo De León, *Mexican Americans in Texas: A Brief History* (Arlington Heights, IL: Harlan Davidson, 1993), 103–105; see also Laura E. Cannon, "Situational Solidarity: LULAC's Civil Rights Strategy and the Challenge of the Mexican-American Worker, 1934–1946," PhD diss., Texas Tech University, 2016; Julia Kirk Blackwater, *Women of the Depression: Caste and Culture in San Antonio, 1929–1939* (College Station: Texas A&M University Press, 1984).

18. Martin Dies Jr., interview by Dr. Ray A. Stephens, May 31, 1966, transcript, 3–4, University of North Texas Oral History Collection, Willis Library, Denton; letter from Hatton Sumners to William E. Borah, November 29, 1935, box 75, folder 8.2, HWSP, DHS.

19. Editorial, *Dallas Journal*, July 28, 1937, box 75, folder 8.18, HWSP, DHS.

20. Letter from Jesse Daniel Ames to Hatton Sumners, March 29, 1937, box 75, folder 8.3, HWSP, DHS.

21. Letter from G. T. Thibodeaux to Hatton Sumners, May 4, 1937, box 75, folder 8.5, HWSP, DHS.

22. Phillips, *White Metropolis*, 116–117.

23. Extemporaneous Remarks of Congressman Hatton W. Sumners at Dinner of the Interstate Commission on Crime, Kansas City, MO, September 24, 1937; Address of Hatton Sumners to Young Democrats Club, May 6, 1938, box 119, HWSP, DHS.

24. *DMN*, February 22, 1937, April 2, 15, and 17, 1937, August 13, 1937, November 23, 1937; Randolph B. Campbell, *Gone to Texas: A History of the Lone Star State* (New York: Oxford University Press, 2003), 391; Green, *The Establishment in Texas Politics*, 69–70. For more on "color-blind conservatism," see, among others, Matthew D. Lassiter, *The Silent Majority: Suburban Politics in the Sunbelt South* (Princeton, NJ: Princeton University Press, 2006).

25. Speech by Sam Rayburn, February 9, 1937, CBS Radio Network, box 3U92, SRP, DBCAH.

26. *Houston Chronicle*, August 21, 1937, box 577, Scrapbook 1937, GMP, SWC; Keith J. Volanto, *Texas, Cotton, and the New Deal* (College Station: Texas A&M University Press, 2004), 86–90.

27. Letter from F. J. Herzog to T. J. Holbrook, February 5, 1937, box 1965/111-1, Thomas Jefferson Holbrook Papers, TSLAC; *Dallas Journal*, March 2, 1937; speech by Thomas B. Love, to Dallas County Agricultural Club, March 8, 1937; miscellaneous letters from Thomas B. Love, box 3E262, Franklin D. Roosevelt Letters, DBCAH; see also Green, *The Establishment in Texas Politics*, 14; Lionel V. Patenaude, *Texas, Politics, and the New Deal* (New York: Garland, 1983).

28. Letter from Thomas Love to Hatton Sumners, March 9, 1937; letter from Thomas Love to Hatton Sumners, May 20, 1937, box 31, folders 8.3 and 8.4, HWSP, DHS.

29. Open letter from T. J. Holbrook to Tom Connally, February 6, 1937, box 1965/111-1, Thomas Jefferson Holbrook Papers, TSLAC.

30. Letter from W. H. Garrett to T. J. Holbrook, February 10, 1937, box 1965/111-1, Thomas Jefferson Holbrook Papers, TSLAC.

31. *DMN*, February 4, 10, 1937, box 1965/111-1, Thomas Jefferson Holbrook Papers, TSLAC.

32. *DMN*, March 3, 1937; letter from Thomas B. Love to FDR, May 14, 1937, box 3E262, Franklin D. Roosevelt Letters, DBCAH. For more on congressional conservatives during this period, see James T. Patterson, *Congressional Conservatism and the New Deal: The Growth of the Conservative Coalition in Congress, 1933–1939* (Lexington: University of Kentucky Press, 1967); see also letter from Thomas B. Love to FDR, June 25, 1938, box 3E262, Franklin D. Roosevelt Letters, DBCAH. Sumners's opposition to the court-packing plan inspired Love to run against Sumners in 1938; *Houston Chronicle*, August 21, 1937, box 577, Scrapbook 1937, GMP, SWC.

33. Letter from Thomas B. Love to FDR, June 1, 1937, box 3E262, Franklin D. Roosevelt Letters, DBCAH.

34. Leuchtenburg, *Franklin D. Roosevelt and the New Deal, 1932–1940*, 237–239; Robert A. Caro, *The Path to Power: The Years of Lyndon Johnson* (New York: Alfred A. Knopf, 1982), 561–565.

35. Letter from Thomas Love to Morris Sheppard, August 5, 1937; letter from Morris Sheppard to Thomas Love, August 9, 1937, box 66, TBLP, DHS.

36. Louis Howe died in April 1936. Thomas T. Spencer, "For the Good of the Party: John Nance Garner, FDR, and New Deal Politics, 1933–1940," *Southwestern Historical Quarterly* 121, no. 3 (January 2018): 254–282; Caro, *The Path to Power*, 557.

37. *Dallas Times Herald*, September 14, 1937, box 59, TBLP, DHS; "Sumners Says He and FDR Are Friendly," "Mr. Sumners Comes Back," undated *DMN*

clippings (c. 1938), box 3E262, Franklin D. Roosevelt Letters, DBCAH; see also Mary Catherine Monroe, "A Day in July: Hatton W. Sumners and the Court Reorganization Plan of 1937," MA thesis, University of Texas at Arlington 1973.

38. Telegram from Allen Wright to Hatton Sumners, February 9, 1937; telegram from D. A. Frank to Hatton Sumners, February 6, 1937, box 31, folder 8.3, HWSP, DHS; Anthony Champagne, "Hatton Sumners and the 1937 Court-Packing Plan," *East Texas Historical Journal* 26, no 1 (1988): 46-49.

39. "The Federal Judiciary," speech by Hatton Sumners, *Congressional Record*, July 13, 1937.

40. Lionel V. Patenaude, "Garner, Sumners, and Connally: The Defeat of the Court Bill in 1937," *Southwestern Historical Quarterly* 74, no. 1 (July 1970): 36-51.

41. Speech by Sam Rayburn, August 23, 1937, NBC Radio Network; speech by Sam Rayburn, summer 1937, Milk Dealers Association, Dallas, Texas, box 3U92, SRP, DBCAH.

42. Unpublished memoir of Marvin Jones, copyright Columbia University Press, box 16, MJP, SWC.

43. *Amarillo Daily News*, September 9, 1937, Scrapbook 2, 1913-1939 (vol. 2), MJP, SWC.

44. *Abilene Reporter*, September 4, box 577, Scrapbook 1937, GMP, SWC.

45. Official Ballot Results for Referendum to Members of the Texas Bar Association, 1937, box 3U92, SRP, DBCAH [Results: against 1,336, for 369]; Leuchtenburg, *Franklin D. Roosevelt and the New Deal, 1932-1940*, 237-243.

46. Letter from W. D. McFarlane to FDR, September 11, 1937, box 2.325/M18b, Hatton Sumners Papers, DBCAH.

47. *Post Dispatch*, July 11, 1937; *Hale Center American*, September 10, 1937; miscellaneous newspaper clippings, box 577, Scrapbook 1937, GMP, SWC.

48. Green, *The Establishment in Texas Politics*, 15.

49. For more on Lyndon Johnson's long political career, see, among many biographies, Caro, *The Path to Power*, and Robert Dallek, *Lone Star Rising: Lyndon Johnson and His Times, 1908-1961* (New York: Oxford University Press, 1991).

50. Robert Dallek, *Franklin D. Roosevelt: A Political Life* (New York: Viking, 2017), 214; Caro, *The Path to Power*, 79-81, 269-277, 308, 340.

51. Address by Lyndon B. Johnson, KNOW Radio, March 11, 1937, box 1, PPPLBJ, Statements of Lyndon Baines Johnson, LBJL; also quoted in Randall B. Woods, *Prisoners of Hope: Lyndon B. Johnson, the Great Society, and the Limits of Liberalism* (New York: Basic Books, 2016), 394-395.

52. Caro, *The Path to Power*, 394-395, 404.

53. *Austin American-Statesman*, March 30, 1937, box 4ZB220, JBP, DBCAH.

54. Speech by Lyndon B. Johnson, Elgin BBQ, September 15, 1937, box 1, PPPLBJ, Statements of Lyndon Baines Johnson, LBJL; Caro, *The Path to Power*, 404, 416-417.

55. Speech by Judge N. T. Stubbs, Johnson City, Texas, April 8, 1937, WOAI Radio, box 2, PPPLBJ, House of Representatives Papers, 1937–1949, LBJL; see also Kenna Lang Archer, *Unruly Waters: A Social and Environmental History of the Brazos River* (Albuquerque: University of New Mexico Press, 2015).

56. Miscellaneous speeches, "Contacts—1937 Campaign," box 2, PPPLBJ, House of Representatives Papers, 1937–1949, LBJL; Caro, *The Path to Power*, 400.

57. Miscellaneous speeches, "Contacts—1937 Campaign"; "Campaign Material, 1937," box 2, PPPLBJ, House of Representatives Papers, 1937–1949, LBJL; letter from Reese Lockett (mayor, Brenham, TX) to FDR, April 11, 1937, box 31, Official File—3: Democratic National Committee, FDRL; Caro, *The Path to Power*, 433, 445.

58. Dallek, *Franklin D. Roosevelt*, 282–283. Upon leaving College Station, the president joined Richardson, Murchison, and a host of others at Elliott's ranch in Fort Worth. According to varying accounts, the group dined on barbecue while negotiating a quid pro quo in which Roosevelt exerted influence on federal prosecutors investigating Murchison on charges of illegal "hot oil" transports, while Richardson agreed to pressure a friend in the Internal Revenue Service to end an investigation into Elliott's tax returns. Such conversations were reportedly common, which explains, in part, Roosevelt's strong protection of the coveted oil depletion allowance, an issue that continued to catalyze Texas oil interests and conservative politicians for decades to come. For more, see Burrough, *The Big Rich*, 141–145.

59. "Tarnish on the Violent Crown," address by Lyndon B. Johnson, KNOW Radio, January 23, 1938, box 2, PPPLBJ, Statements of Lyndon Baines Johnson, LBJL.

60. *Fort Worth Star Telegram*, February 25, 1939; miscellaneous files, box 11, Records of the National Youth Administration, 1935–1937, LBJL.

61. Fireside Chat #13—"Report to the Nation on National Affairs" (speech file 1138A, 1138B), June 24, 1938, box 39, Franklin D. Roosevelt, Master Speech File, 1898–1945, FDRL.

62. See again, for instance, Green, *The Establishment in Texas Politics*; see also Susan Dunn, *Roosevelt's Purge: How FDR Fought to Change the Democratic Party* (Cambridge, MA: Harvard University Press, 2010).

63. Letter from William McGraw to FDR, March 30, 1938; letter from Jimmie Allred to FDR, April 2, 1938; general correspondence, April–June 1938, box 45, OF2, FDRL.

64. Telegram from Myron Blalock to FDR, July 10, 1938; miscellaneous telegrams, box 45, OF2, FDRL. Press coverage of Roosevelt's arrival in Fort Worth on July 10 was inadvertently limited due to an on-the-ground misunderstanding between the *Fort Worth Star-Telegram* and the Secret Service. At the Fort Worth train station, Secret Service agents told reporters, "no photos," intending only

to protect against images of FDR being moved from the train down a staircase. Agents routinely protected the president against images that would have revealed the extent of his paralysis. However, reporters for the *Telegram* incorrectly reported this to mean that no photos would be taken of the president at all. Several days later, Amon Carter contacted the administration to express his frustration over the incident, apologizing for the lack of photographic coverage, while also blaming the Secret Service for the miscommunication. Telegram from Amon Carter to E. W. Starling, July 16, 1938, box 45, OF2, FDRL.

65. Telegram from John Nance Garner to FDR, July 11, 1938, box 45, OF2, FDRL; Spencer, "For the Good of the Party," 272.

66. Letter from FDR to John Nance Garner, November 28, 1938, in Franklin D. Roosevelt, *F.D.R.: His Personal Letters, 1928–1945,* ed. Elliott Roosevelt (New York: Duell, Sloan and Pearce, 1950), 832.

67. Miscellaneous news clippings, July 1938, box 4K149, MMC, DBCAH; Martin Dies Jr., interview by Dr. Ray A. Stephens, May 31, 1966, transcript, 14; telegram from LBJ to Marvin McIntyre, July 10, 1938, box 45, OF2, FDRL; *New York Times,* July 12, 1938, box 4K149, MMC, DBCAH.

68. Informal Remarks by FDR, Fort Worth, Bowie, Wichita Falls, Chillicothe, Childress, Clarendon, and Amarillo, Texas (speech files 1152, 1153, 1154, 1155, 1156), July 10–11, 1938, box 40, Franklin D. Roosevelt, Master Speech File, 1898–1945, FDRL; *DMN,* July 12, 1938; Dallek, *Franklin D. Roosevelt,* 314.

69. Informal Remarks by FDR, Amarillo, Texas (speech file 1156), July 11, 1938, box 40, Franklin D. Roosevelt, Master Speech File, 1898–1945, FDRL; *Shamrock Texan,* July 12, 1938, The Portal to Texas History (Texas Digital Newspaper Program), accessed August 2, 2021, https://texashistory.unt.edu/ark:/67531/metapth526349/?q=The%20Shamrock%20Texan%2C%20July%2012%2C%201938.

70. Political advertisement for reelection, 1938; political advertisement, *Amarillo Globe,* July 21, 1938, Scrapbook 2, 1913–1939 (vol. 2), box 21; "Resume of Main Legislative Activities," campaign brochure (published 1937), box 23, MJP, SWC.

71. Speech by Marvin Jones, 1938, box 21, MJP, SWC.

72. *Andrews County News,* January 1937; *Post Dispatch,* July 11, 1937; *Hale Center American,* September 10, 1937, box 577, Scrapbook 1937; miscellaneous newspaper clippings, box 576, 577, Scrapbook 1938; miscellaneous files and correspondence, folder 21, box 92, GMP, SWC.

73. Campaign newspaper—1928, "Wright Patman Opens Campaign for Congress: Announces Platforms and Arraigns Present Incumbent," box 77B, Wright Patman Papers, LBJL.

74. For more on Patman, see Nancy Beck Young, *Wright Patman: Populism, Liberalism, and the American Dream* (Dallas, TX: Southern Methodist University Press, 2000); for a specific discussion of Patman's campaign in 1928, see Walter

Buenger, *The Path to a Modern South: Northeast Texas between Reconstruction and the Great Depression* (Austin: University of Texas Press, 2001), 225, 240–252.

75. *Mount Pleasant Texas News,* July 20, 1938, box 77C, Wright Patman Papers, LBJL; see again Young, *Wright Patman,* 50, 91–92.

76. Telegram from Wright Patman to James Farley, DNC chairman, July 15, 1938; press release, July 16, 1938, Texarkana, Texas, box 77C, Wright Patman Papers, LBJL.

77. *Paris Texas News,* July 19, 1938; *Mount Pleasant Texas Times,* July 18, 1938, box 77C, Wright Patman Papers, LBJL.

78. Speech by Wright Patman, July 21, 1938, Roxton, Texas, box 77B, Wright Patman Papers, LBJL.

79. Campaign newspaper, "Wright Patman for Congress: For Re-Election, Subject to Action of Democratic Primary, July 23, 1938," box 75A, Wright Patman Papers, LBJL; political announcement of Wright Patman for Representative in Congress, 1938, box 23, MJP, SWC.

80. *Houston Chronicle,* July 22, 1938; campaign advertisement, "The Reasons Why William E. Stone Will Replace T. J. Holbrook," box 1965/111-1, Thomas Jefferson Holbrook Papers, TSLAC.

81. Letter from John Barton, Utley, Texas, to LBJ, March 18, 1938, box 3, Political General, 1938, PPPLBJ, House of Representatives Papers, 1937–1949, LBJL.

82. Transcript of radio address by Maury Maverick, July 20, 1938, WOAI Radio, San Antonio, box 2L60, MMC, DBCAH. See also "Crackpot Files," box 2L50, MMC, DBCAH. This collection includes several letters from constituents parroting Kilday's charges of "radical communism," and includes allegations made by some constituents that FDR was himself a communist. As one writer noted, "We are not ready to trek to Moscow, no matter who attempts to lead us there."

83. *Chicago Daily Times,* July 28, 1938; *Abilene Evening Reporter,* July 28, 1938; *San Antonio Light,* August 11, 1938; *San Antonio Light,* August 22, 1938, box 4K149, MMC, DBCAH.

84. *DMN,* July 18, 1938.

85. Speech by Thomas Love, Opening His Campaign for Congress at DeSoto, Texas, July 2, 1938, box 59, TBLP; *Dallas Journal,* "Tom Love Begins Campaign for Congress Promising to Quit if F. D. Favors Sumners" (undated newspaper clipping, 1938), box 104, HWSP, DHS.

86. *Dallas Journal,* "Sumners' Record on the New Deal" (undated newspaper clipping, 1938), box 104, HWSP, DHS.

87. Letter from Leslie Jackson to FDR, February 17, 1938, box 31, OF3, FDRL.

88. Personal and Confidential Memorandum, from Stephen Early to FDR, June 17, 1938, box 2.325/M18b, Hatton Sumners Papers, DBCAH; letter from

Hatton Sumners to Stephen Early, July 27, 1938, box 103, folder 2.14, HWSP, DHS. Sumners typically sounded loyalist notes during Democratic primaries, becoming more conservative and more critical of liberalism during general elections. For instance, see Address of Hatton W. Sumners, Proceedings: Nineteenth Annual Convention of the Texas Mid-Continent Oil and Gas Association, San Antonio, TX, October 27–28, 1938, box 119, HWSP, DHS.

89. Green, *The Establishment in Texas Politics*, 23; see also James Reston, *The Lone Star: The Life of John Connally* (New York: Harper & Row, 1989), 28.

90. McKay, *Texas Politics, 1906–1944*, 307–320; *DMN*, June 20, 1939, box 3L365, W. Lee "Pappy" O'Daniel Papers, DBCAH; Address of W. Lee O'Daniel, Proceedings: Nineteenth Annual Convention of the Texas Mid-Continent Oil and Gas Association, San Antonio, TX, October 27–28, 1938, box 119, HWSP, DHS.

91. McKay, *Texas Politics, 1906–1944*, 322.

92. John Mark Dempsey, *The Light Crust Doughboys Are on the Air: Celebrating Seventy Years of Texas Music* (Denton: University of North Texas Press, 2002), 38.

93. *DMN*, July 25, 1938, box 3L365, W. Lee "Pappy" O'Daniel Papers, DBCAH.

94. Miscellaneous news clippings (1938); political cartoon, *New York Post*, July 26, 1938, box 4K149, MMC, DBCAH.

95. *DMN*, August 2, 1938; *San Antonio Express*, August 10, 1938, box 3L365, W. Lee "Pappy" O'Daniel Papers, DBCAH. Roosevelt did not aggressively endorse a gubernatorial candidate during the Democratic primary, following advice given to him by Sam Rayburn. Letter from Sam Rayburn to Marvin McIntyre, re: "Texas Trip," box 45, OF2, FDRL.

96. *DMN*, July 28, 1938; *DMN*, August 31, 1938, box 4K149, MMC, DBCAH; Burrough, *The Big Rich*, 134.

97. Letter from FDR to John Nance Garner, November 28, 1938, in Roosevelt, *F.D.R.: His Personal Letters, 1928–1945*, 831–832.

Chapter 5. "My Very Old and Close Friend"

1. Robert Dallek, *Franklin D. Roosevelt and American Foreign Policy, 1932–1945* (New York: Oxford University Press, 1979), 147; see also Alan Brinkley, *The End of Reform: New Deal Liberalism in Recession and War* (New York: Alfred A. Knopf, 1995).

2. Dallek, *Franklin D. Roosevelt and American Foreign Policy, 1932–1945*, 103–119, 530.

3. *DMN*, September 4, 10, 1939; radio broadcast transcript, September 10, 1939, box 2001/138-64; letter from Noble Long to W. Lee O'Daniel, September 7, 1939, box 2001/138-126, RWLO, TSLAC; *Lubbock County Herald*, December 13, 1939, Scrapbook 1939, box 575, GMP, SWC.

4. James Reston, *The Lone Star: The Life of John Connally* (New York: Harper & Row, 1989), 28; *DMN*, January 17, 18, 1939.

5. *DMN*, January 28, 1939; miscellaneous newspaper clippings (1939), box 3L365, W. Lee "Pappy" O'Daniel Papers, DBCAH.

6. *DMN*, July 28, 1938, August 25, 1938; Patrick L. Cox and Michael Phillips, *The House Will Come to Order: How the Texas Speaker Became a Power in State and National Politics* (Austin: University of Texas Press, 2010), 47. For more on the life and times of W. Lee "Pappy" O'Daniel, see Seth Shepard McKay, *W. Lee O'Daniel and Texas Politics, 1938–1942* (Lubbock: Texas Tech Press, 1944).

7. *DMN*, August 12, 1938.

8. Letter from James Perkins to W. Lee O'Daniel, August 20, 1940; letter from W. Lee O'Daniel to Texas Delegation, August 26, 1940, box 2001/138-126, RWLO, TSLAC; *DMN*, December 12, 13, 14, 15, 1938. For more on industrialization in Texas and other southern states during this time, see Bruce J. Schulman, *From Cotton Belt to Sunbelt: Federal Policy, Economic Development, and the Transformation of the South, 1938–1980* (New York: Oxford University Press, 1991).

9. Partial Listing of Radio Broadcast Topics, 1939–1941, box 2001/138-64, RWLO, TSLAC.

10. Radio broadcast transcript, February 19, 1939, box 2001/138-64; radio broadcast transcript, January 14, 1940, Box 2001/138/65, RWLO, TSLAC.

11. General correspondence re: radio broadcasts, June 1939 (3), box 2001/138-66, RWLO, TSLAC.

12. Radio broadcast transcript, April 23, 1939, box 2001/138-64, RWLO, TSLAC.

13. Radio broadcast transcript, May 28, 1939, box 2001/138-64, RWLO, TSLAC.

14. Radio broadcast transcript, June 11, 1939, box 2001/138-64, RWLO, TSLAC.

15. Letter from Joe W. Scott to W. Lee O'Daniel, December 29, 1939; letter from Joseph B. Stratton to W. Lee O'Daniel, December 18, 1939; letter from B. H. Oxford to W. Lee O'Daniel, March 3, 1940, box 2001/138-139, RWLO, TSLAC.

16. Miscellaneous radio broadcast transcripts, box 2001/138-64, 2001/138-65, Radio Broadcast Files, 1939–1941, RWLO, TSLAC.

17. Letter from Anonymous (Bellmead, Texas) to Gov. W. Lee O'Daniel (Folio No. 4); letter from Anonymous (Fort Worth, Texas) to Gov. W. Lee O'Daniel (Folio No. 6); letter from Anonymous (San Antonio, Texas) to Gov. W. Lee O'Daniel (Folio No. 7), box 2001/138-63; letter from Mrs. W. A. Wulf to W. Lee O'Daniel, May 28, 1940, box 2001/138-61, RWLO, TSLAC.

18. "Un-American Activities, General Correspondence, May 1940-June

1941," box 2001/138-61; radio broadcast transcript, March 31, 1941, box 2001/138-66, RWLO, TSLAC.

19. George N. Green, *The Establishment in Texas Politics: The Primitive Years, 1938-1957* (Norman: University of Oklahoma Press, 1979), 29; McKay, *W. Lee O'Daniel and Texas Politics, 1938-1942*, 290; Allison Collis Greene, *No Depression in Heaven: The Great Depression, the New Deal, and the Transformation of Religion in the Delta* (New York: Oxford University Press, 2016), 159, 201.

20. Radio broadcast transcripts, April 23, 1939, Radio Broadcast Files, Box 2001/138-64; radio broadcast transcripts, March 24, 1940, May 26, 1940, January 28, 1940, box 2001/138-65, RWLO, TSLAC.

21. *DMN,* July 31, 1939, July 27, 1940, box 3L365; *DMN,* April 30, 1941, box 3L366, W. Lee "Pappy" O'Daniel Papers, DBCAH.

22. For more on FDR and religion, see again Greene, *No Depression in Heaven,* 130-159.

23. "General Files: Maverick, Maury," box 5, PPPLBJ, House of Representatives Papers, 1937-1949, LBJL; letter from H. B. Fitch to W. Lee O'Daniel, May 22, 1940, box 2001/138-63, RWLO, TSLAC.

24. "Black Congressman Mitchell" is likely Arthur W. Mitchell (D-IL), though the document is unclear.

25. Letter from Earnest Stack to Herman Brown, August 19, 1939, box 5, PPPLBJ, House of Representatives Papers, 1937-1949, LBJL; letter from Kenneth McKeller to W. Lee O'Daniel, February 9, 1940, box 2001/138-126, RWLO, TSLAC.

26. "Sidelights" by Marvin Jones, November 7, 1938, box 24, MJP, SWC.

27. *Lubbock Avalanche-Journal,* June 23, 1939; letter from State Medical Association of Texas to Mahon, March 6, 1939, folder: "Socialized Medicine," box 363; *Lubbock County Herald,* December 13, 1939, Scrapbook 1939, box 575, GMP, SWC.

28. "Six of 23 Texans in Congress Voted with Administration on All Controversial Bills," *Fort Worth Star-Telegram,* August 18, 1939, Scrapbook 1939, box 575, GMP; *DMN,* August 24, 1939.

29. "Six of 23 Texans in Congress Voted with Administration on All Controversial Bills"; *DMN,* August 24, 1939.

30. Miscellaneous newspaper clippings, Scrapbook 1941, box 573, GMP, SWC.

31. Letter from Fred Haile, Loan Agency of the Reconstruction Finance Corporation, Paris, Texas, to George Mahon, December 7, 1936, box 29, GMP, SWC; Dallek, *Franklin D. Roosevelt and American Foreign Policy, 1932-1945,* 103-119, 530; see also, for instance, *DMN,* January 4, 1937.

32. *Andrews County News,* January 1937; miscellaneous newspaper clippings, box 577, 1937; miscellaneous newspaper clippings, box 576, Scrapbook

1938, GMP, SWC; speeches by Morris Sheppard, 1938–1939, box 2G197, MSP, DBCAH.

33. *DMN*, August 24, 1939; *DMN*, September 3, 1939; radio broadcast transcript, September 10, 1939, box 2001/138–64; letter from Noble Long to W. Lee O'Daniel, September 7, 1939, box 2001/138–126, RWLO, TSLAC; *DMN*, November 3, 1939; *Lubbock County Herald*, December 13, 1939; Scrapbook 1939, box 575, GMP, SWC; Dallek, *Franklin D. Roosevelt and American Foreign Policy, 1932–1945*, 180–183.

34. Dallek, *Franklin D. Roosevelt and American Foreign Policy, 1932–1945*, 204–205; Reston, *The Lone Star*, 41, 53–54; miscellaneous letters, "Peace Movement, 1940–41," box 2001/138–139; letter from Wright Morrow to W. P. Hobby, January 19, 1940; letter from S. Tavalocci to W. Lee O'Daniel, May 19, 1940; letter from Joint National Defense of Orange and Mathis Communities to Tom Connally, Richard Kleberg, and W. Lee O'Daniel, July 22, 1941, box 2001/138–126, RWLO, TSLAC; general correspondence, folder "Neutrality, 1940," box 320, GMP, SWC.

35. Democratic National Committee correspondence to Marvin Jones, August 1940; confidential memorandum from Paul Appleby to Marvin Jones, August 8, 1940, box 23, MJP, SWC; letter from C. H. Everett to FDR, August 31, 1940, box 52, OF2, FDRL.

36. Miscellaneous newspaper clippings, box 577, Scrapbook 1937, GMP, SWC.

37. Reston, *The Lone Star*, 41.

38. Campaign promotional letter from Clara Driscoll, E. B. Germany, and the "National Garner for President Committee," February 23, 1940, box 59, TBLP, DHS; *DMN*, April 9, 1940; Seth Shepard McKay, *Texas Politics, 1906–1944* (Lubbock: Texas Tech Press, 1952), 419.

39. *Gainesville* (TX) *Register*, September 10, 1937; Scrapbook 2, 1913–1939 (vol. 2), MJP, SWC; miscellaneous political cartoons by Clifford Berryman, boxes 2W94 and 2W95, John Nance Garner Papers, DBCAH; letter from Clyde Eastus to Steve Early, August 10, 1940, box 31, OF3, FDRL.

40. Assorted speeches by Morris Sheppard, 1940, box 2G196, MSP, DBCAH; "Advance Copy for the Press—Announcement of Hobart Huson of Refugio as 'Write-In' Candidate for Governor of Texas," box 31, OF3, FDRL.

41. McKay, *Texas Politics, 1906–1944*, 330, 419.

42. Press release from Mayor Maverick of San Antonio, May 27, 1940, box 2L49, MMC, DBCAH.

43. McKay, *Texas Politics, 1906–1944*, 419.

44. McKay, 419. Maverick's flirtations with communism cost him ongoing electoral office in San Antonio. However, by 1943, Maverick had parlayed his friendship with Roosevelt into a minor chairmanship within the War Production Board known as the Smaller War Plants Corporation. Letter from Maury

Maverick to Coke R. Stevenson, December 7, 1943, box 4-14/147, Records of Governor Coke R. Stevenson, TSLAC; see also letter from FDR to Maury Maverick, June 5, 1944, in Franklin D. Roosevelt, *FDR: His Personal Letters: 1928–1945*, ed. Elliott Roosevelt (New York: Duell, Sloan and Pearce, 1950), 1514.

45. Letter from Roosevelt Democrat Club of Texas to Maury Maverick, May 1, 1940, box 2L49, MMC, DBCAH; see also general correspondence, box 2L49, MMC, DBCAH. For more on how the politics of the Garner-Roosevelt split unfolded behind closed doors in Texas, see Robert A. Caro, *The Path to Power: The Years of Lyndon Johnson* (New York: Alfred A. Knopf, 1982), 566–579, 590–593.

46. Miscellaneous speeches by Maury Maverick, Spring–Summer 1940, box 2L62, MMC, DBCAH. Despite his loyalty to FDR, and FDR's continued popularity in Texas, civic leaders in San Antonio soon grew tired of Maverick's influence on state and local politics, particularly as that influence seemed increasingly out of touch with the revival of the state's conservative proclivities. In 1941, Maverick lost his reelection bid to former congressional opponent and one-time San Antonio mayor C. K. Quin. Quin defeated Maverick by running a local campaign in tandem with several other candidates who collectively marketed themselves rather bluntly as "anti-Mavericks." Unable to stave off allegations from some that he was sympathetic to communism, Maverick tried to preserve his office through a campaign for "sound city government." It was bland resistance by Maverick's previous standards and ended in failure. Newspaper clippings, *San Antonio Light* and *San Antonio Express*, April–May 1941, box 4K123, MMC, DBCAH.

47. An FDR loyalist and publicly committed New Dealer, Rayburn chose to support his friend, Garner, during the earliest stages of the nomination fight in 1940. Eventually, he succumbed to political reality at the last possible minute, at FDR's personal request. Rayburn's commitment to Garner resulted in significant backlash from liberals in and out of the White House, at least temporarily.

48. "FDR-Garner Fight Stopped: Tempestuous Texas Battle Called Off on Direct Orders of Two Leaders," *Austin Daily Tribune*, April 29, 1940; telegram, Alvin Wirtz to LBJ, April 30, 1940, box 5, PPPLBJ, House of Representatives Papers, 1937–1949, LBJL.

49. *Austin Statesman*, May 1, 1940; *DMN*, May 1, 1940; miscellaneous newspaper clippings, May 1940; telegram, John Sargent to LBJ, April 30, 1940, box 5, PPPLBJ, House of Representatives Papers, 1937–1949, LBJL; Caro, *The Path to Power*, 591–593, 600–605.

50. *DMN*, May 29, 1940; McKay, *Texas Politics, 1906-1944*, 336–342, 419–423.

51. Dallek, *Franklin D. Roosevelt and American Foreign Policy, 1932-1945*, 221–226.

52. Jean Edward Smith, *FDR* (New York: Random House, 2007), 336–342, 442–460.

53. McKay, *Texas Politics, 1906–1944*, 336–342, 426–430; Martin Dies Jr., interview by Dr. Ray A. Stephens, May 31, 1966, transcript, 36, University of North Texas Oral History Collection, Willis Library, Denton.

54. *DMN*, October 11, 1940.

55. Letter from Robert Lee Bobbitt to Sam Rayburn, November 4, 1940, box 23, MJP, SWC.

56. McKay, *Texas Politics, 1906–1944*, 336–342.

57. Letter from Thomas Love to Morris Sheppard, November 8, 1940, box 66, TBLP, DHS.

58. Connally joined Lyndon Johnson's congressional staff in 1939 on the recommendation of J. R. Parten, who as a member of the University of Texas's Board of Regents had become acquainted with Connally when Connally served as president of the UT student body. Alvin Wirtz also aided in the connection. For more, see Reston, *The Lone Star*, 30–31; John B. Connally, interview by Robert Dallek, June 30, 1988, transcript, 3–4, John B. Connally Oral History, Special Interview, Internet Copy, LBJL; see also Caro, *The Path to Power*, 660–662.

59. Miscellaneous newspaper clippings, Scrapbook 1940, box 574, GMP, SWC.

60. Unpublished memoir of Marvin Jones, copyright Columbia University Press, box 16; letter from LBJ to Marvin Jones, July 2, 1941, box 21, MJP, SWC.

61. Letter from C. O. Trent to Martin Dies, May 24, 1940, box 2001/138–61, RWLO, TSLAC; Martin Dies Jr., interview by Dr. Ray A. Stephens, May 31, 1966, transcript, 19.

62. Anthony R. Carrozza, *The Dukes of Duval County: The Parr Family and Texas Politics*. (Norman: University of Oklahoma Press, 2017), 3; Caro, *The Path to Power*, 675–700; McKay, *Texas Politics, 1906–1944*, 348–353; Reston, *The Lone Star*, 60. Behind the scenes, Roosevelt was keen for information on the race. In his quest for news, however, FDR began to suspect some of his once most loyal allies of infidelity. He was particularly concerned about rumors that connected Jesse Jones to anti–New Deal forces in the Texas business community, indirectly pushing Jones to affirm his loyalties via correspondence on the Johnson campaign. For more, see memorandum from FDR to Jesse Jones, March 1, 1941, May 23, 1941, in Roosevelt, *F.D.R.: His Personal Letters, 1928–1945*, 1129, 1159.

63. Reston, *The Lone Star*, 64; McKay, *Texas Politics, 1906–1944*, 352–353. FDR's relationship with Johnson pre-dated LBJ's first campaign for Congress in 1937. He appointed LBJ to run the Texas branch of the NYA in 1935, and later, in 1939, tried to appoint Congressman Johnson to head of the national REA. Johnson declined the offer, choosing instead to stay in the House of Representatives.

64. LBJ campaign brochure, 1941, box 31, OF3, FDRL.

65. Letter from LBJ, May 15, 1941; miscellaneous form letters from LBJ, May 1941, box 15, PPPLBJ, House of Representatives Papers, 1937–1949, LBJL.

66. Campaign flyer, "Friends of Roosevelt," box 31, OF3, FDRL; "1941 Campaign Material"; campaign postcards, "Roosevelt & Johnson," box 15, PPPLBJ, House of Representatives Papers, 1937–1949, LBJL.

67. McKay, *Texas Politics, 1906-1944*, 354, 364. For more on the politics of welfare and motherhood, see again Linda Gordon, *Pitied but Not Entitled: Single Mothers and the History of Welfare, 1890-1935* (New York: Free Press, 1994), 188–207; see also Michelle Nickerson, *Mothers of Conservatism: Women and the Postwar Right* (New York: Oxford University Press, 2012), 1–31.

68. Letter from LBJ to FDR, March 29, 1941, box 12; letter from LBJ, June 21, 1941; miscellaneous letters from LBJ, May 1941, box 15, PPPLBJ, House of Representatives Papers, 1937–1949, LBJL; see also Caro, *The Path to Power*, 714.

69. Miscellaneous letters, "Peace Movement, 1940-1941," box 2001/138–139, RWLO, TSLAC.

70. Letter from "Lyndon Johnson for United States Senator," May 31, 1941; miscellaneous letters from LBJ, May 1941, box 15, PPPLBJ, House of Representative Papers, 1937–1949, LBJL.

71. Campaign ad, Texas Federation of Women's Club, "Federation News," undated, box 15, PPPLBJ, House of Representatives Papers, 1937–1949, LBJL.

72. "Save America First," radio address of Lyndon B. Johnson, May 3, 1941, San Marcos, TX, WOAI Radio, box 3, PPPLBJ, Statements of Lyndon Baines Johnson, LBJL.

73. McKay, *Texas Politics, 1906-1944*, 336–342.

74. "Memorandum to ALL Lyndon Johnson Leaders," May 31, 1941; general correspondence, "1941 Campaign Material," box 15, PPPLBJ, House of Representatives Papers, 1937–1949, LBJL.

75. Campaign ad, Texas Federation of Women's Club, "Federation News," undated, box 15, PPPLBJ, House of Representatives Papers, 1937–1949, LBJL.

76. "These Troubled Times," May 25, 1941, Radio Broadcast Files, box 2001/138–66, RWLO, TSLAC.

77. "Anti-Strike, Anti-Violence Bill," March 31, 1941; "Report on Anti-Strike, Anti-Violence Bill," April 7, 1941; "Spiritual Defense," June 1, 1941, Radio Broadcast Files, box 2001/138–66, RWLO, TSLAC; McKay, *Texas Politics, 1906-1944*, 360–61.

78. *Houston Post*, June 5, 1941, box 31, OF3, FDRL.

79. Telegram from A. M. Goul to Stephen Early; telegram from Stephen Early to A. M. Goul, June 1941, box 3, OF3, FDRL.

80. *Fort Worth Star-Telegram*, June 15, 1941, box 31, OF3, FDRL. Curiously, Thomas Love publicly supported O'Daniel, arguing in part that O'Daniel (and not Johnson) would be the true "yes man" for the New Deal and that O'Daniel would be a "champion of the Drys." "They are both humanitarians and both believe in government by the people and for the people," Love wrote. As he approached the end of his life, clearly out of touch with FDR's preferences,

not to mention the relative tendencies and preferences of the two candidates in play during this specific race, Love's stature as a respected voice in state and national politics was gone. *DMN*, June 24, 1941, box 3E262, Franklin D. Roosevelt Papers, DBCAH.

81. Telegram from FDR to LBJ, June 27, 1941, box 15, PPPLBJ, House of Representatives Papers, 1937–1949, LBJL; Caro, *The Path to Power*, 725–727.

82. Radio address by Lyndon B. Johnson, June 27, 1941, box 4, PPPLBJ, Statements of Lyndon Baines Johnson, LBJL. According to some estimates, Johnson's Senate campaign cost as much as $500,000. For more, see Caro, *The Path to Power*, 718.

83. McKay, *Texas Politics, 1906–1944*, 365; Caro, *The Path to Power*, 729.

84. Robert Dallek, *Lone Star Rising: Lyndon Johnson and His Times, 1908–1960* (New York: Oxford University Press, 1991), 219–224; Carrozza, *The Dukes of Duval County*, 4–6, 47; Caro, *The Path to Power*, 731–740.

85. Letter from Rae Files to FDR, July 2, 1941; letter from J. C. Hinsley to FDR, July 3, 1941; miscellaneous correspondence to FDR, July 1941, box 31, OF3, FDRL.

86. *DMN*, September 11, 1941, box 3L 365, W. Lee "Pappy" O'Daniel Papers, DBCAH.

87. "Roosevelt Sought to Avoid Me So He Hid at Sea, Says O'Daniel," *DMN*, August 16, 1941; "O'Daniel Jibes at Yes-Men, Opposed Extension of Draft: Maiden Speech Breaks Precedent, Draws Ear of Members, Visitors," *DMN*, August 16, 1941, box 3L366, W. Lee "Pappy" O'Daniel Papers, DBCAH.

88. *DMN*, August 20, 1941; "O'Daniel Tells of Confidence with F.D.R.: President Outlined Eventful Meeting with Churchill," *DMN*, August 25, 1941, box 3L366, W. Lee "Pappy" O'Daniel Papers, DBCAH.

89. *DMN*, October 20, 1941, box 3L366, W. Lee "Pappy" O'Daniel Papers, DBCAH; general correspondence, Neutrality Repeal, 1941, box 94, HWSP, DHS.

Chapter 6. *"A Closer Connection with Our Federal Government"*

1. Message to Congress—The State of the Union (speech files 1353A, 1353B, 1353C), January 6, 1941, box 58, Franklin D. Roosevelt, Master Speech File, 1898–1945, FDRL.

2. Inaugural Address of President Franklin D. Roosevelt (speech file 610), March 4, 1933, box 13, Franklin D. Roosevelt, Master Speech File, 1898–1945, FDRL; see also Jefferson Cowie, *The Great Exception: The New Deal and the Limits of American Politics* (Princeton, NJ: Princeton University Press, 2016), 124–156.

3. Labor Day Address—FDR Office (speech file 1380), September 1, 1941, box 61, Franklin D. Roosevelt, Master Speech File, 1898–1945, FDRL; Robert

Dallek, *Franklin D. Roosevelt and American Foreign Policy, 1932–1945* (New York: Oxford University Press, 1979), 285, 530.

4. For more on this period, as well as for a nuanced discussion of the limits of unity, see Michael C. C. Adams, *The Best War Ever: America and World War II* (Baltimore: Johns Hopkins University Press, 2015); see also Kimberly Phillips-Fein, *Invisible Hands: The Businessmen's Crusade against the New Deal* (W. W. Norton, 2009), 26–52.

5. Letter from K. L. Griggs to Mahon, March 23, 1942, general correspondence, box 360, GMP, SWC; Bruce J. Schulman, *From Cotton Belt to Sunbelt: Federal Policy, Economic Development, and the Transformation of the South, 1938–1980* (New York: Oxford University Press, 1991), 43, 55, 98. For more on federal defense contacts in the West, see Roger W. Lotchin, *Fortress California: From Warfare to Welfare* (New York: Oxford University Press, 1992), and Sean P. Cunningham, *American Politics in the Postwar Sunbelt: Conservative Growth in a Battleground Region* (New York: Cambridge University Press, 2014), 17–55.

6. *Muleshoe Journal,* May 14, 1942; George Mahon, miscellaneous newspaper editorials (1942), box 572, Scrapbook 1942, GMP, SWC.

7. Letter from Boyd Scott to Mahon, March 13, 1942, general correspondence, box 360, GMP, SWC.

8. Letter from FDR to Sam Rayburn, February 18, 1942, in Franklin D. Roosevelt, *F.D.R.: His Personal Letters, 1928–1945*, ed. Elliott Roosevelt (New York: Duell, Sloan and Pearce, 1950), 1286–1287.

9. Letter from LBJ to Sam Rayburn, March 25, 1942, box 3U106, SRP, DBCAH.

10. Gregg Cantrell, *The People's Revolt: Texas Populists and the Roots of American Liberalism* (New Haven, CT: Yale University Press, 2020), 427.

11. Letter from Wright Patman to FDR, February 21, 1943, box 3U106, SRP, DBCAH; Nacny Beck Young, *Wright Patman: Populism, Liberalism, and the American Dream* (Dallas, TX: Southern Methodist University Press, 2000), 105.

12. Among many others, see again for more on labor politics and race during World War II, Emilio Zamora, *Claiming Rights and Righting Wrongs in Texas: Mexican Workers and Job Politics during World War II* (College Station: Texas A&M University Press, 2009); see also Kathryn S. Olmstead, *Right Out of California: The 1930s and the Big Business Roots of Modern Conservatism* (New York: New Press, 2015), 227.

13. *DMN,* September 3, 1941; *DMN,* July 11, 1942; "Dallas Hears O'Daniel Tell His Views: Repeats His Claim War Is Not Issue of Campaign, Insists that Communism Is," *DMN,* July 17, 1942; "O'Daniel Says He's a Victim of Propaganda," *DMN,* July 23, 1942, box 3L366, W. Lee "Pappy" O'Daniel Papers, DBCAH; Seth Shepard McKay, *Texas Politics, 1906–1944* (Lubbock: Texas Tech Press, 1952), 365.

14. Robert Dallek, *Franklin D. Roosevelt: A Political Life* (New York: Viking, 2017), 470.

15. John B. Connally, interview by Robert Dallek, June 30, 1988, transcript, 13–14, John B. Connally Oral History, Special Interview, Internet Copy, LBJL; miscellaneous correspondence from FDR to John Connally, 1942; letter from Harold Ickes to FDR, February 3, 1942; memorandum from FDR to Harold Ickes, February 4, 1932, box 31, OF3, FDRL; Dallek, *Franklin D. Roosevelt and American Foreign Policy, 1932–1945*, 360–361.

16. Memorandum from LBJ to FDR, July 27, 1942; letter from Harold Ickes to FDR, July 30, 1942, box 31, OF3, FDRL; McKay, *Texas Politics, 1906–1944*, 375–380.

17. George N. Green, *The Establishment in Texas Politics: The Primitive Years, 1938–1957* (Norman: University of Oklahoma Press, 1979), 39.

18. McKay, *Texas Politics, 1906–1944*, 380–383.

19. Green, *The Establishment in Texas Politics*, 41–42.

20. *Houston Post*, August 22, 1942; McKay, *Texas Politics, 1906–1944*, 385–386.

21. *Houston Post*, August 22, 1942; McKay, *Texas Politics, 1906–1944*, 385–386; memorandum to DNC, December 14, 1943, box 551, Papers of the Democratic National Committee, FDRL; Patrick L. Cox, *The First Texas News Barons* (Austin: University of Texas Press, 2005), 189–201.

22. Miscellaneous newspaper clippings, box 3L366, W. Lee "Pappy" O'Daniel Papers, DBCAH; McKay, *Texas Politics, 1906–1944*, 387–388.

23. Radio speech, November 7, 1938, Campaign for Lt. Governor; campaign brochure, 1938; campaign speeches, July 1938–1940, box 54, Coke Stevenson Papers, SWC; *DMN*, May 9, 1939, box 3L365, W. Lee "Pappy" O'Daniel Papers, DBCAH.

24. Letter from John F. Sturgeon (Pampa) to Coke Stevenson, September 30, 1941, box 38, Coke Stevenson Papers, SWC.

25. Patrick L. Cox and Michael Phillips, *The House Will Come to Order: How the Texas Speaker Became a Power in State and National Politics* (Austin: University of Texas Press, 2010), 38–46; Robert Dallek, *Lone Star Rising: Lyndon Johnson and His Times, 1908–1960* (New York: Oxford University Press, 1991), 315–316; Green, *The Establishment in Texas Politics*, 79–80; McKay, *Texas Politics, 1906–1944*, 395–396.

26. Letter from C. E. Nicholson to Coke Stevenson, June 19, 1942, box 37, Coke Stevenson Papers, SWC.

27. Letter from Lewis Hancock to Hatton Sumners, May 18, 1942; letter from W. W. Biard to Jack Biard, July 7, 1942; letter from Ann Hunter to Hatton Sumners, July 20, 1942, box 105; *Democracy*, June 10, 1942, box 106, HWSP, DHS; *DMN*, July 25, 26, 1942.

28. Miscellaneous newspaper clippings, box 571, box 572, Scrapbook 1942, Scrapbook 1943, GMP, SWC; Dallek, *Franklin D. Roosevelt*, 479.

29. "Gasoline Rationing—Farm and Ranch"—general correspondence; letter from J. O. Green to Mahon, November 27, 1942, box 213; unidentified newspaper clipping (c. November 1942), box 572, Scrapbook 1942, GMP, SWC.

30. Letter from J. G. Evans (Hereford, TX) to Hatton Sumners, December 5, 1942; general correspondence—"Bureaucracy," box 49, folders 1.1–1.21, HWSP, DHS.

31. Green, *The Establishment in Texas Politics*, 55; Dallek, *Franklin D. Roosevelt and American Foreign Policy, 1932–1945*, 443.

32. Richard M. Bernard and Bradley R. Rice, eds., *Sunbelt Cities: Politics and Growth since World War II* (Austin: University of Texas Press, 1983), 162–169, 196–204, 235–238; Sean P. Cunningham, *American Politics in the Postwar Sunbelt: Conservative Growth in a Battleground Region* (New York: Cambridge University Press, 2014), 27–41; see also Gerald D. Nash, *World War II and the West: Reshaping the Economy* (Lincoln: University of Nebraska Press, 1990).

33. Bryan Burrough, *The Big Rich: The Rise and Fall of the Greatest Texas Oil Fortunes* (New York: Penguin Press, 2009), 141–145; Don E. Carleton, *A Breed So Rare: The Life of J. R. Parten, Liberal Texas Oil Man, 1896–1992* (Austin: Texas State Historical Association, 1998); Caro, *The Path to Power*, xxii–xxiii. For more on the competition between LBJ and Elliott Roosevelt, see John B. Connally, interview by Robert Dallek, June 30, 1988, transcript, 15–16, John B. Connally Oral History, Special Interview, Internet Copy, LBJL. According to a story frequently told by Lyndon Johnson, FDR was personally responsible for escalating LBJ's relationship with Brown and Root. In late 1939, Johnson sided with FDR in a dispute with the Texas congressional delegation over whether or not to condemn statements by labor leader John L. Lewis, who had disparaged John Nance Garner during testimony on Capitol Hill. According to the story, Rayburn furiously insisted that Johnson sign a resolution defending Garner, but LBJ refused, and subsequently enjoyed the benefits of frequent visits to the White House and increased support from FDR for construction projects to Brown and Root. James Reston, *The Lone Star: The Life of John Connally* (New York: Harper & Row, 1989), 42–43.

34. Green, *The Establishment in Texas Politics*, 46.

35. *DMN*, March 20, 1944; speech by W. O. Lee O'Daniel, March 23, 1944; "Letters of Clyde Eastus," box 551, Papers of the Democratic National Committee, FDRL; Dallek, *Franklin D. Roosevelt and American Foreign Relations, 1932–1945*, 443–444; Glen Feldman, *The Great Melding: War, the Dixiecrat Rebellion, and the Southern Model for America's New Conservatism* (Tuscaloosa: University of Alabama Press, 2015), 96.

36. Paid political advertisement, Elect Roosevelt Committee, *Austin American-Statesman*, May 23, 1944, box 41, PPPLBJ, House of Representatives Papers, 1937–1949, LBJL.

37. *DMN*, April 4, 1944; McKay, *Texas Politics, 1906–1944*, 432–434. For more on *Smith v. Allwright*, see Darlene Clark Hine, *Black Victory: The Rise and Fall of the White Primary in Texas* (Millwood, NY: KTO Press, 1979).

38. *DMN*, April 4, 1944; McKay, *Texas Politics, 1906–1944*, 432–434. For more on *Smith v. Allwright*, see Hine, *Black Victory*.

39. Minutes of the Texas Democratic State Convention, Austin, Texas, May 23, 1944, box 2.325/A133, Myron Blalock Collection, DBCAH; miscellaneous newspaper clippings, 1944, box 39, PPPLBJ, House of Representatives Papers, 1937–1949, LBJL; Scott M. Sosebee, "The Split in the Texas Democratic Party, 1936–1956," MA thesis, Texas Tech University, 2000, 37.

40. V. O. Key, *Southern Politics in State and Nation* (New York: Vintage Books, 1949), 256.

41. Resolution of the State Democratic Convention, Austin, Texas, May 23, 1944—by Charles E. Simons, Permanent Secretary of the State Democratic Convention, box 363, GMP, SWC.

42. Minutes of the Texas Democratic State Convention, Austin, Texas, May 23, 1944, box 2.325/A133, Myron Blalock Collection, DBCAH.

43. Miscellaneous newspaper clippings, May–June 1944, box 41, PPPLBJ, House of Representatives Papers, 1937–1949, LBJL.

44. Political file: W. Lee O'Daniel (clippings), box 42; *Austin American-Statesman*, July 6, 1944, box 39, PPPLBJ, House of Representatives Papers, 1937–1949, LBJL; Randolph B. Campbell, *Gone to Texas: A History of the Lone Star State* (New York: Oxford University Press, 2003), 406.

45. "Jesse Jones Scores Anti-Roosevelt Demos for Refusing to Bind Electors," *Austin American-Statesman*, July 5, 1944, box 39; miscellaneous newspaper clippings, May–June 1944, box 41, PPPLBJ, House of Representatives Papers, 1937–1949, LBJL; "The Texas Electoral Vote," *Houston Chronicle*, undated, Jesse H. Jones, box 593, GMP, SWC; John B. Connally, interview by Robert Dallek, June 30, 1988, transcript, 15–16, John B. Connally Oral History, Special Interview, Internet Copy, LBJL.

46. "Resolution Adopted by the Pro-Roosevelt Convention, Austin, Texas, Held May 23rd in the House of Representatives, Capitol, Austin, Texas," box 2.325/A133, Myron Blalock Collection, DBCAH.

47. Letter from W. A. Brooks to Ambrose O'Connell, vice chairman, Democratic National Committee, May 26, 1944; letter from W. S. Parker to Sam D. Jackson, July 6, 1944, box 2.325/A133, Myron Blalock Collection, DBCAH; "Clyde Eastus Letters" to Robert Hannegan, DNC, box 551, Papers of the Democratic National Committee, FDRL; Green, *The Establishment in Texas Politics*, 56.

48. Campaign advertisement, "Who Are the Regular Democrats of Texas?," *Houston Chronicle*, September 8, 1944, box 31, OF3, FDRL.

49. Miscellaneous newspaper clippings (Texas); unidentified editorial, "Mr. Roosevelt and the New Deal," September 29, 1944, box 31, OF3, FDRL.

50. Among many others, see again for more on labor politics and race during World War II, Zamora, *Claiming Rights and Righting Wrongs in Texas*; see also Olmstead, *Right Out of California*, 227.

51. McKay, *Texas Politics, 1906–1944*, 432–446. For more details on the 1944 Democratic National Convention, and the negotiations relevant to the Texas delegation, see again Sosebee, "The Split in the Texas Democratic Party, 1936–1956."

52. McKay, *Texas Politics, 1906–1944*, 432–446. See again Sosebee, "The Split in the Texas Democratic Party, 1936–1956."

53. David Cullen and Kyle G. Wilkison, eds., *The Texas Right: The Radical Roots of Lone Star Conservatism* (College Station: Texas A&M University Press, 2014), 1–22; Sean P. Cunningham, *Cowboy Conservatism: Texas and the Rise of the Modern Right* (Lexington: University Press of Kentucky, 2010), 25–26; Green, *The Establishment in Texas Politics*, 49.

54. "President and New Deal are Issues in 10th Congressional Race," *DMN*, July 4, 1944, box 39, PPPLBJ, House of Representatives Papers, 1937–1949, LBJL.

55. "What Is a Democrat?," Political Advertisement Paid for by Friends of Buck Taylor, box 41, PPPLBJ, House of Representatives Papers, 1937–1949, LBJL.

56. Anonymous letter to LBJ, May 26, 1944, attached to undated editorial, Henderson, TX, box 41, PPPLBJ, House of Representatives Papers, 1937–1949, LBJL.

57. LBJ campaign advertisement, July 13–14, 1944, box 39, PPPLB, House of Representatives Papers, 1937–1949, LBJL.

58. *Lockney Beacon*, February 5, 1944, box 593, GMP, SWC.

59. Campaign flyer, "Announcement: A New Blessed Event"; unidentified newspaper clipping, "How Big Business Plotted Texas . . . GOP Worked With O'Daniel to Pack Democratic Convention," undated, box 31, OF3, FDRL.

60. Radio address of D. B. Denney, July 11, 1944, KRRV Radio, Sherman, TX, box 593, GMP, SWC; speech by Sam Rayburn, October 17, 1944, Abilene, TX, box 31, OF3, FDRL; McKay, *Texas Politics, 1906–1944*, 456.

61. This was not the first time that right-wing oil barons asserted themselves into the messy world of Texas politics, nor would it be the last. However, their influence on the rise of Texas conservatism has been overstated. As Bryan Burrough puts it, history has "correctly dismissed" most of them as "fools." Burrough, *The Big Rich*, 56–57, 134, 248–249.

62. Mahon Campaign Message, July 13, 1944; miscellaneous campaign materials (1944), box 593, GMP, SWC.

63. Political correspondence, 1944, box 363; political correspondence, box 349, GMP, SWC.

64. *Lubbock Avalanche-Journal*, July 23, 1943, box 571, Scrapbook 1943, GMP, SWC.

65. *Borden County Sun*, February 18, 1944, box 593, GMP, SWC.

66. "1944 Congressional Campaign Mailers from C .L. Harris"; 1944 Democratic Primary Results, July 22, 1944, box 593, GMP, SWC.

67. Radio address of Hon. Hatton W. Sumners, KRLD, July 5, 1944, 8:30 p.m., box 122, HWSP, DHS.

68. Radio address by Hatton Sumners, WFAA Radio, July 10, 1944; radio address by Hatton Sumners, KGKO Radio, July 17, 1944; miscellaneous speech files, Hatton W. Sumners, 1944; radio address by Carlton Winn, WFAA Radio, July 14, 1944, box 122, folders 8.1–8.4, HWSP, DHS.

69. Political correspondence, 1944, box 106, HWSP, DHS.

70. Political Advertisement Paid for by Bee County Friends of Dick Kleberg; Advertisement by Nueces County Kleberg for Congress Committee, box 5, RKP, LBJL.

71. Letter from Irving Chandler to Richard Kleberg, December 18, 1943; letter from Clyde Booth to Richard Kleberg, January 9, 1944; letter from Daniel Williams to Richard Kleberg, January 25, 1944, box 3, RKP, LBJL.

72. Speech by Richard Kleberg, March 1, 1944, to Texas and Southwest Cattle Raisers Association, box 3, RKP, LBJL.

73. Press release re: "Congressional Speech by Kleberg," May 8, 1944, box 4, RKP, LBJL.

74. Lyle campaign advertisement, July 20, 1944, box 4, RKP, LBJL; Anthony R. Carrozza, *The Dukes of Duval County: The Parr Family and Texas Politics* (Norman: University of Oklahoma Press, 2017), 44; *Chicago Tribune*, December 4, 1944, box 4, RKP, LBJL.

75. Letter from Leonard Piggot to Richard Kleberg, December 5, 1944, "Re: Farewell Speech," box 4, RKP, LBJL.

76. McKay, *Texas Politics, 1906–1944*, 455, 462; Green, *The Establishment in Texas Politics*, 74–75.

77. *DMN*, August 15, 22, 1944; *DMN*, October 1, 11, 19, 22, and 29, 1944.

78. Lewis L. Gould, *Grand Old Party: A History of the Republicans* (New York: Random House, 2003), 298.

79. McKay, *Texas Politics, 1906–1944*, 462.

80. McKay, 454–459; Green, *The Establishment in Texas Politics*, 74–75.

81. McKay, 454–459; Green, 74–75.

82. Statement of Lyndon B. Johnson, November 8, 1944, box 5, PPPLBJ, Statements of Lyndon Baines Johnson, LBJL.

83. Campbell, *Gone to Texas*, 407.

84. Dallek, *Lone Star Rising*, 3–10.

85. Letter from Maston Nixon to Myron Blalock, April 16, 1945, box 2.325/A133, Myron Blalock Collection, DBCAH.

86. For more on New Deal projects in Texas, see, among other sources, the

extensive database maintained at The Living New Deal, livingnewdeal.org, accessed December 9, 2020.

Conclusion

1. Sean P. Cunningham, *Cowboy Conservatism: Texas and the Rise of the Modern Right* (Lexington: University Press of Kentucky, 2010), 1–11.

2. Among many other outstanding works, see Donald T. Critchlow, *The Conservative Ascendancy: How the GOP Right Made Political History* (Cambridge, MA: Harvard University Press, 2007).

3. Arlie Russell Hochschild, *Strangers in Their Own Land: Anger and Mourning on the American Right* (New York: New Press, 2016); J. D. Vance, *Hillbilly Elegy: A Memoir of a Family and Culture in Crisis* (New York: HarperCollins, 2016); Robert Wuthnow, *The Left Behind: Decline and Rage in Small-Town America* (Princeton, NJ: Princeton University Press, 2019).

4. The literature on modern presidential campaigns is vast. For more on George Wallace, see Dan T. Carter, *The Politics of Rage: George Wallace, the Origins of the New Conservatism, and the Transformation of American Politics* (Baton Rouge: Louisiana State University Press, 1995). For more on Barack Obama's identification with Ronald Reagan, see *Washington Post*, January 17, 2008, and *New York Times*, January 22, 2008.

5. Alison Collis Green, *No Depression in Heaven: The Great Depression, the New Deal, and the Transformation of Religion in the Delta* (New York: Oxford University Press, 2016), 201.

6. Radio address re: A National Program of Restoration (Speech File 469), Albany, NY, April 7, 1932, box 9, Franklin D. Roosevelt, Master Speech File, 1898–1945, FDRL.

7. William E. Leuchtenburg, *Franklin D. Roosevelt and the New Deal, 1932–1940* (New York: Harper & Row, 1963), 326–330.

Bibliography

Primary Sources

ARCHIVAL AND MANUSCRIPT SOURCES
Dallas Historical Society, Dallas, TX
    Thomas B. Love Papers
    Hatton W. Sumners Papers
    1936 Texas Centennial Commission Papers
Dolph Briscoe Center for American History, University of Texas at Austin
    Myron Blalock Collection
    James Buchanan Papers
    Tom Connally Papers
    John Nance Garner Papers
    Maury Maverick Sr. Collection
    W. Lee "Pappy" O'Daniel Papers
    Sam Rayburn Papers
    Franklin D. Roosevelt Letters
    Morris Sheppard Papers
    Hatton W. Sumners Papers
Lyndon B. Johnson Presidential Library, Austin, TX
    Pre-Presidential Papers of Lyndon B. Johnson
        House of Representatives Papers, 1937–1949
        Statements of Lyndon Baines Johnson
    Richard Kleberg Papers
    Records of the National Youth Administration, 1935–1937
    Wright Patman Papers
Franklin D. Roosevelt Presidential Library, Hyde Park, NY
    Franklin D. Roosevelt, Master Speech File, 1898–1945
    Papers Pertaining to the Campaign of 1928
    Papers of the Democratic National Committee, 1928–1948
    Papers of the Women's Division of the Democratic National Committee,
        1933–1944
    Papers as President, Official File (OF)
        File 200: Trips of the President
        File 300: Democratic National Committee
        File 400: Appointments
    Papers as President, President's Personal File (PPF)

Southwest Collection/Special Collections Library, Texas Tech University, Lubbock
    Marvin Jones Papers
    George Mahon Papers
    Coke R. Stevenson Papers
Texas State Library and Archives Commission, Austin
    Records of Governor James V. Allred
    Records of Governor Miriam Amanda Ferguson
    Thomas Jefferson Holbrook Papers
    Records of Governor Beauford H. Jester
    Records of Governor W. Lee O'Daniel
    Records of Governor Coke R. Stevenson

ORAL HISTORIES
Lyndon B. Johnson Presidential Library, Austin, TX
    John B. Connally
Oral History Collection, University of North Texas, Denton
    Martin Dies Jr.

NEWSPAPERS, MAGAZINES, AND PERIODICALS
    Dallas Morning News
    Houston Chronicle
    New York Times
    Texas Digital Newspaper Program, "The Portal to Texas History," texas history.unt.edu
    Washington Post

PRINTED PRIMARY SOURCES
Roosevelt, Franklin D. *FDR: His Personal Letters: 1928–1945*. Edited by Elliott Roosevelt. New York: Duell, Sloan and Pearce, 1950.
————. *The Public Papers and Addresses of Franklin D. Roosevelt, 1928–1945*. 13 vols. Washington, DC: U.S. Government Printing Office, 1950.

Secondary Sources

Adams, Michael C. C. *The Best War Ever: America and World War II*. Baltimore: Johns Hopkins University Press, 2015.
Alexander, Charles C. *The Ku Klux Klan in the Southwest*. Lexington: University of Kentucky Press, 1965.
Archer, Kenna Lang. *Unruly Waters: A Social and Environmental History of the Brazos River*. Albuquerque: University of New Mexico Press, 2015.

Badger, Anthony J. *The New Deal: The Depression Years, 1933–1940*. New York: Noonday Press, 1989.

Barr, Alwyn. *Black Texans: A History of African Americans in Texas, 1528–1995*. Norman: University of Oklahoma Press, 1996.

———. *Reconstruction to Reform: Texas Politics, 1876–1906*. Dallas: Southern Methodist University Press, 1971.

Barwinkel, Sarah. "A Legacy in Lubbock: How Three New Deal Programs Left Their Mark on the South Plains." MA thesis, Texas Tech University, 2009.

Beito, David T. *Taxpayers in Revolt: Tax Resistance during the Great Depression*. Chapel Hill: University of North Carolina Press, 1989.

Bernard, Richard M., and Bradley R. Rice, eds. *Sunbelt Cities: Politics and Growth since World War II*. Austin: University of Texas Press, 1983.

Bernstein, Patricia. *Ten Dollars to Hate: The Texas Man Who Fought the Klan*. College Station: Texas A&M University Press, 2017.

Blackwater, Julia Kirk. *Women of the Depression: Caste and Culture in San Antonio, 1929–1939*. College Station: Texas A&M University Press, 1984.

Boorstin, Daniel J. *The Image: A Guide to Pseudo-Events in America*. New York: Vintage Books, 1961, 2012.

Brands, H. W. *The Strange Death of American Liberalism*. New Haven, CT: Yale University Press, 2001.

———. *Traitor to His Class: The Privileged Life and Radical Presidency of Franklin Delano Roosevelt*. New York: Doubleday, 2008.

Brinkley, Alan. *The End of Reform: New Deal Liberalism in Recession and War*. New York: Alfred A. Knopf, 1995.

Brown, Norman D. *Biscuits, the Dole, and Nodding Donkeys: Texas Politics, 1929–1932*. Austin: University of Texas Press, 2019.

———. "Gathering Votes for Cactus Jack." *Southwestern Historical Quarterly* 103, no. 3 (January 2000): 367–378.

———. *Hood, Bonnet, and Little Brown Jug: Texas Politics, 1921–1928*. College Station: Texas A&M University Press, 1984.

Buenger, Walter L. *The Path to a Modern South: Northeast Texas between Reconstruction and the Great Depression*. Austin: University of Texas Press, 2001.

Burrough, Bryan. *The Big Rich: The Rise and Fall of the Greatest Texas Oil Fortunes*. New York: Penguin Press, 2009.

Campbell, Randolph B. *Gone to Texas: A History of the Lone Star State*. New York: Oxford University Press, 2003.

Cannon, Laura E. "Situational Solidarity: LULAC's Civil Rights Strategy and the Challenge of the Mexican-American Worker, 1934–1946." PhD diss., Texas Tech University, 2016.

Cantrell, Gregg. *The People's Revolt: Texas Populists and the Roots of American Liberalism*. New Haven, CT: Yale University Press, 2020.

Carleton, Don E. *A Breed So Rare: The Life of J. R. Parten, Liberal Texas Oil Man, 1896–1992*. Austin: Texas State Historical Association, 1998.

Caro, Robert A. *The Path to Power: The Years of Lyndon Johnson*. New York: Alfred A. Knopf, 1982.

Carrozza, Anthony R. *The Dukes of Duval County: The Parr Family and Texas Politics*. Norman: University of Oklahoma Press, 2017.

Carter, Dan T. *The Politics of Rage: George Wallace, the Origins of the New Conservatism, and the Transformation of American Politics*. Baton Rouge: Louisiana State University Press, 1995.

Cervantez, Brian A. *Amon Carter: A Lone Star Life*. Norman: University of Oklahoma Press, 2019.

Champagne, Anthony. "Hatton Sumners and the 1937 Court-Packing Plan." *East Texas Historical Journal* 26, no. 1 (Spring 1988): 46–49.

Chiles, Robert. *The Revolution of '28: Al Smith, American Progressivism, and the Coming of the New Deal*. Ithaca, NY: Cornell University Press, 2018.

Cowie, Jefferson. *The Great Exception: The New Deal and the Limits of American Politics*. Princeton, NJ: Princeton University Press, 2016.

Cox, Patrick L. *The First Texas News Barons*. Austin: University of Texas Press, 2009.

———. *Ralph W. Yarborough: The People's Senator*. Austin: University of Texas Press, 2001.

Cox, Patrick L., and Michael Phillips. *The House Will Come to Order: How the Texas Speaker Became a Power in State and National Politics*. Austin: University of Texas Press, 2010.

Critchlow, Donald T. *The Conservative Ascendancy: How the GOP Right Made Political History*. Cambridge, MA: Harvard University Press, 2007.

Cullen, David, and Kyle G. Wilkison, eds. *The Texas Left: The Radical Roots of Lone Star Liberalism*. College Station: Texas A&M University Press, 2010.

——— eds. *The Texas Right: The Radical Roots of Lone Star Conservatism*. College Station: Texas A&M University Press, 2014.

Cunningham, Sean P. *American Politics in the Postwar Sunbelt: Conservative Growth in a Battleground Region*. New York: Cambridge University Press, 2014.

———. *Cowboy Conservatism: Texas and the Rise of the Modern Right*. Lexington: University Press of Kentucky, 2010.

Dallek, Robert. *Franklin D. Roosevelt and American Foreign Policy, 1932–1945*. New York: Oxford University Press, 1979.

———. *Franklin D. Roosevelt: A Political Life*. New York: Viking, 2017.

———. *Lone Star Rising: Lyndon Johnson and His Times, 1908–1960*. New York: Oxford University Press, 1991.

Daniel, Josiah M., III. "'What I Said Was 'Here Is Where I Cash In': The Instrumental Role of Congressman Hatton Sumners in the Resolution of the 1937 Court-Packing Crisis." *UIC John Marshall Law Review* 54, no. 2 (Summer 2021): 379–428.

Davidson, Chandler. *Race and Class in Texas Politics.* Princeton, NJ: Princeton University Press, 1990.

De León, Arnoldo. *Mexican Americans in Texas: A Brief History.* Arlington Heights, IL: Harlan Davidson, 1993.

Dempsy, John Mark. *The Light Crust Doughboys Are on the Air: Celebrating Seventy Years of Texas Music.* Denton: University of North Texas Press, 2002.

Dochuk, Darren. *From Bible Belt to Sun Belt: Plain-Folk Religion, Grassroots Politics, and the Rise of Evangelical Conservatism.* New York: W. W. Norton, 2011.

Doyle, Judith Kaaz. "Maury Maverick and Racial Politics in San Antonio, Texas, 1938–1941." *Journal of Southern History* 53, no. 2 (May 1987): 194–224.

Duke, Escal F. "The Political Career of Morris Sheppard, 1875–1941." PhD diss., University of Texas, 1958.

Dumenil, Lynn. *The Modern Temper: American Culture and Society in the 1920s.* New York: Hill and Wang, 1995.

Dunn, Susan. *Roosevelt's Purge: How FDR Fought to Change the Democratic Party.* Cambridge, MA: Harvard University Press, 2010.

Egan, Timothy. *The Worst Hard Time: The Untold Story of Those Who Survived the Great American Dust Bowl.* New York: Houghton Mifflin, 2006.

Feldman, Glenn. *The Great Melding: War, the Dixiecrat Rebellion, and the Southern Model for America's New Conservatism.* Tuscaloosa: University of Alabama Press, 2015.

Fenberg, Steven. *Unprecedented Power: Jesse Jones, Capitalism, and the Common Good.* College Station: Texas A&M University Press, 2011.

Foley, Neil. *The White Scourge: Mexicans, Blacks, and Poor Whites in Texas Cotton Culture.* Berkeley: University of California Press, 1997.

Frank, Thomas. *What's the Matter with Kansas?: How Conservatives Won the Heart of America.* New York: Henry Holt, 2004.

Freund, David M. P. *Colored Property: State Policy and White Racial Politics in Suburban America.* Chicago: University of Chicago Press, 2010.

Fullilove, Michael. *Rendezvous with Destiny: How Franklin D. Roosevelt and Five Extraordinary Men Took America into the War and into the World.* New York: Penguin Press, 2013.

Gilmore, Glenda Elizabeth. *Defying Dixie: The Radical Roots of Civil Rights, 1919–1950.* New York: W. W. Norton, 2008.

Golway, Terry. *Frank and Al: FDR, Al Smith, and the Unlikely Alliance That Created the Modern Democratic Party.* New York: St. Martin's Press, 2018.

Gordon, Linda. *Pitied but Not Entitled: Single Mothers and the History of Welfare, 1890–1935.* New York: Free Press, 1994.

———. *The Second Coming of the KKK: The Ku Klux Klan of the 1920s and the American Political Tradition.* New York: W. W. Norton, 2017.

Gould, Lewis L. *Grand Old Party: A History of the Republicans.* New York: Random House, 2003.

———. *Progressives and Prohibitionists: Texas Democrats in the Wilson Era*. Austin: University of Texas Press, 1973.

Green, George N. *The Establishment in Texas Politics: The Primitive Years, 1938–1957*. Norman: University of Oklahoma Press, 1979.

Greenberg, David. *Nixon's Shadow: The History of an Image*. New York: W. W. Norton, 2003.

Greene, Alison Collis. *No Depression in Heaven: The Great Depression, the New Deal, and the Transformation of Religion in the Delta*. New York: Oxford University Press, 2016.

Grieder, Erica. *Big, Hot, Cheap, and Right: What America Can Learn from the Strange Genius of Texas*. New York: PublicAffairs, 2013.

Hart, Justin. *Empire of Ideas: The Origins of Public Diplomacy and the Transformation of U.S. Foreign Policy*. New York: Oxford University Press, 2013.

Heale, M. J. *McCarthy's Americans: Red Scare Politics in State and Nation, 1935–1965*. Athens: University of Georgia Press, 1998.

Henderson, Richard. *Maury Maverick: A Political Biography*. Austin: University of Texas Press, 1970.

Hine, Darlene Clark. *Black Victory: The Rise and Fall of the White Primary in Texas*. Millwood, NY: KTO Press, 1979.

Hochschild, Arlie Russell. *Strangers in Their Own Land: Anger and Mourning on the American Right*. New York: New Press, 2016, 2018.

Hofstadter, Richard. *The Age of Reform*. New York: Vintage, 1955.

Katznelson, Ira. *Fear Itself: The New Deal and the Origins of Our Time*. New York: Liveright Publishing, 2013.

———. *When Affirmative Action Was White: An Untold History of Racial Inequality in Twentieth-Century America*. New York: W. W. Norton, 2005.

Kazin, Michael. *American Dreamers: How the Left Changed a Nation*. New York: Alfred A. Knopf, 2011.

———. *The Populist Persuasion: An American History*. New York: Basic Books, 1995.

Kennedy, David M. *Freedom from Fear: The American People in Depression and War, 1929–1945*. New York: Oxford University Press, 1999.

Key, V. O. *Southern Politics in State and Nation*. New York: Vintage Books, 1949.

Krochmal, Max. *Blue Texas: The Making of a Multiracial Democratic Coalition in the Civil Rights Era*. Chapel Hill: University of North Carolina Press, 2016.

Lassiter, Matthew D. *The Silent Majority: Suburban Politics in the Sunbelt South*. Princeton, NJ: Princeton University Press, 2006.

Law, Ron C. "Congressman Hatton W. Sumners of Dallas, Texas: His Life and Congressional Career, 1875–1937." PhD diss., Texas Christian University, 1990.

Leuchtenburg, William E. *The FDR Years: On Roosevelt and His Legacy*. New York: Columbia University Press, 1995.

——. *Franklin D. Roosevelt and the New Deal, 1932–1940.* New York: Harper & Row, 1963.

——. *The Perils of Prosperity, 1914–1932.* Chicago: University of Chicago Press, 1958.

Link, William A. *The Paradox of Southern Progressivism, 1880–1930.* Chapel Hill: University of North Carolina Press, 1992.

Lotchin, Roger W. *Fortress California: From Warfare to Welfare.* New York: Oxford University Press, 1992.

MacLean, Nancy. *Behind the Mask of Chivalry: The Making of the Second Ku Klux Klan.* New York: Oxford University Press, 1994.

Marchand, Roland. *Advertising the American Dream: Making Way for Modernity, 1920–1940.* Berkeley: University of California Press, 1985.

May, Elaine Tyler. *Homeward Bound: American Families in the Cold War Era.* New York: Basic Books, 1988, 1999, 2008, 2017.

May, Irvin M. *Marvin Jones: The Public Life of an Agrarian Advocate.* College Station: Texas A&M University Press, 1980.

McArthur, Judith N., and Smith, Harold L. *Minnie Fisher Cunningham: A Suffragist's Life in Politics.* New York: Oxford University Press, 2005.

McCullough, David. *Truman.* New York: Simon & Schuster, 1992.

McElvaine, Robert S. *The Great Depression in America, 1929–1941.* New York: Times Books, 1984.

McGinnis, Joe. *The Selling of the President 1968.* New York: Trident Press, 1969.

McGirr, Lisa. *Suburban Warriors: The Origins of the New American Right.* Princeton, NJ: Princeton University Press, 2001.

McKay, Seth Shepard. *Texas Politics, 1906–1944.* Lubbock: Texas Tech Press, 1952.

——. *W. Lee O'Daniel and Texas Politics, 1938–1942.* Lubbock: Texas Tech Press, 1944.

Miller, Edward H. *Nut Country: Right-Wing Dallas and the Birth of the Southern Strategy.* Chicago: University of Chicago Press, 2015.

Monroe, Mary Catherine. "A Day in July: Hatton W. Sumners and the Court Reorganization Plan of 1937." MA thesis, University of Texas at Arlington, 1973.

Moorehead, Richard. *50 Years in Texas Politics: From Roosevelt to Reagan, from the Fergusons to Clements.* Burnet, TX: Eakin Press, 1982.

Nash, Gerald D. *The Federal Landscape: An Economic History of the Twentieth Century West.* Tucson: University of Arizona Press, 1999.

——. *World War II and the West: Reshaping the Economy.* Lincoln: University of Nebraska Press, 1990.

Neugebauer, Janet M. *A Witness to History: George H. Mahon, West Texas Congressman.* Lubbock: Texas Tech University Press, 2017.

Nickerson, Michelle M. *Mothers of Conservatism: Women and the Postwar Right.* New York: Oxford University Press, 2012.

Olien, Roger M. *From Token to Triumph: The Texas Republicans since 1920*. Dallas: Southern Methodist University Press, 1982.

Olmsted, Kathryn S. *Right Out of California: The 1930s and the Big Business Roots of Modern Conservatism*. New York: New Press, 2015.

Patenaude, Lionel V. "Garner, Sumners, and Connally: The Defeat of the Roosevelt Court Bill in 1937." *Southwestern Historical Quarterly* 74, no. 1 (July 1970): 36–51.

———. *Texans, Politics and the New Deal*. New York: Garland, 1983.

Patterson, James T. *Congressional Conservatism and the New Deal: The Growth of the Conservative Coalition in Congress, 1933–1939*. Lexington: University of Kentucky Press, 1967.

Peterson, Merrill D. *The Jefferson Image in the American Mind*. New York: Oxford University Press, 1960.

———. *Lincoln in American Memory*. New York: Oxford University Press, 1994.

Phillips, Michael. *White Metropolis: Race, Ethnicity, and Religion in Dallas, 1841–2001*. Austin: University of Texas Press, 2006.

Phillips-Fein, Kim. *Invisible Hands: The Businessmen's Crusade against the New Deal*. New York: W. W. Norton, 2009.

Postel, Charles. *The Populist Vision*. New York: Oxford University Press, 2007.

Powers, Richard G. *Not without Honor: The History of American Anticommunism*. New York: Free Press, 1995.

Ragsdale, Kenneth B. *The Year America Discovered Texas: Centennial '36*. College Station: Texas A&M University Press, 1987.

Rauchway, Eric. *The Great Depression and the New Deal: A Very Short Introduction*. New York: Oxford University Press, 2008.

———. *Winter War: Hoover, Roosevelt, and the First Clash over the New Deal*. New York: Basic Books, 2018.

Reston, James. *The Lone Star: The Life of John Connally*. New York: Harper & Row, 1989.

Roberts, Randy, and James S. Olson. *A Line in the Sand: The Alamo in Blood and Memory*. New York: Touchstone Books, 2001.

Schiller, Joseph. "'Don't Sell Texas Short!': Amon Carter's Cultivation and Marketing of West Texas Nature." *Southwestern Historical Quarterly* 121, no. 4 (April 2018): 389–415.

Schneider, Gregory L. *The Conservative Century: From Reaction to Revolution*. Lanham, MD: Rowman & Littlefield, 2009.

Schulman, Bruce J. *From the Cotton Belt to Sunbelt: Federal Policy, Economic Development, and the Transformation of the South, 1938–1980*. New York: Oxford University Press, 1991.

Self, Deborah Lynn. "The National Youth Administration in Texas, 1935–1939." MA thesis, Texas Tech University, 1974.

Self, Robert O. *All in the Family: The Realignment of American Democracy since the 1960s*. New York: Hill & Wang, 2012.

Shales, Amity. *The Forgotten Man: A New History of the Great Depression*. New York: HarperCollins, 2007.

Slotkin, Richard. *Gunfighter Nation: The Myth of the Frontier in Twentieth-Century America*. Norman: University of Oklahoma Press, 1998.

Smith, Jason Scott. *A Concise History of the New Deal*. New York: Cambridge University Press, 2014.

Smith, Jean Edward. *FDR*. New York: Random House, 2007.

Sosebee, Scott M. "The Split in the Texas Democratic Party, 1936–1956." MA thesis, Texas Tech University, 2000.

Spencer, Thomas T. "For the Good of the Party: John Nance Garner, FDR, and New Deal Politics, 1933–1940." *Southwestern Historical Quarterly* 121, no. 3 (January 2018): 254–282.

Sugrue, Thomas J. *The Origins of the Urban Crisis: Race and Inequality in Postwar Detroit*. Princeton, NJ: Princeton University Press, 1996.

Sullivan, Patricia. *Days of Hope: Race and Democracy in the New Deal Era*. Chapel Hill: University of North Carolina Press, 1996.

Timmons, Bascom N. *Garner of Texas: A Personal History*. New York: Harper & Brothers, 1948.

Trachtenberg, Alan. *The Incorporation of America: Culture and Society in the Gilded Age*. New York: Hill & Wang, 1982.

Vance, J. D. *Hillbilly Elegy: A Memoir of a Family and Culture in Crisis*. New York: HarperCollins, 2016.

Volanto, Keith J. *Texas, Cotton, and the New Deal*. College Station: Texas A&M University Press, 2004.

Whisenhunt, Donald W. *The Depression in Texas: The Hoover Years*. New York: Garland, 1983.

Williams, Daniel K. *God's Own Party: The Making of the Christian Right*. New York: Oxford University Press, 2010.

Woods, Randall B. *Prisoners of Hope: Lyndon B. Johnson, the Great Society, and the Limits of Liberalism*. New York: Basic Books, 2016.

Worster, Donald. *The Dust Bowl: The Southern Plains in the 1930s*. New York: Oxford University Press, 1979.

Wright, Lawrence. *God Save Texas: A Journey into the Soul of the Lone Star State*. New York: Alfred A. Knopf, 2018.

Wuthnow, Robert. *The Left Behind: Decline and Rage in Small-Town America*. Princeton, NJ: Princeton University Press, 2019.

———. *Rough Country: How Texas Became America's Most Powerful Bible-Belt State*. Princeton, NJ: Princeton University Press, 2014.

Young, Nancy Beck. *Wright Patman: Populism, Liberalism, and the American Dream*. Dallas: Southern Methodist University Press, 2000.

Zamora, Emilio. *Claiming Rights and Righting Wrongs in Texas: Mexican Workers and Job Politics in Texas during World War II*. College Station: Texas A&M University Press, 2009.

Index

old-age pensions, 167, 169–170. *See also*
  Social Security
O'Rourke, Beto, 240

Palmer, A. Mitchell, 126
Parr, George, 234
Parten, J. R., 219
Patman, Wright
  1928 House campaign, 31–32
  1938 House campaign, 155–157
  political views, 31–32
  support for FDR and the New Deal, 9,
    155–157
  support for labor, 209
Patton, Nat, 82, 121, 235–236
Pearl Harbor attack, 204
pecan-shellers' strike, 130
personality, in politics, 10–11
Philadelphia Record, 85
Pickett, Tom, 236
political cartoons, *133*, 163, *176*, 181,
  223
populists/populism
  FDR's appeal in 1932, 43–44
  Sam Rayburn as, 52
  Texas farmers and, 58–59
  Texas political culture and, 6, 13, 241
  See also individual politicians
Porter, Paul A., 115
Porter, Winslow, 28
preparedness. *See* military preparedness
presidential campaigns and elections
  of 1928, 5, 18–19, 23–25
  of 1932, 27, 35–48
  of 1936, 115–120
  of 1940, 179–191
  of 1944, 236–237
  of 2020, 240
  FDR's margins in Texas, 5, 48, 120, 189,
    237
progressives/progressivism
  FDR's appeal in 1932, 43–44
  Thomas Love's views, 28
  Wright Patman's views, 31–32
  Morris Sheppard's views, 32–33
  Texas political culture and, 13
  See also liberals/liberalism
Prohibition Party, 28
Prohibition politics

1928 presidential election and, 18–19,
  23, 24
1932 presidential election and, 40, 42–43
Tom Connally's 1934 Senate campaign
  and, 77
Thomas Love and, 18, 24, 28–29
Public Utility Holding Company Act of
  1935, 86
"purge" of 1938, 150–163

Quin, C. K., 80

race
  1928 presidential election and, 23–24
  antigovernment backlash and, 126–127
  FDR's record on, 85, 95–96
  New Deal and, 85, 124
  political influence of Ku Klux Klan,
    20–21, 23, 29
  Texas Centennial and, 95–96
  Texas political culture and, 11–13,
    126–127, 132
  Texas Regulars and, 226
  See also civil rights; white supremacy
"racketeering," 207
radio
  FDR's mastery of, 11
  LBJ's 1941 Senate campaign and, 199
  LBJ's holdings in, 219
  Pappy O'Daniel and, 169–170
  third term movement and, 184
rationing mandates, 218
Rayburn, Sam
  1932 House reelection, 52–53
  1932 presidential campaign and, 41, 46
  1936 House campaign, 97–98, 121
  1936 presidential campaign and, 119
  as Confederate-sympathizing populist, 52
  court-packing controversy and, 140
  as Democratic strategist, 190
  on executive reorganization, 134
  neutrality politics and, 179
  NLRB investigation resolution and, 176
  political cartoons depicting, *133*, *176*, *223*
  securities legislation and, 82
  support for FDR and the New Deal, 53,
    86, 97–98
  "Texas Harmony" agreement and, 182,
    185

"Sell Texas" program, 168
Shamrock Texan, 154
Sheppard, Morris, *189*
  1932 presidential campaign and, 45
  1936 Senate campaign, 100–101, 120
  AAA and, 62
  court-packing controversy and, 137
  death of, 191
  Ku Klux Klan and, 21
  military preparedness and, 178
  political views, 32–33
  promotion of FDR's third term, 182
  support for FDR and the New Deal,
    70–72, 87–88, 100–101
Smith, Al, 18–19, 23–24, 25, 40, 128
Smith, Howard W., 175
Smith, Walter P., 88
Smith Committee, 175–176
Smith v. Allwright, 221
Social Security, 89, 109
special elections
  LBJ's 1937 election to the House,
    143–149
  Pappy O'Daniel's 1941 election to the
    Senate, 191–204
Stack, Earnest, 174
State Medical Association of Texas, 175
State of the Union addresses
  of 1935, 83
  of 1941, 205
states' rights
  antilynching bill and, 131–132
  Texas Regulars and, 224, 231
Sterling, Ross, 48–49
Stevenson, Coke, 214–215
Stone, William E., 157
strikes, 130. *See also* labor politics
Stubbs, N. T., 145
Sumners, Hatton W.
  1936 House campaign, 103–106
  1938 House campaign, 159–161
  1942 House reelection, 216
  1944 House campaign, 232–233
  anticommunist and antilabor views,
    232–233
  as congressman, *158*
  court-packing controversy and, 138–139
  criticisms of the New Deal, 106
  Ku Klux Klan and, 21

  as Miller Group member, 56–57
  opposition to antilynching bill, 131–132
  opposition to rationing mandates, 218
  patents moratorium proposal, 26
synthetic rubber manufacturing, 168

tariffs
  Hawley-Smoot Tariff of 1930, 34, 37
  Reciprocal Tariff Act of 1934, 66
taxes
  James Buchanan's views, 51
  conservative opposition and debates,
    88–89
  debates during WWII, 208
  increases under Hoover, 34, 37
  George Mahon's views, 79
Taylor, Buck, 227–228
Teacher Retirement System of Texas, 120
Tejanos, 130
Tennessee Valley Authority (TVA), 100–101
Texas
  Centennial, 91–96
  congressional districts, *30*
  counties, *16–17*
  cowboy trope and, 13
  Depression's economic impact in,
    26–27
  enduring legacy of the New Deal in,
    238–239
  FDR's margins in, 5, 48, 120, 189, 237
  identity and cultural fluidity of, 6
  Ku Klux Klan and, 20–21
  popular support for FDR in, 1–5, 9–10,
    73, 119–120, 188–189, 229, 238
  Roosevelt Recession and, 142
  wartime economy and, 178–179,
    207–208, 219
  WPA spending in, 87
Texas and Southwest Cattle Raisers
    Association speech, 233–234
Texas Centennial, 91–96
Texas congressional delegation
  court-packing controversy and, 134–142
  neutrality debates and, 177–179
  NLRB investigation resolution and, 176
  voting habits analysis, 177
  See also individual politicians
Texas Democratic Party
  1940 state conventions, 185–186, 187